THE HAWAIIAN HORSE

Authentic illustration of a vaquero seated on a saddle that reflects the transition from bulbous Mexican horn and cantle to the refined form typical of the paniolo Hawaiian tree.

THE HAWAIIAN HORSE

DR. BILLY BERGIN AND DR. BRADY BERGIN

UNIVERSITY OF HAWAIʻI PRESS
HONOLULU

Printed in the United States of America

22 21 20 19 18 17 6 5 4 3 2 1

Library of Congress Cataloging-in-Publication Data

Names: Bergin, Billy, author. | Bergin, Brady, author.
Title: The Hawaiian horse / Dr. Billy Bergin and Dr. Brady Bergin.
Description: Honolulu : University of Hawai°i Press, [2017] | Includes bibliographical references and index.
Identifiers: LCCN 2016011324 | ISBN 9780824837440 (cloth ; alk. paper)
Subjects: LCSH: Horses--Hawaii--History.
Classification: LCC SF284.U5 B47 2017 | DDC 636.1009969--dc23
LC record available at http://lccn.loc.gov/2016011324

University of Hawai'i Press books are printed on acid-free paper and meet the guidelines for permanence and durability of the Council on Library Resources.

DESIGNED BY MARDEE MELTON

This book and the efforts put into its production are dedicated to Arthur Morgan Brown to honor his tireless enthusiasm and perseverance to improve horse quality in the Hawaiian Islands.

Morgan, as he is more commonly known, stands apart from other horsemen and ranchers for his dedication to the advancement of animal health as a major component of livestock improvement. As owner and manager of A Lazy B Ranch, he championed the Quarter Horse, American Paint Horse, and the Charolais breed of beef cattle in a manner that drew statewide attention to these breeds. His efforts showcasing these breeds through horse shows, clinics, and sales were heroic. Most impressive was his consistency in embracing and applying animal health techniques to maximize the production, growth, and welfare of his animals, which placed him above his peers. Morgan is an exemplar of animal health and welfare of the highest order.

CONTENTS

FOREWORD

If you've ever been interested in the horse, or even history, or Hawai'i, this is the book for you. It is my honor to be asked to write this foreword of *The Hawaiian Horse,* written by Drs. Billy and Brady Bergin. So saddle up, because this is a wonderful ride across a long journey through history, culminating with today and the horse in Hawai'i.

Drs. Billy and Brady Bergin have eloquently and with thorough documentation uncovered what few of us would ever think about living in Hawai'i and seeing a horse. My personal introduction to the horse in Hawai'i came in 1989 when I was recruited to train the young horses for Parker Ranch. In the mid-1990s, as the horse herd foreman for Parker Ranch, I would have the opportunity to spend several weeks at a time with Dr. Billy Bergin, and we would go through every single horse on Parker Ranch together taking field notes, deworming, and vaccinating (four shots for each horse and over five hundred head of horses!). Needless to say, we spent some interesting time together with horses. Some of the topics unique to Hawai'i are shared within.

Along this trail, you'll also find some hidden gems, but look up because the high mountaintops that we will be "riding" toward will come quickly, first with the ports of entry of the horse into the Americas. You'll soon be riding alongside the vaquero, followed up by the vaquero Hawaiiano and the *paniolo* and witness their unique way of working cattle with the Spanish influence.

Not only is this a book about the Hawaiian horse, but Drs. Billy and Brady Bergin take us out beyond our own horizon to look at other native horse populations in Australia and New Zealand. This gives us a better understanding to our own local equine ancestors, such as the legendary "Mauna Kea" horse, as well as our often misunderstood Waipi'o Valley horse and the nightingale donkeys.

Prior to the industrial revolution, there was a grand need for the horse, donkey, and mule in providing Hawai'i's people with the day-to-day staples carried by these tireless workers. The horse has obviously risen to eminence among these three animals, but after reading on we will all have an appreciation for the price paid and sacrifices made for the people of Hawai'i by the mules and donkeys as well.

One of the most unique things covered in this book is the in-depth look at livestock transportation worldwide and, in particular, the awe-inspiring recounting of horse transportation through history. If you've ever lacked for adventure, this should fill your cup.

As we continue to blaze the trail through history, you will meet the men and women who played key roles in the development of the horse in Hawai'i. You couldn't find better people to ride alongside!

The impact of the two world wars influenced the horse we have today. We learn firsthand about the vital role horses played from the Civil War through World War II. We also learn what traits, size, and colors were preferred for military use, such as bay, chestnut, sorrel, and black, and why. Imagine having an entire company of military horses made up of a single coat color!

Through these lessons of war, the United States Remount Service was born. "Remount" is defined as a fresh horse that is to replace a lost or disabled one. This became a universal term in horse circles, referring to the US military horse in context. This season for the horse in Hawai'i was a season of great leaps forward in all areas of fine horse breeding. The stallions placed nationwide with ranchers already equipped with bands of broodmares saw the quality influx from America's finest Thoroughbreds, Standardbreds, American Saddlebreds, Morgans, and Arab stallions. Hawai'i's ranchers were perfectly poised to become solid beneficiaries and providers to the US Remount Service and its need for good horses nationwide. This high point jumpstarted what would lead to the next season of fine horsemanship in Hawai'i. We see the sport of military polo grow and later become a popular domestic sport. Polo became a rich part of Hawai'i's horse history; some horses went on to international fame.

As a result of these developments, horse sports in Hawai'i began to flourish. Drs. Billy and Brady Bergin relate, as we ride along the trail, the beautiful history of the pā'ū riders, the older days of horse racing in Hawai'i, and some of its more colorful characters, as well as the planting, nurturing, and blooming of rodeo and high school rodeo in Hawai'i, due in no small part to the White, Bergin, and FitzGerald families.

It would be unlikely that a book written by two veterinarians would not include material on horse health issues peculiar to Hawai'i. Based on these chapters alone, I would encourage every horse owner in Hawai'i and beyond to watch carefully where we ride now. Hawai'i is a unique environment, and we're in good hands with the information pioneered by bold visionaries and held properly in the hands of our current veterinarian population. Along this trail, Drs. Billy and Brady Bergin share an in-depth look at unique issues, diseases, and conditions peculiar to the tropics.

I particularly appreciate the firsthand, fair, nonbiased, but well-informed view of the current overpopulation issues facing horses and donkeys nationwide. We certainly have our bands of feral animals here, but to really understand the "big picture" it's good to have a guide on this subject. There are honest, well-thought-out questions, and no sidestepping of the situation we find ourselves in as horse owners, breeders, and stewards.

As a lifelong student of the horse, I find that this book has been a real joy to read. I hope you enjoy it as well. Often, when I was training horses at Parker Ranch, people came from around the world to the breaking pens and asked, "How did horses get to Hawai'i?" Now we can all be well equipped to answer.

As we pull up our horse and pause for a moment of reflection, I wholeheartedly agree with Drs. Billy and Brady Bergin that to understand where we are and where we are going, it is important to know where we come from.

Aloha,
Lester Buckley
Kamuela, Hawai'i

PREFACE

The place of the horse in Hawai'i's postcontact history has long been worthy of celebration. Recording the history of the donkey and mule in agricultural and ranch contexts in a comprehensive and documentary manner is also long overdue. Inquiries into these historic facets are frequent but usually met with only scattered resources of knowledge. This book intends to provide a comprehensive, colorful background of these topics that allows the reader to come away with a thorough understanding and appreciation of the fascinating history and critical role of these animals in Hawai'i.

Such historic chronicling relies upon limited resources of printed or published materials that are found by searching files of plantations, ranches, and private individuals. Equally important are the voices of elders whose clear recollections of their parents' and grandparents' involvement bring to light vital insight into the challenges, successes, and tragedies faced by Hawai'i's stewards of the family Equidae, genus *Equus.* These voices will now be heard.

The impact of the Spanish influence and Mexican vaquero mentorship on Hawai'i's budding ranching and plantation industries and cowboy genre is summarized in a single word: *paniolo.* With this Hawaiianization of the term *español,* Spain is given due credit as the world's undisputed cradle of horsemanship. While the national image of the American cowboy is an Anglo, Hawai'i speaks of the *paniolo,* which in title alone honors the Spanish influence, while the man himself could be from a variety of ethnicities. This begins with Native Hawaiian *kanaka maoli* and blends with multiethnic bloodlines of Japanese, Chinese, Korean, Portuguese, Spanish, Galician, Puerto Rican, Filipino, and yes, Caucasian horse people. These men and women honor the *caballo* (horse) as the iconic symbol of human mobility in a progressive and productive society set in a tropical locale. This book now honors these men and women of Hawai'i.

Most impressive was the rapid transformation of the seafaring Polynesian to the mounted *paniolo,* where in the space of two to three years, the vaquero mentor, with due pride and satisfaction, molded a skilled and competent protégé to steward the agricultural, ranching, military, and societal needs of the Islands from that point forward. Progress over the span of more than two hundred years would not have come about without royal blessing, governmental oversight, military needs, sporting interests, and agricultural and ranching pursuits, as well as the dedicated efforts of key individuals. *The Hawaiian Horse* details this worthy journey.

As the first horses arrived with mustang blood freely flowing in their veins, the Islands called for improved strains that originated from Arabia, Australia, Britain, France, Germany, and India, while the American continent supplied landrace breeds such as the Morgan and later the Quarter Horse.

Despite periodic overabundance of common horses by the mid-1880s, the love of the horse in Hawaiian society is best reflected in the *wahine holo lio,* the elegant yet regal *pāʻū* rider, boldly racing across the countryside in colorful regalia. This was the beginning of the historic genre of the *pāʻū* rider, which has reached professional status in modern-day Hawaiʻi.

Gratitude for the profound improvement in the quality of horses, donkeys, and mules must in large part be extended to the emerging plantation industries. Managers (*luna*) needed quality mounts, as they oversaw thousands of acres of land yielding tons of sugar and pineapple. The drayage of product, fertilizer, seed cane, building materials, and personnel was handled effectively by the beasts of burden, the donkey and mule.

The territorial government was effective in safeguarding the health of these animals, in addition to fostering improved nutrition and breeding of the critical mass of Equidae that served agricultural industries as well as private businesses and individual owners.

Beyond the cavalry, military influence on Hawaiʻi's horse scene spanned both world wars, enhancing the sports of polo and dressage while fostering rodeo through highly qualified personnel, elevating these events to a level of professionalism that the Islands enjoy today.

Two men of Hawaiʻi share the spotlight in pioneering the advancement in quality of the horse, donkey, and mule. First is A. W. Carter, the "Trustee of Trustees," who ably guided the horse, donkey, and mule programs to greatness, not merely for the Parker Ranch but on behalf of neighboring ranches and plantations, as well as the military and sporting interests of mainland and foreign markets. The exemplary work of Dr. J. C. FitzGerald from a veterinary standpoint is nothing short of heroic in stamping out animal disease while fostering appropriate nutrition in the production of Hawaiʻi's emerging horse and mule industry. He went further, personally importing premium Thoroughbred stallions, such as Sileo, that stood proudly and productively at Maui's top breeding stations.

Hawaiʻi was blessed with equestriennes of the highest order in Haku Baldwin on Maui and Amy Rich on Oʻahu. These women are celebrated not only for their personal horsewomanship but for their life of devotion to developing equestrian skills in the youth of their respective home islands.

Hawaiʻi's use of the horse in performance activities is notable. Racing, even in the absence of pari-mutuel wagering, provided profound incentive for bettering the blooded horse, the Thoroughbred, which expanded beyond racecourse markets to polo, military, and dressage venues. Rodeo enthusiasts continue to hold the national championship of steer roper Ikua Purdy in a "Duke Kahanamoku–like" mysticism, as Hawaiian contestants continue to thrive in mainland rodeo victories. Youth rodeo has very effectively underscored this confidence in the abilities of Island-born contestants who relish success in mainland competition.

Horse health issues, especially those specific to the Hawai'i environment, are described in a historic as well as current manner, while the plight of the unwanted horse and donkey is elaborated upon in a mainland as well as local context.

Insight is the key in the closing epilogue of this work, which looks at what the future holds for the role of the horse. This especially applies to recreational use of horses here in the Islands, where the stunningly beautiful landscapes often remain beyond reach of most in a sensitive environment that we also want to preserve in its pristine state. The horse community must be uniformly informed and concerned about the future of the Hawaiian horse world. We hope that this documentary review of Hawai'i's horse history will help us to be good stewards in the future. We need to know where we came from to know where we are going.

ACKNOWLEDGMENTS

As always, we first extend gratitude to our wife and mother, Patricia Cockett Bergin, affectionately known as Toots. Far beyond her role as silent editor, her dedicated attention to the mission of recording the history of Hawai'i's ranching and *paniolo* legacy is paralleled by our love for one another, our children, grandchildren, and wide array of dear friends. Not once, while writing ranch history over the past two decades, did she neglect her professional role as a leading educator in Hawai'i's public arena. To describe her as a skilled multitasker is woefully inadequate.

We must honor Patrick Ching, Hawai'i's foremost equine artist, for sharing the thought of coauthoring a book on horses in Hawai'i over a decade ago. His approach was very artful, and ours was of a more scholarly persuasion. We never did launch a combined project, but credit for the idea of a Hawaiian horse book clearly goes to Patrick.

Always there with expertise in graphics were Matt Pearce and Neil Morris of Waimea Instant Printers. Their advice and technical support was superb. Dick Solmssen, Michael Olival, and Diana Webb were instrumental in gathering horses of mountain and valley breeding for the DNA project. Peter Baldwin and Robin Jensen of the Haku Baldwin Center are to be thanked for their enduring help in gathering background of Haku, the legendary horsewoman of Maui, whom we regret not having the honor of knowing better in her lifetime. Henry "Tippy" Ah Sam deserves recognition as "Hawai'i's cowboy artist" for his artful representation of the Hawaiian Tree Saddle series, which shows its layered accoutrements from start to finish, including the *lala,* the vestige of the vaquero's saddle overlay, the *mochila.* A cowboy in his own right, he is also recognized for the years of service to many of the Island's prominent ranches. Otto Ziegler of Missouri provided extensive background on the draft horse, particularly the Belgian breed, in Hawai'i's history. When it comes to polo, Lester Maruoka and Freddy Rice were forthright in sharing photos, history, and specific knowledge on the equestrian sport. Judy Folk and the Dick Ednie family were great sources of polo history and enthusiasm.

We thank three contributors: Dr. Lisa Wood for her input, collegiality, and love for horses that matches ours; Lester Buckley, who served as an inspiration for this book given his enduring quest for advancing horsemanship in the Islands and beyond; and Valerie van der Veer, who provided thorough input on the armed forces' involvement in rodeo and horse club activities.

In the field of photography, genuine appreciation is extended to William J. Andrade Sr., Gene Balzer, John Cross, Chris Hartwell, Michal McClure, Ethan Tweedie, and Jock Goodman.

Another generation of Bergins is responsible for the enduring love for horses, and hence they have played a part in composing this book. For this we thank sons and brothers, Bill, Chris, and Holi (deceased). Reinforcing this love for horses are their spouses, Lori, Iwalani, and Tiffany, whose passionate care for the noble animal surfaces in daily deeds and conversation.

Finally, as senior author, my deepest gratitude is expressed to John Holi Ma'e, who introduced me to the horse and nurtured my aloha for this special animal, serving as inspiration for several generations of Bergins.

Dr. Billy Bergin
Waimea, Hawai'i

CHAPTER 1

ORIGIN OF THE EQUINE SPECIES

While humans are said to have originated in what is now Africa, North America may well have been where many animal species—most notably the horse—originated. The early-age rain forests and verdant valleys likely provided the ancestral home of the equine species and its subspecies, the ass. A browser of forage, the early equine was well suited to swamp country given its multidigited hind and forefeet. After thousands of years of trekking through vast tracks of rocky plains and savannahs covering hundreds of miles in migration, a single-toed equine emerged by natural selection, as the more fleet footed early horse took shape into its modern form and function. In Britain, fossils indicate that a pony-like equine species existed 100,000 years BCE.

The North American continent has long been considered the cradle of the equine species, but the evolution of the functional horse likely occurred in the Eurasian steppes, where the species flourished for thousands of years.

Preserved fossils found abundantly in the Bighorn Basin of Wyoming provide evidence of America's first horse, *Sifrhippus sandrae,* which lived 56 million years ago. According to scientific classification, they were not at all like the present-day mustangs of Wyoming; they were small creatures about the size of the house cat that browsed on leaves rather than grazing on grass.

Recent studies of fossilized horse teeth by researcher Matthew Mihlbachler and others reveal that the timeline of changing tooth features paralleled major changes in the climate of North America. Equine dental fossils as ancient as 55.5 million years ago reveal that the horse shifted from a diet of leaf and fruit eating to grazing on grass. Further changes in the horses' molars that occurred around

33 million years ago reflect environmental changes from a moist-forested, fruited landscape to expansive grasslands, where grazing abrasive forage demanded sharper-pointed dental cusps for prehension (biting) and mastication (chewing). Tooth height was enhanced some 18 million years ago, as the surface of the molars became better suited for chewing tough plants—mainly grasses that contain silica particles that wear down teeth. Harsher, colder climate conditions added further forage abrasiveness, accelerating dental changes over the last 5 million years as the modern horse further evolved.

By 12,500 BCE, the horse had all but disappeared from the continent of North America as a result of severe climatic changes and predation by dogs and large cats. With the passing of the Ice Age, however, the horse had guaranteed its continued presence in the world by migrating west via the preexisting land bridge connecting Alaska with Siberia and Asia. When the ice cap melted and the land bridge was covered by the rising sea, the Bering Strait (as we know it today) became an ocean barrier separating Alaska from Siberia and Asia. Asia became the new home of the horse, where it thrived and spread into the Middle East, Africa, and Europe.

In the ancient caves of Iberia (Spain and Portugal today), wall paintings reflect the presence of haltered horses. Land that once connected the Shetland Islands (an archipelago off northern Scotland in the Atlantic Ocean) with Scandinavia was also inundated, providing an isolated home for small horses that eventually became a separate breed. This horse has existed since 8000 BCE. Swamplands formed a bridge for animal and human transit between England and Europe. Between 6500 and 3000 BCE, the bridge became submerged and formed a strait that became the English Channel. Migratory pathways that gave way to the Bering Sea and English Channel guaranteed that the equine would survive into modern history as a significant companion of man. Horse and humans were mutually introduced in 5000 BCE, the relationship likely one of hunter and food source.

Recent findings by archaeologists working on the Kazakh steppes of Kazakhstan suggest that by 3600 BCE, pastoral tribes may have been the first to domesticate, bridle, and mount these early equines. Under true domestication, these early horses went beyond being solely a meat source to providing milk in the form of koumiss—fermented mare's milk, still enjoyed by horsemen of Central Asia. Most striking of all findings is the presence of bit wear—traumatic erosion of molar teeth and mandibular bone—in skeletal remains found in archaeological diggings in this region, which is occupied by the semisedentary Botai culture. These tribes expanded the horse's value beyond food to become beasts of burden, as well as sources of locomotion. Bit wear suggests that they used mouthpieces to secure horses for bridling and harnessing, further suggesting that they were becoming working animals.

It is reasonable to assume that the wild horse served primarily as a food source. Horseflesh continues to be used today in well-developed countries such as Belgium, France, and Germany as a delectable source of protein. Once horses became apprehensible, either by trapping or snaring, humans recognized their utility as a means of advanced mobility, given their athleticism and endurance.

Noted author of equine publications Dr. Robert M. Miller poignantly describes progress in domestication of the horse in *The Revolution of Horsemanship and What It Means to Mankind,* coauthored by Rick Lamb: "The Battle-Axe people of Britain, by 3000 B.C. were found to have used the horse for packing, as well as draught purposes. Thanks again to cave artists, the Appaloosa color pattern appeared in Egyptian and Greek art by 1400 B.C. Celtic invasions over vast continents further applied the horse's domestic, albeit military use by 800 B.C. when they brought their war ponies to the Iberian Peninsula by 800 B.C. and to Ireland by 500 B.C." (Miller and Lamb 2005).

The last of the truly wild horses are the mustangs of North America, the brumbies of the Australian outback, and the Kaimanawa horses of New Zealand. Attitudes regarding feral horses vary dramatically throughout the world. The kiang horses of the Himalayas are considered sacred, while the brumbies Down Under are considered a disposable species and a great nuisance. The government of New Zealand, however, has taken an aggressive management role to preserve the Kaimanawa mounts.

By perhaps 1200 CE, Polynesian voyagers had migrated by double-hulled canoe from their homeland of Havaiki in the Society Islands to Hawaiʻi in the north, New Zealand in the south, Rapa Nui (Easter Island) in the east, and outliers in the western Pacific—in all directions of the compass. Also by this time, Vikings of Scandinavia had not only pillaged the world by warship but had selectively bred the Norwegian Fjord Horse as a distinct breed known today for its adaptation to arctic climates.

As superb navigators, the "Vikings of the Sunrise" (as Polynesian voyagers have been called [Buck 1938]) established transpacific migratory patterns all across the Pacific Ocean. Soon village people of Hawaiʻi were farming produce and fruits, hogs, dogs, and chickens. During this same period, the Moors (a conglomerate of Muslim military forces) invaded Spain, bringing as many as one hundred North African Berber mounts with them as war horses. These horses, of superior cavalry quality, readily mated with native Iberian stock to create some of the world's noted breeds. By the second voyage of Christopher Columbus in 1493, the horse, likely a Spanish Barb, was reintroduced into North America some fourteen thousand years after the original species had all but disappeared. According to historian Charles F. Lummis (1936), "The Spanish introduction of the horse, mule, burro and ox to America marked the longest stride so many people, in so short a time have ever taken in the arts of transportation." Frederic Remington, renowned cowboy artist,

This poetic capsule by Scott Wells (pers. comm.) sums up the progressive relationship of horse and human over the many centuries:

Pre-Horse-Toric Man

In Days of Old, when folks were naked
And lizards stood sixty hands,
Men lived in caves and carried clubs
And scavenged across these lands.
They lived on bugs and leaves and grass
And seldom tasted meat,
For if they wandered far from home,
They's likely to get eat.
See, their mountain lions had teeth like
 sabers
And a meat-eatin' dinosaur
Could eat a mammoth at a single meal
And go out and hunt for more.
Folks lived scared, and rightly so,
For they were small and weak
And lived in a land of giants
Whose appetites they tweaked.
But there was one creature then
Who was agile, strong and fleet
And he'd outrun or out-maneuver
Those who craved his meat.
They called him "horse" and one day came
When a man jumped on one's back.
Before he knowed, at high speeds he'd rode
Across the valley and back.
From that time on, horses and humans
Have helped each other out.
Mounted, a man could carry a club
And wield hisself some clout.
He could ride up beside a bigger beast
And knock him in the head,
Or otherwise molest him
'til the thing was dead.
And them ancient Indians where we now live,
They were plenty savvy,
But all they had was tame coyotes
To drag their little "travvies"
'til the Spaniards came, a-huntin gold
And turned some horses loose.
Soon after that, the Red Man,
He developed the cayouse.
With horses he could follow herds
And move his family 'round
And leave the snows that winter blows
For a better huntin' ground.
And when the East was urban
And the West was wild,
Them townfolks wanted steaks,
So horsemen gathered longhorns
From the plains and the cedar breaks.
And if folks needed to send their mail
Or travel from east to west,
They could go by boat around the Cape,
But a horse-drawn stage was best.
Now they say Man's brain set him apart
And altered history's course.
But if you ask me, what changed it all
Was the day he rode the horse.

~ **SCOTT WELLS**

also attests to the importance of the horse in his article, "Horses of the Plains," in the *Century,* a popular quarterly in 1889:

> One thing is certain: of all the monuments which the Spaniard has left to glorify his reign in America, there will be none more worthy than his horse. . . . The Spaniards' horses may be found today in countless thousands, from the city of the Montezumas to the regions of perpetual snow; they are grafted into our equine wealth and make an important impression on the horse of the country. . . . They have borne the Moor, the Spanish Conqueror, the Indian, the mountain man and the vaquero through all the glories of their careers. (Remington 1889)

Southeastern Portal of the Horse

In 1493, Columbus arrived in the Caribbean islands with horses, donkeys, and mules. Sailing on behalf of King Ferdinand and Queen Isabella of Spain, the explorer reintroduced a long extinct species that enhanced life in the New World in perpetuity. Spanish royalty clearly intended to ship the finest horses from Andalusian horse farms and military garrisons, but lancers (light cavalry armed with lances) of the exploratory voyage took a different tack. Aboard ship went commonly bred horses of utilitarian use and background. Andalusian and Barb horses formed the bulk of the manifest, while the *garrano* (Galician), the *sorraia* (Portuguese), and the jennet mounts filled out the consignment.

These were not the stabled, pampered, conditioned mounts of the Spanish knight, the lancer. Whether by practical wisdom or neglect of duty, the lancer chose for shipment horses and jackasses of toughened range-bred mounts, wiry but of easy-keeping nature. The small Barb horses predominated, weighing eight hundred to nine hundred pounds and measuring thirteen to fourteen hands in height. They are short-backed mounts with prominent withers, an angled croup (sloping hip), and low-set tail. Such a conformation lends itself to greater maneuverability: the horse can bring its hindquarters well beneath its torso, allowing a springlike ability for bursts of speed, quick turns, and pivots.

The sure-footed Barb horse was gifted with jet-black upright hooves of good size and texture. To a degree, their hooves are oversized relative to their small frame. This was advantageous, given the environment of their home, which varied from savannah to arid coastal plains. Though their heads are coarse, large, and somewhat convex in profile (Roman nosed), these horses of rural Iberia had innate cow sense underscored by common sense. Survivors by nature, they were built to work hard on little feed and water. The lancers were indeed wise to send these hardy survivors to the New World. The tropics of the Caribbean offer an abundance of poor-quality forage, low in protein, carbohydrates, minerals, and fiber, yet high in moisture. The classic heavy mounts of the Spanish knight would have languished on such a substandard diet,

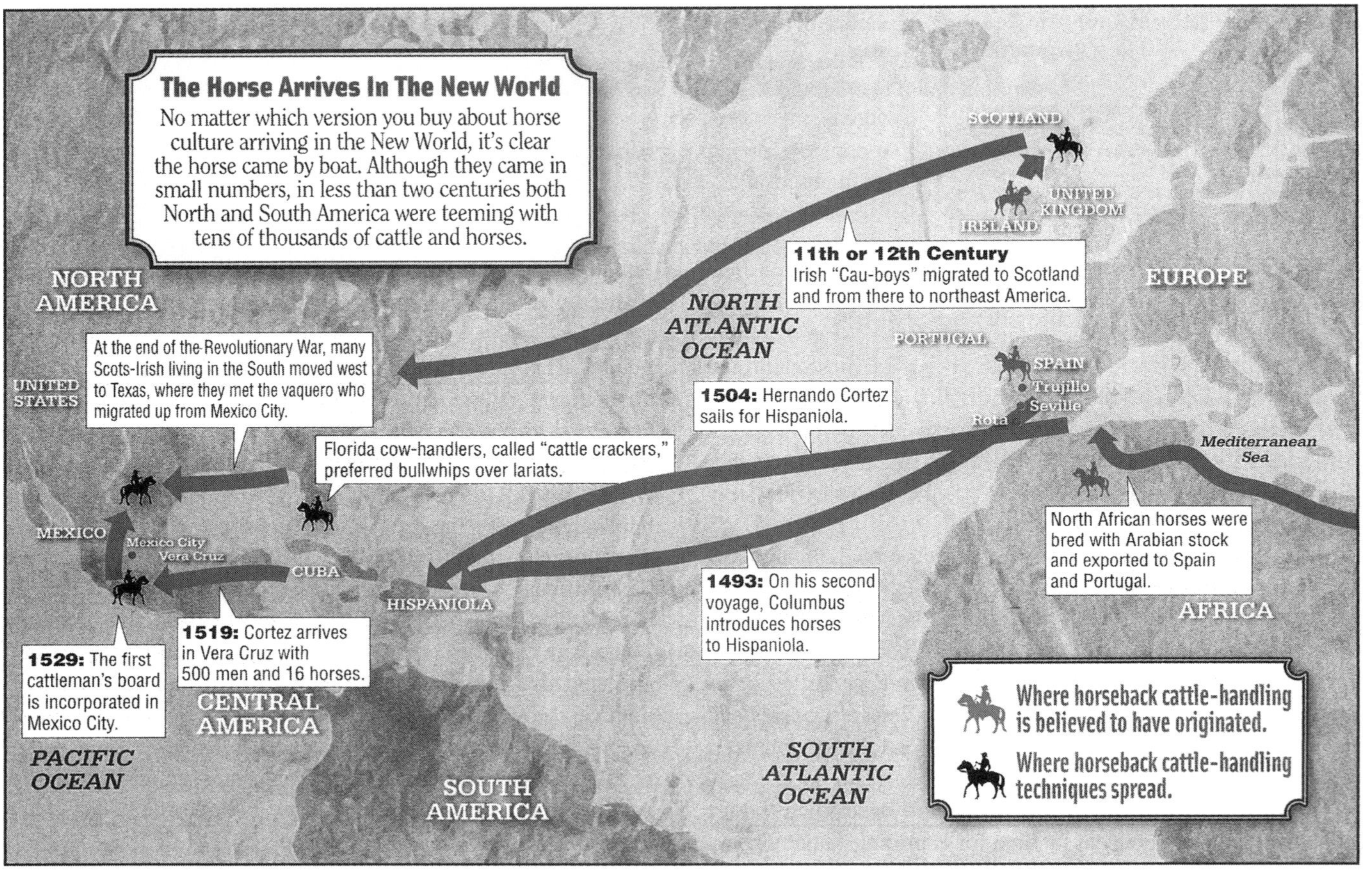

{1.1} *Origin of livestock handlers of the Americas. Scotland, Ireland, and Spain significantly influenced exportation of horses as well as expertise in using the horse to handle cattle.*

while the Barb horse, once acclimatized, flourished in numbers.

It is interesting to note that the name "Andalusia" might suggest that the region of Andalusia was the sole source of the breed. In modern Spain, however, this breed is found in every one of Spain's fifty-two provinces.

A symbol of national identity, the purebred Spanish horse developed a formal place in equestrian history when the Purebred Spanish Horse Breeders Association of Spain (ANCCE) was founded in 1972. Purebred Spanish Horses (Pura Raza Español or PRE) gained even greater formal attention in 1973 when the Royal Andalusian School of Equestrian Art (Real Escuela) was created to preserve the traditional training methods of Spanish horses. Reaching the world stage by the 1990s, Spain fielded its first international dressage team.

Hosting the World Equestrian Games in 2002, the Andalusian city of Jerez de la Frontera provided the venue for international recognition of the Spanish horse as a desirable sport horse breed.

Spanish breeders are striving for larger-framed mounts, with mares of at least 15 hands and stallions reaching 15.2 hands, while adhering strictly to preserving the purity of the breed and the most typical traits. Many sport horse experts describe the Spanish horse as best in the world when it comes to the collected gaits—particularly the *passage* (slow-motion trot) and *piaffe* (a trot in place). Good temperament is a prepotent trait of the Spanish breed.

At the 2014 Real Escuela performances, the majestic gray mounts, appearing to weigh 1,100 pounds on average, demonstrated both *piaffe* and *passage* gaits with the grace of a ballet. Most impressive was witnessing these magnificent animals rearing up on their hind legs and actually walking on two legs in time with the music. The temperament of the dappled stallions was good throughout. The prestigious school attracts approximately five to six hundred applicants annually. Only four fortunate individuals are selected for a four-year program of study each year.

Columbus' second voyage and subsequent voyages by other explorers included mares in shipments. While the Spanish horsemen held in disdain the use of mares and fillies for riding, their use as pack and breeding animals was well accepted. Soon royal horse farms sprang up in the Caribbean islands. On the island of Hispaniola (Haiti/Dominican Republic), a band of broodmares—sixty strong, Spanish-bred dams—formed a nucleus for export of offspring. By 1515, this farm began delivery of colt crops to outlying islands and eventually to the North American continent.

In 1521, Ponce de León delivered the first shipment of horses, donkeys, and mules to the shores of Florida. Of this consignment, fifty were island-bred Spanish colonial horses. These mounts were greatly preferred by the mounted entourage of explorers, as they were well acclimated to the environment of high humidity and rainfall, wet, washy forage, and muddy footing. By this juncture, the Native American Indians of the southeast were eyeing the means of becoming mobile warriors. Horse importation continued, with Ferdinand DeSoto arriving with three hundred horses in 1539 near present-day Tampa Bay. Meanwhile, to the southwest, the conquest of Mexico had brought the conquistadors and their Spanish mounts. This campaign would give birth to the vaquero, the buckaroo, and cowboy culture.

Southwestern Portal of the Horse

Hernán Cortés landed in Vera Cruz, Mexico, in 1519 with a large contingent of mounted conquistadors and their entourage of attendants, including indentured grooms. Instead of second- or third-generation island-bred mounts enjoyed by southeastern continental explorers, Cortés' men rode directly imported

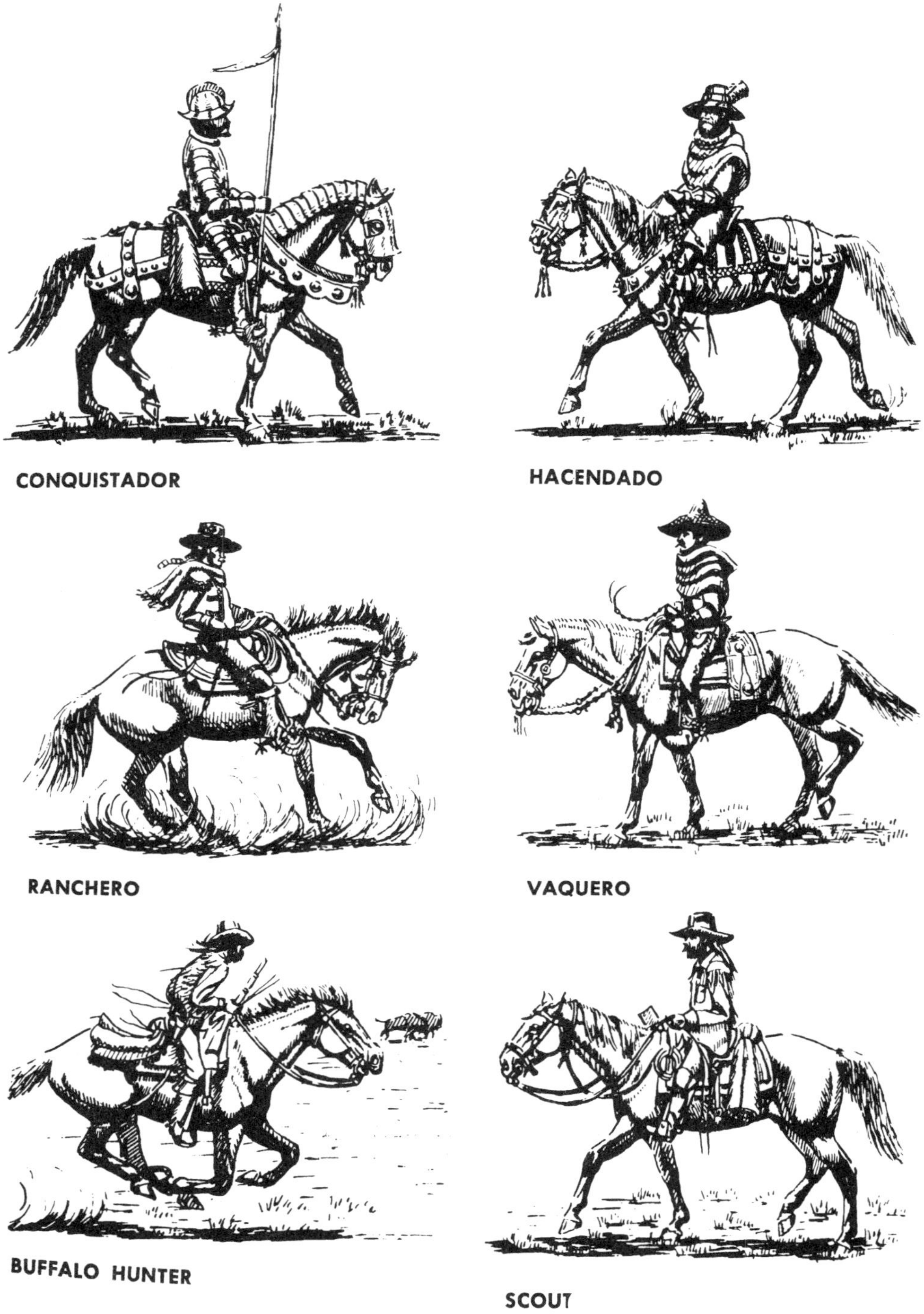

{1.2} *Mounted on a Spanish Barb. Seated on a war saddle between a high, hornless pommel and cantle, the conquistador and his horse (top left) are decked out in typical armor. This illustration shows the evolution over time that led to the American cowboy.*

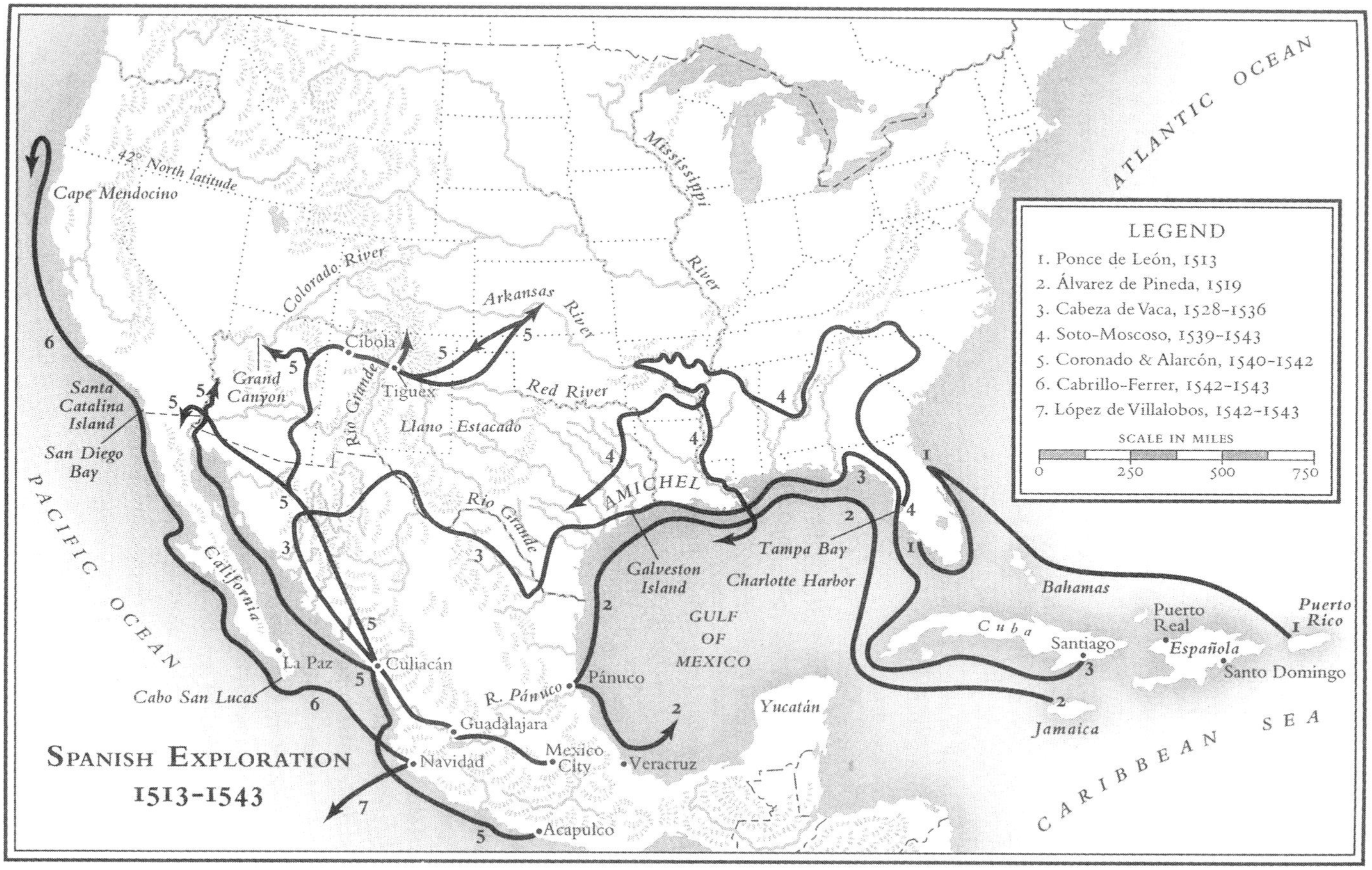

{1.3} *Exploration of the continent of North America by the Spaniards was extensive. They brought with them their horses and horsemanship, changing the Americas forever.*

horses of Andalusian, Barb, and *garrano* breeding. Some were pinto colored, but most were duns, chestnuts, and bays.

Historian Joe B. Frantz wrote of the landing in glowing terms:

> More than four hundred and fifty years ago that magnificent conquistador, Hernan Cortes, landed at the place of the true cross, Vera Cruz, with sixteen purebred Spanish horses.
>
> A herd of Spanish cattle followed two years later. Even though their arrival produced wonderment in the hearts and eyes of the peeking Indians, the real excitement lies in the enduring significance of that moment in history. (Frantz and Choate 1955)

A distinct advantage of the southwestern portal was the abundance of rich, palatable forage of high fiber and low moisture. Further, the cultivation of corn (maize) by the native farmers provided a superior source of concentrated feed. The admixture of legumes with the indigenous grains reinforced diet quality equal to or greater than the Spanish motherland. Provided with rest and recuperation after arrival, the Spanish warhorses were readily acclimatized to their new home. Subtropical desert warmth coupled with low humidity and rainfall underscored the environmental qualities so enjoyed by the horses, donkeys, and mules.

Cortés, like Columbus, brought a contingent of mares for packing and breeding, but they were pressed into service instead of reproduction, as the conquistadors forged inland, fanning out to South, Central, and North America from their point of disembarkation in the Gulf of Mexico. Vera Cruz continues as a major port to the present day.

Cortés, Francisco Vásquez de Coronado, and other parties that followed were far more zealous in their desire to explore the unknown than their southeastern counterparts such as Columbus, De Soto, De Leon, and others that followed them. To their credit, the eastern explorers provided the impetus for launching cattle ranching in vast lands that would become the southeastern United States. These Spaniards referred to the district known as Guale, which would include much of modern-day Florida and Georgia. By 1600, Guale boasted several large civilian ranches or haciendas, seventy-nine Catholic missions, eight towns, and two royal haciendas. But these figures paled in comparison to progress that came with the conquest of Mexico and its expansive missionary and military campaigns.

Northeastern Port of Entry for European Horses

American horse history often dwells on English importations, omitting contributions of the French. Frank Forester, in his 1857 publication, *The Horse of America,* provided background on French and Dutch imports, as well as and English:

> In 1604, M. L'Escarbot, a French lawyer, brought horses with other domestic animals, into Arcadia, and, in 1608, the French, extending colonization into Canada, introduced horses into that country, where the present race, though it has somewhat degenerated in size, owing probably to the inclemency of the climate, still shows the blood, sufficiently distinct, of the Norman and Breton breeds. In 1609, the English ships, landing at Jamestown, brought, beside swine, sheep and cattle, six mares and a horse, and in 1657 the importance of increasing the stock of this valuable animal was so largely recognized, that an act was passed prohibiting its exportation from the province. In 1629, horses and mares were brought into the plantations of Massachusetts Bay by Francis Higginson, formerly of Leicestershire, from which county many of the animals imported. (Forester 1857)

Forester credited Holland as the source

{1.4} *Percheron stallion, Picador 27370.*

of the first heavy draft horse arriving on American soil:

> New York received its first horses in 1625, imported from Holland by the Dutch West India Company, probably of the Flanders breed, of which, however, few traces seem to exist, unless it be in the Conestoga horse of Pennsylvania, which, I think, shows some affinity to that breed, either directly or through the English dray-horse, which is understood to be originally of Flemish origin. (Forester 1857)

The influence of horse breeding systems of France, according to Forester, was found as far west as Illinois, the gateway to the American Midwest.

> In 1750, the French of Illinois possessed considerable numbers of French horses, and, since that time, as the science of agriculture has improved and advanced, pure animals of many distinct breeds have been constantly imported into this country, which have created in different sections and districts distinct families easily recognized; as the horses of Massachusetts and Vermont, admirable for their qualities as draft horses, both powerful and active, and capable of quick as well as heavy work—the Conestogas, excellent for ponderous slow efforts in teaming and the like—and the active wiry horses of the West, well adapted for riding, and affording mounts to most of the American cavalry. (Forester 1857)

Impact of the Spanish Colonial Mount

Whether the Spanish Barb horse entered the Americas via the southeastern or southwestern portal of entry, it is clear that the Spanish mount is the progenitor of many breeds and subbreeds of South, Central, and North America.

Over time, diligent research and record keeping by serious equine breeders, geneticists, and historians have resulted in significant evidence, often supported by DNA (deoxyribonucleic acid) findings, that the blood of the Spanish Barb circulates through the ancestral veins of the horses of the Americas. Some examples of these horses include the following:

Appaloosa	American mustang
American Paint Horse	Sulfur Herd of Utah
American Quarter Horse	Cebat Herd of Arizona
Pinto horse	Kiger Herd of Oregon
Florida Cracker	Pryor Mountain Herd of Montana and Wyoming
Morgan	Hawaiian horse (not confirmed)
Wilbur Cruce Strain of Arizona	Paso Fino
Nokota Herd	Peruvian Paso
Feral horse of Western Canada	Carolina Marsh Tacky

Evolution of the Mustang Horse

Whether they roam the deserts of Nevada-Utah, the mountains of Oregon, Montana, or Wyoming, the mustang of the American continent differs little from those found on the steep slopes of Mauna Kea or the deep valleys of Waipiʻo and Waimanu on the Big Island of Hawaiʻi. They are all descendants of domestic horses gone wild. This could also be said of the feral horses of Mexico, Canada, Australia, and New Zealand.

"Feral" is the biologist's name for animals that moved from a domestic setting to a wild state, regardless of species. Traditional farm and ranch livestock—the bovine (cattle), the ovine (sheep), the caprine (goat), and the porcine (hog)—all have feral counterparts, as does the horse. Of these, only the feral hog is found in all fifty American states.

Left to their destiny, feral animals over several generations develop a characteristic phenotype (physical appearance): "lean and mean," based on their "fight or flight" physical and neurological mechanisms. Those inborn and acquired mechanisms serve as means of self-preservation in the face of real or perceived threat. This leads to the Darwinian axiom of "survival of the fittest": the lean, mean *corriente* steer escapes the snare of the vaquero's lariat, while the errant but robust Hereford yearling is readily roped and hogtied by the Wyoming cowhand.

In the gradual process of becoming feral, skeletal as well as muscular changes occur. The rib cage becomes narrower than well sprung, resulting in a deeper thorax. The line of the vertebral column, no longer parallel to the ground, slopes downward to a narrower pelvic frame. While the bones of the limbs maintain their density, the height of the animal is compromised, resulting in smaller total body frame. A feral animal is always smaller than its forebears or domestic counterparts. The single equalizer here would be stepped-up nutrition of a current generation as opposed to its ancestral counterparts, rare though this instance may be. Other explanations for the smaller frame size of feral animals are rampant inbreeding and the absence of selective mating toward superior genetic combinations. Poor forage and inadequate minerals, however, remain primary factors.

The heads of feral animals lengthen and their muzzles become narrower. Nostril diameter, however, remains a patent counterpart to lung capacity in part of the "fight or flight" mechanism. The feral horse has a somewhat coarse head that is crowned by good-sized ears and a convex nose bridge. Rarely are the eyes large, brown, and round, as found in better-bred horses.

Hooves tend to remain large, black, and upright in these horses. The bipeds of other livestock tend to become claw footed. In all cases, the terrain of the rain forest, rugged canyons, and arid inland and coastal ranges provides natural trimming for the feral animals that race about in pursuit of food or when being pursued by a predator.

In the male, musculature of the chest and shoulders remains stout for offensive and defensive purposes. Their hips, albeit narrowed, provide propulsion from loin and limb muscles that generate early and lasting speed. In the female, the udder becomes smaller and more closely imbedded in her groin. Her milk is richer in quality but lessened in quantity. In the multiparous or litter-bearing species such as the hog, the sow delivers only four to five piglets, while domestic piggeries expect ten to twelve from each brood sow.

In terms of coat color, the more camouflaged the skin and hair, the greater the survival rate. Loud-colored feral animals are highly visible to man or animal predators and are thus more easily captured or killed. Pinto-colored feral livestock were readily depopulated, leaving a gene pool of black, brown, dun, fawn, or brindle coats. Even Indian warrior predilection for calico ponies reduced the pinto gene pool, as free-roaming reproductive opportunities were reduced. Despite this, pinto-colored horses are not uncommon in mustang herds throughout North America.

Roles of the Conquistadors and Missionaries

In the conquest of Mexico, cattle were imported in large numbers over several sailings. Three Spanish strains were introduced: the *prieto,* the *ganado,* and the *retinto.* These strains were hardy and temperamental, relating closely to the bloodlines used in production of fighting bulls. Cattle were taken along on missions in

South, Central, and North America as a portable meat pantry, but their numbers were few compared to those that escaped into the wild. Spain's incursion into South America was harshly military, and conquest of the native tribes was a dismal failure. The indigenous tribes often rustled horses and cattle, but more were lost by abandonment by the conquistadors' hurried escape from marauding bands of Indians. Forester provided a graphic background in his 1857 account:

> It must have been the case, in the bloody wars of Mexico and Peru, where the battles more than once went disastrously for the Spaniards, that warhorses, their riders being slain, would recover their freedom, and propagate their species rapidly, in the wide, luxuriant and well-watered plains, where the abundance of food, the genial climate, and the absence of beasts of prey capable of coping with so powerful an animal as the horse, would favor their increase. (Forester 1867)

In their northerly explorations, the conquistadors wisely adopted the spiritual thrust of the Christian missionaries and thus successfully developed Mexico and northern territories into Spanish holdings. Despite the spiritual theme, conquest did not come without hard work and sacrifice. In 1540, Francisco Vásquez de Coronado arrived in New Spain (Mexico and California) in his quest for Cibola, the City of Gold. Pressing north, he and his large entourage were likely the first Europeans seen by the Indians in what is now the United States. Aside from the contrasting image of the conquistadors, the Native American was enamored with the mounts upon which they rode.

Historian Joe B. Franz provides the following perspective in his commentary for Bill Wittliff's photographic collection on the vaquero:

> In the beginning they thought he was human, or even superhuman. When later they learned that the Spanish horseman could be separated and that the horse was actually an animal, they still regarded him with awe and fear. When finally they learned that they could ride him, the Spanish overlords proclaimed laws that forbade the Indian from climbing astride. An attitude of servility is hard to maintain in a man sitting fourteen hands high above the crowd. Servility belongs to a man afoot or on his knees. A man who keeps his gaze down when on a horse is likely to look you straight in the eye.
>
> Yet they overcame the first fears, and they overcame the restrictive laws, and they became the vaqueros—men who could ride with the best, mounted men whose exploits with horses and cows have been told throughout the world, men who taught the later North American cowboy how to run an empire from "the hurricane deck" of a Spanish mesteño. (Wittliff 2002)

Two things set the vaquero apart from other forms of stock tending: use of the reata (lariat) to control and gather livestock and incorporating the *cabeza* (dally horn) on the saddle tree. The dally horn served as a portable snubbing post to which the end of the lariat was attached in the process of roping and apprehending a *buiso* (wild bull).

While the early Mexican saddle maker is credited for converting the bulky conquistador saddle to a functional saddle tree with a dally horn, the reata may have been in the Americas long before the Spaniards landed with horses. Woven from sisal, manila, or maguey fibers, the early reata served a distinct purpose in battle. Later lariats of spliced rawhide were brought to bear in apprehending wild horses, cattle, hogs, and bears by the newly minted bronze race.

The function of the lariat has traditionally been credited to the Indians of Mexico as an asset to apprehending and handling of cattle. However, Lummis reports otherwise.

In his publication *The Spanish Pioneers and the California Missions,* Charles H. Lummis reports of clashes by the conquistadors with Peruvian Indians as early as 1537 in which lariats (reata) were used by the native tribesmen to rout their invaders. In Juan Pizzaro's challenging conquest of Cuzco, his men were fiercely repelled by native warriors' effective use of sling stones and reata, the latter weapon likely woven from fibrous vines, sisal, maguey, and manila. "As cattle were introduced, the dried hides offered a stronger more malleable and durable strand to be braided by four or more plaits into a very functional rope for lariat use" (Lummis 1936).

By edict, the Spanish government, their explorers, and missionaries outlawed the Indian from becoming mounted. The Spaniards logically feared the pandemonium that could result from horse-bound Mexican and American Indian tribes that had come under their control as indentured slaves under the guise of Christianity. It was the Gila Apaches and southern tribes that first came into contact with the Spanish horse. Interestingly, in 1541, Viceroy Mendoza allowed allied chieftains to ride horses as they led their tribesmen. This marked the starting point of the Native American horse culture. As early as the 1590s, horses brought into the northern region of Mexico were often stolen by Apache and Comanche warriors, falling now into the hands of the Plains Indians, who were rapidly thrust from a pedestrian culture into a sophisticated and wide-ranging mounted society of the Great Plains.

As cattle populations expanded along the missionary pathways moving north and east from Mexico, the native peoples were pressed into service as stock tenders. Working afoot among hordes of increasingly wild cattle, they were ineffective, and this pressure brought about the rescission of the edict barring the natives from horse use. The native rider immediately bonded with the horse from Mexico through the western part of the North American continent with uniquely natural grace. Concurrently, Spanish caballeros took native women as wives, and the bronze race (mestizo) was born.

{1.5} *Once mounted, using minimal tack and saddlery, the Native American displayed horsemanship of superb ability. Note the early prototype with high pommel fore and aft.*

Jerald Underwood, in *Vaqueros, Cowboys and Buckaroos,* is eloquent on the topic:

> Imagine if you will a situation in which a Spanish conquistador takes as his wife an Indian woman. To this couple is born a little boy. He rides on a horse in a cradle strapped to his mother's back. Later he rides in front of her, clinging to the horse's mane with his little hands. His mother holds him to keep him from falling off. This little boy absorbs the feel and smell of the horse. As he grows larger, the boy rides with his father and later gets his own horse. By the age of ten the boy becomes an accomplished rider. He is part of the horse; the horse is part of him. The boy is neither Spanish nor Indian. He is a member of a new bronze race: he is Mexican. This young man can ride as no one in North America has ever ridden before: He is the true centaur of the New World. (Clayton, Hoy, and Underwood 2001)

Francisco de Ibarra, a Spanish explorer of the 1550s and 1560s, wisely chose the grassy plains and fertile river bottoms of present-day Durango and Sinaloa states of Mexico. With his vast herds of horses and cattle flourishing, he sought further adventure. He crossed the Sierra Madre mountain range, and in spite of tragic losses of men and animals, he founded a thriving Hispanic community. In a few short years, repetitive Indian attacks brought the mission into abandonment. Two decades later, Hernando de la Trigo sought to reincarnate the mission, only to find that in the interim, feral horse and cattle numbers grew to about ten thousand head. Crossing the Rio Grande into south Texas, the explorers encountered mounted Indians frequently. Permanent settlements were established in present-day New Mexico by the Juan Onate expedition of 1598. By 1700, mestizo and Indian horsemen were commonplace all across Central and North America's western half. Traffic went both ways: the Shoshone tribes frequented trading pathways from present-day Oregon to the Aztec capitol of central Mexico. The Shoshone, like the Apache, Kiowa, Comanche, and Cherokee tribes, as well as the Mexican natives, had transformed themselves from a pedestrian society to a culture of skilled horsemen. The same conversion of a barefoot Native Hawaiian stock tender to a mounted Polynesian cowhand would begin in 1833, when the bronze centaur, the Mexican vaquero, ventured to Hawai'i, giving birth to a culture appropriately called *paniolo.*

CHAPTER 2

VAQUERO INFLUENCE

Cattle ranching became well established throughout present-day southwestern United States, thanks in large part to the Catholic mission and presidio systems that came with the Spanish conquest of old Mexico. Like the beads of a rosary, missions dotted the landscape from Mexico to northern California, converting the natives to Christianity while transforming the mestizo into a working cowhand with horsemanship skills of legendary proportion. The missionaries from Mexico taught horsemanship and cattle ranching techniques to the Dieguenо, Ipai, and Tipai Indians by the early 1700s. These aboriginal California tribes were not as warlike nor nomadic as their Apache and Comanche counterparts. Their nature was somewhat compatible with the missionary and vaquero genres. The founding of Mission San Francisco Solano in 1823 linked the remarkable cordon of more than twenty missions of Alta (upper) California from San Diego north to Sonoma Valley. Conveniently scattered, these missions were situated a day's journey apart on foot.

In a few words, Joe B. Franz aptly sums up the significant role of the vaquero: "In time, the progeny of those first cattle and the men who chased and herded and worked them over vast open ranges from sure-footed and well-reined ponies would provide the New World her most enduring legend: the Vaquero, the cow-worker, the Cowboy" (Franz and Choate 1955).

Like the King's Trail circling the Big Island of Hawai'i, El Camino Real became the King's Highway of New Spain. This seven-hundred-mile pathway joining the Harbor of the Sun with the Valley of Seven Moons that began as a mere trail between missions eventually became a heavily trodden passage for the arrival of Mexican colonists into Alta California. This was long before the gringos came,

{ 2.1 } *Classic profile of a vaquero riding shoreside.*

a time when the era of the squeaking *carreta* (oxcart) was replaced by mounted caballeros clad in serape and sombrero, riding on saddles of spruce adorned with carved leather and silver inlay. Not far behind the landed gentry rode the working vaquero, often clad in common cloth, sandaled feet, and astride a utilitarian but horned saddle.

Soon, mule trains (*atajos*) with securely packed saddles (*aparejo*) succeeded the lowly burro as freight transporters. With progress, mule trains of fifty to sixty head, each bearing a three-hundred-pound packed saddle, meandered northward with the constant bellow of the Mexican mule skinner, "*Hippa mula!*"

In the era leading up to King Kamehameha III's decision to bring skilled vaqueros to mentor Native Hawaiians in cowboy life skills, feral horse herds in California had grown significantly. According to Mariano Guadalupe Vallejo, military leader, politician, and rancher in early California, by the year 1806 horse numbers within the valleys of San Jose and Santa Clara were so large that it became necessary to kill seven or eight thousand. In the following year, thousands more were driven ruthlessly into the sea at Santa Barbara. This horrific act was repeated in Monterrey shortly thereafter, as feral horses were ravaging the meadows of forage needed by the some 420,000 head of cattle owned by prominent ranchers. The territory already boasted a population of 62,000 working horses, mules, and donkeys. While old California rancheros were plagued with such oversupply of feral horses, the island nations of Hawai'i, Australia, and New Zealand were receiving their first horse importations.

Still, the vaquero was simply an early-day cowboy, living on meager wages. He worked for the landed gentry, the elite caballero of proud Spanish heritage that developed an equally significant form of horsemanship, the *charro*. The *charro* saddle, complete with ornate accouterments, was a decadent fixture compared with the skeletal Spanish tree of the lowly vaquero, an indentured servant attached to the hacienda ranchero. Even less ornate was the saddle of the Native American Indian, which had a thin tree hewn from soft wood and bound with cloth, rawhide, and buckskin, with minimal attachments. It recalled the age of the Moorish invasion of Iberia, when saddles were of scant structure and design.

The evolution of the vaquero saddle (*silla vaquera*) as well as the Western stock saddle counterpart spanned both world hemispheres. The concept of the saddle, a fixture adjoining man to his mount, spread from its birth in ancient Persia through Europe and North Africa, culminating on the Iberian Peninsula (old Spain). Spain by the early Middle Ages had become world renown as a center for breeding fine horses. All developmental forms of horse tack logically rode the coattails of progress in horse production, especially when related to the mounted knight and military excellence.

The conquistadors entering Vera Cruz in 1519 were well appointed with Moorish *jineta*-type combat saddles. This saddle had a high, steep cantle that formed a crescent-shaped butt-board wrapping around the rider's rear and hips. The front of the saddle was adorned with a bulky, hornless pommel that came up nearly as high as the cantle. Such a seating arrangement nearly entrapped the knight in his saddle. It was suited only for combat and not cattle work.

Richard W. Slatta, in *Cowboys of the Americas* (1990), reflects on vaquero life. Some of the information in this section is based on his observations.

As livestock production flourished in New Spain (Mexico and California), so did the demand for competent vaqueros appropriately mounted and equipped. The Spanish combat prototype underwent drastic modification in form and function to suit the vaquero, who spent countless hours, days, and weeks on the vast desert and mountain ranges attending to cattle, horses, and sheep, a challenge that could only be met on the back of a wiry steed. Vaquero responsibilities required long hours in the saddle doing work of intensity, skill, and finesse, such as roping a wild *buiso* (unbranded jack bull) for branding and castrating.

The Mexican *silladero* (saddle maker) refined the combat cantle into a low profile, comfortably concaved rear seat for his client, the working vaquero. Most significantly, he built a *cabeza,* or dally horn, by vertically extending the forward piece, the pommel. It was the *cabeza* (head) upon which the vaquero would *dar la vuelta* ("take a turn," anglicized to "dally") his lariat after roping a wild steer. The mestizo saddle maker stripped much

{ 2.2 } *Mounted on a trusty donkey with full vaquero regalia, the vaquero displays the protective* armas *covering his legs from pommel to* tapadero, *precursor of the cowboy's chaps.*

{ 2.3 } *William Harry Naleilehua Purdy, father of Ikua Purdy, stands with his mount. Note the rawhide-braided tack and lālā-covered saddle, as well as his* botas *(jackboots).*

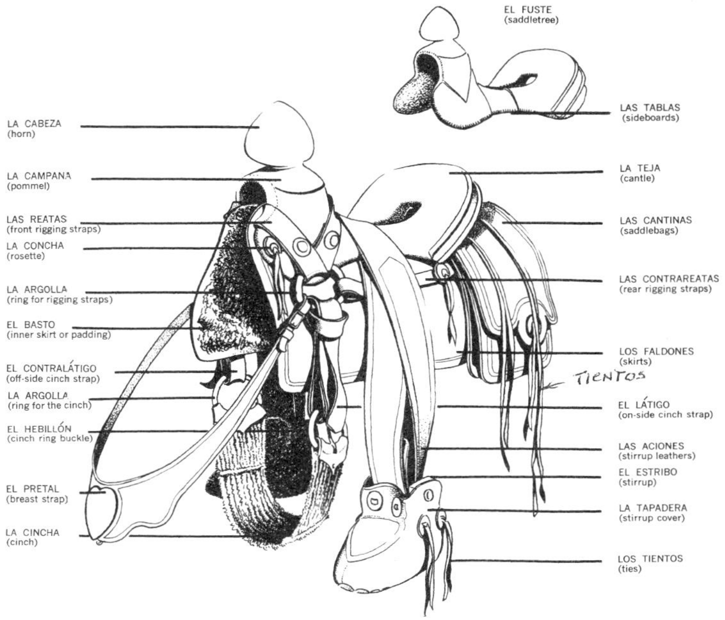

{ 2.4 } *The vaquero invention of the* tapadero *covering of the stirrup gave lasting protection to his feet, boots, and spurs, an accoutrement still used in today's cowboy gear, two centuries later.*

{ 2.5 } *The Mexican* silladero *(saddle maker) modified over time a work saddle, giving greater comfort and functional beauty to the vaquero's prime tool of his trade. This well-worn model likely lasted for decades of hard use.*

of the heavy leather and metal armor but retained practical Spanish accoutrements including a rump cover, albeit refined from an *anquera* (over the rump and down the flanks) to an *anquerita* that became a duckbill-shaped tail piece (*cola de pato*). The heavy leather draping over the saddle seat and stirrups was trimmed into the tidy *mochila* that dropped through slots over the horn and cantle and bordered the periphery of the saddle skirt. The vaquero saw the need to retain the heavy leather that hung from the pommel and draped over the rider's legs. With native ingenuity, the saddle *armas* maker converted the attached *armas* to the *chaparreras* then worn by the vaquero as the early prototype of modern-day chaps. Also retained were the saddle skirting (*faldones, basto*) and long stirrup leathers (*aciones*), with attendant fenders coming later. With practical wisdom, the stirrup foot piece (*estriba*) was enclosed with heavy rawhide or leather to house and protect the feet of the vaquero, who could ill afford footwear beyond the slipperlike *huarache* or rudimentary jack boots (*botas*). The protective housing became the *tapadero*.

By the mid-1700s, vaqueros across old Mexico had developed work saddles

{ 2.6 } *A horseman from Waimanu Valley, Solomon Kala was a sought-after saddle maker for his technique and the functional beauty of his product. Note the "form fitter" style with enhanced winglike swells at the base of the pommel. The cantle and seat are covered with leather, while the skirting beneath the tree is trimmed with tapalike stamping* (laukuni).

to their needs and taste, with some regional differences in details. Early on, the saddle horn resembled a hemisphere, a ball with a flat top. This was the forerunner of the saddle horn of the northern Mexico vaquero, who enjoyed a bulbous or pear-shaped *cabeza*. By the mid-1800s, the vaquero saddle horn was flattened. developing a squat, platelike appearance.

With regional differences abounding, the California vaquero preferred a narrower, less bulky horn with somewhat of a neck, which could be more easily dallied or tied upon with a lariat. This is the likely prototype of the vaquero saddle brought to the Hawaiian Islands in 1833 (Slatta 1990).

One must suppose that in those times, the vaquero, a working cowboy, gradually gained prominence as an iconic image of old California. The vaquero loved nothing more than a flashy, fast, and beautiful mount. Like all cowboys, they had their favorites. The first choice among all mustangs captured happened to be the palomino, with its light cream-colored coat and silver-white mane and tail. It was the dapple gray and chestnut horses that were targets for capture and training into sound but attractive cow horses. To the Hawaiian *paniolo,* feral mounts were sought after more for their size and conformation, as browns, bays, and blacks were most plentiful.

Once secured in the Islands, the horse provided an image of caballero grace not unlike the days of old California. Reverend Walter Colton's recently published account, *Three Years in California* (1846–1849), describes the horse-riding habits of the "gay caballero":

> A Californian is most at home in his saddle; there he has some claims to originality, if not in character then in costume. His hat, with its conical crown and broad rim, throws back the sun's rays from its dark, glazed surface. It is fastened on by a band which passes under his chin, and rests on a red handkerchief, which turbans his head, from beneath which his black locks flow out upon the wind. . . .
>
> His feet rest in stirrups of wood, carved from the solid oak, and which are extremely strong and heavy. His saddle rises high fore and aft, and is broadly skirted with leather, which is stamped into figures, through the interstices of which red and green silk flash out with gay effect. The reins of his bridle are thick and narrow, and the headstall is profusely ornamented with silver plate. His horse, with his long flowing mane, arching neck, broad

chest, full flanks, and slender legs, is full of fire. He seldom trots, and will gallop all day without seeming weary. (Colton 2007)

The vaquero saddle was about to undergo a metamorphosis, as the Hawaiian saddle maker improved the prototype but retained the "slick" appearance of the saddle tree, as though the Lord made the horse with this graceful accoutrement already in place.

Regardless of the regional variations, the fork (the inverted Y forming the pommel shoulders and horn) of the Mexican tree (sometimes referred to as a Spanish tree) remained "slick." A slick fork has flattened sides that slope about forty-five degrees from the horn downward laterally. Using the Mexican tree as a prototype, American saddle makers often embellished the forks by bulking out the fork shoulder with wood, leather, and padding. This is described in cowboy circles as a "swelled fork." In some cases, it became an extreme embellishment of the fork shoulders into what was called a "form-fitter." With a high cantle in back and a form-fitted fork at the front, the bronco buster was often entrapped when the horse threw himself to the ground, just as the combat saddle of the conquistador similarly entrapped the knight. To the vaquero and later the Hawaiian *paniolo,* the freedom of movement of the slick fork was paramount as a safety measure. Soon, detachable "bucking rolls" were made to swell up the slick fork if a rider so desired. Noted horseman Godfrey Kainoa is one such user.

Rigging of a saddle refers to the physical features that attach it to the horse. Leather straps around the pommel area converge below to a large metal ring (*argolla;* in Hawaiian, *lina ʻaweʻawe*) three to four inches in diameter. This creates a single forward rigging from which a leather strap (*latigo; ʻili huki*) is suspended and threaded through a cinch ring. The cinch (*cincha; kaula ʻōpū*), usually made of fiber or fabric, partially encircles the lower girth line of the horse's chest behind the elbows. The rigging on the far (right) side also threads through the opposite cinch ring. Tightening the two *latigos* "cinches" the saddle to the horse.

{2.7} *Detachable in nature, bucking rolls give the rider a degree of security when riding a broncky colt. Note the darker bulbous roll behind the saddle horn.*

Adding a second cinch or rear cinch (*harriguera; kaula keko*) created a double

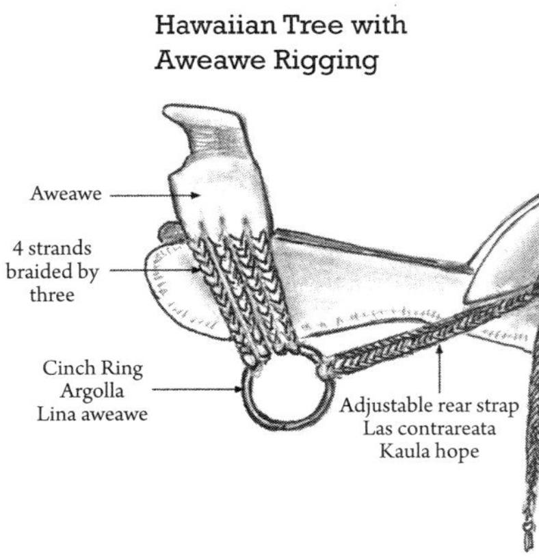

{ 2.8 } *A barren rawhide-covered saddle tree.*

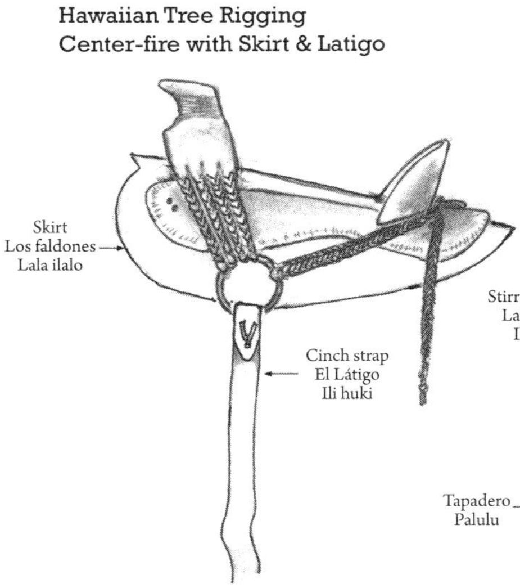

{ 2.9 } *Saddle tree with* ʻaweʻawe *(braided fore rigging),* ʻili hope *(rear rigging strap),* ʻili huki (latigo), *and skirt* (pale ilalo).

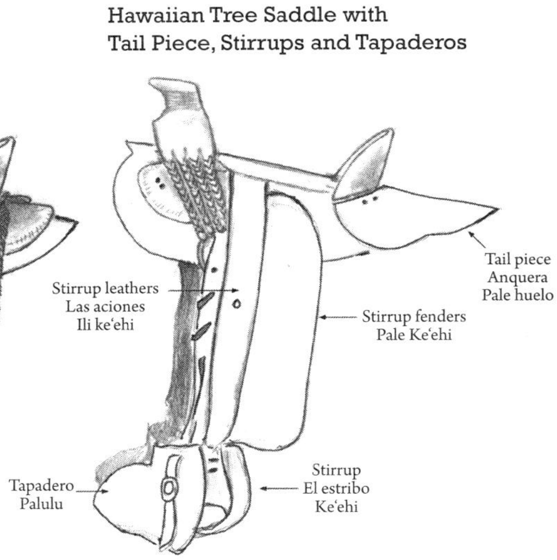

{ 2.10 } *Saddle tree with* ʻili keʻehi *(stirrups),* palulu (tapaderos) *and* pale huelo *(tailpiece) added.*

rigging. The American cowboy and saddle maker are credited with this improvement, which makes the saddle far more secure under heavy roping use. By the late 1800s, cowboys rode double-rigged saddles commonly on both sides of the Rio Grande. A leather component that formed a seat cover (jockey) provided the rear rigging suspension by attaching cinch rings on the near (left) and far corners. Again, *latigo* straps are suspended from each side by threading through rear cinch rings. The rear cinch was made of heavy leather or rawhide, with three- to four-inch rings on each side.

The most significant modification made by the Hawaiian saddle maker was the development of a front rigging of superior strength and flexibility. It is called an *ʻaweʻawe* rigging, the Hawaiian term meaning "tentacle." Hawaiian saddles were basically patterned after Spanish saddles and traditionally had taller, wider horns, slightly higher cantles, and braided front rigging straps. Hawaiian saddle makers did not use cured leather for most of the saddle, as rawhide was not only hardier and more readily available but withstood moisture much better. It is said that the *ʻaweʻawe* is the strongest saddle rigging made, and it was adapted as part of the Hawaiian saddle because the cured rawhide could withstand the high humidity in Hawaiʻi and not rot. Pat Bergin recorded the step-by-step construction of the Hawaiian tree saddle in an article written forty years ago after interviewing master saddle makers of that time.

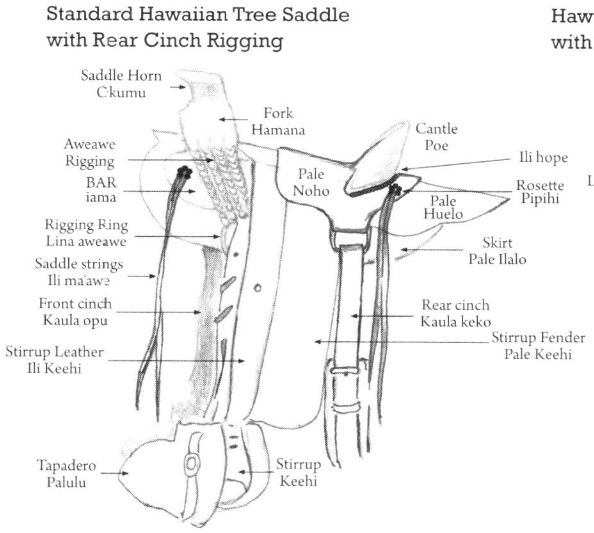

{ 2.11 } *Saddle parts identified, including* hapa lālā *(half jockey) and* kaula keko *(flank cinch).*

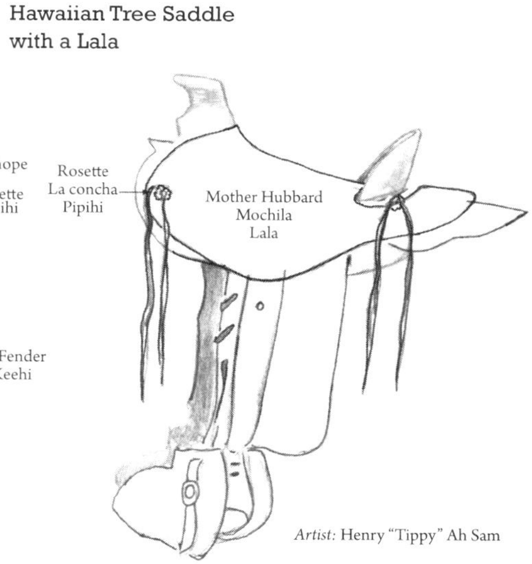

{ 2.12 } *Saddle parts identified, including* hapa lālā *(half jockey) and* kaula keko *(flank cinch).*

{ 2.13 } *Horse hitched in old California. Note vaquero saddle with duckbill-shaped tailpiece* (cola de pato; pale huelo) *and* mochila (lālā *in Hawaiian*).

Hawaiian Saddle Making

By Patricia Bergin (circa 1975)

The saddle maker held a central position in early Hawaiian communities dependent on ranching. In larger ranch communities, it was not uncommon for two or more individuals to perform saddle-making tasks. These men frequently serviced smaller surrounding ranches as well as the larger ranch that employed them. Retired or disabled cowboys frequently became saddle makers later in their careers. On the other hand, there were those men who took an interest in the skill very early in their youth. Nonetheless, each became a master of his art and style. They were true artisans whose legacy endured far beyond their natural lives.

One of these individuals was Manuel Miranda of Kūkaʻiau Ranch on the Big Island. A self-taught saddle maker, Manuel learned the craft simply by observation, trial and error, and improvising his own tools. He provided saddle making services to the Kūkaʻiau Ranch in addition to his other ranch responsibilities. Most of the information for this article was obtained through firsthand interviews with Mr. Miranda and other community members who have an interest in the Hawaiian saddle.

{ 2.14 } *Manuel Miranda, a Kūkaʻiau Ranch cowboy and saddle maker, mounted on his cow horse Jim, which did double duty as a plow horse in times of need.*

Construction of a saddle from start to finish can easily take two hundred hours or more, excluding the drying seasoning process for the rawhide, which takes approximately six months depending on the weather. An experienced custom saddle maker can turn out about five to six completed saddles each year. Hawaiian saddles are patterned after Mexican vaquero saddles and traditionally have taller, wider horns, slightly higher cantles, braided front rigging straps called *ʻaweʻawe,* a rounded skirt and tailpiece, and are primarily constructed more of rawhide than of cured leather. Rawhide is not only hardier and more readily available, but it withstands moisture much better. The *ʻaweʻawe* is known to be the strongest saddle rigging made and was adapted as part of the Hawaiian saddle because cured rawhide could withstand the high moisture in Hawaiʻi and not rot. The average seat from brim of the cantle to the back of the horn is about fifteen and a half inches, and the width varies with the conformation of the horse. Older trees were narrower because horses were basically Thoroughbreds with narrower backs and taller withers. Today, trees are flatter and rounder to fit the backs of Quarter Horses. Life expectancy for Hawaiian tree saddles varies, but it can be thirty or more years depending on the care taken to keep them in good condition. More often than not, the tree itself remains in perfect condition long after the leather has rotted away. In the hands of the Hawaiian tree aficionado, these revered trees are refurbished, covered in leather, and pressed into service for yet another *paniolo* (Hawaiian cowboy) or pleasure rider.

Constructing a saddle from start to finish requires specific materials and follows a step-by-step process. Basic raw materials include the following:

1. Native wood for the bars and cantle cut into lengths approximately twenty-four inches in length and two inches thick
2. One forked branch of *neneleau* (sumac) or *hau* for the fork and horn
3. Cured rawhide to cover the tree
4. Cured goatskin for lacing
5. One tree form or mold
6. Dowel pins to join the wooden tree
7. One strip of rawhide approximately eight feet long and five to six inches wide for the *ʻaweʻawe* rigging
8. Four brass rings for the rigging
9. One pair of wooden stirrups for *tapaderos*
10. Cured leather

The *first step* in making a saddle is the selection and harvesting of wood for the tree. There are approximately twenty-one varieties used by Hawaiian saddle makers, some of which are mentioned here:

neneleau (sumac)	*naio (false sandalwood)*
hau	*māmane*
kuawa (guava)	*ʻinia (pride of India)*
manakō (mango)	*Portuguese cyprus*
ʻōhiʻa	*ʻōhai (monkeypod)*
kiawe (mesquite)	*koa (not used often because the dowels squeaked)*

Older, dry, fallen trees were usually selected as there was less likelihood for the wood to warp when being seasoned.

There are four parts to the saddle tree: the two bars, cantle, and fork. The bars and cantle can be made of any wood variety mentioned above. The fork and horn, however, are usually carved from a forked branch of *neneleau* or *hau* because they are strong, light woods that resist cracking or splitting. Both of these woods are difficult to obtain, as they usually grow in deep, dangerous gulches and take two men to harvest; one man to go down and cut it, and another to haul the cut pieces up by rope. The wood is then cut into pieces about twenty-four inches long and two inches thick. The bars and cantle are usually carved from these pieces. The fork and horn usually follow the natural contour of the forked branch and are shaped in one continuous piece. All of these are carved and smoothed to fit the wooden mold. The length of the seat usually remains about the same on the mold—fifteen and a half inches—and the width is easily adjusted by moving lengthwise guides outwardly for a flatter, rounder tree. After these four pieces are carved to fit the form, they are joined together by *kauila* (buckthorn) wood dowels. The finished tree is then allowed to dry for about six months. Any warping or flaws that can hurt the backs of horses are corrected during this period.

The *second step* involves covering the seasoned tree with rawhide. The rawhide is cut into several pieces using a pattern. The cut rawhide is then soaked in water until softened, then left aside for about four hours to remove most of the water. This softened hide is then molded to fit the tree and laced into place with goatskin. Covering the seat is an important step. One large piece is used to cover both the pommel and seat first, then underside pieces are added. The goatskin lacing is usually obtained from arid sources, stripped into approximately three-eighths-inch widths, soaked in water, and then stretched before it is used for lacing. Upon completion, the rawhide-covered tree is sun dried and allowed to contract. Application of the *ʻaweʻawe* is the next step and essentially follows the same procedure.

{ 2.15 } *Master braider Henry Silva of Maui stretching a newly braided five-strand* ʻaweʻawe. *"Maui style" usually has five strands and five plaits.*

A wet strip of rawhide approximately eight feet by five inches is wrapped around the horn twice, down the fork, and stripped into four stripped strands that, once braided by three, go through and *under* the brass rings to join again at the point of origin. This, too, is allowed to dry thoroughly. This style is common to Big Island *ʻaweʻawe* braiders and called "four by three"—four strands braided by three. Maui braiders use a "five by five" style.

The *third and final step* is the addition of cured leather pieces. Using cardboard patterns as guides, the skirting, seat with rear rigging rings, stirrup leathers, fenders, tailpiece, and *tapaderos* are cut and applied to the completed tree. All materials and supplies for this third step are usually obtained through mainland or local saddle equipment suppliers. When asked why wooden stirrups are purchased instead of handmade, each person interviewed stated that stirrups are difficult to make as they must be steamed and dried into appropriate shapes. Manuel Miranda is one of the few who started to make his own stirrups, but he too claimed that the difficult process is hardly worth the time and effort when stirrups are easily obtained for a small cost.

This, then, is the basic saddle. Other decorative markings are added as desired. Lacking proper tooling equipment in the early 1900s, Miranda devised his own out of wood and metal. A wooden line marker he crudely made in 1918 has lasted until today. The metal cutter he created for the edging was fashioned in 1910. He also shaped the broken tip of an old file into a V, which was also used to smooth edges of cured leather. Other equipment included a leather vise for sewing leather pieces together and a marking machine that marked and molded leather more easily than handmade instruments.

Today, a wooden tree patterned after the Hawaiian tree can be purchased through several companies. Called a Hamley Parker Ranch tree, it is somewhat better quality than those made locally. The Hawaiian tree has certainly come a long way from the $10 rawhide-covered trees offered by a Chinese saddle maker from Waipiʻo Valley in the early 1900s.

The Spanish tree, a prototype perfected by time, hard use, experience, and crafters' skill, is truly a mestizo product; Iberian in origin, Mexican in realization, nevertheless perpetual in its contribution to cowboy life, the cattle industry, and Western heritage. Richard E. Ahlborn in his Smithsonian Institute essay "Horizons of the Western Saddle," said it best: "This tree was the foundation of all Mexican stock saddles from later colonial times to this day. Its presence in the United States by 1830 to 1860 only documents the reliance of American military and western stock saddles on some Mexican prototype." Ahlborn went on to acknowledge the importance of recognizing the cultural significance of the evolution of this saddle: "The fact of the Mexican working saddles continental diffusion from the colonial period to the present suggests the capability of certain 'ideal' forms to satisfy a variety of human tasks and social values within a continuously extended environment" (Ahlborn 1980).

By 1833, the "extended environment" came to include the Hawaiian Islands, where the Native Hawaiian saddle maker made further improvements, refining the Mexican prototype to establish another enduring one, the Hawaiian tree. This Polynesian prototype has remained relatively unchanged over the past 175 years. Once again, we witness man's ingenious modification of an instrument, the saddle, to suit the needs and tastes of a given community culture that lies in the middle of the Pacific Ocean, some three thousand miles due west of its seat of origin in old Mexico.

{2.16} *The typical Hawaiian tree saddle (circa 1920) stands as a prototype that in perfection of style has survived well over a century of ranch life with little or no change. Identical saddles are commonly seen today on working ranches.*

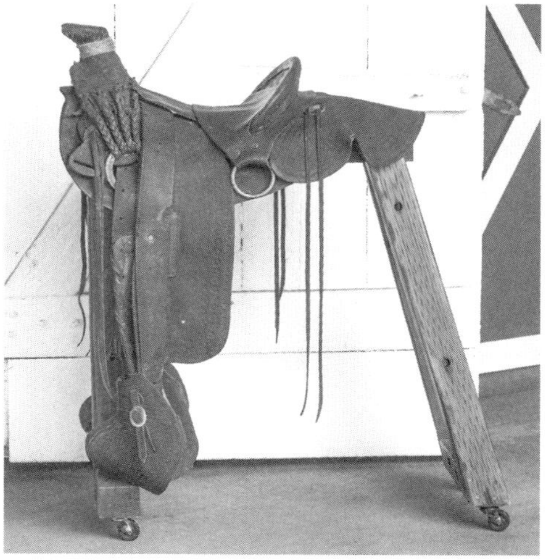

{2.17} *This saddle, made by Manuel Miranda of Kūka'iau Ranch, is typically* paniolo *and belongs to John Holi Ma'e.*

Coming of the Vaquero Hawaiiano

Three decades passed after the first horse came to the Islands before another wave of horseflesh arrived and the *paniolo* role and history of the cattle and horse industry began. At the time, livestock shipping was approaching a gentler, more caring level. The arrival of the vaquero with his *montura* (horse gear) and string of mounts to the shores of Hawai'i was made possible by the royal request of Kauikeaouli—King Kamehameha III. A year earlier, the king was hosted by a ranchero Californio to enjoy a typical Mexican rodeo, which, in the true sense of the word, was a roundup of vast herds gathered by mounted horsemen, the vaqueros. Kamehameha was captivated by the swift and graceful lariat loop of the lithe and able horsemen in roping and casting longhorns in the process of branding, castrating, and earmarking.

What the king witnessed as swift, efficient, and relatively humane processing of cattle by the vaqueros was a far cry from the labor-intensive method of the Native Hawaiian and *malihini* (newly arrived) bullock hunters. After the *kapu* (taboo) protecting the *pipi 'āhiu* (wild cattle) was lifted, pioneer cattlemen such as John Palmer Parker I and W. W. (Jack) Purdy led teams of natives to the high mountain ranges, where the feral bullocks would be dispatched by a muzzle-loaded rifle. Often, the wounded bullock would wander a mile or two before being brought down by another gunshot or cattle dogs. At this site, skinning and boning of the bullock began the salting process. Casks of salt carried on the backs of the *maka'āinana* (commoners) were emptied, as large slabs of fresh beef were vigorously salted by hand rubbing (*lomilomi*). The empty salt casks were tightly repacked with salted beef, and the bearers headed back to the central *kauhale* (village). When multiple casks were gathered, they were transported by the dozen via oxcarts to the calm bays of ocean ports such as Kawaihae on the Big Island or Lahaina on the Island of Maui, where whaling ships replenished their stores with preserved beef. Honolulu also served as such a depot. Later, all these ports became vital in the export of tons of kegged beef to supply the 1849 Gold Rush beef markets of California.

The Hawaiian king was aware that he had ample talent in the native community, horse numbers to support it, and most critically, a huge population of wild cattle that plundered island farms, villages, and meadows, to convert the pedestrian stock tenders into willing, mounted, and skilled vaqueros. He realized that, with appropriate mentoring, naturally athletic Hawaiians were capable of converting a cumbersome, struggling beef industry into a major export industry. By royal decree, King Kamehameha III called for vaqueros from California to come to the Islands in 1833, probably unaware that he not only launched a major industrial/agricultural industry but also founded the Hawaiian *paniolo* culture that would parallel the image and skill of the vaqueros of New Spain and America's West.

The *vaquero hawaiiano* (those bound for the Islands) guaranteed their successful entry into the Hawaiian cattle industry by bringing their own mounts. More than likely, these mounts were of mustang origin typical of the Spanish Barb—small (13 to 14 hands/700 to 800 pounds), wiry, and athletic, with extensive experience in cow horsemanship, roping, snubbing, casting, and even bulldogging of wild cattle equal to or greater than their size and weight.

Care of these horses aboard ship was at a higher level than common stock for two reasons. First, they were traveling at the invitation of royalty, and second, the vaquero's appreciation for his beloved companion, the *caballo,* meant close attention to its daily care. Vaquero stock tenders brushed down salt- and sweat-encrusted coats, cleaned and rebedded mangers, and fed and watered the mounts twice daily. While embarkation in California meant dockside loading, the vaquero was apprehensive about casting his mounts overboard in Kawaihae Bay for the swim to shore. There was no alternative, as the harbor had not yet developed dockside disembarkation of livestock.

The vaquero and his extensive *montura* of saddles, lariats, bits, bridles, whips, and blacksmithing tools were brought ashore in outrigger canoes. The vaqueros readily befriended the Native Hawaiian people. They were formally received by the king himself, as well as by established cattlemen such as John Palmer Parker and Jack Purdy and by Charles Beckley, the king's *konohiki* (regional agent), who also looked after cattle of royal ownership and was an integral part of the reception for the Mexican cowboys.

{2.18} *Kamehameha III is credited with bringing to the Islands California vaqueros who mentored Native Hawaiians to become mounted* paniolo.

While the king returned to Waimea village by carriage, the vaqueros were provided fresh local mounts to drive their seaworn strings of horses twenty miles *mauka* (inland), where they were turned out in verdant meadows for a monthlong rest. The vaqueros were first headquartered at Hanaipoe, a cowboy camp nestled against the northern face of Mauna Kea.

In these Native Hawaiian cowboy candidates, the vaqueros found four existing conditions that gave their native charges a comparative advantage: innate athletic ability, advanced craftsmanship skills, fearless posture, and a willingness to learn.

In the interim, the vaquero contingent met and bonded with more than a dozen of the king's choice candidates for training in the use of the horse and lariat for the capture and eventual reduction of the hordes of *pipi ʻāhiu*. In addition to the king's men, about a score of able-bodied men volunteered, some with limited experience around horses, donkeys, and mules.

Native Hawaiian Athletic Ability

The Native Hawaiian of that era was a man of the sea and the mountains. Whether swimming, diving, or paddling canoe,

{ 2.19 } *National champion steer roper Archie Kaaua aboard his top mount, Diamond Jim. Note leggings on Kaaua and* lālā *on his saddle.*

the *kanaka maoli* (native) engaged in constant physical activity and conditioning, with mountain treks for hunting and gathering adding to the equation. A diet based on fish and fiber helped maintain excellent body condition.

A high degree of hand-to-eye coordination was developed in most Hawaiian people, as witnessed in precontact and subsequent feats of war, war games, athletic challenges, and even the art of hula. In postcontact Hawaiʻi, conventional athletics—especially volleyball, softball, baseball, basketball, football, and soccer—have showcased the Hawaiians for their innate hand-to-eye coordination. Specifically, the Hawaiian embraced roping as a skill of national prominence in the case of the 1908 World Championship of Ikua Purdy in the Cheyenne Frontier Days (Daddy of 'em All) Rodeo in Wyoming. Placing third and sixth in competition were Archie Kaʻauʻa and Jack Low/Billy Spencer respectively. Hawaiian team ropers continue to excel to the present day on a national level. Little did the vaquero know that the product of his mentoring would be world championship ropers only seventy-five years later.

Advanced Artisans

The Polynesians who voyaged to Hawaiʻi were propelled by winds that pressed against sails woven by the native hand, suspended by cords of *aho* (sennet) that were braided by those same hands. The masts mounted upon the double-hulled, oceangoing canoes were carved by the ancestors of Hawaiians for their epic journey to the north and a new home.

The wood carver that hewed the vessel from lengthy logs and magnificent trees also made hand-hewn vessels for food and water. The Polynesian craftsmen also worked with a denser medium, that of hard stone or basalt to make warheads and weapons for combat, as well as poi pounders, *kukui* oil lamps, and mortars and pestles with salt-drying stones in times of peace. When the vaqueros arrived, these skills were still being maintained as a way of life.

The Native Hawaiian's transition from a seafaring man to a mounted *paniolo* blended both worlds in common phrases and names of equipment. The names of major saddle tree parts are adapted from those of the outrigger canoe. The prominent front piece that adorns the bow of a canoe is often called an *'ōkumu,* a term used for the saddle horn. The actual outriggers on a canoe are referred to as *ama,* which resemble the right and left underplates (sidebars) of the saddle seat; these bars are called *iama* or *ama.* The rear seat piece (cantle), *poe* in Hawaiian, takes its name from the semiround splashboard that adorns the fore and aft of the canoe deck. Lines and cordage are called *laina,* which for a *paniolo* can refer to his lariat or reins. *'Alu ka laina* is an order to slack your reins or rope. Such naming cognates were common as the Hawaiian seaman evolved into a cowhand.

These newcomers redirected the Hawaiian craftsmen to carve the saddle tree from *neneleau* (sumac) wood, the dowel to join its parts from the *kauila* tree, and the fork or *hāmana,* the cantle (*poe*), and the bars or sideboards from the *iama.* From royal blacksmiths such as Charles Cockett, blacksmithing was readily learned by the *kama'āina* (native born), and soon bits and spurs were produced. These works were described as *'āmala* (armor), made using the forge (*kapuahi*), anvil (*kuahao*), tongs (*'ūmi'i*), file (*apuapu*), and hammer (*hāmale*). Headstalls (*kaula waha*), halters (*pūnuku*), reins (*laina*), and martingales (*makīnikela*) were readily made from braided rawhide (*'ili*) or sennet cord (*laina aho*).

{2.20} *Joe Pacheco, third-generation* paniolo, *braiding a rawhide lariat in a manner passed down from vaquero mentors of his grandfather's time.*

The vaquero, equipped with a dried and cured cowhide, surrounded himself with interested braiders and demonstrated how, with a spiraling blade cut, a single hide could yield more than two hundred feet of rawhide plait. The rawhide

{ 2.21 } *Hawaiian cowboy with* lauhala *(pandanus leaf) hat at Kealakekua Bay.*

strips were carefully carved at a uniform two-centimeter width, skived (cut on a beveled edge), then stretched and dried. Beneath the shade of a *lauhala* (pandanus) grove, the vaquero would braid four strands (*ma'awe*) of rawhide into the first Hawaiian *lariata* (*kaula 'ili*) eight fathoms long, fitted with a *honda* (*kīpuka*) and restretched. Beneath the same *lauhala* tree, the natives kept busy watching while weaving a *pāpale lauhala* for themselves with a lofty crown and widened brim that mimicked the sombrero of their mentors.

Soon the Native Hawaiian cowboy was christened "*paniolo,*" by the *po'e Hawai'i* (people of Hawai'i) in due honor, respect, and gratitude to their Hispanic mentors who equipped them with saddle and tack, lariat and leggings, hat and bandana, and training to harvest the unruly king of the mountain—the wild bullock.

Spanish Method of Harvesting Cattle

Prior to the arrival of the vaquero, the methods used by Parker, Purdy, and others to gather wild cattle were tedious, labor-intensive, and minimally productive. The vaquero, on the other hand, took his team of *paniolo* to the mountains on horseback, where cattle were roped and hog-tied by three legs (*kūpe'e*) or snubbed and tied by the horns to a stout tree (*po'owai'ū*) for an overnight cooling-off period.

Traditionally, vaqueros waited a day before moving live cattle to the main corral. The process allowed cattle to move on their own volition with appropriate prodding, pulling, and encouragement. The *paniolo* enjoyed the *alaka'i* method in which the bull, upon release from tether, was led down the mountain several miles to corrals located at headquarters. The *pini* method, also of Mexican origin, was commonly used, though not nearly as exciting as the *alaka'i*. In this case, a gentle home-raised bullock was "pinned" (hence the name *pini* in Hawaiian) by neck rope up against the untethered bull. An initial skirmish between the bull and his new mate was soon settled, as the gentle ox headed home over the next day or two. Arriving at the home corral, the gentle *pini* was separated from the wild bullock, which was set aside for market along with his mountain mates that had been

{2.22} *The dress, tack, and saddlery of these Native Hawaiians all show strong vaquero influence, including the* tapaderos *and leggings.*

delivered a day before by the swift, exciting, but dangerous *alaka'i* method.

Gathering wild bullocks in villages such as Waimea on the Big Island gave rise to an efficient process: the cattle were slaughtered in a central location that could accommodate salting and kegging of beef, curing the hides, and rendering the by-products. Soon, tannery services were born alongside the rendering plants. The oxcarts gave way to horse and mule draft teams hauling the kegs of beef, tallow, rawhide, and leather by wagon to Kawaihae for export. The Spanish method of cattle marketing was a boon to the early Hawaiian cattle industry.

Los Caballos

The imported vaquero workhorse looked much like the *lio maoli* (existing horses of Hawai'i) in appearance, endurance, and hardiness. While both horses descended from feral stock, the stallion was the gender for the Latino horseman, while the *paniolo* were comfortable riding mares, likely the offspring of imported Barb as well as local stallions. These offspring were a concentrate of like genes of feral origin but from different backgrounds. The vaquero mounts were heavily endowed with cow sense by birthright, and training came naturally. The common Hawaiian horse likely never experienced the herding, roping, snubbing, or leading of cattle, being of domestic or feral nature. However, with the infusion of genes from the Spanish Barb, the Hawaiian horse readily developed more of a "cow horse" attitude that remains today. For the willing *paniolo,* the learning curve was steep, but before long he excelled in cattle work and horse handling.

CHAPTER 3

LIVESTOCK BOUND FOR THE ISLANDS

The first major recorded transoceanic shipping of horses, donkeys, and mules occurred in 1493 when, on his second voyage, Columbus reintroduced the equine species to the Americas. Gavin Menzies' *1421: The Year China Discovered America* (2008) relates the voyages of Admiral Zheng He, who allegedly sailed fleets of military vessels to the Americas, including loads of cavalry mounts. No evidence, however, supports the permanence of such horse exportations, if they occurred at all.

Embarkation facilities in Spain may well have afforded dockside gangway loading of Columbus' animals, as opposed to the alternative of being lifted aboard from shore using body slings and hoisted overhead by a system of booms and pulleys. Hammocklike slings in box stalls slightly suspended the horse from the deck to offset the rolling pitch of the seas. Rings and ropes secured the sling and mount to the ship's framework. The horses' forefeet were loosely tied together. The deck provided no shade or protection from the salt spray, the beating sun, or torrential storms. The effect of these storms frequently resulted in severe limb and torso injuries. Severely injured animals were commonly tossed overboard. Death losses varied between 25 to 50 percent on journeys to distant destinations such as the Caribbean, which took as long as a hundred days. Upon arrival in the calm tropical bays, the horses, donkeys, and mules were disembarked by being shoved overboard and forced to swim to shore and their new home.

Over the ensuing two centuries, transoceanic transport improved significantly, as several nations and cultures became noted pioneers in his endeavor. Livestock care improved, with more spacious quarters and better feed. While holds beneath the deck lacked ventilation in warm weather, animals were kept below in temperate or arctic zones. Horses were afforded individual stalls and mangers that were small but secure. Mules and donkeys were loosely placed in common pens, as were cattle, sheep, and goats. Hogs were provided with shaded space, as they are less tolerant of heat and salt water.

By the mid-1800s, a Danish family brought transoceanic shipment of livestock to a newer and higher level. A loyal Dane named Carl Clausen began shipping hogs by sailing ship in 1864. Clausen set a high standard for animal care and transport—and for client satisfaction. Adherence to this golden rule likely explains why Clausen's Corral Line remained in business for a long time, maintaining its reputation as the leading livestock shipping line of the world. Animal care and client satisfaction were Clausen's historic mandate.

{ 3.1 } *Horses and cattle leaving Spain may have enjoyed being loaded out via a docked ship with a boom and sling or gangway ramp, a luxury lacking in disembarkation on shallow shores of distant lands.*

{ 3.2 } *A horse suspended in a stanchion with feet hobbled.*

{ 3.3 } *Tall ships entering Kealakekua Bay. Cattle and horses arrived in Hawai'i between 1793 and 1803. Note the towering cliffs in the background.*

Between Columbus' voyages and the birth of the Corral Line, thousands of livestock had encircled the world. For most of those centuries, Britain ruled the seas. Britain was also a great source of blooded stock of Thoroughbred horses, Hereford bulls, Suffolk sheep, and Hampshire hogs.

British command of the open seas included the Pacific Ocean, culminating in Captain James Cook's discovery of the Hawaiian Islands, which he named the Sandwich Islands. Cook's discovery of these islands in 1778 was followed shortly by Captain George Vancouver's delivery of California mission cattle in 1793. The proliferation of these longhorns is described in detail in *Loyal to the Land: The Legendary Parker Ranch, 750–1950* (Bergin 2004). A decade passed before Richard Cleveland and Captain William Shaler delivered horses to the Islands. The environmental and nutritional challenges facing both species were overwhelming, making their survival and propagation remarkable events.

The choice of the longhorn from the California mission system reflects practical wisdom. Pampered British show sires, cows, and heifers would have perished in the washy foraged meadows, with no supplement of corn or barley available. The choice of Cleveland and Shaler's Hawai'i-bound mounts was likely based on the practical desire to guarantee survivability. Hardy, easy-keeping, reproductively sound mounts were the likely candidates, just as the Polynesian voyager chose like-endowed hogs, dogs, and chickens to ensure their survival and propagation in their new island home, Hawaiʻi.

The merchant ship *Lelia Bird* brought the first horses to the Hawaiian Islands. The ship made two stops along the way. A stallion and mare in foal were obtained from a missionary priest at the ship's first stop at Mission San Borgia (Baja California) on May 20, 1803. Traveling to Cabo San Lucas, a second mare in foal was purchased and added to the retinue. Within a month, the ship arrived at Kealakekua Bay in Kona, Hawaiʻi, where a mare, the first horse ever seen in Hawaiʻi, was disembarked. Proceeding on to Maui, the ship landed the remaining mare and stallion—likely at Lahaina.

P. Quentin Tomich in his work *Mammals of Hawaii* (1986) shares insight on the subject, as reported by H. W. S. Cleveland, son of Captain R. J. Cleveland, from published journals of his father, *Voyages of a Merchant Navigator of the Days That Are Past* (1886). Captain R. J. Cleveland is credited, along with Captain William Shaler, with bringing the first horses to Hawaiʻi. Cleveland describes the reaction of Kamehameha I, for whom the horses were intended as a gift: he "only remarked that he could not perceive that their ability to carry a man quickly from one place to another would be sufficient compensation for the great amount of food they would necessarily require." It wasn't long, however, before the king acquired a royal mount that carried the *aliʻi* with regal countenance.

There are conflicting details about the relationship between R. J. Cleveland, described as having captained the *Lelia Bird,* and the actual captain of the vessel, Captain William Shaler. In 1886, H. W. S. Cleveland described the relationship of his father and Shaler as partners in the purchase of the ship itself in Hamburg, Germany. The decision about who was to be captain was settled "by tossing a copper" (coin). Although Shaler won the toss, Cleveland's name appeared on the ship's papers as supercargo (the officer in charge of commercial concerns on a voyage).

Soon horses became plentiful throughout the Islands, likely due to ongoing shipments from California to Hawaiʻi. Available for rent from livery stables, horses for a dollar a day seemed the going rate. By the mid-1800s, horse numbers began to grow, but quality of the mounts declined from indiscriminate breeding and loose, casual ownership. In an 1854 "Report of the Committee on Horses" to the Royal Hawaiian Agricultural Society (RHAS), C. G. Hopkins described conditions on Oʻahu: "About one-half of the horses on the Island are never used for any purpose but multiplication,—are never bitted or backed,—are born, live and die without being of any advantage to anyone, or having served any purpose, useful or ornamental, but the impoverishment of the land, and the propagation of a nuisance." Hopkins' protests of the poor quality and management of horses in Hawaiʻi did not go unnoticed by the RHAS, which developed a progressive posture in reducing the population of common stallions by encouraging neutering as an alternative to a harsh "stallion tax" that was imposed.

The quality of horses throughout the Islands, however, remained common, because the native community continued to enjoy loose ownership and control of their horses in a manner not unlike that of the Plains Indians of continental America. They had no incentive to improve strains of the saddle, carriage, and draft horses, as few of them were inclined toward businesses such as livery, taxi, cartage, or drayage.

Two decades hence, little seems to have changed in horse quality and care. Upon disembarking in Honolulu in 1873, Isabella Bird observed about two hundred horses dockside, each with a Mexican saddle (likely a Hawaiianized version) standing in the sun. Her assessment, in the eyes of a British horsewoman, was not positive:

> Outside this motley, genial, picturesque crowd about 200 saddled horses were standing each with the Mexican saddle, with its lassoing horn in front, high peak behind, immense wooden stirrups, with great leathern guards, silver or brass bosses, and coloured saddle-cloths. The saddles were the only element of the picturesque that these Hawaiian steeds possessed. They were sorry, lean, undersized beasts, looking in general as if the emergencies of life left them little time for eating or sleeping. They stood calmly in the broiling sun, heavy-headed and heavy-hearted, with flabby ears and pendulous lower lips, limp and rawboned, a doleful type of the "creation which groaneth and travaileth in misery." All these belonged to the natives, who are passionately fond of riding. Every now and then a flower-wreathed woman, in her full, radiant garment, sprang on one of these animals astride, and dashed along the road at full gallop, sitting on her horse as square and easy as a hussar. (Bird 1964)

Arrival of Donkeys and Mules in the Islands

The donkey, *Equus asinus* or *kēkake,* traces its origin to Assyria, where it was domesticated some five thousand years ago. For centuries, the donkey has been the workhorse for mankind throughout the world.

The ancestors of the modern donkey are the Nubian and Somalian subspecies of the African wild ass. Following domestication around 4000 BCE, the donkey became vital to agriculture as a pack animal, a farming implement, and in some cases a dairy producer. The equine species became extinct in the Western Hemisphere during the Ice Age, but they were reintroduced to the Americas by Spanish explorers. However, the first actual donkeys, four jacks and two jennies, were imported by Christopher Columbus in 1495. Despite the early introduction to America, the donkey did not enjoy widespread distribution until it was found to be a useful pack animal by miners and gold prospectors of the mid-1800s.

Britain, in its seventeenth-century quest of colonial expansion, set out on exploratory missions with sensible stowage of animal and plant life. The donkey may rank alongside the very British subjects aboard ship in terms of importance. Credit, however, needs to be given to the Spanish explorers disembarking in New Spain with horses, cattle, hogs, poultry, dogs, sheep, goats, and the donkey arriving during the sixteenth century (1519). According to Lummis, as quoted by Brookshier, a prolific writer around the turn of the twentieth century, "Two thirds of the New World would hardly have been civilized yet, without him [the donkey]. Also, as far as Spanish America goes . . . the burro has been the corner stone of history and the father of civilization" (Brookshier 1974).

None of the Spanish colonial donkeys of New Spain made their way to the Hawaiian Islands. It took the British to bring them.

The arrival of the donkey in the Islands came a full twenty-two years after the first horse.

In 1825, Richard Charlton left Falmouth, England, with a crew of ten sailors on his brig *Active* with four donkeys aboard destined for the Sandwich (Hawaiian) Islands. The long voyage across the Atlantic, down along the eastern seaboard of South America, through the stormy waters of the Magellan Strait, spanning the eastern Pacific Ocean, and on to the port of Honolulu took three months. While Charlton disembarked the brig with due ceremony appropriate to a recently appointed first British consul for the Hawaiian Islands, the donkeys were afforded a less pompous reception. These first few donkeys were landed on Oʻahu, where they were sold at auction shortly after they arrived. However, by 1847 donkeys were found in common use as pack animals in the bullock hunting industry on the Big Island, bearing kegs of salt and beef, as well as hides from the hunting grounds of Hilo. The noble horse had been in the Islands for more than two decades, and the native community was likely amused by the short-statured, long-eared cousins of their own mounts.

The explanation for Alta California failing to be the first to ship donkeys to the Islands was an early nineteenth-century restriction against exporting any breeding animals, including jackasses. Fortunately, this restriction was not applied in 1803 when mares and stallions left Baja for the Kingdom of Hawaiʻi. When the stricture was lifted in 1879, it was thirty years after Hawaiian donkeys were exported to California to supply the gold miners of 1849. During the Gold Rush, the Hawaiian Islands were a dependable source of livestock, including horses, mules, donkeys, bullocks (draft oxen), hogs, and fowl. Sweet potatoes, rice, sugar, salt, and tobacco were also export items.

At home in the Islands, the donkey was adorned with a *noho ʻāmana,* the typical cross-buck pack saddle upon which loads would vary: taro, rice, coconuts, firewood, papayas, coffee, pineapple, sugarcane, wool, sandalwood, lumber, and sometimes a rider.

As the bullock-hunting industry blossomed on the Islands, it was cowhides, goatskins, salt beef, and salt pork that kept the pack strings moving from the mountains to the coast to meet sailing ships docking for freight and provisions. The first sugar mills employed donkey power for grinding cane, as the burro beat a circular path around the two cylindrical stone rollers. Early Chinese immigrants in the cartage trade found the donkey to be a dependable and economic draft animal.

While donkeys became feral on Kaua'i and Moloka'i, only Hawai'i Island has remained home to wild burros into the new millennium.

The donkeys increased in significant numbers and were put to general use as pack animals in all segments of agricultural endeavors on all inhabited islands. Steadfast beasts of burden, donkeys and later mules became best known as enduring pack animals in the rice and taro paddies. Historically, donkeys also played a significant role in the development of the coffee industry in Hawai'i. Without these worthy animals, the coffee industry would not have survived. This reputation lasted more than a century, as the role of these animals was replaced by the surplus military jeep after World War II.

Significant packs of feral donkeys still remain on the Big Island—the Kona Nightingale of the Ka'ūpūlehu-Kīholo areas of North Kona and the Waikoloa Village area of South Kohala. The latter band, which had grown to about six hundred head, graze on private and Parker Ranch lands adjacent and to the southeast of Waikoloa.

{ 3.4 } *Kuka'iau Ranch cowboy John Holi Ma'e with a team of pack mules that carried lumber to high elevation sites for building redwood water tanks.*

{ 3.5 } *Sired by mammoth jacks of Kentucky out of imported Percheron mares, Parker Ranch in the early 1900s produced top-quality draft mules such as this one, weighing 1,290 pounds at only three years of age.*

Frank Brookshier (1974) shares some interesting points about donkeys that can be summarized as follows:

- Among Hawai'i's common folk is a legend that burros never die. The Hawaiian people have a saying about the donkey: "*ola mau loa*" (he lives forever).
- Donkeys can live forty to fifty years of age.
- The jenny lives longer than the jack.
- In Hawai'i, the donkey is a Kona Nightingale, in Colorado a Rocky Mountain canary, in Arizona a desert contralto.

Enter the mule—*Equus asinus* x *Equus caballus.* The mule is born out of the union of a jackass and a horse mare. A hinny is sort of a mirror image—a product of mating a horse stallion with a jenny donkey. While both products are commonly called mules, the hinny is blessed with a fuller horselike tail switch and a more tractable disposition. Due to incompatible chromosome series in each parent species, both the mule and hinny are sterile, unable to reproduce. Thus mules never attain a true feral state, as their ability to reproduce in the wild is not possible. No doubt abandoned mules can flourish in a wild state, no longer in a domestic environment, but their sterility means that they cannot produce offspring. Mules can also be born from the union of feral horses and donkeys in the wild, but as a generation they are self-limiting.

Whether the first mule in the Islands was imported or born to a horse and donkey already in Hawai'i is uncertain. To the

{ 3.6 } *Top-flight Belgian and Percheron mares were imported by Parker Ranch to produce draft horses and mules for ranch, plantation, and war purposes. On the left stands the champion Percheron mare Alline from Kansas State College, a popular source for top draft horse prospects.*

{ 3.7 } *A Kentucky mammoth jack. Over the years, A. W. Carter, trustee of Parker Ranch, imported jacks that became sires of hundreds of work mules used throughout the territory.*

{ 3.8 } *Imported by Grove Farm, Kingsman Monarch, a Percheron stallion, became the mainstay stud for draft horses and mules on Maui and Kaua'i.*

Hawaiians, a mule was referred to as *hoki* or *piula* and was considered a respectable means of transportation, packing, and even ranch work. By the 1880s, the Hawaiian Islands abounded with mules, as they became the pack and draft animal of choice in the burgeoning sugar industry. Demand greatly exceeded supply, and by the early 1900s they were brought in by the hundreds. In 1908 alone, over 750 mules were imported, 100 of which were reserved for military use.

A. W. Carter of Parker Ranch recognized the mule market strength and began an intensive breeding program, crossing Kentucky mammoth jacks on Percheron mares for draft mules. For pack mule production, the same jacks covered grade Thoroughbreds to produce ideal animals for plantation and military use. With the end of the world wars and the beginning of the mechanization era, donkeys and horses went by the wayside.

Comparison of Feral Horse Issues in Other Island Nations

Hawai‘i, Australia, and New Zealand share a common history: all were new homes to an imported species—the equine—which forever altered the agricultural and cultural history of these island nations. Stock tenders, formerly afoot, were made mobile, and freight was moved en masse overland. Moreover, the Aborigine, the Maori, and the Native Hawaiian adopted the noble species as their own treasured companion. Sadly, they all witnessed the conversion from domestication to the feral state when community and government concern for environmental degradation arose.

Paralleling these events was the growth of preservation societies bent on preserving feral gene pools, putting these animals to practical use and appropriately rehoming as many as possible. Sanctuaries sprung from kindly and sympathetic sources that advocated for population control through humane channels.

Australia's Feral Horses

Horses and donkeys arrived with the first fleet of Irish and British settlers to Australia. Arriving in 1788, horses' entry into this island continent took place fifteen years before the Kingdom of Hawai‘i would be so honored. The term "brumby" is attributed to several sources. First, a Sergeant James Brumby released his horses when he left New South Wales for Tasmania in 1804. Second, the Aboriginal word for "wild" is *baroomby.* And third, "brumby" is derived from the Gaelic *bromaigh,* which has the same meaning. In this case, the reader's choice is an unchallenged privilege.

Brumbies are said to descend from a variety of horse ancestors, including the "Caper" horse of South Africa, the Timor pony of Indonesia, the British pony, as well as Arabian, Thoroughbred, and draft horse breeding.

The first recorded release/escape of domestic horses (Brumby in 1804) marked the beginning of a thirty-year span that brought about wild horse distribution to all regions of Australia. By the 1860s, brumbies were formally considered as pests by critics, while a good many were converted to work and saddle mounts and draft/military purposes. Unfortunately, by the new millennium more than 400,000 feral horses roamed parts of Australia. Over the past fifty years, feral horses have become the source of 30 percent of Australia's horse meat exports.

Balance is being sought between the environmentalists, humane care interest groups, and the Australian government to bring overpopulation under control. Negative environmental impact caused by the brumbies includes soil loss, compaction and erosion, trampling of vegetation, chewing on tree bark, and spreading invasive weeds, causing the Australian government to consider drastic control efforts (Plummer 2013).

Australia's feral horse problem is characterized as the most severe in the world. By 2009, the brumbies grazed throughout Australia's countryside, with about a hundred thousand in Queensland alone. Thousands are dying in drought spells.

Like their American counterparts, brumbies produce a foal every two years, while spending from 50 to 75 percent of each day grazing. Despite a 20 to 25 percent annual die-off, the overall growth of brumby numbers has reached alarming proportions and is described as an extreme threat in Queensland. In this state, one station alone shot three thousand of them to reduce competition with domestic stock, contamination of water supplies, and threat to people as they wander through villages and campsites.

Recently, the Australian government approved aerial shooting as a last resort for population control, with a goal of reducing numbers by ten thousand. Further plans call for reduction to expand to tens of thousands, as they are perishing in extended drought-ridden areas of the outback (Plummer 2013).

On a positive note, the brumbies are credited with keeping trails clear for bush walkers, rescue personnel, and service vehicles. Interestingly, the Aboriginal people consider the brumby part of their cultural and demographic identity, just as the *kamaʻāina* families of Waipiʻo Valley believe the Waipiʻo horse to be a historic fixture representing the heritage of the verdant valley, to be left alone despite occasional crop damage to taro farmers.

Feral Horse of New Zealand, the Kaimanawa

Horses entered New Zealand in 1814, eleven years after Hawaiʻi and twenty-six years after Australia's importation of equines.

By 1876, the Kaimanawa Range of the North Island had become inhabited by feral horses, which had in years past escaped or had been released from sheep stations and cavalry bases. New Zealand's only true wild horses have grazed the rugged Kaimanawa Range south of Lake Taupo for more than a century.

It is no wonder that the Maori people have a strong cultural kinship with these wild horses. The first recorded horse in the central North Island was a royal gift to the son of Te Heu Heu Tukino by Tamati Waka Hene of Hokianga in 1844.

The word *kaimanawa* means to "eat the wind," and in Maori culture it signifies that the brave must survive on their own resources even when food is depleted and the future doubtful. The brave shall endure by eating the wind they breathe and endure to victory. "Wind biscuits" is a colloquial term in Hawai'i for the diet of nutritionally deprived horses.

The Maori *hapu* (extended family grouping) of the wild horse range views the wild horse as a *kaitiaki,* a spiritual guardian, much as the Native Hawaiian views a shark or owl as their *'aumakua.* Efforts by this group are centered on having the Kaimanawa horse protected as a "Taonga" —a national treasure of New Zealand.

Groups such as Save the Brumbies (Australia), Kaimanawan Wild Horse Trust (New Zealand), Mālama Waikoloa Nightingales (Hawai'i), Hawai'i Horse Rescue, and others were borne from the minds, elbow grease, and pocketbooks of reasonable people seeking a reasonable resolution.

Progress in Humane Shipment of Horses

Maritime activity of the world was in command of the British, as colonization of faraway lands seemed a mandate during these expansive times. Just as Captain George Vancouver landed cattle in the Hawaiian Islands in 1793, his colleagues were seeding other parts of the world with flora and fauna for future pantry usage.

By 1788, as noted, horses were delivered to Australia, and in 1803 and 1814 the equine species landed in Hawai'i and New Zealand, respectively. The British Admiralty was clearly methodical in recording findings as well as records of successes and failures of shipping techniques. With storms and shipwrecks notwithstanding, the survival rate of animal and plant life in shipping was a critical gauge of success.

Australia's early importation of horses was duly critiqued when survival rates were as low as 50 percent. During the ensuing century, Australia rose to become a major exporter of quality saddle, coach, draft, and military horses to India, South Africa, the Philippines, and China, using excellent horse husbandry and good planning that reduced death losses to zero. It was learned through trial and error that the most common cause of these losses had been poor management due to lack of adequate stall space, fodder, ventilation, exercise, and cleanliness.

The Australian Method

In their resolve for better outfitting of ships, shipping authorities insisted that horses be preconditioned in dry lots and over a week to ten days, given the very feed and water to be used on board to facilitate ready acclimatization once en route. Feed would be withheld the morning of embarkation. Once loaded in their respective mangers, the first maritime meal was served immediately, establishing a psychological comfort level to monitor in what would be their home for the next several weeks. Shipping stalls were generous in size—eight feet six inches long and two feet nine inches wide—providing comfort to even the stoutest artillery or draft horse.

Extra stalls were kept vacant for doctoring, exercise, or isolation in the event of illness. Upper decks were cleared of ropes, lines, and tackle to make daily exercise of horses functional on the top deck, while their mangers below were cleared, disinfected, and freshened with new bedding.

Finally, the Australian horse shipper insisted on a horse-to-man ratio of one groom per twenty horses on board, allowing for adequate attention to each animal over a given day. Such thoughtful and humane practices undoubtedly became the norm for livestock transport in the ensuing decades. Failure likely meant that some component of the prescribed regimen had been neglected.

Overseas Transport of Military Horses and Mules

Teddy Roosevelt, in his autobiographic work chronicling the Spanish-American War, dwelled in detail on the challenges of getting railcars of cavalry horses to Tampa for shipment off to Cuba. It is no wonder that his observation on the disorderly preparation, feeding and watering, and loading on and off steamships of cavalry mounts and pack mules had an impact on shipping protocol as World War I was viewed on the distant horizon.

In his book *The Rough Riders* (1902), Roosevelt reflected on his frustration with disembarkation methods of the military mounts: "Meanwhile from another transport, our horses were being landed, together with the mules, by the simple process of throwing them overboard and letting them swim ashore, if they could.... One of mine was drowned. The other, little Texas, got ashore all right."

With World War II well underway, the US Veterinary Corps was well staffed with some of America's most qualified equine practitioners. By this juncture, overseas transportation of horses and mules was highly regulated and approached scientific excellence.

Lt. Olin Anderson (1942) wrote about the intricacies of such voyaging. He was the transport veterinarian on the US Army Transport *Meigs,* a cargo vessel remodeled for animal transport. His observations are the basis of the information that follows.

The *Meigs* left San Francisco November 13, 1940, for Manila via Honolulu, with 264 horses and mules and one private mount to disembark on Oʻahu.

The horses were shipped to the West Coast from both Fort Robinson and El Reno Remount Depots and stabled at Fort Mason just four miles from the Presidio. Once stockpiled preshipment, it was a feat of experience and strategy that moved all 264 animals through Golden Gate Bridge traffic using a "floating picket line." Suspended between two trucks, a three-quarter-inch steel cable was suspended with crossbars of one-by-four-foot wooden straps bolted to the cable at eight-foot intervals. With spring snaps linked to each end of the crossbars, twenty animals could be moved at the same time, two abreast, without congesting more than one lane of bridge traffic. Using two floating picket lines, all 264 animals were moved within a seven-hour span, with one mounted rider accompanying each line.

Upon arriving shipside, each horse was unsnapped and led individually up the loading chute onto the ship and down into the hatches onto the first deck below the main deck. Each horse had a stall two feet wide and six feet long, with overhead clearance of eight feet.

Ventilation was accomplished by means of exhaust fans, portholes, and deck ventilator pipes. Wind scoops in portholes enhanced ventilation.

Healthwise, the trip to Manila via Honolulu was uneventful. The Honolulu-bound private mount (likely a Schofield Barracks officer's polo pony) was loaded by a "flying stall," a typical portable box stall moved by an overhead boom lifting the unit from ship to dockside.

Unloading the horses at the Manila port was an easy task. The animals needed no urging to abandon ship. Philippine scouts led each mount down the gangway on to the Army Transport Dock and onto barges for transshipment to the front lines at Corregidor. Other than being sea-leg weary, the horses traveled well, gaining weight over the monthlong voyage.

Clearly, much headway was made by World War II in ocean transport of horses,

{ 3.9 } *A young Thoroughbred stallion imported into Kawaihae via a "flying boxstall." After being craned off the ship onto a longboat, here it is offloaded on a wharf.*

mules, and donkeys. With progress in military transport, World War II was the beginning of air transport, with hundreds of US mules flown to Burma.

In accordance with customary practice, only hay (no grain) was fed for the first three days at sea, and water was provided freely.

All of the horses were manually clipped after leaving port, removing excess hair before the animals began sweating. When passing through the doldrums, this provided further comfort, as there was less ventilation on those days.

Exercise was accomplished daily by leading a number of mounts around the deck while the empty stalls were cleaned and rebedded. Weekly application of pine tar to their hooves and frogs maintained excellent hoof health. Manpower was provided by forty enlisted men detailed as stock tenders. A special assistant to the transport veterinarian served as an aide-de-camp (Anderson 1942).

CHAPTER 4

THE HORSE IN HAWAIIAN SOCIETY

The early horses in Hawai'i were likely intended as "royal reserve"—gifts for the king. Royalty soon recognized the enhanced countenance given a man or woman on horseback. Horses' care and husbandry was as good as could be expected. Subsequent shipments of horses, donkeys, and mules quickly raised the level of awareness of the image and function of the species. The horses' closeness to the landed Hawaiian gentry paralleled that of the Spanish don in old Mexico. Early Hawaiian historian John Papa I'i (1959) wrote that as a child, he had frequently observed King Kamehameha I riding to his Nu'uanu farmlands astride his personal mount, Kawaiolaloa. The donkey, and to a lesser degree the mule, developed a commonplace ownership role, in addition to their draught and packing functions.

As for the *ali'i,* they saw merit in seeking superior blood lines. King Kalākaua brought home from Kentucky a railcar load of quality Thoroughbreds. As the turn of the nineteenth century approached, however, the best horseflesh brought to the Islands came through the orders of the emerging sugar, pineapple, and ranching interests under the regulatory auspices of the Territorial Board of Commissioners of Agriculture and Forestry, detailed later in the book.

The common horses of Hawai'i grew in numbers, like the longhorn stock, to the point of losing their domestic status in favor of remote valleys and steep, rocky mountain enclaves, where they propagated in gay abandon. On the other hand, owning horses was a status symbol among the *maka'āinana,* so their proliferation eventually became a nuisance.

Between 1803 and 1822, horse numbers grew via natural propagation and periodic imports of common horses. The quality of horseflesh began to improve by

Horses Seized as Spoils of War

When Kaumuali'i, chief of Kaua'i, died without leaving clear instructions for the distribution of the lands of Kaua'i and Ni'ihau, it caused a skirmish between the warriors of Kaua'i and those of Hawai'i who were sent to enforce distribution of property according to the wishes of Kamehameha. In 1825, the Battle of Wahiawa (Kaua'i) was significant because the spoils of war included seized horses and cattle. Historian Samuel M. Kamakau described what occurred:

> Large numbers of Kauai soldiers had gathered on the battleground, but they were unarmed save with wooden spears, digging sticks, and javelins. Many women were there to see the fight. The men acted as if death were but a play thing. It would have been well if the gods had stepped in and stopped the battle. No one was killed on the field, but as they took to flight they were pursued and slain. So Kia'i-makani, Na-ke'u, and their followers met death. For ten days the soldiers harried the land killing men, women, and children. Humehume had ridden away to the mountains with his daughter and his wife, Pake. Many fled to the mountains until amnesty for all was declared. Kalai-heana neither killed nor injured any prisoner, neither did Hoa-pili or Ka-lani-moku. All the rest took prisoners and brought them to Oahu and even to Maui and Hawai'i. A great deal of property was taken, among other things horses and cattle, which had become numerous on Kaua'i because the foreigners had given many such to Ka-umu-ali'i. (Kamakau 1992)

the exemplary importation of a blooded broodmare by Reverend William Ellis in 1822. Local breeders in 1825 sought superior bloodlines for mule production when they imported four English donkeys. The grandfather of renowned Parker Ranch trustee/manager A. W. Carter, Captain Joseph Carter, imported a boatload of blooded California horses in 1838, a full ten years after the French ship *Le Heros* delivered seventeen premium mares for local breeders. In 1884, Aubrey Robinson of Ni'ihau Ranch imported top-flight Arabian horses from Arabia and India. Horses on the island of Kaua'i were so plentiful that they became spoils of war.

With the 1833 arrival of the team of vaquero mentors came their strings of horses of utility mustang breeding and innate cow sense. It is likely that their Native Hawaiian protégés realized that the wiry Mexican ponies had something that the pampered mounts of the *ali'i* lacked: endurance, hardiness, and easy-keeping qualities.

Understandably, the *maka'āinana* took note that these smaller, easy keeping mounts suited them just fine. By 1852, the Royal Hawaiian Agricultural Society (like the modern-day Department of Agriculture) realized that the oversupply of such useless horses bordered on nearly twelve thousand common cayuses that nobody seemed to own or care for. The kingdom imposed a tax bill of $1 per stallion per year. Like many modern-day tax bills, the Stallion Bill of 1852 had unintended consequences: Native Hawaiians who could not pay the tax in some cases ate the horses instead. Despite further taxation, by 1879 horse and mule numbers in the Islands grew to nearly thirty thousand.

In the following excerpt from P. Quentin Tomich (1986), the author relates the early history of the horse in Hawai'i, quoting from Isabella Bird's 1890 account:

> The Hawaiians took readily to the loose ownership and use of horses in a manner mildly comparable to that of the Plains Indians, and this must have contributed to the foregoing objections of those desirous of maintaining and improving strains of saddle, carriage, and draft horses....
>
> Adoption of the horse by the natives was, however, not immediate after its arrival, especially outside of O'ahu, for Bird relates that when the missionary Titus Coan came to Hilo in 1835, in succeeding years he visited outlying villages on foot because, "Horses were only regarded as wild animals in those days." Nor were they used in that era for dragging timber from the forests to build churches, for the Hawaiians themselves did this work. Bird observes also of the natives of Honolulu in 1873, "... the passion for riding, in a people who only learned equitation in the last generation is most curious." And, "Except for short shopping distances in Honolulu, I have never seen a native man or woman walking . . . and I have seen men take the trouble to mount horses to go 100 yards."
>
> Further notations bear a similar theme. On Kaua'i, when a mount was caught in quicksand it was abandoned because it was "only a horse."
>
> The Hawaiian horse must have been somewhat reluctant to take to the wild and often roamed about settlements, which may have led to [Bird's] observation that "Horses are abundant and cheap on Kauai: a fairly good one can be bought for $20.... Indeed the horses seem to outnumber the people." (Tomich 1986)

In his research, Tomich found very little information on feral horses. He attributes the lack of information to the attention that was focused on stray, half-owned mounts that wreaked havoc on villages. He quotes C. S. Judd (1936) for an assessment of the feral horses of that time.

> Wild horses were never so abundant as wild cattle on Mauna Kea but they have been there in feral state since soon after their introduction in 1803.
>
> These horses were very hardy animals, strong for their small stature and had excellent feet. The last of them were driven out of the Mauna Kea forest reserve in 1932 but there are two or three still in one of the upper paddocks of the Parker Ranch on the land of Humuula. (Tomich 1986)

Tomich surmises that horses, unlike wild cattle, probably experienced greater difficulty surviving in the wild and were more likely to be captured and returned to domestication. He reports that in a two-year period prior to 1925, only one wild horse was removed from forest reserves, two in 1927, and six in 1929.

While continued shipment of horses from Spanish California provided a plentiful supply on O'ahu, where they could be rented for a dollar a day by 1825, the

Neighbor Islands gradually became home to nondomesticated horses by 1835. This made inexpensive horses accessible to Native Hawaiian communities and brought about a significant change to the Hawaiian way of life, as the passion for being on horseback was becoming a tradition even for the common man or woman.

Tomich presents further details of uncontrolled horses on Kaua'i:

> G. Swedberg (personal comm., 1964) found on Kaua'i that at one time a fair number of horses ranged uncontrolled above Kekaha Town and west of the Kōke'e Road. These animals undoubtedly bred in the wild but were not a true feral population. Tinker (1938, p. 116) probably refers to this group of horses, which disappeared sometime after 1937. Another Kaua'i population, consisting of a few short-coupled, large-headed, and heavy-footed horses, occupied the bottom of Waimea Canyon near the Kukui Trail and in the Hanalei-Hā'ena Region for as far in the past as local residents could remember, according to Swedberg. These horses had undergone some genetic selection in the wild. A hazy ownership of them was claimed, but they were not managed in the usual sense as domestic horses.

In 1934, a group of Makawao horsemen attempted to capture a band of Maui mustangs. According to H. Frederick "Freddy" Rice, the band was driven *makai* (seaward) from their high, dry home in the cinders above Mount Haleakalā's timberline. The feral horses were herded down into forested ranch lands that were thoroughly infested with *pāmakani,* a thick, tenacious, and leafy shrub that covers the meadows and ravines in high mountain pastures. In a less than well-orchestrated feral horse drive over an uncharted forest reserve, the band of mustangs was driven over a steep ravine, falling about ninety feet to their death, forfeiting any chance for the Makawao cowboys to capture, tame, and train any of the *lio'āhiu.* No one knows what became of the remaining mustangs. The opportunity has been lost to preserve the genetic makeup of these feral mounts.

Tomich further reports the following:

> J. S. Medeiros, (pers. comm.) states that Maui feral horses once roamed in the Erehwon Ranch adjacent to the west end of Haleakalā National Park, and the upper reaches of Haleakalā Ranch in the same region. These animals were present as late as 1942, and as many as ten were known there about that time. They did not venture into Haleakalā Crater as is assumed by Yocom (1964, p. 25). Stray horses occupied Lāna'i at various times, and the last of these were hunted out in 1951–1952 with the last of the cattle, according to Medeiros.
>
> For Moloka'i, N. K. Pekelo, Jr. reports (pers. comm., 1965) that unbranded horses had ranged in Hālawa Valley since the 1946 *tsunami;* there is no history of truly feral horses on that island.

Thomas A. Woods, PhD, executive director of the Mission Houses Museum

{ 4.1 } *An artist's depiction of wild horses being driven off a cliff to their deaths.*

and an authority on agricultural history and its preservation, has worked closely over the past two decades with the Kona Historical Society (KHS) to chronicle ranching history in the districts of North and South Kona.

In a fall 2008 KHS publication, *Ha'ilono,* Woods reported extensively on the Hawaiian Kingdom's property taxes on land and livestock. For our purposes here, information gleaned from Woods' account relates to ownership of horses, donkeys, and mules in the North Kona District through the year 1890.

While the forthcoming snapshot of the horse, donkey, and mule numbers of North Kona provides genuine insight into the importance of such animal ownership among the Native Hawaiian people, it may not be comparable to other parts of the kingdom. The reason is amply stated in a letter from D. H. Nahinu to the governor of Hawai'i Island dated August 8, 1877: "Steep and rocky, Kona was ill-suited to plantation agriculture, and at this time, many cattle and mules have been moved to cane growing areas. While this clearly points to plantation agriculture's strong demand for draft mules and beef, it also reflects on Kona's historic role in ranching per se, given its untillable terrain more suited to cattle and coffee, industries that depend heavily on the horse and ass."

Woods' research illuminates livestock numbers and ownership according to major ethnic groups; that is, Native Hawaiian as opposed to haole (Caucasian) ranchers. Tax rates for all subjects, however, were uniform: milking cows $15, beef cattle $7, horses $25, and mules $40 per annum. Woods notes that

> As early as 1849, tax ledgers of Native Hawaiians of North Kona provided a glimpse into the emerging shift of livelihood from hunters/gatherers/farmers to livestock ownership as a means of survival in economic and social contexts. Hawaiians owned 88 percent of the cattle, 92 percent of the horses, and 96 percent of the mules. By 1881, a *paniolo* and associate of H.N. Greenwell, Kekoanui of 'Ō'oma, owned 18 horses, four mules and three donkeys. Throughout the 19th century, Hawaiians continued to own an overwhelming majority of horses. By 1890, 248 Hawaiians were taxed for 72 percent of all horses owned in the district. A Hu'ehu'e *paniolo* named Makini, owned 60 horses with another North Kona horseman, W.M. Kailianu, owning another 28 mounts. As Portuguese immigrants moved into the ranching scene of Kona, horse inventories were kept quite low while cattle, especially dairy types, expanded in significant numbers giving birth to modern day ranching names of note such as Deniz, Duarte, Freitas, Gaspar, Gomes, Gouveia, and Rapoza.

Enter the Pā'ū Rider

While the KHS report by Woods is a narrow geographic glimpse of horse, donkey, and mule ownership during the monarchy, the value lies in the reflection of what the Native Hawaiian community felt about horseflesh: a species that brought status and productivity to one's

{4.2} *An array of* pāʻū *riders in 1909, representing the Island of Molokaʻi, prepares for a gala procession in Honolulu.*

lifestyle, an ethnic endearment to one of God's greatest creatures. Isabella Bird wrote about the joy of horseback riding in Honolulu in 1873:

> There were hundreds of native horsemen and horsewomen, many of them doubtless on the dejected quadrupeds I saw at the wharf, but judicious application of long rowelled Mexican spurs, and a degree of emulation, caused these animals to tear along at full gallop. The women seemed perfectly at home in their gay, brass-bossed, high-peaked saddles, flying along astride, bare-footed, with their orange and scarlet riding dresses streaming on each side beyond their horses' tails [see plate 1], a bright kaleidoscopic flash of bright eyes, white teeth, shining hair, garlands of flowers and many-colored dresses, while the men were hardly less gay, with fresh flowers round their jaunty hats, and the vermilion-coloured blossoms of the Ohia round their brown throats. Sometimes a troop of twenty of these free-and-easy female riders went by at a time, a graceful and exciting spectacle, with a running accompaniment of vociferation and laughter. . . . Many of the women were in flowing riding dresses of pure white, over which their unbound hair, and wreaths of carmine-tinted flowers fell most picturesquely. (Bird 1964)

{ 4.3 } *An elegant equestrienne, the* pāʻū *queen poses at attention, her proud gray gelding gaily adorned in* maile *lei.*

{ 4.4 } *A modest but able* pāʻū *rider gathers her reins before entering the procession.*

{ 4.5 } *A solemn* pāʻū *queen poses with her shoulder-branded mount.*

{ **4.6** } *Regal in countenance, two* pāʻū *riders pause for a photo. To the left stands W. C. Bergin holding his son, W. N. Bergin. W. C. was Billy's grandfather and Brady's great-grandfather.*

Reflecting a more elitist and royal view of the aura and majesty of being astride a fine horse, J. A. Cummins, a Hawaiian chief and *konohiki* (lord) of Waimānalo, detailed a two-week journey circling the island of Oʻahu in 1875. Cummins was summoned to ʻIolani Palace on October 10 by Queen Emma, who requested a grand tour of the island, visiting each district to greet her subjects personally. By November 5, Cummins had organized a mounted cavalcade with the queen mounted on his pedigreed parade horse named Kekonikauikanahele, which would be at her disposal for the next fourteen days. Cummins rode as an outrider to the queen's immediate right. Nearly forty years later, Cummins (1913) wrote about his adventure:

> After breakfast the cavalcade was put in order. It consisted of one hundred and forty women riding astride, dressed in the brightest colors the stores of Honolulu afforded. The pa-u or riding habit of the women consists of a long piece of bright print wrapped around the hips and extending down to the stirrup from whence it flares out behind when the horse is in motion.
>
> The impression as we swept through the streets on our dashing horses must have been gorgeous. Her majesty and myself led the procession, followed by her mother and other chiefs. The streets of Honolulu were thronged with people to witness the grand sight, and it would appear that the whole city and many from the country had turned out to see the departure.

{4.7} *Draped in a bright white* pāʻū, *this rider sits proudly on her* lakana *(chestnut) mount.*

Stopping at different venues for overnight rests, the mounted entourage grew larger at each daybreak. Cummins provided for huge lūʻau, hula, surfing, and fishing activities along the way. On October 7, he presented horse racing: "On the 7th I decided to give an exhibition of my trained horses,

{ 4.8 } *Out for a Sunday ride, mounted couples strike a natural pose. Note the flowing* pā'ū *apparel.*

and other sports were introduced at Hunananiho. I had then eleven horses under training, all of which were thoroughbreds; and four jockeys. The races were very good, and as Hawaiians are lovers of the sport the whole party had a rare treat."

The following morning began with no less pageantry: "After another grand breakfast on the eighth, the whole party being ready, we made a start for Kaneohe by way of Alele. It was a great crowd, all mounted on horseback and all dressed in various bright colors, with many beautiful leis. The cavalcade was led by six mounted knights in red with burning torches. Many people stood on the Pali to witness the course of the procession."

As the growing procession of mounted *ali'i* and *maka'āinana* alike left for Kahana, Cummins reflected on the hospitality as well as the growth of the cavalcade: "Here a Chinese, Apakana, and his Hawaiian wife, Mary, a sister of Kamakini, received us all very warmly and had made great preparations for our entertainment. To see two hundred horses tied out in the grounds and their accoutrements on fences and trees, alone was a novelty."

As the cavalcade approached Honolulu, the gaiety intensified accordingly:

> The cavalcade was formed for the ride towards Honolulu. It was one of the most beautiful sights ever seen, to look back on the procession from the uplands; and Her Majesty continually looking back at the bright colored procession which followed us, four abreast. There were three hundred women with gaudy leis of bright flowers and *maile* wreaths, their horses also decked out with evergreens. The horses pranced and looked well, the women looked fat and smiling and every face was wreathed in smiles.

The final leg of the tour was a genuine reflection of the magnitude of the ranks of O'ahu's dignitary-filled population and the splendor created by beautiful flowers and handsome horseflesh:

> After the luau we resumed our march towards town, the Queen on "Kekonikauikanahele" and I on "Taiehu," which was a most beautiful white horse with red spots the size of a dime. Her Majesty and the horse were covered with leis of lehua and pikaki, and every one of the seven or eight hundred were likewise bedecked with leis. We led the procession, followed by the whole cavalcade, along King street, up Richards and along Beretania to Her Majesty's house. All dismounted and bade Her Majesty farewell, and I took my men home to Waimanalo, having been fifteen days on the merriest, wildest jaunt of my life.

By 1900, feral horse herds were found in varying degrees on all islands except Kaho'olawe. With the birth of the sugar and pineapple industries, horses, mules, and donkeys of superior breeding were imported in large numbers. The progressive livestock industry followed shortly thereafter and sought larger, faster purebred mounts for cattle work, relegating the Hawaiian horse, called the "*kanaka* horse" in a derisive tone, to its remote homes and hideouts. Like the mestizo and Indian horsemen, the Hawaiian horse was caught and tamed for use on an as-need basis by the common populace and not the landed gentry. Since these times, the term "Hawaiian horse," while not reflecting an actual breed, refers to the steed of common, sometimes feral, and inbred origin that carries the *hi'ona* (phenotype) and *koko* (genotype) of small, wiry, and hardy mountain and valley horses.

The impact of the Spanish Barb continued after the vaquero left Hawai'i and their horses behind. The Islands' broodmare populace, feral and otherwise, was readily settled by several of the *caballo* Californio, spreading the cow horse instinct throughout the Islands.

CHAPTER 5

THE MAUNA KEA BREED IS BORN

In early 1932, a lead foreman of Parker Ranch's vast mountain range of Humu'ula, Willie Kaniho, ventured to a verdant wild horse hideout, Pu'u Lahohinu (Hill of the Shiny Stallion), in search of a long-storied black stallion. Coming upon one of several bands of feral brood mares in the upper reaches of Keanakolu, Kaniho and his men could hear the shrill cries of stallions in battle. Within a mile of Pu'u Lahohinu, they found the black stallion in mortal combat with another much older male.

Seizing the moment, Kaniho rode directly into the melee, only to have the black stallion turn on him—just what the experienced horseman wanted. With the stallion in hot and close pursuit, Kaniho snared him with a swift, long, backhanded loop neck catch and rode off at ninety degrees, pitching his prey to the ground in a harsh roll. Coming up right behind the stud was Joe Pacheco, looping his *kaula'īli* over the hind legs of their prey, which promptly rose in a failed attempt to escape. The ropers tightened their lariats, bringing the stud crashing to the ground and out of wind.

Now fore footed (roped by both front legs) by Henry Ah Fong, the stud was stretched taut while other *paniolo* dismounted and, with a pair of lariats, fashioned a *pūnuku* (halter) to lead the stallion home to Kalaieha, Humu'ula's headquarters. With one cowboy on the lead rope and one on the rear lariat, it was a raucous trip across the mountain, with the stallion in constant, hoarse shrills of objection. When not rearing, he was rolling over or slapping his haltered head with his forefeet.

With the calm, patient Henry Ah Fong at lead rope, the stud was afforded the time it took to accept his capture and follow the lead. By the time they reached Pu'u 'Ō'ō paddock, the stud was

{5.1} *A respected cattleman and leader of men, Joe Pacheco's love for fine horses was an enduring passion. His skill with a lariat came with the grace of a vaquero.*

in submission and broke to lead. In a secure Kalaieha corral, he was released with a drag rope of stout *malina* (sisal rope) attached to a heavy-duty mule halter.

For a mate, Kaniho turned in an old draft mare weighing nearly twice that of the stallion. Only the sound of soft neighs and an occasional squeal came from the corral. The black stallion was home for good in the year 1932.

Willie Kaniho's intent in capturing the stallion was practical. Preservation of the feral Hawaiian horse was an unexpected result. Kaniho sought after the hardened hooves of black granite that were a characteristic and a prepotent trait of feral horses that quickly became known as the Mauna Kea breed.

Horse breeding on Parker Ranch, especially during the time of A. W. Carter, was a tightly controlled program, with Pukalani Stables being the stallion station near the ranch headquarters. But Kaniho, already recognized for his wisdom and leadership, was granted much leeway as the long-standing boss of Humu'ula Sheep Station, the largest and most remote of all sections. He asked that he be granted, for cross-breeding purposes, a Percheron mare of good size and temperament, with minimal white marks and solid black feet. A veteran horseman

{5.2} *A top ranch hand, Henry Ah Fong was a quiet, bright, and talented leader of men and a good roper to boot.*

{5.3} *The Parker Ranch cowboy gang heads home from Humuʻula after a wild horse roundup.*

of the horse department, James "Palaika" Brighter, had just the horse: an eighteen-hundred-pound jet-black daughter of Gladiator, the imported Percheron stallion. As this cross produced some filly and stud colts, Willie patiently waited for a stallion foal that complemented the best traits of each parent. In 1938, his wish was granted—a jet-black colt was born and christened "Mauna Kea."

In the breeding career of the Mauna Kea stallion at Humuʻula, his home was Huikau, a large paddock where he readily covered (bred) a band of a dozen broodmares, retired mounts of the cowboys of that station. Before long, some of Mauna Kea's offspring were observed as working cowhorses, and cowboys of the main ranch were impressed. Hartwell Carter, upon assuming the ranch reins from his father, called for Mauna Kea to be brought home to headquarters to enter the formal breeding program. Kaniho, however, insisted that Mauna Kea stand at Humuʻula Sheep Station. His sire, the wild black stallion of Puʻu Lahohinu, had been long gelded, serving at length as a dependable workhorse for Take Horie at Humuʻula Sheep Station. Upon retirement, he was led back and released where he was found—the Hill of the Shiny Stallion.

Besides Puʻu Lahohinu, the slopes of Mauna Kea had two other bands of wild horses: one at Puʻu Mali above Hanaipoe and the other at Kahoupuokane above Pōhakuloa. Whether these three bands ever comingled remains a mystery, but with these numbers ever increasing, a decision to depopulate them was made in 1932. Traps that were set up and wild horse drives were only moderately effective. Kahoupuokane, with its stone pen

{5.4} *A 1920 view of Pukalani Stables. Once a thriving ancient Hawaiian village, Pukalani evolved into the horse center of Parker Ranch. The pen in the foreground was replaced with a sale barn in 1975. By 2011–2012, it became the Hale ʻAina dining hall of the Paniolo Heritage Center of Paniolo Preservation Society.*

{ 5.5 } *James K. "Palaika" Brighter, mounted on a half-bred Belgian/Mauna Kea gelding, proudly displays the products of a sheep hunt.*

nestled high at the timberline, was blessed with a spring for water trapping, a system designed by Willie Kaniho, readily rid the southern slope of the mountain of feral horses. These bands wreaked severe havoc, as the paddocks on the plains of Pōhakuloa (land sections Ka'ohe III, IV, and V) were the resting area for draft horses that often returned to work with feral foals at their side.

On the far western flank of the lands of Ka'ohe lay the boundaries of Ke'āmuku (*makai*) and Pu'u Wa'awa'a Ranches (*mauka*). Robert Keakealani Sr. often shared his familiarity with this intermountain triad where the Mauna Kea, Mauna Loa, and Hualālai slopes converge in a common plain that was the *alahele* (pathway) by which he would lead strings of Hind-purchased Pu'u 'Ō'ō Ranch colts back to ranch headquarters at Pu'u Wa'awa'a. He was clear in his assessment that the feral horses of Mauna Kea crossed the plains of Ka'ohe and became established in the upper reaches of the North Kona ranch, in an area called Kīpuka Lio 'Āhiu (Wild Horse Canyon). This arid, high-elevation desert was nicknamed "The Valley of the Seven Moons," as it boasts seven large, crescent-shaped craters, the largest of which is the grassy Kīpuka Lio 'Āhiu. According to Robert, the senior Native Hawaiian horseman, this band of wild horses never became

permanently established due to drought and lack of consistent access to water.

The remaining nests of feral horses of Mauna Kea were finally corralled using retired workhorses as imposed mates. The *lio lahoʻāhiu* (feral stallions) were more than willing to be herded into large stone corrals when accompanied by gentle mares. With no viable market for the feral horses, ranchmen disposed of them humanely.

The legend of the Mauna Kea horses was not to be lost in history, however. Notable preservationists of the Mauna Kea breed and other Hawaiian horse strains, including the Waipiʻo/Waimanu horse, kept the name of the native feral horse at the forefront either by breeding programs or usage. Three of these men were Dr. David Woo (deceased), a prominent Big Island physician; George Kealoha (deceased) of Kūkaʻiau Ranch; and Dick Solmssen of Hawaiʻi Preparatory Academy's horse program. Short biographical sketches of these men and how they contributed to preserving the Hawaiian horse breed and its history follow.

{5.6} *It was Willy Kaniho who had the wisdom of incorporating the rugged, flint-hooved character of the Mauna Kea strain of wild horses into the Parker Ranch mainstream of bloodlines.*

Three Champions of the Mauna Kea Horse

T. David Woo, MD

Born on November 8, 1907, in North Kohala, David Woo aspired at a young age to

{5.7} *Thanks to the foresight, wisdom, and passion of Dr. David Woo, the history, DNA, and bloodlines of the Hawaiian horse have been preserved in perpetuity. His neck rope tying process indicated need for improvement.*

become a medical doctor. Upon completing high school in Kohala, Woo went on to graduate in premedicine from the University of Hawai'i in 1929. He received his medical degree at St. John's University in Shanghai in 1935. He was ahead of his time in medical progress in the Islands, electing to combine training in Eastern and Western medicine at both St. Andrews and St. Luke's hospitals in China from 1935 to 1937. Returning to practice in Hawai'i in 1938, he became a plantation physician, serving the Kohala and Hāmākua communities, including Parker Ranch, where he served as medical director. Dr. William N. Bergin (Billy's father and Brady's grandfather) was Woo's colleague and friend. He was also a plantation physician, and he and Woo complemented one another's professional services for several years before forming a partnership, the Hilo Medical Group.

When Billy was a ten-year-old boy in 1950 with a deep love for horses, his father introduced him to Dr. Woo, telling him of Woo's concern that the Hawaiian horse was nearly extinct and about his mission to preserve the breed. Woo owned a small ranch in Āhualoa, where he stood a stallion for his small band of broodmares. He also bred outside mares, provided they were typical "*kanaka* horses." Young Bergin was privileged to spend weekends with him in Āhualoa, where he met Woo's herdsman, a kind and handsome Hawaiian man named John Waihee.

The name of the Woo outfit was the Double U Double O Ranch. By the time Bergin left for college in 1958, Dr. Woo's stallion is said to have produced more than thirty foals, which were purchased for nominal prices by homesteaders and hunters. He developed a registry for the Hawaiian horse, the Royal Mauna Kea Mustangs. While the American Quarter Horse was just coming into popularity and the Thoroughbred and Morgan-crossed horses were the mainstay of ranch and rodeo horses, Dr. Woo's efforts and perseverance, which lasted as long as his stud could serve mares, were instrumental in the preservation of the Hawaiian horse breed. In many ways, Dr. Woo provided the inspiration that moved young Bergin toward a career in horse care, as he observed Woo using a variety of Western and Eastern medicaments on his horses. Another point of inspiration for Bergin was to develop his own brand. The subject arose when Woo was queried about the brand on his horses, which was the male symbol (♂). With a slip of paper from a feed sack, Woo sketched the male symbol at first, then artfully rotated the arrow to be straight up while opening the bottom of the circle, producing a "spur" brand that graces the hips of many fine rodeo horses that the Bergin family has produced. On February 11, 1952, young Bergin registered the brand with the Territorial Board of Commissioners of Agriculture and Forestry. Bergin was eleven years old and paid the $2.00 fee out of his allowance. It has now been registered for more than sixty years.

Cowan-Smith and Stone (1988) capture Woo's interest in preserving the Hawaiian horse breed in his own words: "My interest in breeding mustangs in Hawaii paralleled that of the Brislawn brothers in Wyoming. They were concerned with preserving the history of the Spanish horse on the mainland and began the Spanish Mustang registry. In Hawaii, I registered my horses as Royal Hawaiian mustangs." Woo later changed the registry to Royal Mauna Kea Mustangs.

Dr. Woo's search for native Hawaiian horses of pure stock took him around the Big Island, where he found breeding stock in Pololū, Waimanu, and Waipi'o Valleys, as well as Kalapana, Wood Valley, and Hīlea Valley. In the once remote fishponds of Kaloko Makai in North Kona lived a lone feral stallion with a small band of mares. Several pockets such as this were considered by Woo, but lack of access or proof of ownership hampered acquisition and preservation. Trips to Kaua'i, Lāna'i, Maui, and Moloka'i were successful in locating more *kanaka* horses, but transportation difficulties limited access to these animals.

Woo made a vital contribution to the history of the Hawaiian horse by describing a standard of conformation. His phenotypic description stands today as appropriate, as it was based upon a territory-wide examination of Hawaiian horse resources.

BILLY & PAT BERGIN

{5.8} *Registered spur brand for W. C. Bergin, passed down to succeeding generations.*

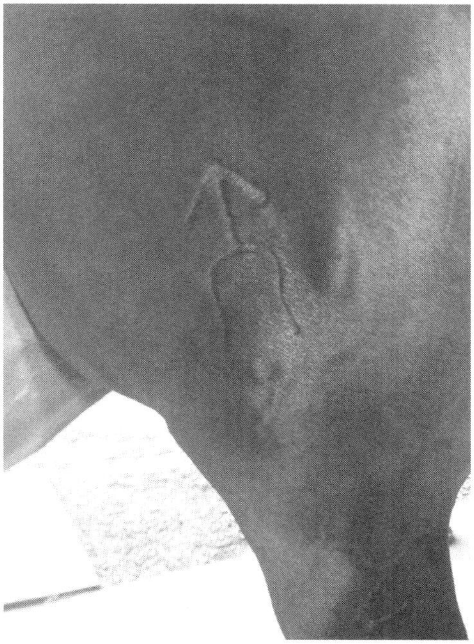

{5.9} *The spur brand placed on the left hip of Bergin-bred horses is well depicted on Brown Sugar, a noted barrel-racing horse.*

For height, if a horse stood only twelve hands, it was on the small side; if it stood fifteen hands, it was on the large side. Weight should be between six and nine hundred pounds at maturity (five years) for the standard he set for the Royal Mauna Kea Mustang Registry. In Woo's judgment, a typical Hawaiian horse stood fourteen hands tall and weighed about eight hundred pounds.

Heads were described as slightly larger relative to their body frame than the typical ranch horse of the day. Ears were also larger and eyes smaller by comparison. Longer heads were prone to be Roman-nosed. Wide in the muzzle, the upper lip seemed longer than the lower and crowned with a pair of narrow but readily flared nostrils.

In profile, the "*kanaka* horse" displayed a short and thick neck that met significantly high withers, merging with a short back that ended in a sloping rump and low tail set. Viewed from the rear, the horses appeared "rafter rumped" (gable hipped or *'ōkole hoki*) and "cat hammed" (thin gluteal thigh muscle groups). Viewed from the side, their deep chests of good length met sloping shoulders. Viewed from the front, the brisket was narrow and met the forelegs as an inverted V. The forelegs emerged from the lower chest in close proximity. Cannon bones fore and aft left moderate forearms and gaskins respectively. The legs were endowed with significant bone size and density, as were the fetlocks and pasterns, which were supported by relatively large black hooves. The upright hooves had significant wall and sole thickness. Well-concaved soles met the vortex of the frogs in a well-seamed fashion.

Woo's color patterns typically included the bays, browns, blacks, grays, roans, and chestnuts as the most common coat colors. Sorrels, buckskins, and pintos were less common, as were palomino horses. Woo's prize stallion was a palomino that seemed to meet all of the conformational standards, carrying the owner's brand on the left gaskin.

Woo's band of Hawaiian horses, entirely made up of Big Island stock, was eventually liquidated in the twilight years of the fine country doctor, whose heroic efforts kept the noble Hawaiian mustang from certain extinction. Fortunately, his mission was carried on by other horsemen.

George Kealoha, Paniolo o 'Umikoa

Another significant person responsible for the preservation of the Hawaiian horse is George Russell Kealoha, a lifelong cowboy of Kūka'iau Ranch Ltd., headquartered in the mountain village of 'Umikoa on the Big Island's Hāmākua Coast.

George was the second eldest son of Samuel Kealoha and Maraea Wela. Sam Kealoha was a Kūka'iau cowboy who produced six children, half of them daughters of beauty and three sons who were all *paniolo.* Paul, the eldest, and George spent their entire careers as Kūka'iau Ranch cowboys. Youngest brother Milton, better known as Chubby, worked as a cowboy for a few years upon returning home from a stint in the US Army. He later left this life for a career with the State of Hawai'i Fish and Wildlife Division.

{5.10} *Sam Kealoha (in white shirt) with his three* paniolo *sons (left to right): Milton (Chubby), George, and Paul.*

George's mother was a product of a marriage between a Tongan man named Vea and a Hawaiian woman named Anakalea. Besides Maraea, two sons were born of this union—Walter and Dan Wela. The Tongan name was Hawaiianized to Wela. Walter's career began as a cowboy on Kūkaʻiau Ranch Ltd., and later he became a career figure in the travel industry as a tour bus driver, while his younger brother Dan went to work for Hawaiian Airlines, eventually heading up the Hilo operation before retiring.

The union of Sam and Maraea, despite producing six children, was not a lasting one. The boys stayed periodically with their father, and the girls were scattered among other relatives. George's middle sister, Laverne, was formally adopted by John Holi Maʻe and his wife, Esther, who were childless. They also adopted another niece, Verna Mae Ako. Later, when I became *lawe hānai* (informally adopted) of the Maʻe household, I always considered Laverne and Verna Mae to be my calabash (nonblood related) sisters. They were as pretty then as they are today, and it was a pleasure and honor to be considered part of their *ʻohana*.

For George, his early childhood years were not easy times due to chronic respiratory disease. He also lost his mother when he was only six years old. By age ten, frequent hospital stays were still needed to prop up his failing health. Although Kūkaʻiau Ranch's health benefits were sponsored by its sugar counterpart, Hāmākua Mill Company, the extended periods of hospitalization were frowned upon by the parent

{ 5.11 } *Brother-in-law of Sam Kealoha, Walter Wela was a respected uncle of the Kealoha children. Here Walter is photographed decked out in his wool chaps in front of Maulua Camphouse with his Winchester rifle, dog, and horse.*

company, Theo H. Davies and Co. Our father/grandfather, W. N. Bergin, MD, was the plantation physician from Pa'auilo through Laupāhoehoe, and he personally drove little George from Pa'auilo Dispensary after an allowed stay of several days to the dispensary at 'O'ōkala for a similar period of recuperation. When that period was exhausted, my father took him to Laupāhoehoe Hospital, where George again could find healing support. When that hospital stay was exhausted, my dad repeated the cycle, placing George again at Pa'auilo Dispensary, then 'O'ōkala, and on to Laupāhoehoe Hospital. This poignant vignette came from George himself, as my father never shared this story of his boundless devotion to the health and welfare of a sickly boy, extending heroic but due care in the face of rigid plantation constrictions.

By his early teens, George matured into a wiry, fit, and handsome young man who yearned for the life of a cowboy like his father, Sam, and uncles Holi Ma'e and Charlie Mahuna. The Kūka'iau Ranch foreman, Joe Correia, was a great horseman and revered cow boss who was raised and groomed by the Horner family. George went to work at the ranch as a fourteen-year-old boy when Roger Williams managed the outfit. Williams, like Correia, was an easy person to respect. They were both firm and formal, but they were very considerate leaders.

George was assigned a small string of horses, mostly gentle leftovers from senior cowboy strings. These were Morgan/

Standardbred crosses that, like Parker Ranch cow horses, were long-distance horses noted for their stamina throughout a long and full day of cowboy work. Sired by prominent remount stallion High Wire of Standardbred lineage, the Kūka'iau cow horses were commonsense types of mounts—not broncky, and they took to cattle work with ease and enjoyment. Browns, bays, and especially blacks were common coat colors. Uncle Holi's entire string was made up of solid black mounts, both geldings and mares.

George took an early interest in the Hawaiian horse, and he was privileged to become familiar with both the Mauna Kea strain and the Waipi'o Valley type of feral horse. In his memory, it was the Pu'u Mali brand of Mauna Kea horses that was most colorful, having roans, grays, and buckskins. The buckskins were of the darker variety, often with dorsal stripes of dark hair. Some of these had dorsal crosses over their withers and horizontal stripes on their upper forelegs. Such striping could well be a genetic throwback to the mustang-type mount that came down through the Iberian horses brought to America by Cortés. The Sorraia variety was largely buckskinned with dorsal stripes, crosses, and foreleg striping.

Although the Pu'u Mali band had been depopulated by the time George joined the cowboy ranks of Kūka'iau Ranch, he was vivid in his memories of how it was done. The final remnant band of mares with foals at their side was less than twenty head after the stallions were roped and gelded. In 1932, Donald MacAlister, ranch manager at the time, insisted on offering these feral horses for sale. He enlisted George's father and Charlie Mahuna Sr. to take the horses to ranch headquarters, where they were halter broken and "tidied up." Each *paniolo* led a string of nine or ten horses, some with foals at their side, down to the villages of Hāmākua. MacAlister's orders were to head toward Hilo until all were sold. According to George's father, MacAlister was delighted that some of the older mustangs brought as much as $40. This is testimony to MacAlister's Scottish penchant for good business, and it avoided the cruel act of simply killing the whole band once they were seized with the Pu'u Mali horse trap.

{5.12} *Though sickly as an infant, George Kealoha grew to become an able-bodied and highly respected* paniolo, *horseman, and historian.*

A young Billy Bergin first became aware of the cowboy skills of George and his brothers when he joined the household of John Holi Ma'e in 1949. George's brother Paul, robust and handsome, had just returned home from the army.

{5.13} *Candy Girl, daughter of Kūka'iau Ranch Standardbred sire High Wire. Candy Girl was a winning race mount, proudly shown here by owner/jockey "Old Man" Hasegawa in 1925. When not in competition, the mare was used under harness by Hasegawa, peddler of confectioneries, hence her name.*

Early developers of what is known today as Kūka'iau Ranch Ltd. were the Horner brothers. Many of their early stallion importations were of the finest Standardbred (trotter) bloodlines in America, such as the Hambletonian 10, Bellfounder, Mambrino, and Messenger. Further importations also went back to the foundation sires of the finest trotters, such as Orion, Impecatuer, and Adrian, the latter of which sired nearly a hundred foals for the Horners by 1928.

Kūka'iau Ranch horses were known for their dark colors, long backs, and stamina over long distances to and from work sites along the eastern slopes of Mauna Kea from Hanaipoe to Maulua. As a later complementary stud, High Wire, a remount stallion, became the ranch's leading sire, making the ranch a prime resource for cavalry mounts. John Holi Ma'e and Willy Miranda were logically assigned by then ranch manager Donald MacAlister to start many of the remount prospects, taking pride in their colts being praised by the remount committee for their gentle nature and polished reining qualities.

{5.14} *Top Kūka'iau Ranch teamster Charlie Mahuna attending two draft horses used to haul timber. Charlie and Sam Kealoha led a string of the last feral Mauna Kea horses for sale on the Hāmākua Coast.*

George, as always, was lithe, lean, and graceful. Just as handsome as his older brothers, Chubby was yet to return home from the service. He had lost his boyish chubbiness by then, but like in all country families, his childhood nickname was forever.

George was a fine all-around cowboy; but he was first a horseman. This quality emerged in his early years at 'Umikoa, when he was dutifully mentored by his Uncle Holi. George also read a lot about horses and was willing to apply modern techniques. While he had his pick of the finest colts on the ranch, he always had a *pono'ī* (self-owned horse) or two on his string and was proud that they were Hawaiian horses descended from either the Pu'u Mali line or, more likely, the Waipi'o Valley strain. He preferred color in his *pono'ī* mounts, while his ranch string was made up of sorrels, chestnuts, and eventually palominos when Coco Billy (American Quarter Horse Association) became the stallion standing at Kūka'iau Ranch.

George was a popular figure at the annual Honoka'a Rodeo, held at the arena on Memorial Day since 1955. He struck a stoic pose as flag judge, always mounted on a well-groomed and well-mannered *pono'ī*, usually a strawberry roan. He was also the flag judge of choice for Hilo and Kona rodeos. By the mid-1950s, George began in earnest to breed select Hawaiian horse broodmares to Waipi'o stallions in an effort, like that of Dr. Woo, to preserve the breed. He was in a position of respect as a fine horseman throughout the

{ 5.15 } *George Kealoha mounted on his* pono'ī *(owned) Hawaiian horse. The Kealoha brothers were frequently found at Hawai'i Saddle Club rodeos, where George served as flag judge and brother Paul performed as calf roper.*

Islands and for his quiet crusade to keep the Hawaiian horse heritage in a prominent place in Hawai'i's *paniolo* history.

Typically *paniolo,* George was quite talented musically, especially in slack key guitar (*kīhō'alu*) and country-western genres, as were his brothers and sisters. When ranch managers hosted special guests, sisters Myrtle and Laverne were often present to serenade the visitors. George preferred quieter renditions expressed in small family circles, rarely venturing beyond this close group. As was customary with most ranch families, music was an evening pastime, even after the advent of rodeo and television to 'Umikoa Village. With homes located in close proximity of one another, it was not uncommon to hear George's father, Sam, playing slack key in concert with his neighbor Arthur Johansen for hours on end while seated on their cottage veranda. In the stillness and quiet of a foggy 'Umikoa night, the entire village enjoyed their joint rendition of the beautiful and haunting Hawaiian love song "'Imi Au Ia 'Oe." These impromptu concerts that included spontaneous versions of mountain music instilled in George a lifetime appreciation for *paniolo* music.

As George entered retirement to look after his three-hundred-acre Hawaiian Homes Ranch, he was intent on maintaining his campaign to keep the Hawaiian horse image to the forefront. His daughter Georgiann, equally a lover of horses, has taken over the ranch in dutiful fashion, still respectful of the oversight provided by her dad. The history of the Hawaiian horse has been carried forward into a new century due to the enduring support of George Russell Kealoha, memorialized in this poem by his adoring daughter:

Umikoa Paniolo

Umikoa paniolo—
A wise old man is he.
He wears a beat up cowboy hat,
A red bandana 'round his neck.
Old faded jeans, and leather chaps;
Cowboy boots and silver spurs.
Upon his trusted horse he rides;
And works so hard each day.
Umikoa paniolo–
Proudly sits upon his horse,
And gazes at free roaming cattle—
Which graze upon the fine green lands of Mauna Kea.
I know where his heart is at—
His home—
This will forever be.
This fine old man has taught me much,
And shown me wonder and beauty—
Much unknown to many.
This is the last true paniolo of Umikoa—
A legacy of his time.
How I adore this fine old man.
For he is no other—
But my dear old Dad.

GEORGIANN L. KEALOHA
NOVEMBER 5, 1982

Franz "Dick" Solmssen

Likely the seniormost faculty member of Hawai'i Preparatory Academy (HPA), Dick Solmssen rightfully deserves praise as the father of the horse program at the esteemed private school in Waimea on the Big Island.

Born in 1935 in Berlin, Franz Solmssen was destined for a life with horses. Uncomfortable with life in prewar Germany, the Solmssen family moved to the United States in 1939, settling in Summit Hill, New Jersey.

Despite a bout with polio, young Solmssen's attraction to horses landed him in his first horse show. At age ten, he placed in the Junior Essex Troop Horse show. In 1949 he moved up a few notches, entering the Newark Horse Show and winning his class as he prepared to enter high school at the Darrow School in upstate New York. His love for horses never waned, but the rigor of Trinity College directed his focus toward academics, and he earned a bachelor's degree in 1957.

A teaching opportunity became available at Hawai'i Episcopal Academy (now Hawai'i Preparatory Academy) in Kamuela, a budding college preparatory institution that emphasized horsemanship as part of the extracurricular activities. Upon arriving on campus in the fall of 1958, Dick first immersed himself in preparation for a lifetime career in teaching high school English literature and Spanish.

Known by then as Mr. Solmssen to his charges but as Dick to the community,

{ 5.16 } *Smokey was a typical* kanaka *horse purchased for $50 from Jonika Perreira. Smokey transported young Billy, pictured here, all over Hilo, from Wainaku to Ho'olulu Park and from Waiākea Uka to Boiling Pots in Kaumana and down across Hilina Pali in Ka'ū.*

his exemplary academic career spanning more than four decades was matched by his contributions to the horse culture of the island of Hawai'i. In his own words, "We had the use of six horses, most of them owned by James Spencer, foreman of the county road crew and senior warden of St. James Church. The horse program involved saddling a few horses and riding through town (there were no shopping centers) toward Mauna Kea for a few miles and then riding back to school" (pers. comm.).

In its fledgling years, the horse program at Hawai'i Prep depended on donated horses, a policy that naturally did not attract top-of-the-line horseflesh in the Islands. As a matter of fact, Billy Bergin's first boyhood mount was a horse named Smokey, a genuine Hawaiian horse purchased from Jonika Perreira for $50. The horse was later given to Holi Ma'e when Billy graduated to bigger and better mounts through high school. Smokey was a typical "*kanaka* horse" with big hooves, sloping narrow hip, decent withers, a short neck, and a large Roman-nosed head, a solid dark brown with a small star—but he was a good horse. Holi, in turn, donated the horse to HPA for students to ride. When twenty-seven years old Billy, now a DVM, returned to Waimea after ten years in Kansas and Kentucky. "Ole Smokey" was still going, a little stiffer in gait, with grayish-white hair around his eyes and muzzle but the same black feet—unshod but in perfect shape.

Dick's interest in horses was enhanced by his friendship with several Parker Ranch cowboys, including Allen Lindsey, Jiro Yamaguchi, Teddy Bell, and Joe Hui. This invited opportunities for him to join the cowboy gang on major cattle drives, brandings, and even camping at Keanakolu when the crew worked the Humu'ula Sheep Station section of the ranch. During those early years, the cowboys christened him "Rawhide," borrowed from the popular television series of those times.

By 1967, Dick had developed a well-regarded horsemanship program including Western and English pleasure, hunter/jumper classes, and polo. It was during this period that he began a breeding program on the campus with donated mares and lease arrangements, using Parker Ranch Thoroughbred stallions crossed on mares that carried the bloodline of the noted feral Humuʻula stallion, Mauna Kea.

Dick did a lot to encourage and develop improved academy horses. His skill and interest in the sport of polo strengthened his mission. It was still a struggle, however, until a kindly gentleman named Isami Goto bought at auction a Parker Ranch horse as a donation to HPA. The filly turned out to be one of the last known daughters of the legendary Humuʻula stallion Mauna Kea. This was a defining moment in Dick Solmssen's life, launching his passionate interest in the Mauna Kea line of the Hawaiian horse and his crusade for the preservation of this special line of horseflesh.

The filly purchased by Ichiro Goto was Amaryllis, daughter of Mauna Kea out of a Morgan Parker Ranch mare sired by Junior. Under her mane, she carried the "8" brand, reflecting her sire Mauna Kea. Amaryllis was put to good use on the campus, but more importantly she became the matriarchal cornerstone of the bloodline of Mauna Kea. Her direct grand-offspring excelled in performance over the past three decades, regardless of which sire or grandsire was utilized.

In a 2010 Hawaiian horse DNA campaign, Dick and the HPA horse program provided for testing of more than twenty horses that traced back to the legendary mountain stallion Mauna Kea. While Dick's career on campus, which continues part-time beyond its fifty-year span, is marked by high peer and student respect for academic excellence, his contribution to the preservation of the genotype of the feral horse of old Hawai'i is an epic parallel. He joins *paniolo* George Kealoha of Kūkaiʻau Ranch and Dr. David Woo of the Royal Mauna Kea Mustangs: all three men are duly credited with keeping alive the heritage of the Hawaiian horse into the new millennium.

In 2012, Dick was honored with the Mānā Award from Veterinary Associates, Inc., at the Hawaiʻi Horse Expo, recognizing his lifetime contribution to the betterment of the horse.

{5.17} *Dick Solmssen, a perennial figure on the campus of Hawaiʻi Preparatory Academy. Dick's role in elevating horsemanship of the youth has spanned more than fifty years. It was during his tenure that he preserved the genotype of the Hawaiian horse.*

A DNA Study of the Hawaiian Horse

After spending our lifetimes around horses, from show stallions to feral *kanaka lioʻāhiu* (wild native horses), we (coauthors Billy and Brady Bergin) became interested in determining if there was a genetic link between the Hawaiian horse and early Spanish mounts imported from California. We conducted comprehensive DNA studies on Island horses that met the conformational standards (phenotype) and genetic (genotype) histories compatible with the Spanish mounts that reached the Sandwich Islands between 1803 (Cleveland and Shaler) through and beyond 1833. Aware of the challenges we faced locating these animals, we planned to survey a minimum of up to seventy-five horses in our study.

Inspired by the fine DNA work of Dr. Phillip Sponenberg of Virginia Tech University and Dr. Gus Cothran of Texas A&M University, we completed the DNA work in time to include the findings in this book on the Hawaiian horse. To set the stage for this undertaking, Sponenberg provided an overview of Spanish mustang heritage and the Barb horse in America.

Observations of Dr. Phillip Sponenberg

Dr. Sponenberg's overview begins as follows:

> Colonial Spanish horses are of great historic importance in the New World. They descend from horses introduced from Spain during the age of the conquest of the New World. They are a direct remnant of the horses of the Golden Age of Spain and that type is mostly or wholly extinct now in Spain. Our Colonial Spanish horses are therefore a treasure chest of genetic wealth from a time long gone. (Sponenberg 1992)

In North America, more than one registry association has borne the mission to preserve the Colonial Spanish horse, typically incorporating the term "mustang." The Spanish Mustang Registry, formed in 1957, is one of these organizations. Sponenberg aptly addresses the fact that not all of these horses came from feral (free-roaming) sources:

> Colonial Spanish horses are rarely referred to by this name. The usual term that is used is Spanish Mustang. The term Mustang generally carries with it the connotation of a feral horse, and this is somewhat unfortunate since many of these horses have never had a feral background. The important part of the background of these horses is that they are Spanish. These [are] descendants of the horses that were brought to the New World by the Conquistadors, and include some feral, some rancher, some mission, and some native American strains (tribal). (Sponenberg 2011)

Sponenberg sheds further light on the history that could provide the genetic pathway through the vaquero-*paniolo* link of imported Mexican cow horses in 1833:

> The original horses brought to America from Spain were relatively selected. These first came to the Caribbean islands, where populations were increased before export to the mainland. In the case of North

> America the most common source of horses was Mexico as even the populations in the southeastern USA were imported from Mexico rather than the Caribbean. (Sponenberg 2011)

Reaffirming this DNA link would give credence to the idea that the missionaries were a source for horses, as opposed to feral horses with the common denominator being of Spanish colonial origin. The missionary connection is supported by the fact that the first horses brought to Hawaiʻi by Cleveland and Shaler came from Mission San Borgia and Cabo San Lucas in in Baja California (Franciscan missions). In the 1833 shipload of cowboy horses were some belonging to mounted servants of the missions of Monterey—further pointing to missionary origins.

Sponenberg raises two other points. One is the designation of the Spanish colonial horse as a "landrace" type population, a term that also applies to the Hawaiian horse. Landrace is a local Hawaiian variety of a once-domestic equine species that developed over the last two centuries, largely by natural processes and by adaptation to environmental and cultural surroundings. Landraces tend to be genetically and physically diverse from formal breeds.

The second point made by Sponenberg could apply to the demise of the Hawaiian horse DNA in the Aloha State:

> From the original and consistent Spanish base were developed the more common breeds that are associated with the American West: American Quarter Horse, Paint, and Appaloosa. These have been largely separated on the basis of color, but were originally part of a population that included all of these colors. As selection has proceeded in these breeds with continuous outcrossing to Thoroughbreds and Quarter Horses the original Spanish influence has become minimal. (Sponenberg 1992)

This point may explain the results of the DNA study on the Hawaiian horse.

In an effort to ascertain the presence of DNA components in hair samples of Hawaiian horses with the mustang phenotype, we launched a 2010 study with support of a DNA Analysis of Feral Horses in Hawaiʻi from the Paniolo Preservation Society, a 501(c)(3) nonprofit foundation dedicated to preserving ranching heritage in the Islands.

Horses that arrived in 1803 via Cleveland and Shaler were acquired from Catholic missions serving Cabo San Lucas and Baja Point in New Spain (Mexico). Although mustang in immediate origin, these horses descended from Spanish horses brought to the Americas via Hernán Cortés in 1519.

As these horses grew in profusion throughout North America and the West, recent progress in DNA analysis has confirmed their mustang/Spanish horse connection. The United States presently has nine confirmed bands. The Bergin study hoped to add Hawaiʻi to the list of historically connected horse communities.

We analyzed hair samples of seventy-five head of horses that matched the phenotypic (conformation) mustang appearance and had a history of descending from Mauna Kea mountain stallions or from the valleys of Waipiʻo and Waimanu, the last holdouts of feral horses in Hawaiʻi. Laboratory work was conducted by the Animal Genetics Laboratory of Texas A&M's College of Veterinary Medicine.

Two major sources for horse samplings of the Mauna Kea and Waipiʻo Valley horses came from Franz "Dick" Solmssen of Hawaiʻi Preparatory Academy and Waipiʻo on Horseback owner Michael Olival and his able assistant, Diana Webb. We are grateful for their assistance with the project. Without their enthusiastic support, the DNA undertaking would have lacked critical mass.

While the DNA results point more to a Thoroughbred than Spanish origin of the sampled representatives, the project, at minimum, established a baseline for the makeup of the Hawaiian horse, which may best be described as a landrace population as opposed to a specific breed. Technical details of the study can be found in appendix A.

Waipiʻo Valley, while located in a remote corner of the Big Island, played a significant role in horse history, affecting the entire island state.

CHAPTER 6

THE HISTORIC ROLE OF HAWAI'I'S VALLEYS

In precontact times, the wetland valleys of Waipi'o, Waimanu, and Pololū in North Kohala provided extensive taro production. Whether for the warriors serving the *ali'i* or for export to neighboring villages of the uplands, the *lo'i kalo* (taro terraces) of these valleys were vital to early Hawaiian agricultural productivity. Villages distant from Waipi'o Valley were spared decimation in times of extended drought during the era of Kamehameha I due to the valley's flowing waters.

With the advent of the horse, but especially the donkey and mule, Waipi'o Valley and its sister *awāwa* (valley) Waimanu expanded distribution of taro and routinely served villages in all of Hāmākua and Waimea. Pololū Valley served *nā kauhale* (the villages) of Kohala. By 1875, the donkey was replacing the horse as a pack animal. Still used today for riding and breeding, the horse has been ever present in these valleys.

Just as cattle production appropriated the early Mauna Kea horse, commercialization of taro farming created a special purpose to the lowly donkey and its hybrid counterpart, the mule. By the turn of the nineteenth century, more than 275 mules, donkeys, and horses were in use in the valleys of Waipi'o and Waimanu.

The Waipi'o horses that we know of today are likely descendants, with significant admixture, of the valley horses of the late 1800s and early 1900s. By 1910, donkeys and to a greater extent mules were the bearers of produce out of the valley and remained so for the next half century.

At the end of World War II, the military jeep was introduced to the valley, and over the next decade some of the horses, donkeys, and mules were "turned out" to

{ 6.1 } *This aerial view captures the depth, width, beauty, and shoreline of Waipi‘o Valley, lying between towering walls of lava.*

subsist on their own, with very loose ownership responsibility. Unlike their hybrid counterparts, the horses and donkeys were free to reproduce, with very limited domestication. The horses maintained a mustanglike appearance and attitude. When caught, gentled, and trained, these animals are known for their hardiness and utility as cow horses, pack animals, and hunting mounts.

As for the donkeys and mules, they have established iconic status in the valleys of Waipi‘o, Waimanu, and Pololū. The important part they played in the history of the Big Island is discussed further here and in the following chapters.

The Chinese Connection

With the arrival of the immigrant plantation workers came the need for rice production, another staple for which the valleys, especially Waipi‘o, are well suited. With the wave of people came those skilled in farming the wetlands, and Waipi‘o became home to many, especially those of Chinese heritage. Many of them were experienced farmers of rice and taro

{ 6.2 } *Even to the present day, a common sight is the casual comingling of horses, donkeys, and mules from the shore to the deeper haunts of the magical valley of Waipi'o.*

{ 6.3 } *Holi and Esther Ma'e touring Waipi'o Valley on horseback (1935).*

root in their homeland. Still evident today, the names of Ah Puck, Lau Kong, Loo, and Mock Chew herald the legacy of valley life.

Two of these families stand out among the many Chinese/Hawaiian farmers of Waipi'o: Mock Chew for his industriousness and Akaka for surviving challenges of great magnitude.

Ah Chew Mock, who later changed his name to Mock Chew, was born in Canton, China, in 1877 and took his first job as a ranch hand in Waimea, Hawai'i. By 1900 he was farming rice and Hawaiian *kalo* (taro) for poi in Waipi'o. Industrious by nature, he farmed these food staples commercially, while Akaka exported the product from the valley floor by horse, donkey, and eventually mule trains of five to six pack animals.

While rice was conveniently bagged for packing, taro was cleaned, steamed, and peeled before pounding into a baggable cakelike form called *pa'i 'ai.* These cakes were wrapped in ti leaves for protection before placing into cloth rice bags and heavy burlap sacking of about 105–110 pounds per unit. A pack animal transported two of these units, so a train of six mules carried a total payload of about 1,200 pounds of *pa'i 'ai* per trip. By 1920, Mock Chew opened a poi factory in Honoka'a town, where Mālama Market is currently located.

{ 6.4 } *With each mule packing a 300-pound payload for a daylong round-trip to the rim of Waipi'o Valley, it was a highly productive undertaking for man and beast.*

Two trails served the Waipi'o mule trains. The conventional route exists today, meandering up the oceanside cliff to reach Kukuihaele village. From this point, poi and rice brokers filled orders for villages as far south as 'O'ōkala, down the Hāmākua Coast.

The historic Mud Lane trail served the Waimea-bound mule trains. The mule trains climbed an equally steep and winding trail up the massive *kualapa* (ridge) on the *mauka* side of famed twin falls Hi'ilawe, the *wailele* (waterfalls) so celebrated in love songs and legends of old Hawai'i. At the top of the ridge, the trail intersected with Mud Lane, the aptly named track between Kukuihaele village *makai* and Waimea's scattered communities *mauka*. This route served many *kauhale* in the Waimea area, including Hanaipoe, Lālākea, Mahiki, Mānā, Po'okanaka, and Pu'ukapu on its eastern flank. In the west, the main village of Waimea became a distribution point through merchants, such as Akona Store, that served the area from Kawaihae to Waiki'i.

The Mock Chew Poi Factory consistently processed three tons of *pa'i 'ai* daily, converting the cake form to baggable poi. Households would again *ho'owali* (mix by hand and massage with water to appropriate consistency) the poi before placing in a large bowl for collective consumption.

While Ah Chew, known as the "Taro King" of Waipi'o, passed away in 1955, there were several other Chinese immigrant farmers of significance during this early period of rice and poi production. One of these men was a man named Akaka, whose strings of horses, mules, and donkeys were decimated by glanders, a highly contagious and fatal zoonotic (transferable between animal and man) disease caused by the bacterium *Psuedomonas mallei*. A febrile disease causing fevers as high as 105 degrees, it results in ulcerations of the nasal passages, thick

nasal mucoid discharge, swelling of the lymphatic glands in the area of the throat, and eventual death; in some cases, euthanasia is necessary to prevent further spread.

Glanders wreaked havoc during the American Civil War (1861–1865) on both Confederate and Union sides, decimating military horses and mules to the point of immobility of cavalry, pack, and draft resources. The eventual birth of the US Remount Service at the dawn of World War I was largely a result of institutional memory of glanders' tragic role.

In Hawai'i, the Board of Commissioners of Agriculture and Forestry was established, with Albert Waterhouse as chairman. Hawai'i's territorial regulatory

{ 6.5 } *Fording the stream was a pleasure in good weather but a risky undertaking during stormy times and flooding. Sam Mock Chew wends his way home from taro delivery to the valley's brim.*

{ 6.6 } *Skillful loading and frequent inspections were the hallmarks of good packers, whether they worked in Appalachia, the Rockies, or Hawai'i's steep valleys. Here a mule tender prepares to load out his train.*

forces were organized within the board in 1905 as the Division of Animal Industry under the direction of a Danish veterinarian named Victor Norgaard. An Irish veterinarian, Dr. J. C. FitzGerald, was the territorial assistant (and later Maui island deputy), while Dr. J. Elliot, a British-trained veterinarian, was appointed to the island of Hawai'i.

It was Dr. Elliot who ascertained that glanders came to the island in 1895 via a load of mainland imported mules destined for the Hāmākua series of sugar plantations, including Kukuihaele on the upper bluff lands bordering Waipi'o. By 1898, Elliot confirmed the presence of the disease using the Mallein skin test, which provides conclusive detection prior to the advent of clinical signs. Euthanasia of glanders-positive Equidae is the only recourse. The disease established itself in Waipi'o Valley, bringing rice and taro farming to its knees. It left no means of transport other than the backs of the farmers, their family members, and hired hands.

The first outbreak in the valley occurred in 1907, and FitzGerald headed up the diagnostic efforts. Norgaard, in a July 1907 report, noted these efforts to contain the spread of glanders. Described in detail in *Loyal to the Land: The Legendary Parker Ranch, 750–1950* (Bergin 2004), the following excerpts are from this first volume of the series covering the history of Parker Ranch:

{6.7} *Over the vast ranges at midday rode the lunch boy, or "pa'i 'ai man," to catch up with the cowboy gang and deliver their "meal on the run" during a cattle drive break.*

While there, Dr. Fitzgerald received information that there were a number of sick mules in Waipi'o Valley, wherefore he proceeded to that place to investigate. He found 9 cases of acute glanders, all in mules belonging to a Chinese rice planter, Akaka. All of these animals were destroyed and the remaining mules belonging to the same party were placed in quarantine in a separate pasture.

Dr. Fitzgerald also ascertained that a larger number of horses and mules had been dying from glanders in Waipi'o Valley during the last few weeks before his arrival, and, considering that nearly all of the animals from this valley are used to carry rice and *pa'i 'ai* all over the Hāmākua districts from Kamuela to Pā'auhau, the situation was sufficiently serious to warrant that steps be taken without delay to prevent the further spread of the disease.

A wireless message was sent to the Parker Ranch requesting that no horses or mules from Waipi'o Valley be allowed to pass the Hāmākua gate and that the pack train, which once a week brings *pa'i 'ai* to the Parker Ranch and to the stores at Kamuela, be met with wagons at said gate. At this place the provisions were transferred from the pack animals to the wagons and the pack train instructed to return immediately to Waipi'o Valley and remain there until further notice. (Norgaard 1907)

FitzGerald, in December of that year, filed the following status report:

> I left for Kukuihaele on December 11th and immediately proceeded to organize a party to accompany me into and beyond Waipio Valley. I succeeded in getting together three cowboys, one interpreter and two policemen, with whom I went into the valley on the 12th. On the 13th and 14th we rounded up all horse stock in Waipio Valley, a total of 192 head. Among these was one case of acute glanders, which was destroyed, while 16 animals were slightly suspicious. These all submitted to the mallein test, but as none of them reacted they were released.
>
> On the 15th we went up the trail on the further side of the valley and rounded up the entire plateau including the 12 gulches located there. We found only 10 horses, one of which was affected with glanders and was destroyed. The 16th was spent in Waimanu valley where 30 animals were examined and one destroyed for glanders. We then returned to Kukuihaele and on the 17th and 18th rounded up and inspected all of the outside animals in the neighborhood, as well as all of the plantation stock. Among the outsiders one case of glanders was found and destroyed. After examining the plantation stock of Honoka'a, which was found to be free from the disease, I returned to Honolulu. (FitzGerald 1907)

Sadly, glanders flared up again in 1912, generating a report from Norgaard reflecting the seriousness of this episode:

> On October 30, 1912, a wireless message was received from the manager of the Kukuihaele plantation, Hamakua, Hawaii, stating that an epidemic had broken out among the horses and mules in Waipio Valley and requesting that the Territorial Veterinarian be notified which was done immediately. Glanders was suspected at once, but as the message seemed to indicate that the recent heavy rains in the district might be a contributing cause and as the death of seven horses within a short period pointed to some acute infectious disease, such as epizootic laryngitis, the glanders theory seemed doubtful, even though the seriousness of the situation was realized. Waipio Valley or Gulch is an absolutely isolated district approachable only by way of a rough, steep trail, descending a thousand feet or more at an angle of 40 to 45 degrees from a point a short distance north of the village of Kukuihaele, where the plantation stables, with more than 250 head of mules and horses, are located. The transmission of infection to the plantation animals was therefore imminent, and the same applies to the adjoining string of plantations, stretching south along the east coast of Hawaii, as well as to the Parker Ranch, all of which are visited regularly, twice a week, by pack trains from Waipio Valley carrying rice and pa'i 'ai. (Norgaard 1912)

Another excerpt from the first volume of *Loyal to the Land* describes the tragic impact glanders dealt to Akaka:

> In both outbreaks, the focus of infection came from the stables of the prominent

> Chinese rice and taro farmer named Akaka. Akaka's operation had barely managed by purchasing available horses and mules from neighboring farmers in the valley. Apparently during the period between epidemics, glanders had been reduced to a mild incidence, and the locally raised mules had some natural immunity. This changed drastically when Akaka purchased twelve young pack mules from Parker Ranch and put them to work packing his produce up to Kukuihaele. The Parker Ranch mules were obviously immunologically naïve, for within three months all had died of glanders and an epidemic broke out among neighboring taro farmers. (Bergin 2004)

On October 30, 1912, Norgaard himself left Honolulu by steamer, but not before a wire was sent to A. W. Carter advising the reinstitution of safeguards that had protected the ranch during the 1907 outbreak. Norgaard also ordered the Territorial Department of Health to station twenty-four-hour personnel, with support from Sheriff William M. S. Lindsey of Waimea, at the mouth of the valley to detain and segregate any suspicious animals coming out. Upon arriving himself, Norgaard aptly described the challenge ahead:

> The first day in the valley was exceedingly disagreeable, a constant pouring rain necessitating the continuous use of oil skins and making the trail dangerous. Several times my horse slipped and nearly sent me headlong over the pali. However, we reached the bottom safely but the mud and rain made the work slow and exceedingly disagreeable. After inspecting the isolated cases, the rest of the animals belonging to Akaka were examined, and several had to be pronounced suspicious. . . .
>
> During the following days an attempt was made to inspect all the horses, mules and donkeys in Waipio Valley, and it is believed that all the animals were seen. In rounding up both owners and animals the Hamakua police lent valuable aid, supporting the Board of Health inspector and his assistants in securing a complete list of names of the owners and the number of animals belonging to each. (Norgaard 1912)

By 7 a.m. the following day, Akaka's pack train arrived, using twelve horses bearing two large bags of rice each. These were all Akaka had left for pack animals, and even these horses showed early signs of glanders. They were relieved of their freight and marched back to the valley floor to join the rest of the condemned pack animals. Norgaard describes the disposing of these condemned horses and mules in graphic detail:

> The animals were, therefore, ordered sent to the beach where I shot them in such positions as to leave the bodies below the high tide line which, the native assured me, would cause the carcasses to be carried out to sea by the receding tide.
>
> A strange sight was presented at this place, seldom visited by anybody except for the purpose of disposing of dead or dying animals. Here bones and skulls were

> littering the beach, many of them still retaining traces of flesh and ligaments, indicating that they had but recently died. Four white bleached skulls were found having bullet holes in the forehead, evidently the remains of those which were killed in this place five years ago. In several cases the skulls and neck vertebrates were found tied with a rope to a large rock, without indication of injury to the skull either by bullet or axe, showing clearly that the sick or dying animal had been taken to the place and left to die without the mercy of a death blow. Considering that a majority of the bones and carcasses must have been carried out to sea, the number of those remaining in sight was a sure indication of a very high mortality among the horse stock of the Valley, which has never been known to exceed 200 head. (Norgaard 1912)

The combined efforts of the territorial government, the sugar industry, and Parker Ranch were exemplary, not only in stamping out glanders but in safeguarding the future of taro and rice production while restoring the pack mule resources of farmer Akaka. Another excerpt from *Loyal to the Land* details these efforts:

> A. W.'s concerns were not limited to infecting ranch horses and mules; they focused also on the human famine that would result if Waipiʻo's intensive taro and rice production was rendered undeliverable from the valley save for the backs of men. A severe shortage of these vital foodstuffs would certainly hamper the productivity of the cowboys, as well as risking the health and welfare of ranch families. The bulk of the villages in Hāmākua, from Kukuihaele in the north to ʻOʻōkala in the south, would be similarly deprived.
>
> Norgaard and Carter divided the challenge of resolving the crisis. While Norgaard immediately launched aggressive mallein testing on all Equidae between Kukuihaele and Kohala in search of unexposed pack animals to replace the large Akaka string, Carter implored the territorial government to indemnify Akaka for destroyed pack animals and purchase of replacements. Norgaard gave Carter direction for securing indemnification, but it was A. W.'s influence and perseverance that saw it through to fruition. (Bergin 2004)

Akaka's woes were compassionately described in a supportive memo from Norgaard to Albert Waterhouse, then chairman of the board:

> I am up against a problem that in a way is new to me, and I take the liberty to lay the matter before you, and, if you deem necessary, I should very much like to have the Attorney General's opinion thereon. The facts are simply these:—Mr. Akaka, an aged Chinese rice planter in Waipio Valley, has glanders among his horse stock to an extent unprecedented in this Territory. What his losses have been previous to a few months ago I can only surmise, but of twelve young mules purchased at Waimea about four months ago not a single one remains; all have died from glanders. When I was here three weeks ago I destroyed 6 horses and 1 mule, all affected with typical

glanders and now, having tested with mallein his remaining twenty-seven head of horses I have found twenty four of them to be suffering with glanders. Now, the law, that is, the rules and regulations of our Board, is plain enough on the subject, saying that any horse or mule found by the Territorial Veterinarian to be affected with glanders or farcy shall be destroyed the carcass disposed of premises disinfected, and so forth at the owners expense. . . . There are, however, conditions and circumstances, not to mention precedents, which seem to me to demand more explicit instructions or authorization before I proceed as indicated. Mr. Akaka was a comparatively rich man a few years ago, but through mismanagement of his business here, while on a visit to China, he returned to find himself very much reduced financially, in fact almost ruined. Unfavorable conditions made it difficult for him to regain what he had lost in spite of generous support from his friends, and the present difficulty which finds him indebted to the extent of $9,000.00 can result only in bankruptcy, if he is deprived of the means wherewith to harvest and market the now ripe crop of 55 to 60 tons of rice. Without any assurance of indemnification by the Government, I am told it will practically be impossible for him to borrow any more money wherewith to replace his work animals, without which the present crop and possibly the following one will be a total loss. Under these conditions you will undoubtedly understand why I am desirous of reassurance in regard to the apparently plain course outline by our rules and regulations. As an American citizen, Mr. Akaka must have some inalienable rights, covered by constitutional or other laws, guaranteeing him against the deliberate though legal destruction of his means of making a legitimate living—pro bono publico—

Now Mr. Waterhouse, if, after reading this, you have come to the conclusion that I am borrowing trouble and that I should not bother the members of the board with such details after receiving plain instructions to enforce the law, I will only ask you to imagine yourself in my position, with an old man, palsied and with tears running down his face begging me to spare at least some of his animals, explaining over and over again in his nearly unintelligible pidgin English the unfortunate position he is in—and I doubt you would fancy yourself in my place. To me there is something awfully unjust in ruining the old man for the benefit of the community, and I have done what I could to get the neighboring plantations to help him out with a view to reimbursement by the coming legislature. (Bergin 2004)

Waterhouse—with nudging from A. W.—responded positively, ordering the appraisal of stock and the cost of replacing the Akaka stables and outbuildings. Norgaard then reported,

Upon my return I was pleased to meet Mr. O. L. Sorenson, Assistant Manager of the Parker Ranch, who informed me that he had been designated to act as an agent for a number of plantations, as well as for

> the Parker Ranch and the Hawaiian Irrigation Company, for the purpose of purchasing horses wherewith to enable Akaka to harvest his rice crop, thereby saving him from bankruptcy. (Bergin 2004)

Norgaard's appeal was not in vain. Akaka was made whole by these efforts, and the cupboards of the villages of Hāmākua and Waimea were restored with rice and taro from the fertile fields of Waipiʻo Valley. Little is known today of Akaka's twilight years. No family members (if any) have stepped forward with added history. In contrast, the Waipiʻo/Chinese Mock Chew clan, whose ancestors survived glanders, world wars, floods, and tsunamis, entered the new millennium celebrating their heritage with pride.

The Sproat Influence

No discussion on mules and valleys of Hawaiʻi would be complete without including the Sproat family of North Kohala. For that matter, any discussion of native music, storytelling, or rodeo in the Islands will eventually include the Sproat name.

Jacob William Sproat came to Hawaiʻi as a mercenary during the overthrow of the Hawaiian Kingdom in 1893. While he had no allegiance to either side of the tragic deposing of Queen Liliʻuokalani, his initial posture was in support of abandoning the kingdom in lieu of succession via a territorial government of the United States, of which he was a citizen. Once aware of the moral inequity of the overthrow, Sproat left the campaign, moving to Hawaiʻi Island. At one point, the senior Sproat owned a thirty-acre homestead in Waimea.

Shortly after the turn of the century, Sproat was employed by Parker Ranch as a teamster working out of Waikiʻi, where corn farming covered several thousand acres. A genuine mule skinner from Missouri, Sproat's reputation as a master of mule husbandry drew him to North Kohala and the Kohala Ditch Company. While in Kohala, he met a Native Hawaiian woman, Clara Kalehuaopele Raymond, whom he took as his wife. Clara was the granddaughter of Ramon Baesa, a vaquero brought to the Islands in 1833 by Kamehameha III. With their union, Jacob and Clara launched a succession of five subsequent generations whose name in Native Hawaiian circles is revered in many genres beyond the trusty mule: music, ranch life, rodeo, history, legend, and the Mormon faith. One of their more prominent sons, William Kāneākalā, was born in Mahiki, a verdant forest above Waipiʻo Valley celebrated in the verses of the ballad, "Hole Waimea."

The Sproat name is synonymous with the famed Kohala Ditch. Over a seventy-year span, three generations of the family oversaw Kohala Ditch operations. They began with the senior Sproat in 1917, when he became foreman of operations for the ditch—a water resource very dependent on mule service to manage a twenty-six-mile course consisting of fifty-seven tunnels and six miles of open ditch. As water flowed toward the plantations of Kohala, flumes were the conduits built to carry it over the steep *kahawai* (gulches). Measuring six feet in depth and seven feet in width, the flumes were mounted on trestles of wood and concrete. The meandering flumes were caulked and tarred, while the tunnels and open ditches were lined with cement and carefully laid stones, artfully crafted by Japanese contract workers and masons.

In repair and maintenance chores alone, the mule was the vehicle of choice for packing and personal transport, wending their way along the cliffs on a five-foot-wide pathway. Beyond repair and maintenance, supervising large crews under risky work conditions and conducting rescue missions, Sproat managed to raise a splendid family, including his protégé William Kāneākalā "Bill" Sproat, who replaced Jacob when he retired in 1928.

North Kohala sugar plantations beckoned Bill Sproat to move there and assume a much broader responsibility—maintenance of the Kohala Ditch system as it emerged from the *nā'ahawa* (waterheads) high on the northern face of the Kohala Mountain Range. His wife, Beatrice Rodenhurst, a Native Hawaiian of North Kohala, became the quiet matriarch of a family that reared noted individuals in mule tending, irrigation, music, the Mormon faith, and rodeo. Born of this union were sons Dale, Kindy, Buzzy, and Kamaka and a lone sister, Bea.

In continuing the Sproat bond with the trusty mule, Buzzy carried the torch forward. A former paratrooper, truck driver, and lumber worker, he returned to Hawai'i's outback, this time Moloka'i

{ 6.8 } *Home from Awini for a long weekend, Bill Sproat enjoys four of his five children.*

{ 6.9 } *Kindy Sproat carried forth the family tradition of mule skinning and meaningful Hawaiian music.*

instead of his *one hānau* (birthplace) in the valleys of North Kohala. The Moloka'i connection began in 1973 when a Moloka'i party was attempting to launch a Grand Canyon–like mule ride down the Kalaupapa Trail. When Papa Bill and Buzzy flew to the Friendly Isle to assess the opportunity, the younger Sproat found a new home and lifetime career astride a trusty mule. Buzzy eventually became owner of the trail outfit with Roy Horner, a business partner. A key guide on the trail is Buzzy's son Sale, a top cowboy in his own right, who was named the 2003 Hawai'i High School Rodeo Association' Champion Bull Rider.

Keeping horses, donkeys, and mules in good health remained a challenge for decades to come. Sadly, Buzzy Sproat died unexpectedly in 2014. The newspaper announcement of his passing aptly described the muleteer as a "legend."

CHAPTER 7

HORSE HEALTH ISSUES

Many of these considerations of health extend beyond the horse to include donkeys and mules. Moreover, such observations bridge well over a century of time, as they include the views of veterinarians, ranch managers, horsemen, and trainers from the nineteenth century to the present. While the veterinarians share a combined experience of nearly a century of horse practice in the Islands, their love for horses has been deeply embedded since their youths.

Placing horse health issues in order of importance, nutrition is the leading issue, followed by parasitism, foaling issues, infectious and allergic diseases, and finally by dental, skin, and hoof problems.

Nutrition and parasitism are traditional leaders of health issues in horses of Hawai'i. Foaling problems, dental issues, infectious and allergic diseases, along with skin and hoof problems, also plague the species but to a lesser degree. Fortunately, all of the above are preventable and manageable conditions with today's medical expertise. Many of the predisposing conditions are universal to all regions of the world with horse populations. Hawai'i's tropical climate, with its high forage moisture, high rainfall and humidity, volcanic soils of variable mineral composition, and common presence of wetlands, largely bears responsibility for nutritional deficiency and ubiquitous parasitism.

In the following section, we provide insight into problems associated with nutritional deficiency that impact horse health.

Early Diagnostic Findings

Tropical Degeneracy

From a historical standpoint, one must appreciate that when horses arrived in 1803, global knowledge regarding proper feeding was nearly two thousand years old, if one considers the cultivation of oats as the universal choice and source of the Arabian horse tender. Lacking the environmental conditions for cultivation of alfalfa, let alone oats, a horse of Hawai'i browsed on leafy grasses of sparse nutritional content and high moisture. A century later, Dr. J. C. FitzGerald of Maui aptly described such nutritional deficiency as the cause of "tropical degeneracy." Imported adult horses, unless acclimated, lose body condition rapidly, while young studs never achieve their growth potential.

Coupling this deficiency with forage grown on the volcanic soils of the Islands, which is sporadically low in calcium, phosphorus, magnesium, and copper, the Hawaiian horse is challenged by depressed bone growth, ossification, and metabolism, leaving cartilage with impaired protective and regenerative qualities. Under severe conditions, these pressures result in epiphysitis (inflammation of the growth zone), curb (inflammation of the long plantar ligament of the hock joint), and joint malformation.

Big Head Disease

By far the most severe manifestation of mineral deficiency in the Hawaiian horse is big head disease (BHD) and its attendant issues. This condition was described in an early report of the Territorial Board of Commissioners of Agriculture and Forestry. The third volume of *Loyal to the Land* (Bergin 2008) briefly details the condition: "Bighead (Osteomalacia) is a disease of horses caused by deficiency in calcium or the disruption of the interrelationship between calcium and its counterparts phosphorus and magnesium. When calcium metabolism is upset, inadequate blood levels result, and bone growth and density begin to fail. It is usually manifested dramatically in the head, where spongy expansion of bones resulted in the descriptive name."

BHD is found on all islands with horses in which the deficient diet is not addressed. Certainly, over the last century, the condition has been studied and restudied, resulting in a plethora of noteworthy probable causes and preventive advice. Noteworthy in these studies were the high levels of oxalic acid in forages where BHD is found. Oxalic acid binds the available calcium in the grass, and over a period the horse's blood level reflects deficiency, and the hormone parathormone signals in a compensatory effort—the leaching of calcium from the bones, especially those of the head that enjoy a profound blood supply. Kikuyu grass, a ubiquitous and palatable forage, is especially high in oxalic acid. Oxalic acid, coincidentally, is responsible for the itchy tingling sensation in the mouths of people that consume inadequately cooked taro, causing the *mane'o* (itching) effect.

Actual cases of BHD have occurred, however, in pastures producing high levels of available calcium. Phosphorus is moderately unavailable in Hawaiian rangelands. and magnesium deficiency is not uncommon. Magnesium is a vital metabolite that regulates calcium and phosphorus absorption. BHD has occurred under conditions when more than adequate calcium intake

is accompanied by phosphorus and/or magnesium deficiency.

Hence, our cautious and conservative opinion is that BHD can occur under calcium, phosphorus, and magnesium deficiency as well as conditions that disrupt the interrelationships of these three vital macrominerals.

Diagnosis of Big Head Disease

Blood samples measuring calcium, phosphorus, and magnesium are of little diagnostic help because the parathyroid gland constantly regulates these mineral levels by absorption from consumed nutrients and reabsorption from bone and several body organs. Blood levels that appear adequate may reflect what has been demineralized from bone rather than dietary intake.

Unfortunately, clinical signs of BHD appear after the animal is chronically affected. Two sites are the first indicators: the maxillary bones beneath the eyes that seemingly bulge to the level of the orbit, and the mandible, which thickens midshaft to more than an inch. As the disease progresses, the bones of the face thicken to the point of grotesqueness, while the jawbone

{7.1} *A broodmare (foreground) with big head disease. Note disfiguration of the facial bone structure and poor condition due to malformation of maxillae, mandibles, and dental array.*

{ 7.2 } *Note the contrasting thickness of the affected big head mandible (left) with that of a normal horse of similar age (ventral view).*

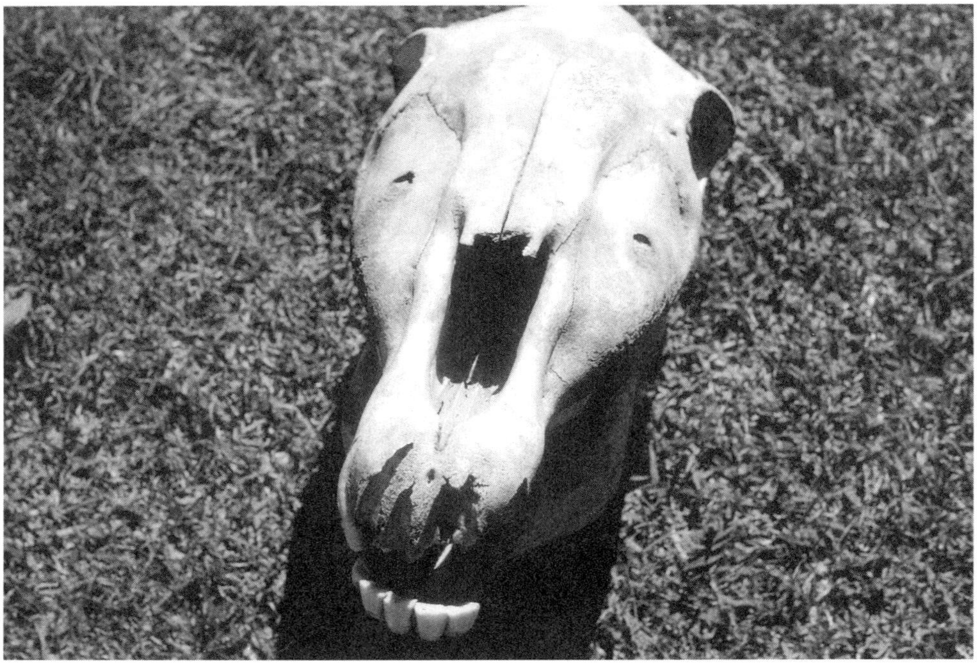

{ 7.3 } *Frontal view of a big head skull shows enlargement of the whole skull.*

doubles in thickness. Progressive demineralization of these facial bones requires that they thicken to support the same functions. With malformation of the maxillary and mandibular bones comes malocclusion of the associated upper and lower dental arcades, especially the premolar and molar teeth. At this point, mastication of grain and forage is severely compromised.

On postmortem and laboratory examination, these bones appear as hard sponges, hence the name *Osteomalacia spongiosa*. All joints of the limbs become rickety, and spontaneous fractures can occur when exercise is forced.

Prevention of Big Head Disease

Under typical stable conditions, a diet that includes alfalfa certainly avails calcium in more than adequate amounts. Horse owners who supplement the diets of their mounts with any of the mainstream products, such as Clovite, provide minerals in a traditionally balanced way.

Under range conditions, horse owners are wise to provide the Hawaiian Horse mineral mix available at feed stores to their mounts. The mix has been developed not for only BHD prevention but for fulfilling the daily requirement for growth maintenance and performance of horses in the Islands. Developed by equine practitioners and University of Hawai'i animal nutritionists, this supplement, when fed routinely, has made BHD a rarely reported condition. Individuals who have attempted to second-guess the parathyroid gland with bone meal, calcium tablets, and home remedies have met with severely disappointing results. Staying with an established, broad-based quality supplement is not only less costly, but it has more consistent results.

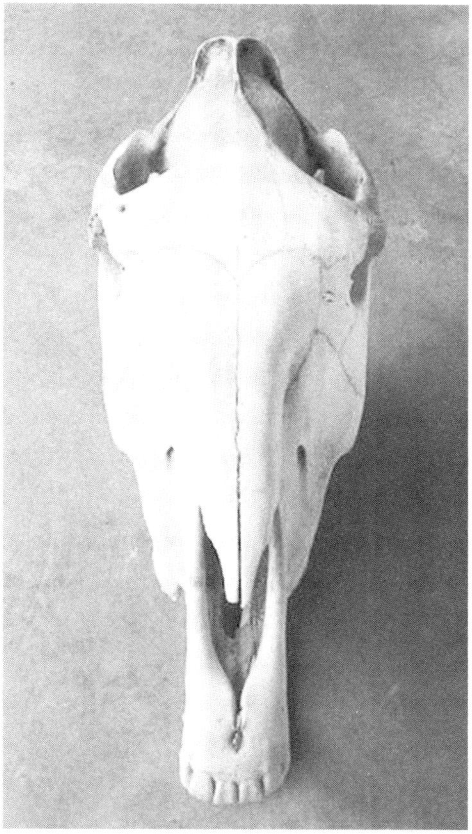

{7.4} *Frontal view of a normal skull.*

Prognosis and Treatment of Big Head Disease: Chronic Conditions

Once well established, BHD remodels the bones of the head to the point of no return, as the dental functions are profoundly diminished by malocclusion of incisors and especially premolar and molar teeth arrays. Prehension (biting) and mastication (chewing) of forage, cubes, pellets, and granular feed becomes severely impaired, as do subsequent digestive processes.

Joints and bones of the limbs are severely compromised by the demineralization process, making grazing a nearly impossible chore. Simple tasks of moving down an embankment or unloading from a trailer can bring about limb fractures. As a whole, BHD when well developed is incurable, with an irreversibly poor prognosis.

Often a horse owner reports that his mount seems stiffened in gait or mildly lame in different limbs at different times. As often, one may notice what appears to be recession of the prominence of the eye while bridling a horse, because the maxillary bone has thickened around the orbit. Another horseman may complain of difficulty bitting the horse due to its unwillingness to relax the jaw enough to accept the port of the curb bit. Still other horse folks detect a very mild loss of condition and vigor, despite good health care. A lay horse dentist is horrified by causing a mandibular fracture when placing his speculum into an unwilling mouth and cranking it open.

The dependable means of early BHD detection well ahead of the above described progression has to do with palpating the midshaft of the mandible below the row of molars. The jaw of an average one-thousand-pound horse can be readily palpated for thickness by placing the thumb and forefingers along the sides of a midshaft mandible, just as we would our left or right jawbone.

A horse's mandible is not much thicker than that of a two-hundred-pound man: a little more than an inch. A horse with early BHD with only the history of gait stiffness will already exhibit abnormal thickening of the mandible to 1.5 to 2.5 inches well before the bones of the face (maxilla) begin to thicken. While balanced supplementation may help in these cases, we know of two cases of early BHD that returned to normal in bone health and function by merely exposing them to the coastal range of North Kohala, notably Puakea.

A gelding went from a stiff-gaited mount with mildly enlarged mandibles to total resolution after an eight-month rest in the rich lands of Puakea. Similarly, another ranch horse, an Appaloosa gelding from Pu‘u Wa‘awa‘a Ranch, where BHD is an endemic problem that borders on epidemic proportions in the absence of the Hawaiian Horse mineral mix, spent a year at Puakea and came home slick and fat, with normal mandibular and facial bones. This gelding also returned to a full workload.

In our qualified opinion, certain rangelands, though rare, enjoy an appropriate balance of soil and forage minerals. Puakea is a rare gem.

Oral Issues

Dentistry

The significance of dental health in horses matches that of nutrition, with one single qualifier: all horses can lose body condition when nutrition is compromised, while only some horses develop dental disease to a degree that noticeably affects their overall health.

This is not to say that every horse deserves dental care, but points to the fact that body condition and prehension, mastication, and deglution (swallowing) can appear normal when dental treatment has never been prescribed or attempted. However, as a preventive measure, dental care of horses may be a deterrent to subclinical ailments that can include dental disease, colic, choke, and difficult bitting and reining.

Hawai'i offers unique challenges to dental health in horses, as more than three-fourths of these animals live on fibrous, abrasive, and bulky forage that accelerates tooth wear. Vog (volcanic fog) and volcanic acid rain further aggravate dental health, especially in horses that live downwind. Silica dust particles are readily observable, adhering to forage in dense vog conditions. When combined with high atmospheric levels of hydrogen sulfide and sulfuric acid, these conditions have correspondingly contributed to a significant rise in equine dental disease since Kīlauea volcano began its current eruption more than thirty years ago. Collaboration between horse owner and veterinarian for prevention and treatment of dental disease has never reached greater importance than in the last quarter century.

Choice of veterinarian for horse dental care is particularly important, as expertise can vary significantly in this area. Brady's essay that follows looks at this subject and provides insight for horse owners (revised from an article previously published in *Mālama Lio Magazine* in 2009).

NOT ALL DENTISTS ARE CREATED EQUAL

Dr. Brady Bergin

The majority of us understand that equine dental care is an integral part of routine horse health care. It ranks up there with nutrition, exercise, vaccinations, parasite control, and hoof care. What began over a hundred years ago as a relatively simple procedure involving only manual files has now advanced to a technologically based science being performed by highly skilled and trained personnel—veterinarians and nonveterinarians alike. However, there is a distinct difference in the level of skill and knowledge among these individuals. Recently there has been a bit of a debate in the horse world as to who should provide dental care to the horse. In fact, this debate has become so intense that it has ended up in the court system of some states. This essay is designed to assist the horse owner in making an educated decision when choosing who will perform dentistry for their horse.

Essentially, an owner has two general categories to choose from: a veterinarian who performs equine dentistry or a nonveterinary professional, also referred to as an equine dental technician, an equine dental specialist, an equine dentistry consultant, or a lay dentist. The next section compares these two groups regarding some important points a horse owner should consider when making this decision. In reviewing the points below, it is essential to remember that the experience and skill among individuals can differ significantly based upon the quality and quantity of their training.

NOT ALL DENTISTS ARE CREATED EQUAL

(continued from previous page)

Table 1.

Comparison of veterinary and nonveterinarian dental care

Veterinary dental care	*Nonveterinarian dental care*
Applying to veterinary school requires a bachelors degree or a certain number of prerequisites, depending upon the university.	Attending most equine dentistry schools requires NO specific degrees or prerequisites. Some require a minimum age of 18 years and a high school diploma or GED.
All US veterinary schools are four-year programs. Within the veterinary curriculum are required lectures covering the basics of equine dentistry as well as more advanced hands-on elective courses and clinical rotations. Following veterinary school are optional opportunities to further specialize with an internship (one year) +/- residency (three years). Some veterinarians do attend a dentistry school for further training.	Each equine dentistry school sets up its own curriculum and program. To obtain a basic level of certification requires an average of approximately 200–300 hours of course work and hands-on training, whereas a master's level of certification requires approximately 900–1,000 hours. The level of certification depends on the amount of education.
Education is in depth and covers all aspects of veterinary medicine, including equine dentistry. The amount of education pertaining strictly to equine dentistry depends upon the university and individual interest.	Education is specific for equine dentistry. It includes oral anatomy and function in addition to dental abnormalities and equilibration ("floating").
Becoming a licensed veterinarian requires passing a standardized national veterinary board exam as well as the state board exam for any state in which one practices veterinary medicine.	There is NO standardized testing to become certified. Some schools have their own methods for testing and determining if an individual has earned certification.
It is legal for a licensed a veterinarian to perform equine dentistry in every state.	It is ILLEGAL in some states for an individual to perform equine dentistry as a trade without veterinary supervision or consultation. Laws vary between states on who is allowed to practice veterinary dentistry.
Continuing education is required to maintain licensure, which allows opportunity for further training and advancement.	Continuing education is recommended but NOT required to maintain certification.
It is legal for veterinarians to administer prescription medications such as tranquilizers, antibiotics, pain medication, etc.*	Administering any prescription medication without specific veterinary direction is ILLEGAL in every state. *Therefore, absolutely no equine dentistry professional should be administering tranquilizers or any other prescription medication without veterinary supervision.**
Able to obtain further diagnostic testing, such as X-rays or lab work.	Must refer further diagnostics to a veterinarian.
Able to provide follow-up care if complications arise during or following a procedure.	Often unable to provide appropriate or medical follow-up care.
Focus is on the whole horse and how dental health fits into the overall health of the horse.	Focus is primarily on dental health.
Liability insurance is required in the event of a complication.	Liability insurance is recommended, but not required.
COST—depends on the individual.	COST—depends on the individual.

*Administering tranquilizers legally requires a veterinarian for good reason. There are numerous risks involved with what appears to be a relatively simple procedure.

NOT ALL DENTISTS ARE CREATED EQUAL

(continued from previous page)

- Assessing cardiovascular status: Most veterinarians will check the patient's vital signs and listen for any arrhythmias or heart abnormalities prior to administering a sedative to any patient.
- Using the appropriate dosage—young vs. geriatric: Different-sized and -aged horses will respond dramatically differently to a tranquilizer. Choosing the right type of sedative and knowing how much to use is critically important. The same amount isn't safe for every patient.
- Appropriate placement: All sedatives are designed to be given intravenously (IV). Accidental intra-arterial administration is fairly easy to accomplish, as the carotid artery lies just deep to the jugular vein. Intra-arterial administration of a sedative can lead to severe seizure activity and in the worst-case scenario to heart failure.
- Having the ability to administer an anesthetic reversal medication is beneficial for safety precautions.

The American Association of Equine Practitioners as well as the American Veterinary Medical Association exist to protect and enhance the health and welfare of horses and other animals. Both organizations consider dentistry on horses (animals) as part of the practice of veterinary medicine, and therefore it should be performed by licensed veterinarians in accordance with the specific state veterinary practice acts. Legislation regarding equine dental procedures is complex and varies between states. The Hawai'i Revised Statutes, Chapter 471, Sections 1 and 2, define the "practice of veterinary medicine" to include the surgical, medical, and *dental* care of animals and specify that only a licensed veterinarian in this state is allowed to practice veterinary medicine. Any person convicted of violating these sections shall have committed a misdemeanor and could be subject to fines and imprisonment (471-15). The Hawai'i State Board of Veterinary Examiners understands that not all veterinarians in this state are able and willing to perform proper equine dentistry and therefore allows nonveterinarians to perform these procedures under the direction of a licensed veterinarian.

Equine dentistry is far more complex than simply rasping down some sharp edges. The motorized equipment and various medications utilized to perform these procedures carry risks, and if not performed without proper understanding may lead to permanent complications. Just because an equine dental professional is certified doesn't always mean they are well qualified. Likewise just because a veterinarian performs equine dentistry doesn't mean they've received adequate training. Owners should take the time to understand and learn who is the most qualified to provide the best quality care for their horse's mouth.

Next, Billy describes his experience in dealing with a chronic dental problem among horses (revised from two articles published in *Mālama Lio Magazine* in 2010).

LAMPAS

Dr. Billy Bergin

Lampas is a chronic thickening of the gum line immediately behind the upper row of incisor teeth.

As a boy growing up in ranching circles of the Big Island, I remember hearing elder horsemen speak of an affliction in the mouths of hard-keeping horses called lampas. I presumed that these pidgin-speaking horsemen were pronouncing a word that is spelled and properly pronounced as "lampers" in correct English. I found I was wrong on both counts. In *The Last Forge in Lismore,* Paddy Vaughn details the condition from an old farrier's viewpoint:

> The farrier himself provided certain specialist services in the care of horses. Lampas was a disease of the gums which caused much discomfort to the horse. It was a swelling of the gums in the form of blisters which rose higher than the teeth so that the horse was prevented from eating and became thin as a consequence. To cure this, a special tool was used consisting of a length of iron with a bend at one end. The horse's mouth was opened and a hammer handle inserted to keep it open. The iron was heated and applied to the blisters, and salt was then rubbed in. I saw this done on many occasions. Today the cure is far more humane, in the form of an injection or a stomach drench, and is administered by a vet. (Vaughn 1994)

For the sake of local tradition, I retain lampas as the choice of spelling. To the Native Hawaiian cowboy, lampas is called *iukupu,* pronounced "you-coopoo."

The term "lampas" is found in horse literature more than two centuries ago. While it seems to have a Hispanic sound to it, lampas is reported in veterinary literature throughout northern Europe. In modern-day American veterinary literature, the term is applied to an acute inflammatory condition much unlike what is described in Hawai'i, where the lesion of lampas is considered a chronic thickening (hypertrophy) of the gum of the anterior (front) palate of the horse immediately posterior (behind) the row of upper incisor teeth. Lampas of genuine proportions thickens the upper gums downward beyond the biting line of the upper and lower rows of incisors, hampering the "bite and cut" process of a grazing horse. Hence, the horse inefficiently grazes in the manner of a cow (which has no upper incisor teeth), using a "bite and pull" manner that yields less grass and therefore a lessened dietary intake.

While in veterinary school, I queried the professors of anatomy, pathology, and equine medicine and surgery as to their knowledge of lampas. Their interpretation of the condition matched current literature, which describes the condition as an acute but transient inflammation of the upper palate in young Thoroughbred horses subjected to a highly concentrated grain diet used in early training.

LAMPAS

(continued from previous page)

When I described the condition in aged, hard-keeping horses of a dense calluslike crescent of the gum behind the superior incisors, the professors were perplexed. When I described the method of treatment of excising this crescent-shaped callus by carving it out with a red-hot curved iron in a patient that had been cast and tied, they were aghast. When I described the topical after-treatment as dousing the excised palate with a handful of Hawaiian salt (rock salt), they were mortified. In short, the revered Dr. James Coffman discharged my rendering of lampas and its treatment as a "figment of some quack's imagination and dealt with in a most barbaric manner." Somewhat bewildered, I was left to assume that these thickened, obstructive, and callused gums were a natural growth and not a clinical or surgical issue at all.

When I came home to practice in 1968, I received more than occasional requests to "cut the lampas" from horses of clients who were usually traditional *kama'āina* (native-born) horsemen. Without even a peek into the animal's mouth, I quickly declined out of fear of being branded as a "quack" (unlicensed, unqualified, misinformed), willing to subject a patient to such a barbaric procedure. I had learned my lesson well from Dr. Coffman.

Further literature review was not encouraging. Dr. C. B. Michener (1907) was frank in his condemnation of lampas treatment: "Burning the lampas is barbarous and injurious and it should never be tolerated." As for the condition itself, Michener was even less accommodating: "It's an affliction of a stableman's mind rather than of the horse's mouth."

After about three years of practice, I was approached by a close acquaintance, a ranch cowboy who knew of my disdain for the subject of lampas. He brought in his fourteen-year-old cream-colored palomino rope horse that had failed to improve in condition either from my thorough dental workup or from his regimen of frequent deworming and an intensified feeding program. He was fully aware that I had already discharged the lampas lesion as "normal" despite his description of grain-spilling and difficulty grazing. The cowboy got my attention when he pleaded with me to "just try, just to see what happens" if I removed the lampas surgically. He promised he "would not tell nobody, no matter what!" It was hard to say no to someone as persuasive in his appeal.

Late the following afternoon we met at the Parker Ranch Surgery Barn, where the horse was placed in a stock and sedated following a thorough mouth washing. With a wedge speculum, I secured the jaws open, allowing ample visual and manual access. After thoroughly infusing the lampas lesion with a local anesthetic, we rested a few moments while I cautioned the cowboy to expect things to get a little bloody.

As he held the sedated horse's head up high, using a scalpel I made a single four-inch-long incision along the palate parallel to the lampas callus, then curved the blade forward to trim along the back surface of each of the six superior incisors. With a thumb

LAMPAS

(continued from previous page)

forceps, I grasped and removed the lampas with a minimum of trimming. Once removed, it appeared to be about the size of my little finger. Upon cross-section, the callus was like gristle in texture and dull pink in color. The bleeding was profuse, as the cowboy released the mount's head that now hung low from the sedation. The horse was seemingly free from pain throughout the procedure. Normal clotting time is about eleven minutes, and the patient followed suit accordingly. The usual tetanus toxoid booster was administered, and the patent's evening meal of heavily soaked alfalfa pellets was consumed with gusto. By morning, the surgical area had closed to a narrow band a half-inch across the posterior surface of fully exposed teeth, now rendered capable of "biting and cutting" the ample available forage. Total surgical healing was complete within a week's time.

Cherokee Rose was the name of the horse, and Alvin Baptiste was the cowboy. He presented the patient to me a few weeks later, fully filled out and with a shiny coat. His condition now intact, Cherokee Rose lived a productive life into his twenties, no longer spilling grain and grazing with ease.

Compared to their mainland counterparts, horses on the Big Island, up until thirty or forty years ago, lived on forage alone, with little or no quality supplements such as grain or forms of complete feed or hay. Could this constant diet of roughage cause the development of calluses as a defensive barrier that eventually outgrew its usefulness into becoming a physical hindrance to prehension and mastication? Or did we have certain grasses that were so abrasive that building a lampas callus was the only way to graze adequately?

In subsequent years, I became quite an advocate of using the "lampectomy" where it was indicated. I readily got over the apprehension instilled in me since the days of veterinary school. I coined the term "lampectomy" to describe the process of excising the callus growth, just as the term "lumpectomy" is used to describe a minor surgical procedure used in cancer diagnosis and treatment in all species. I was intrigued by the Hispanic nature of the spelling and pronunciation of the term "lampas" and wanted to preserve it, despite finding it in early Irish literature; after all, the Spaniards are the progenitors of today's cowboy.

While my search for the derivation of the term and the ancient and agreeably barbaric method of treatment continues, I note that the procedure seemed to be relegated to the farrier/blacksmith, who in many ways was the progenitor of the modern-day veterinary practitioner. More than likely, the malady was first recognized by the Moors, and "lampas" is therefore Arabic in origin; the Moors would have brought the term with them to Spain. From there, the Spanish and Portuguese later introduced "lampas" to the Americas, whence, finally, it was introduced to Hawai'i.

Over the last four decades of my Big Island practice, it would be reasonable to speculate that more than two hundred hard-keeping mounts have benefited from the procedure.

LAMPAS

(continued from previous page)

While I remain prudent in advising the client that the treatment for lampas is neither reported nor supported by veterinary literature, save for the knowledge of now very senior horsemen coupled with my personal experience, it has returned to the forefront of collaborative efforts to make the life of a horse comfortable and useful over a much longer span.

Some significant observations were made regarding the procedure. Foremost was the rapid healing process where, within a week, the surgical site completely healed, matching the rest of the palate that reaches the deeper cavern of the mouth. Second was the rapid return of a horse to being bitted in comfort. While I recommended a week of convalescence, many horses were pressed into duty in a day or two after surgery, with the rider describing no untoward effects. Third, the return of the horse's condition to one of thrift and vigor coupled with a shiny coat was a routine result, absent any underlying conditions such as weed intoxication, cancer, or other problems.

Two lessons were learned on the subject of lampas. First is to never disregard the knowledge and experience of elders in all fields of agriculture and its attendant sciences. Second, be willing to take some risks in helping a friend or patient. You might be pleased with the mutual reward. Alvin Baptiste and Cherokee Rose gave me such an opportunity.

Next, Brady offers an essay on equine choke (revised from an article previously published in *Mālama Lio Magazine* in 2009).

UNDERSTANDING EQUINE CHOKE

Dr. Brady Bergin

A COMMON EQUINE EMERGENCY CALL that my practice receives is for the horse that is choked. Among these calls, there is often a misinterpretation regarding what the horse is truly experiencing. Most if not all of us know exactly how unpleasant it feels to be choking. Fortunately, what occurs in the choking horse is something quite different.

There is a distinct difference between a person choking and a horse choking. In people, choking is basically an obstruction of airflow into the lungs that prevents breathing. Rather than a foreign object being lodged in the airway, the condition in horses involves an obstruction of the *esophagus,* most commonly with food or bedding. Therefore it should be clear that a choking horse can still breathe normally, but it cannot eat or drink. This should still be considered a serious emergency to the horse owner, even though it is not as immediately critical as the condition in people.

It is helpful to know how a horse eats in order to understand what is occurring with an esophageal obstruction. When a horse takes a bite, it uses the lips and incisors (front

UNDERSTANDING EQUINE CHOKE

(continued from previous page)

teeth) for prehension (grasping). The tongue then carries the "unchewed" food back to the premolars and molars for mastication (chewing). Their unique chewing cycle forms a bolus, which is moved over the tongue further back into the pharynx. There, as the horse swallows, the esophageal sphincter opens, while the epiglottis and arytenoids close to prevent food from entering the trachea. Once in the esophagus, which lies on the left side of the neck, muscular contractions help to move the chewed, saliva-soaked food bolus down into the chest cavity, through the diaphragm, and into the stomach.

Causes

Teeth: Horses with dental problems are definitely predisposed to an esophageal obstruction because they are not chewing their food well enough. Sharp enamel points, loose or missing teeth, or other malocclusions can limit appropriate chewing due to pain or mechanical causes.

Diet: Horses have become obstructed on all types of feeds, but some are more common than others. Dry pelleted feeds or dry sugar beet pulp are easily swallowed with very little chewing and can expand once saturated with saliva. Dry alfalfa cubes swallowed whole have been the source of my most difficult cases. Other food objects associated with choke include carrots, apples, corn cobs, or even hay or thick grass if consumed too quickly.

Eating Behavior: Certain horses have eating habits that will make them more prone to an obstruction. Most commonly, horses "inhale," "vacuum," or bolt their food. Some of these do it out of habit, excitement, or because of competition with another horse nearby. This can also occur when a horse is exposed to something new, as in stall bedding or an unfamiliar feed. Their inquisitive nature can also get them into trouble by consuming nonedible objects.

Clinical Signs

Knowing what signs to look for can make a difference in the outcome and ease of treatment. Listed below are the symptoms associated with an esophageal obstruction:

- Disinterest in eating or drinking
- Coughing or gurgling
- Nasal discharge—usually feed material from both nostrils

UNDERSTANDING EQUINE CHOKE

(continued from previous page)

- Drooling
- Extending head and neck in a downward direction
- Repeated attempts to swallow
- Dehydration
- Elevated heart rate

Note that occasionally the obstruction can be felt on the left side of the neck. If any of these symptoms appear and there are signs the horse might be choked, the veterinarian should be called immediately. Removing any food and water at this time is also a good idea.

Diagnosis

Every veterinarian will have his or her own approach to diagnosing and treating an esophageal obstruction. Most of the time, he or she will begin the evaluation with a physical exam followed by inserting a nasogastric (stomach) tube. Sedation (tranquilization) might be required or preferred. This is performed by inserting a semirigid tube up one of the nostrils into the esophagus and on down to the stomach. If the tube is unable to enter the stomach, then an obstruction is likely present.

Another approach is with the use of endoscopy. With this approach, an endoscope is guided into the esophagus the same way as the nasogastric tube. The benefit of endoscopy is that it allows the veterinarian to visualize the obstruction and evaluate the condition of the esophagus. The mucosal lining of the esophagus can become ulcerated and weak from a long-standing obstruction, increasing the likelihood of further complications.

Treatment

A number of obstructions can clear on their own just by removing food and water and allowing the horse to relax. However, it is still very important to notify the veterinarian to decide if further treatment will be required. In acute cases, a reasonable approach to treatment is sedating the horse in order to relax the esophagus and allow the obstruction to pass on its own. Some veterinarians will also administer spasmolytics at this time to gain further relaxation by reducing the spasms of the esophagus. The veterinarian will decide how long to allow this treatment to work before moving to the next step. It's important to know that the longer the horse is obstructed, the higher the chance of serious complications.

If this approach proves to be unsuccessful, then more aggressive treatment is warranted. The next step is pumping water through the nasogastric tube to gently lavage (flush) the obstruction to break it apart and/or push it along. The horse needs to be heavily sedated, with its nose toward the ground, to allow the water to follow out its nostrils

UNDERSTANDING EQUINE CHOKE

(continued from previous page)

and not into the trachea. Some veterinarians will pass a second tube into the trachea to prevent inhalation of water and feed material during this procedure. Care must also be taken not to apply excessive force with this procedure in order to avoid lodging the obstruction even tighter or rupturing the esophagus. This will typically clear most obstructions; however, for more difficult cases, using endoscopy instruments to pick apart the mass can be beneficial. Surgical removal is another option if the obstruction is located prior to chest cavity; however, it is typically avoided if at all possible due to the post-operation complications with healing.

WARNING: No one should ever run a water hose up the nose or down the throat of a horse in an attempt to clear an obstruction. It is more likely that water will shoot down the trachea and into the lungs, resulting in pneumonia or drowning.

Complications

Most episodes of esophageal obstruction resolve uneventfully, but complications may occur. The incidence of complications is directly related to the time it takes to resolve the obstruction. Without being able to eat or drink, the choked horse can become dehydrated rather quickly. Intravenous fluid therapy might be necessary in some cases to restore hydration. The close anatomical proximity of the openings to the esophagus and trachea makes accidental inhalation of feed material, saliva, and water relatively easy. This creates the risk of developing aspiration pneumonia. Prophylactic, broad-spectrum antibiotics are prescribed on a case-by-case basis, but if pneumonia develops, it will need to be treated aggressively.

Esophageal ulceration is another potential complication. Usually this results from severe cases that cause inflammation and damage to the esophageal mucosa. As the ulceration heals, scarring occurs, which can result in an esophageal stricture (narrowing of the diameter of the esophagus). Strictures pose a problem for the future in that they may lead to chronic or repeated obstructions.

Prevention

Below are a few tips for preventing a horse from developing an esophageal obstruction. Prevention is much easier than correction. It is always best to consult with the veterinarian to decide the best course of prevention.

- Always provide clean water.
- Have the horse's teeth examined annually.

UNDERSTANDING EQUINE CHOKE

(continued from previous page)

- Maintain regular dental care recommended by the veterinarian.
- Cut apples, carrots, and other treats into small pieces.
- Introduce a new feed gradually.
- When stalled, discourage horses from eating the bedding.
- Soak high-risk feeds (alfalfa cubes, beet pulp) in water to soften.
- Discourage bolting of food: spread the feed out, or place large obstacles (large, smooth stones, salt blocks, etc.) in the feed bin, forcing horses to slow down and eat around them.

As with humans, feet play an important role in the overall general health of horses. While horses have four hooves to bear weight, it is truly remarkable how so small a surface area can support over a thousand pounds of weight. It is no wonder that hoof health is critical to the health and well-being of horses. Here Brady shares some perspectives on common hoof problems in Hawaiian horses.

HOOF PROBLEMS

Dr. Brady Bergin

Horses in Hawai'i have skin and hoof problems related to humidity and ground moisture, while nutrition plays an equally important role in growth and body maintenance requirements.

As a rule, horses throughout the island chain that grow and live on the windward sides, where the trade winds and attendant humidity and rainfall keep range animals in high-moisture environments, seem to have more diseases of the hooves (and skin) than their leeward counterparts. At higher elevations, however, weather patterns bring cloud banks with fog and rain, which also invite attendant health problems in leeward pasturelands, such as in Kona and Ka'ū on the island of Hawai'i.

Hoof bruising and cracking are prone to all unshod horses throughout the state, especially in windward areas. Hoof bruises are commonly called "stone bruises," "gravel," and "*palawai*" (stone bruise; fetid water) by local horsemen, while farriers and veterinarians refer to the affliction as subsolar abscesses. Some healers use hoof knives to pare out and drain the abscess to avoid linear rupturing of the hairline above the coronary band. These fissures eventually grow horizontally down the hoof wall and complicate the shoeing in months ahead.

HOOF PROBLEMS

(continued from previous page)

Another course of hoof bruise treatment is early detection and placing the horse on phenylbutazone for a few days, averting the horizontal fissuring along the hairline and foot. Apparently the anti-inflammatory drug causes absorption of the sterile abscess while providing profound pain relief.

Most aggressive treatment involves packing the hoof with medicaments and wrapping with gauze, vet wrap, and duct tape.

As a contributing author, Dr. Lisa Wood comes with excellent credentials. She has been a Big Island mixed veterinary practioner for more than a quarter century. A well-known surgeon for both small and large animals, her expertise in equine surgery draws frequent referrals. Dr. Wood shares her knowledge on appropriate foaling protocol in the following essay previously published in *Mālama Lio Magazine* in 2010.

FOALING GUIDELINES

Lisa Wood, DVM

While Hawai'i enjoys sunshine year-round, mares are still routinely bred to foal in the spring to summer months. Many breed registries still regard January 1 as the official birthdate for show eligibility, thus foals born as close as possible to that January 1 date are at an advantage in growth and maturity. In addition, mares are generally cycling more regularly during the longer spring and summer days, contributing to more successful breedings at that time.

The average length of pregnancy for a mare is between 335 and 342 days. The maximum range for mares is anywhere from 320 to 365 days. Beyond those limits, the veterinarian should be consulted for any possible risks.

One Month Ahead

As the foaling date approaches, owners should be sure that mares have been appropriately dewormed and vaccinated. Vaccinations given four to six weeks prior to foaling will help to boost the quality of the colostrum, or first milk, that the foal receives. It should be noted that mares should have already received vaccinations for equine herpes-1 at five, seven, and nine months.

Mares should be located in the area where they are expected to foal. This allows the mare time to relax and become familiar with her environment. Pastures and troughs should be relatively clean, with adequate fencing. Owners should check thoroughly

FOALING GUIDELINES

(continued from previous page)

for any hidden dangers, such as old wire, protruding posts, nails, and the like. If a foaling stall is available, the stall should be completely disinfected and dried out. Straw is the preferred bedding, as shavings may cause damage to the newborn's eyes or become clogged in the nostrils.

Some of the items owners may wish to add to their emergency kit include the following:

Towels	Emergency number for vet
Betadine or 1–2% iodine solution	Flashlight
Scissors/dental floss	KY Jelly
Tail wrap	Exam gloves
Foal nipple and bottle	Fleet enema

One Week Ahead

As the expected foaling date draws closer, owners may observe a softening of the muscles around the tailhead and a relaxation of the vulva. The mammary glands may become engorged, and there may be leakage of milk. Some mares may go off feed or seek solitude. "Waxing" is the formation of yellowish droplets of sticky fluid over the ends of the nipples. This may be observed twenty-four to forty-eight hours prior to foaling.

Foaling itself can be divided into three stages: labor, delivery of the foal, and delivery of the placenta.

Stage I: Labor

This phase can last anywhere from two to twenty-four hours. Signs include restlessness, looking at the belly, getting up and down, sweating, and frequent urination. These signs can often mimic colic signs. Owners should be alert, and if signs are severe or last longer than expected, a veterinarian should be consulted.

Stage II: Delivery of the Foal

This stage should last about fifteen to thirty minutes and is marked by strong, forceful uterine contractions. The white water sac may be present as the foal makes its way out the birth canal. Normal presentation includes two feet, face down, with one slightly ahead of the other. The next structure visible should be the foal's nose at about the level of the knees.

FOALING GUIDELINES

(continued from previous page)

If the foal does not progress through the birth canal within twenty minutes, or if the foal does not present with two feet and a nose, the veterinarian should be contacted immediately.

Most mares will deliver lying down, but some may choose to stand. If the mare is standing, gently hold her to prevent her from walking and possibly injuring the foal during delivery. Avoid any unnecessary disturbances to the mare, as this may prolong delivery.

Stage III: Delivery of the Placenta

The mare's placenta should be passed within the next three to four hours. During this period, the mare may lie down and uterine contractions may again be observed. Nursing may also stimulate contractions. Once the placenta has passed, it should be evaluated for any tears or missing areas. There should be one tear where the foal has come through.

Mares that retain their placentas for longer than three to four hours are at risk of infection and possible laminitis. Oxytocin may be administered by the veterinarian to aid in expelling the placenta. In prolonged cases, further care including uterine lavaging, antibiotics, and anti-inflammatories may be necessary.

Post-foaling

Upon delivery, both mare and foal may rest quietly for some time. If the foal still has the water sac over its head, owners should quietly remove it. If the foal is breathing normally, retreat and allow mare and foal to bond without interruption. If the foal is having difficulty, place the foal on its chest, wipe the nostrils clear, and vigorously rub the foal's sides with a towel. Otherwise, mom and baby should be observed with as little interference as possible.

The umbilical cord will usually break once the mare stands or as the foal attempts to get up. Once the foal is standing, the cord should be dipped in iodine to help dry it up and prevent infection.

Foals should be standing within one hour of birth and should be suckling within two to three hours. It is critical that foals receive the first milk or colostrum within the first six to twelve hours of life. If the foal is unable to suckle within this time period, the mare should be milked and the foal bottle-fed twelve to sixteen ounces of colostrum.

Finally, the first manure from the foal is called meconium and should pass within four to six hours of birth if the foal has been nursing. The meconium may be dark greenish brown or yellowish brown in color. Signs of impaction include straining and flagging of the tail.

FOALING GUIDELINES

(continued from previous page)

Contact the veterinarian for advice concerning enemas.

Mare owners may wish to have a wellness exam performed on the new foal and mom after twenty-four hours. Foals should be examined for any birth defects, such as umbilical hernias, cleft palates, and heart murmurs, as well as for adequate colostral transfer. Mares should be checked for bruising or tearing of the birth canal and milk production. Concerns regarding rebreeding may also be addressed at this time.

The birth of a healthy foal is a combination of good luck, good genes, and good preparation. After months of anticipation, mare owners are understandably anxious about their investment. Fortunately, mares have been giving birth unassisted for thousands of years, and in most cases owners will wake excitedly one morning to the welcome sight of a new addition, proudly and awkwardly following its mom through the pasture!

As a whole, horse health in the Islands is exceptionally good. For more than a century, the Division of Animal Industry played a significant role in keeping Hawaiʻi healthy and free from disease. But for the dedication and vigilance of these men and women, Hawaiʻi might not be the beautiful equine paradise that we know today. Working quietly in the background to control and eradicate disease, their work was bold and daring, and it continues even to the present day.

CHAPTER 8

THE TERRITORIAL GOVERNMENT'S ROLE

In his seminal 1929 work, *A Survey of Livestock in Hawaii,* Dr. L. A. Henke was complimentary in reporting Hawai'i's advancements in horse production: "Hawaii has long been famous for its outstanding horses[,] some of which have made notable records not only in island competition but in mainland contests as well. Horse breeding and racing, often called the 'sport of kings,' has long been very popular in Hawaii[,] particularly during the latter part of the nineteenth century. Hawaii's polo players and horses are favorably known wherever the game is played."

In 1904, the territorial government established the Division of Animal Industry (DAI) as a formal arm of the Board of Commissioners of Agriculture and Forestry. The primary role of the division was guarding, through import and export inspection, the integrity of animal and plant health status of the entire Territory of Hawai'i.

Specific to livestock, the role was expanded from post import inspection and testing to preshipment staging on the West Coast for serious diseases such as glanders in horses, jackasses, and mules and tuberculosis and brucellosis in cattle. Prior to preshipment inspection, Hawai'i had become a dumping ground for the dregs of the livestock communities of the western states of America. DAI's role in the eradication of horse diseases in the Islands was nothing short of heroic. The Federal Bureau of Animal Industry not only blessed the DAI's double testing and eradication programs but provided the preshipment (West Coast) regulatory service as a gesture of support.

The DAI's service was enhanced far beyond fire-walling the Islands from diseased importations. It proactively encouraged programs to improve the quality of breeding stock throughout the island chain. Moreover, the territorial government welcomed the involvement of federal forces beyond the Bureau of Animal Industry to include the US Quartermaster's Department, the US War Department, and the US Remount Service in safeguarding the health and improving the quality of equine populations.

In the first third of the 1900s, three territorial veterinarians promulgated animal health regulations while enhancing the quality of the equine species, including donkeys and mules, through extensive outreach to plantations and ranches advising them of the improvements. This personal and professional involvement brought about remarkable enhancements in the form of vastly improved horseflesh, as well as attaining sustainability of the industries of sugar, pineapple, and ranching needs for horses and mules. This service was paralleled by attending to military needs for a constant supply of quality mounts, draft horses, and mules.

Dr. Victor Norgaard, a Danish-trained veterinarian of high repute, headed up the Division of Animal Industry. He was ably supported on Maui by Dr. J. C. FitzGerald, a British-trained veterinarian, who extended his coverage to include Molokaʻi, Lānaʻi, and Kauaʻi. Dr. J. Elliot, another veterinarian with British ties, first served the port of Hilo and eventually the entire Island of Hawaiʻi.

A chronological array of reports from these leaders provides a glimpse into the past as they plodded forward. Dr. Norgaard, in his 1907 *Annual Report,* provides a frank assessment of the status quo:

> *Horses.* A scarcity of horses prevails in the Territory and prices have consequently gone up to a considerable extent.
>
> Seven stallions were imported, only one of which was a heavy draft animal (Percheron). As heavy draft animals are needed more than any other horses in these Islands, it is to be hoped that the coming year will see the introduction of more draft animals for breeding purposes.
>
> Among the rest may be mentioned two German Coach stallions, two large well bred trotting stallions and one aged, but well bred running stallion. As neither trotters or runners are bred here (the trotting sport is unknown and running races only indulged in to a very slight context) the latter animals were possibly introduced with a view to improving the cow ponies, so that some time in the distant future, the resulting mares may be used with additional importations in the production of road horses (carriage), for which there is limited but constant demand.
>
> The remaining imported horse stock was, with the exception of a few choice carriage and saddle horses, very ordinary. One shipment of twenty-two mares, imported for mule breeding, had some very good animals among them, but, taken all together, the importation of horse stock during 1907, so far as quality is concerned, was far below what might be desired.
>
> There are less good horses in Honolulu than in any other city in the United States of the same population and wealth

> and there is less interest taken in horse flesh than in almost any small city on the mainland which is the more remarkable as there are excellent roads and beautiful drives in and around the city.
>
> An annual fair for the exhibition of live stock, supported by the Territory and the counties, would, no doubt, help to revive the interest in horse breeding and keeping, both for sport and utility.
>
> *Mules.* Four hundred and eighty-five mules were imported in 1907, as compared to two hundred and ninety-five during 1906, and two hundred and forty-five in 1905. The animals, as a general rule, were younger and of better quality than those of the immediate preceding years, but the prices were higher than ever before. At a conservative estimate the average cost was $245 per head, landed in the Territory, or an aggregate of $118,825.
>
> The great increase in the number imported is, no doubt, due to the fact that many plantations refrained from buying mules on account of the high prices until they were absolutely forced to do so, and there is little doubt that the coming year will see still greater importations in this line, as a large percentage of the mules on hand are getting old and decrepit.
>
> The high price of mules will, without question, remain unchanged for several years to come, as the demand for these animals on the mainland seems to be increasing steadily. Relief must, therefore, be looked for from the breeding and raising of mules in the Territory, and the importation of eight jacks would seem to indicate that a serious attempt is now being made to make the mule industry a factor of importance in the Islands. (Norgaard 1907)

Norgaard emphasized the animal husbandry aspect of improving mule stock in the Islands in the 1908 *Annual Report:*

> To produce first-class mules a certain amount of concentrated feed must be given, and as young mules must be broken to harness and their muscles developed through steadily increasing work before they can be considered finished plantation mules, this process of breaking and developing can be made profitable by making them produce their own feed. Suitable tracts of land should be selected on every breeding farm or ranch especially with a view to irrigation. These lands may be plowed, harrowed and planted, and the crops harvested and hauled by the young mules, care being given not to overwork them.
>
> When it is further considered that it requires practically the same length of time to raise a mule as to raise a steer, and that when ready for market the former is in strong demand at five times the price which the latter often goes begging, there can be little doubt that mule breeding in this Territory will prove profitable to the stock raisers and ultimately, in regulating the prices by a constant and abundant supply, prove beneficial to the planters and agriculturists.
>
> The total importation of mules was 750 head as compared to 485 head during 1907 and 295 head during 1906. Of this total a little more than 100 head were

imported by the United States Quartermaster's Department and cannot, therefore, strictly speaking, be considered in the same class as mules purchased for sugar plantations or for other purposes as they were simply transferred from one military post to another.

> The steady increase was predicted in my two previous reports and undoubtedly [will] continue for at least one more year more or until the sugar plantations have obtained their full quota of work animals, the same having been allowed to diminish on account of the great increase in the price of mules during the past few years.
>
> As a general rule the mules which arrived here during the past year were of a better class than those received during the preceding years and were, as a rule, of good size and on an average of satisfactory ages that is from four to eight years old. (Norgaard 1908)

The importation of quality horseflesh was routinely sprinkled with draft horse aspects, as Norgaard further reported in 1908:

> The total number of horses imported, 157 head, was about the same as that for the preceding year, 139 head. There were only six stallions among these animals as compared to seven for the preceding year.
>
> Of these six stallions, there were only two worth mentioning, an imported Percheron stallion, weighing more than a ton, and a German Coach stallion, both splendid animals and imported by Mr. A.W. Carter for the Parker Ranch.
>
> Of the rest of the horses 34 were for the Quartermaster's Department, 10 were breeding mares for Kapāpala Ranch and the rest were either driving or work stock.
>
> A scarcity of horses prevails in the Territory and prices have consequently gone up to a considerable extent. (Norgaard 1908)

The Heavy Horse of Hawai'i

As for the details of the first true draft horse coming to the Hawaiian Islands, diligent research has yielded no clues. While the Territorial Board of Commissioners of Agriculture and Forestry describes imports occurring under their jurisdiction starting in 1905, it is very likely that plantations, ranches, and transporters (freight movers) were calling for heavy draft horses during the second half of the previous century.

Distinction must be made between the carriage horses and the true draft model. The German Coach Horse was simply a bigger, heavier version of the saddle horse used singly or in teams to pull light to moderately heavy carriages loaded with people and goods. Over the ensuing century, German Coach stallions sired many cow horses reserved for heavy work such as wild cattle gathers, brandings, or *hō'au pipi* (swimming cattle to longboats). The choice sires of such massive cow horses were the draft stallions, with Percherons and Belgians being the most popular breeds.

The draft breeds' major role was pulling heavy wagons over rough terrain for long distances. Where mule power would require six to ten pairs in tandem, full or half-bred draft horses in single or double tandem could achieve the same horsepower. In fairness to mule teams, however, they readily outflanked the draft horse teams when it came to pulling the cane-laden sleds of freshly hand-cut sugarcane out of the steep hillsides and low-lying, muddy valleys. Both served such draying functions with expedience as they replaced the obsolete oxcart.

In terms of popularity, the Percherons and Belgians were likely equal, while the Shires and Clydesdales were uncommon.

While the more refined Percheron breed lent itself better to producing uniform progeny of "part-heavy" (often mispronounced "pot-heavy" in local parlance) horses that formed the ideal of the best of both worlds, the Belgian blood seemingly blended better at producing a cow horse attitude. For dray horses, either of the half-bred draft horse types worked fine.

On a national level, the draft breeds have recently gained popularity for interesting reasons. With the nation's growing ecological awareness that much of the heavy equipment used in modern agriculture is destructive to terrain, it has been

{8.1} *As recently as the early 1960s, the trusty mule was called upon for draft work where vehicles could not go. This mule moves irrigation flumes at Pi'ihonua for the* hanawai *(irrigation work) of an independent sugarcane farmer selling cane to the Hilo Sugar Company Mill.*

{ 8.2 } *Wailuku Sugar Company continued to use mules well into the 1980s to bring seed cane to the hand-planting crews.*

{ 8.3 } *A Belgian sire of ideal proportions and conformation that stood at Kansas State College.*

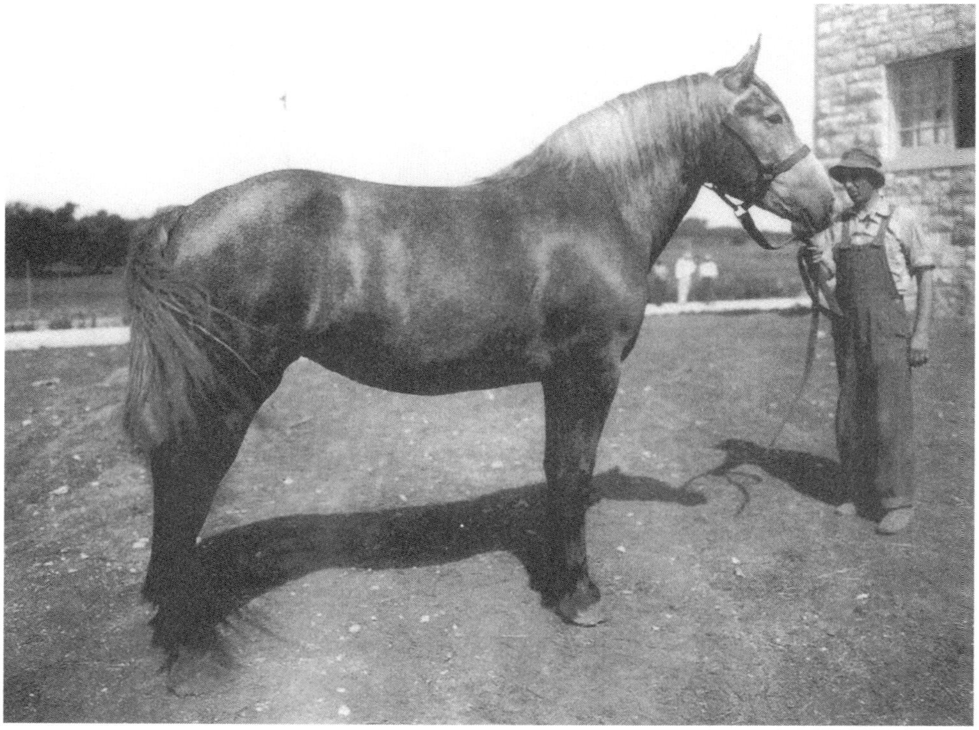

{ 8.4 } *The Percheron breed produced excellent ranch cow horses given its inherent conformation features of lighter muscle mass, rangier frame, and enhanced agility.*

noted that the draft horse causes only mild soil disruption.

From an economic standpoint, the draft horse provides homegrown power that runs on home-raised fuel, while enriching the soil in the form of manure.

Aesthetically, the draft horse reflects beauty in motion, even to the eye of a novice beholder. Nostalgia becomes a parallel emotion as we recall the lives of our grandparents and great-grandparents, whose robust and tanned forearms grasped the multiple pairs of reins that guided the course of the great team horses of their times. These emotions drive the advertising successes of companies such as Anheuser Busch, which presents the Clydesdale teams in an iconic manner.

The Belgian Horse

Avid draft horse historian Otto Ziegler (pers. comm., March 24, 2009) offered historic information on the Belgian breed and how it significantly influenced the Hawaiian horse industry:

> I also wanted to tell you that the first horse in the *Belgian Stud Book,* Vol. I was Jumbo 1 Dark bay, foaled in 1881 and imported August 25, 1885 by Wabash Importing Co. Wabash, Indiana. Wabash Importing

would have been the three Jews that I told you started the Belgian Corp. The next 28 horses registered were imported by them.

The basic colors were bay, brown, roan, black and a few greys. The sorrel was almost unheard of in Belgium in the early 1900s. And this was true in what was being imported. However the greys vanished fairly early. And the blacks also. Although in my 64 years dealing with the breed I did see one black Belgian stallion, and he went through an Amish sale at Arthur, Illinois. I want to get back to roans. The roans came in two different forms. Some were blue roans and some different shades of red roan. As can be expected the blue roans would all have black manes and tails and black legs. But the red roans could have red legs and manes and tails. There were still some roans here in the United States during the 1940s that had black points. But this was bred out of them some way.

Ziegler shared some insight on ideal conformational aspects of a top draft horse:

> When you get to the hocks, that is a different story than saddle horses. You want the hocks together and then straight down to the hoof. But not "Cow Hocked". The fetlocks should be together. But the hoof can turn out slightly. The reason for this goes to pulling heavy loads. In a dead pull the hocks tend to turn out and the horse loses power. It's pretty hard to win in a line class (halter class) with a wide hocked horse. It's like anything else, there are tricks to any trade.

Ziegler also noted the relative size (in hands high: HH) of the draft breeds: "The Belgian, Percheron, Clydesdale and Shire all have their 19 HH horses and they have smaller ones also. The World's Largest Horse is still held by the Belgian. There are horses as tall as him but not as massive."

Ziegler also reported on a draft stallion shipped to Hawai'i in 1937:

> The one Belgian stallion I could trace was Perfection 20858. A sorrel foaled May 12, 1933 and bred by Frank L. Stream, Creston, Iowa. The horse was sold to Grant Good, Ogden, Iowa then to R.G. Henke of Stewartville, Minnesota. And then Grant [Good] bought him back and sold him November 12, 1937 to Parker Ranch, Alfred W. Carter Trustee, Kamuela, Hawai'i.
>
> They must have started using him as soon as they got him in 1937 as I have a copy of a letter from L. Radcliffe Greenwell to Lester Good stating that he was doing quite well in his new home, and that they had bred some mares with him. The letter does not say if these were draft mares or not.

On a historic note, Greenwell's family ranch, Palani Ranch Ltd. in North Kona, Hawai'i, purchased a son of Perfection out of a Thoroughbred mare and stood him with their broodmares for nearly twenty years. Yielding progeny of quarter-bred Belgian cow horses over many years, Palani Ranch continued to be a resource for part-heavy mounts sought after by the industry. In 1960, Palani

{ 8.5 } *Three Percheron fillies imported by Parker Ranch in 1907.*

{ 8.6 } *Stationed at Pukalani Stables, this imported, registered Belgian stallion named Jumbo was crossed on Parker Ranch mares. The flaxen-maned palomino was a popular sire.*

Ranch again purchased a young half-bred roan Belgian stud, this one out of a mare by Naniloa, a popular cow horse sire on the Parker Ranch. When Greenwell retired from the legendary Hawaiian spread and returned frequently to his home ranch, he wasn't alone in appreciating the added value of keeping some draft blood in working cow horses. While at present, Palani Ranch progeny are about one-sixteenth to one thirty-second Belgian, they represent a popular sale item in the periodic horse dispersal sales.

A son of Palani Ranch's roan stud Circus Boy, sent to Kaupō Ranch on Maui to upgrade their workhorse breeding program, presented a minor kink in the reputation of Palani's part-heavy horses. An offspring of this stallion, a gelding named Kaupō Aloha, became notorious in rodeo circles for never being ridden to the eight-second bell. Humiliating the downed rider even more, he would prance a high-tailed, high-stepping victory lap around the Oskie Rice Rodeo Arena in Makawao, Maui, before retiring to his pen. The crowds went wild applauding Kaupō Aloha.

Other ranches that retained some draft blood in their workhorses included both McCandless Ranch and Hawaiian Ranch Company on the Big Island. The former outfit, noted for its intensive efforts to depopulate the hordes of wild cattle on the southern slopes of Mauna Loa, utilized a plantation-bred gray Belgian stallion that spread his progeny over several foal seasons out of a variety of mares from mustang types (*kanaka* horses) to compact Morgans.

{8.7} *Circus Boy, a quarter-bred Belgian stallion sold by Palani Ranch to Kaupō Ranch, sired many good workhorses, with one exception: his son Kaupō Aloha became a rodeo star in the Maui circuit, having never been ridden to the eight-second bell.*

Hawaiian Ranch Company was an amalgamation of three outfits: Ka'alu'alu, Kapāpala, and Keauhou Ranches, each of which came with significant horse history. The third volume of *Loyal to the Land* (Bergin 2009) describes the ingenuity of the manager of the combined ranches, Fred Schattauer, in producing an ideal bullock type heavy cow horse for the wild and rough country of Ka'ū:

> Aware of the need for a special type of cow horse for Ka'ū's terrain, Schattauer brought in a large-framed, heavily boned Appaloosa stallion from Washington State. Chief White Cloud was more than sixteen hands in height and weighed twelve hundred pounds. He was mated with Percheron broodmares acquired shortly after 1949, when the sugar plantations were depopulating horse and mules at bargain prices. Soon Hawaiian Ranch was known

for their "part-heavy" Appaloosa horses that were noted for their strength, stamina, calmness, but mostly their bulldozer-like ability to plow through brush, ferns, and forests, skipping over tree molds, *piha'ā* (tree trunks), *pohā* (sink holes) and treacherous lava tubes in avid pursuit of a mustang bull. My lasting memory of Schattauer is on his favorite mount, "Boar," a fourteen-hundred-pound half-Percheron *apowai* (brownish grey) gelding. He introduced a whole new way of directing cattle drives. Not only is slower better, but in the end, slower is faster as you gather cattle at their pace, giving the lead cows a chance in their own meandering way, to bring in the whole herd, not just overheated remnants.

Ziegler (pers. comm., March 24, 2009) closed his draft horse discussion with a report of a large shipment to the Islands: "The last Belgians I have record of going to Hawai'i were eleven head bought at the Indianapolis sale March 4, 1987. Bought by Merland Carlson, Agent, Turlock, California. These were all mares." These Belgian mares may have been part of a large order placed by the Marriott Kaua'i Resort, where wagon-drawn tourists would enjoy the scenery. Clydesdales and Percherons were also included. A sadly misguided venture, the wagon tour program collapsed financially, and the draft horses were dispersed at a fraction of their value. Most unfortunate was the well-intentioned buyers' lack of knowledge of the very special upkeep required of these massive steeds in terms of adequate nutritional intake, as well as hoof and coat care. Some died as mere shadows of the great and proud horses they once were.

By the turn of the new millennium, the Fiftieth State could no longer boast of any significant presence of draft breeding, save for a limited presence of those pressed into service as "sport horses."

Horse Importation Nightmares

State veterinarian Victor Norgaard's *Annual Report* for 1907 includes notes on the hardship horse shipping created during early importation:

> A shipment, consisting of 64 mares and two jacks, arrived in Honolulu on October 16th 1907. In spite of a very pleasant trip, with no rough weather and no sickness among the animals, nine of them died en route, simply from weakness and exposure. A veterinarian, who happened to be on board, stated that at one time more than thirty animals were down, and as soon as one was gotten up another would go down, and so on until nine had been thrown overboard, dead.
>
> A majority of those which arrived here alive were barely able to cover the mile and a half between the place of landing and the quarantine station. One animal was found upon arrival to suffer from pneumonia and had to be shot. A number lay down immediately after reaching the station, most of them never to get up again, and when it was found that a majority of the consignment could masticate nothing but bran mash, the downers were put out of misery without delay. (Norgaard 1907)

{ 8.8 } *Broken-down mares illustrate a poorly executed consignment of imported mainland horses. The entire consignment was humanely destroyed after arrival at the Honolulu Quarantine Station. This drew the Territorial Division of Animal Industry (TDAI) into a more active role in regulating livestock importation and transportation.*

{ 8.9 } *Another mare from the doomed consignment that left the West Coast already crippled by a chronic hoof infection. TDAI officials called for more stringent preshipment inspection and testing to avoid unfortunate tragedies such as this in the future.*

A shipment of equines from the West Coast was fraught at times with loads of animals that never should have left the mainland to begin with. In his 1910 report, Norgaard bemoans such errors:

> A shipment of mares, which were brought in here for breeding purposes during the latter part of 1910 deserves special mention, that it may serve as a warning to other horse or mule breeders, who are inclined to think that the mare is of minor importance in the production of a colt, so long that the stallion or jack is of good quality. A certain ranch company placed an order in San Francisco for 75 mares and 2 jacks, the mares to cost $75 per head and the jacks $1200 each. No exact specifications, or at least written agreement, were made. At any rate, there seems to have been some misunderstanding and the result was that an attempt was made to fill the order with broken down city mares and cripples, unfit for work of any kind. (Norgaard 1910)

Unfortunately, the rancher failed to conduct minimal due diligence and was swindled by an unscrupulous horse trader.

Dr. John Charlton FitzGerald

Beyond any doubt, no single veterinarian did more than Dr. J. C. FitzGerald in improving horse quality in the Territory of Hawaiʻi, especially for the island of Maui. We should quickly add, however, that his role in stamping out glanders, which especially plagued the Big Island's Waipiʻo Valley, was equally heroic.

His 1910 observations on the horse industry, especially the Thoroughbred, are noteworthy:

> The Cavalry and Artillery Regiments of the United States stationed on Oahu create a steady demand for high class remounts and artillery horses. The increasing demand for polo ponies with breeding and speed is also a factor; lastly, the renewed interest in racing is a source from which to draw a goodly profit, if the right kind of animal is forthcoming. Taking all in all, the encouragement to the breeders to invest in high class breeding stock was never greater that at the present time. It was feared that the innovation of the automobile would cripple the horse breeding industry, but the reverse has proved to be the case and horseflesh is higher in the Islands today than ever before and the demand for high class animals has increased.
>
> It has been frequently demonstrated in horse breeding, especially in thoroughbreds, as among these, better facilities are offered for testing the results of breeding, that sixty percent, lies in the dam. The breeding operations of many of the most successful breeders of America and Great Britain have been conducted on these lines with no meager results.
>
> Two very noteworthy importations of horses and mares for breeding purposes have been made to this Island during the past biennial period. One of some forty grade Percheron mares all bred to a purebred Percheron stallion, was accompanied by two registered Percheron stallions. These were imported by Mr. L. von

{ 8.10 } *Dr. J. C. FitzGerald, a leader in horse health and improvement.*

{ 8.11 } *Built to serve plantations and ranches of central Maui, the Spreckelsville Veterinary Hospital was a critical force in keeping both horses and mules in sound condition.*

{ 8.12 } *The interior of the surgery room at the Spreckelsville Veterinary Hospital included a water bath where horses such as this gray saddle horse could be bathed and soaked in water treated with hoof medicaments.*

{ 8.13 } *The medical dispensary of the Spreckelsville Veterinary Hospital was readily supplied with appropriate medicaments. Note Dr. FitzGerald's saddle and tack in the left corner.*

Tempsky of the Haleakalā Ranch as nucleus for a band of draught horses from which the plantations may be supplied.

The second consignment of note was thoroughbred stock and consisted of a stallion, four mares and four yearlings. These animals were purchased by Mr. H.A. Baldwin with a view of improving the class of animals used for saddle purposes, and breeding stallions to be distributed on the different ranches.

"*Sileo*," a seal brown stallion, 16.3 hands, weighing 1250 lbs., with over 8 ½ inch bone below the knee and is undoubtedly the largest and best bred animal in his class ever brought to the Hawaiian Islands. (FitzGerald 1910)

Ever a champion of the Thoroughbred horse, FitzGerald was just as passionate in defending our country, of which he became a compatriot. His words reflect these values:

The value of this importation, with proper handling, is unquestionable and it is to be hoped that other breeders will follow the good example and make importations of thoroughbred stock, while the American market for them is such that they can be purchased for about half their real value, owing to legislation prohibiting racing in the major portion of the United States. Many adverse criticisms have been made and are frequently heard in reference to thoroughbred blood, but it is the only source from which any real improvement to saddle stock can be reasonably looked for. This is clearly demonstrated by the breeding methods adopted by the Governments of the powers of the world in breeding remounts. In citing a few instances where most costly thoroughbred stallions are being used for this purpose, mention may be made of the acquisition of "Henry of Navarre," "Octagon," "Footprint" and "Tipsand," by the United States Breeding Bureau. These animals were presented to the nation by Mr. August Belmont, who, as a breeder of world-wide fame, could see the necessity of strengthening the country's defenses, through building up the standard of the remount. (FitzGerald 1910)

Citing a local example of such noble efforts to upgrade horseflesh, FitzGerald stated, "An instance of this method for the betterment of horse breeding may be quoted from this island. A well bred stallion of good bone and quality has been stationed in the Makawao district by the courtesy of Mr. H.A. Baldwin.

{ 8.14 } *Coppit, a prize-winning Thoroughbred broodmare imported by Dr. FitzGerald. She became the dam of many fine colts for Maui's polo and racing crowd. She won the Light Broodmare Class at the First Maui County Fair in 1916, garnering Blue Ribbon, Special, and Silver Cup Awards.*

{ 8.15 } *Advance Guard was an outstanding Thoroughbred sire imported by H. A. Baldwin that stood at stud at several Maui locations. At the first Maui County Fair in 1916, Advance Guard II won two classes: Imported Saddle Stallion and Champion of all Light Horse entries.*

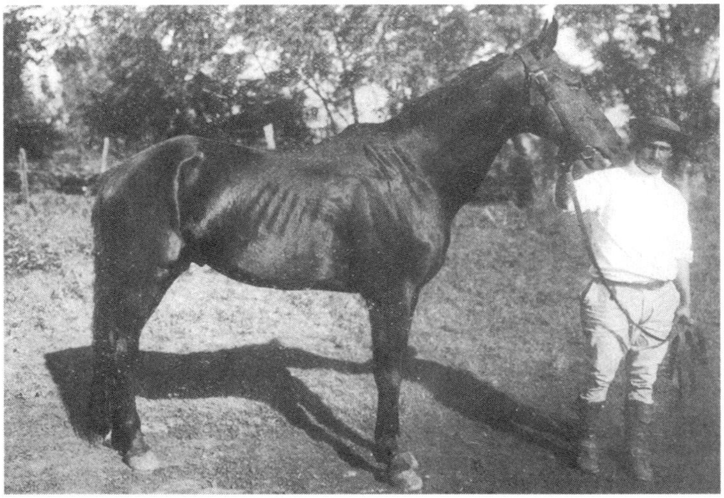

{ 8.16 } *Imported by H. A. Baldwin, Sileo stood 16.3 hands and weighed 1,250 pounds. A grandson of St. Simon, the super sire of Great Britain's Thoroughbred world, Sileo produced fine offspring noted for speed and level-headedness.*

This animal will be bred to a number of approved mares free and should prove a valuable addition to the district."

FitzGerald reported on horse improvements on Kaua'i as well as Maui:

> This season Sileo will be stationed on the Grove Ranch, while the Hamakua Poko stud farm will use the sire "Harvester," who has been lent through the courtesy of Mr. Charles Lucas, his owner. This animal was bred by Mr. A.B. Spreckels at the Napa Stock Farm, California, and is a full brother to the great horse "Voorhees."
>
> During the past two years great strides have been made in the character of breeding stock, among which may be mentioned:— The purchase of a Mammoth Jack by Kekaha Plantation. This plantation has always taken a great interest in stock breeding, especially saddle horses, and light mules. It has demonstrated beyond a doubt the feasibility of raising mules for saddle and packing purposes, and there seems to be no reason why, if larger mares were available, work mules could not be raised. The small mules raised at Kekaha are superior to the ordinary horse for saddle purposes, they keep up on less grain and last longer.
>
> The McBryde Plantation now raise all their own saddle horses, the stud headed by "Romeo," a "Sunnyboy" colt, originally bought from the Koloa Plantation. The type of horses raised here are well adapted to all kinds of plantation work, though not large, running to about 800 pounds.
>
> Koloa Plantation in 1911 purchased a thoroughbred colt whose get is most promising. In addition to this they still have their old stallion "Rebel Chief" and a Shire. This Shire has been in stud for some years, and Koloa Plantation buys no more mules, and has not for five years, doing nearly all their work, with horses raised at home. The geldings and mares average from 1150 to 1300 lbs., which is sufficient proof that horses of good size can be raised in these Islands.
>
> To prove what can be done by selection and good sires, however, one must notice the horses raised by Mr. W. Hyde-Rice on his ranch. There are at least three six-line teams of mares averaging 1450 to1500 pounds apiece, in addition to all the other horses he uses on the plantation and for other work.
>
> This has been the work of years, by careful breeding of imported mares, and selection from their progeny. The horses at present working here are the get of Solum, a Shire.

{ 8.17 } *Senator B, a direct son of Sileo, won the Saddle Stallion Class for Hawaiian-bred entries at the first Maui County Fair in 1916.*

{ 8.18 } *Oneonta, a two-year-old bay filly, won the Hawaiian-bred Light Horse Class at the first Maui County Fair in 1916.*

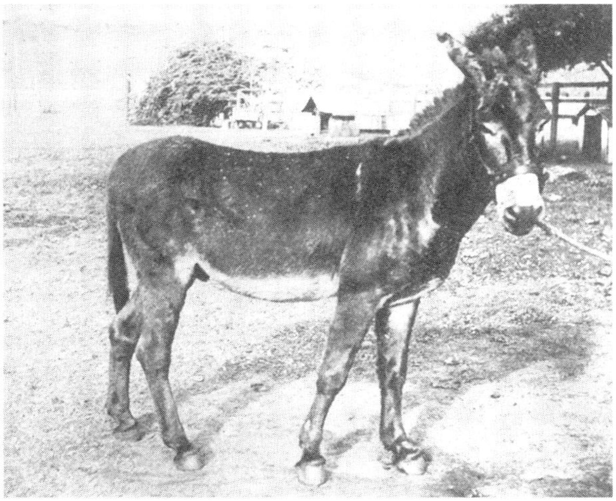

{ 8.19 } *Imported by Līhu'e Plantation Company, this Tennessee-bred jack was a notable sire of both pack and draft mules for the island of Kaua'i.*

{ 8.20 } *Imported by W. H. Rice Sr., Solum, a Shire, served as a popular sire of draft horses for both ranch and plantation use.*

{ 8.21 } *William Hyde Rice Sr. was a prominent Kaua'i agriculturist responsible for importing fine horses and cattle.*

The saddle horse end is being attended to by the purchase of a splendid Arabian stallion that is now in service on their ranch.

The Makee Sugar Company continues its breeding of thoroughbreds but have made no recent importations of new stock.

The Kilauea Plantation Company has entered into the breeding of draught animals by the purchase of a Percheron stallion, eight mares, mostly Percheron, and some Clydes and Shires. In addition to this their native mares have been bred and the grades are large and of beautiful type, and show that in three or four years more Kilauea will also be producing its own draft stock. (FitzGerald 1912)

In conjunction with Lihue Plantation, Mr. W. Hyde-Rice has recently purchased a Belgian stallion to be used in his stud. This is a big horse weighing about 1900 pounds and great things are expected of his colts.

In addition Mr. Rice acquired last year the celebrated stallion "Workman," well known 5 and 6 years ago on the Eastern tracks and Cuba. He has been in stud less than a year so nothing can be said as yet of his success as a breeder.

Lihue Plantation Company has used the same stallion for a number of years at the Lihue Ranch and with corresponding results. In addition they have recently purchased eight heavy mares from the Coast, which, with those they have raised themselves, put them in a position in a very few years to raise their own draft horses. In addition to this mares are also bred to an imported jack with good results.

FitzGerald's words aptly describe the territory-wide efforts to improve horse and mule quality.

Horse Production on the Island of Lāna'i

The Story of Lana'i (Munro 2007) presents the account of early rancher and conservationist George C. Munro, who managed Lāna'i Ranch from 1911 to 1930, covering the island's livestock history in thorough detail. His views on horse and mule production are noteworthy:

In the early days of ranching, the Hawaiians ran horses on the uplands and watered them at the wells of Kaunolū and Kaumālapa'u. They probably often went short of water. Raised under these rough conditions, the horses were very hardy and were

> renowned for their stamina. The ranch, under the Lanai Company, raised horses and mules, and continued to raise horses under the Baldwins and the Hawaiian Pineapple Company, eventually providing horses for the plantation until riding horses were no longer used. (Munro 2007)

Munro made several observations on mule and donkey husbandry that defy traditional attitudes and methods:

> In order to breed mules when it started in 1910, the Lanai Company brought two Kentucky jacks with other importations from California. The venture did not turn out well, but one jack was still there in 1911. Some mules were afterwards sired by him with ranch mares. There were several Hawaiian donkeys on the ranch. The imported jack killed the small one when they got together one time. The Hawaiian jenny was kept as far from the imported jack as possible, out of his sight in the uplands. It was not considered good practice to allow a jack used for mating with horse mares to mate with his own kind. Our jack had other ideas and sensing that the jenny was there, he opened several gates, traversed several miles of country between, and mated with the small donkey. The Hawaiian jenny had several foals to him. However, it did not spoil the jack for raising mules. We afterwards ran a stallion and a jack, one of his offspring, together with a herd of mares and raised mules and horse foals in one herd. On one occasion, a mare was found with a horse foal and a mule foal suckling her. There was no proof that she was the mother of the ill-assorted twins, but she was mothering them, and the inference was that they were hers. Strange to say, when driven to pens, neither the stallion nor the jack considered the other a rival; they ignored each other completely. (Munro 2007)

Even Munro's description of peaceful coexistence between a stallion and jack defies traditional attitudes:

> On ranches where two stallions are allowed to run on one stretch of open country, some of their habits are found to be very interesting. Each has a section of range for his harem, and when released from the pens, the stallions round up the mares of their respective harems and take them off. Young fillies left in the herd unweaned are driven out when they reach breeding age, and they join the other herd, a natural provision against inbreeding. The stallion's habit of adroitly letting his successive droppings fall in one pile is probably intended as a marker to warn the other stallion off his beat. The stallion and the jack, however, did not trouble to divide the herd and remained peaceably together. (Munro 2007)

Munro expressed humane care as a deeply held emotion, even when the odds for success were dismal:

> It is known to be very difficult to save a horse that breaks a leg. Once, a cowboy was starting out to work, when his mount's leg snapped. It had evidently been kicked

{ **8.22** } *Gold Oak, one of five US Remount Service stallions standing at Parker Ranch, excelled as a sire of race horses, polo ponies, and cavalry mounts.*

by another horse while in the pen, and the bone cracked when put under the extra weight. We lowered the wires in the fence of a small paddock by the road where she was and carefully led her through. She was left undisturbed and the leg healed—not a straight mend, but the leg was usable, and she raised colts for the ranch.

There were many adventures and sometimes fatalities with the animals in gently weaning foals and training young animals to the saddle, but we had no serious accident with the men. (Munro 2007)

Observations of Dr. Victor Norgaard on Horse and Mule Production

The island of Hawai'i in many ways accommodated some of the most dramatic advances in horse and mule production. Hawai'i is blessed with vast mountain ranges replete with rich grasses and legumes with minimal rainfall. "High and dry" describes the valued upper lands of Waimea, Hāmākua, and parts of Ka'ū, supplying remount breeding meadows to Parker, Kūka'iau, and Kapāpala Ranches, where wild oats, sweet vernal, Rhodes, and brome grasses thrived among native and imported legumes.

The Big Island had another comparative advantage as the home of the Parker Ranch and its manager, A. W. Carter, a renowned leader of Hawaiian range management. Carter happened to love the sight of a fine equine, be it a race horse, cow horse, or draft mule. In the same series of *Annual Reports* referenced earlier,

Norgaard was unabashed in his appreciation for the advances in livestock production led by A. W. Carter.

> On the Island of Hawaii a considerable number of large mares have been raised by the use of imported Percheron and Shire stallions. These mares are now being bred to imported Kentucky jacks and as the high mountain pastures contain a great variety of nourishing grasses and the cool climate is ideal for the purpose, there is every prospect of mule raising being added to the livestock industry of the Territory.
>
> An abundance of saddle horses are being bred in the Islands, and have found favor with the local military authorities as mounts for cavalry.
>
> A transaction of considerable import to the local live stock industry took place recently when a considerable number of island bred horses were purchased for cavalry mounts to be used by the forces stationed here. Though the matter has been under consideration for a long time and was highly recommended by the officers stationed here and who had learned to appreciate the high spirited surefooted native horses, it seemed that there were insurmountable obstacles emanating from elsewhere, until suddenly the barriers were let down. The horses purchased were all bred on the Parker Ranch on Hawaii and it is confidently expected that these horses will prove so satisfactory as to establish a demand for many more at remunerative prices.
>
> A number of stallions of the German Coach, Belgian and Clydesdale type have

{ **8.23** } *Sir Galahad III was sired by Teddy out of Plucky Liege. He was the sire of Parker Ranch's top Thoroughbred sire, Ormesby.*

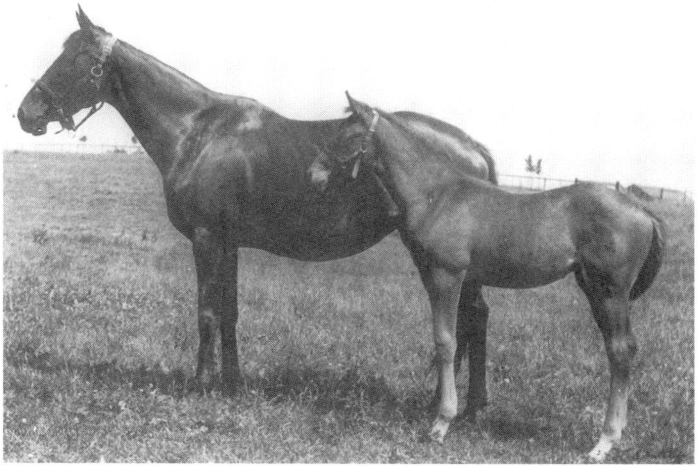

{ **8.24** } *Chewink, a Parker Ranch mare by Celt out of Bobolink, with a Sir Gallahad III foal at her side.*

{ 8.25 } *Two of six mammoth jacks imported by Parker Ranch for A. W. Carter's highly successful mule production program.*

been imported during the past two years. These importations should be continued and every encouragement given to bringing such animals into the Territory as it is by such means that improvement of the various types will take place and enable the different ranches to supply the demand for such animals.

Six exceptionally fine Jacks have been imported by Mr. A.W. Carter for the Parker Ranch for the purpose of mule breeding. It is to be hoped that this industry will make rapid strides and that in a comparatively short time the large ranches will be in a position to supply, in part at least, the demand of this Territory for this valuable class of work animals and keep in circulation within the Territory a large part of the thousands of dollars which are annually being expended in the purchase of mules from the Mainland. The Parker Ranch at least is in a position at the present time to breed a high class of mules and every encouragement should be given to promoting this important industry so long advocated by this Division.

From the beginning of the sugar industry mules have been imported here in ever increasing numbers and demand for them will continue so long as that industry is in existence. But up to the present time the Territory has never produced these animals in appreciable numbers, except in so far as pack mules (450 to 700 lbs.) were concerned. As far back as 1906 this Division began urging the breeding of larger mules here, it having been conclusively shown that such animals could be raised here, when sufficiently large mares were used. To produce the mares here first and then import pedigreed jacks for mule breeding, appeared a very risky undertaking, requiring from six to nine years before the first crop of mules would be of marketable age, and still, a careful analysis of the question satisfied Mr. Carter of the Parker Ranch that this was the only sane solution of the problem. He therefore

{ Plate 1 } *With a shy smile, the* pāʻū *queen sits elegantly upon her well-groomed chestnut mount.*

{ Plate 2 } *Mounted on her favorite horse, Speedy, Pat Bergin depicts Queen Kamāmalu at the 1972 Old Hawai'i on Horseback pageant in Kamuela. West Hawai'i contractor Guy Lam serves as escort.*

{ Plate 3 } *Noted horsemen Morgan Brown and Alex Penovaroff depicting the American cowboy and vaquero in Old Hawai'i on Horseback presentation.*

{ **Plate 4** } *A talented artist, Pat Ching is a skilled bullfighter, safeguarding fallen contestants. He deflects the charge of the son of the great bucking bull Rocky. Ching is credited for inspiring the authors to write this book on the Hawaiian horse.*

{ **Plate 5** } *Colorful poster depicting the notable characters involved in producing the Great Waikoloa Rodeo and Races.*

{ **Plate 6** } *The seminal 1988 HHSRA Finals program chronicled the First State Finals competition, complete with events and names of participants.*

{ Plate 7 } *Little Dan Miranda. As a son of Morag Rice Miranda and Ken Miranda, no finer rodeo and ranching heritage could exist. Namesake of his paternal grandfather, along with his maternal grandfather, Freddy Rice, Dan is living testimony to the multigenerational tradition of cowboy life.*

{ **Plate 8** } *Donkeys struggle to survive in the barren wasteland of Waikoloa, devoid of feed and rain.*

{ **Plate 9** } *The feral donkeys adapted readily to the bountiful forage of Waikoloa but suffered starvation in times of drought.*

{ Plate 10 } *At the Pu'u Mahoelua Corral at Waiki'i Ranch, a full day of work staffed by volunteers neutered more than eighty donkeys.*

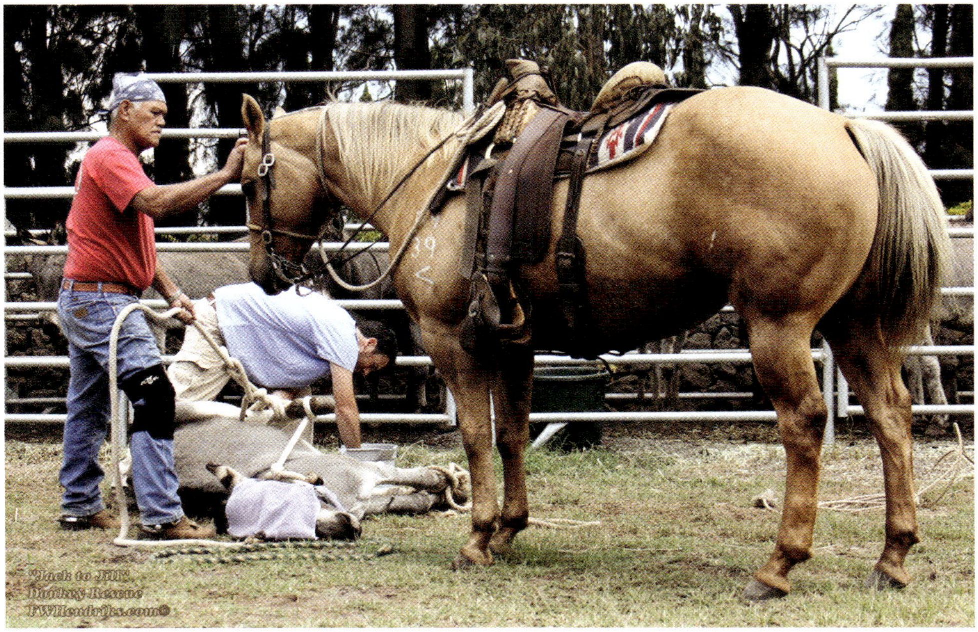

{ Plate 11 } *Sonny Keakealani teamed up with Dr. Brady Bergin from the onset of the project, providing superior animal husbandry skills and employing safety precautions at all times.*

{ Plate 12 } *Mark and Amy Meyers, owners of the Peaceful Valley Donkey Rescue facility, supervised loading more than 100 Waikoloa donkeys onto the Pacific Airlift aircraft. The rescue facility is now based out of Texas.*

{ Plate 13 } *A small band of donkeys remains in the Waikoloa rangelands. A modern-day watering device provides safe, conservative service to a more manageable herd held in reserve at Waikoloa.*

{ **Plate 14** } *Designed and built by Ken Miranda, the breeding barn of ʻĀina Hou Animal Hospital houses Salt Point, a great-grandson of Secretariat, three broodmare stalls, and a 20 × 20-foot breeding parlor.*

{ Plate 15 } *In the spacious breeding parlor, a protective bar effectively separates the mare and attendant during the teasing process.*

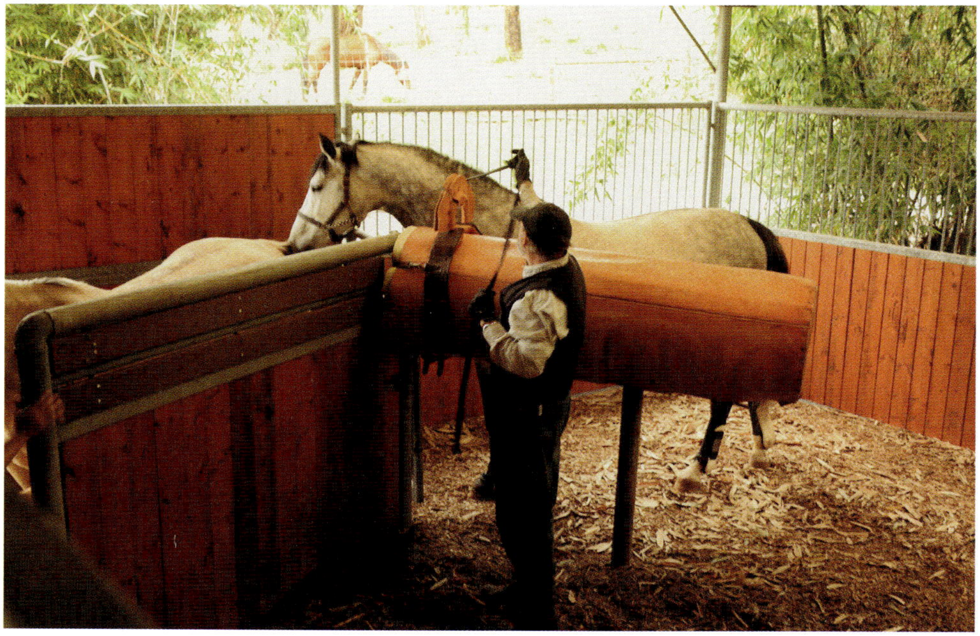

{ Plate 16 } *When aroused, a trained stallion mounts a "phantom mare" used for semen collection that may enable insemination of up to three mares.*

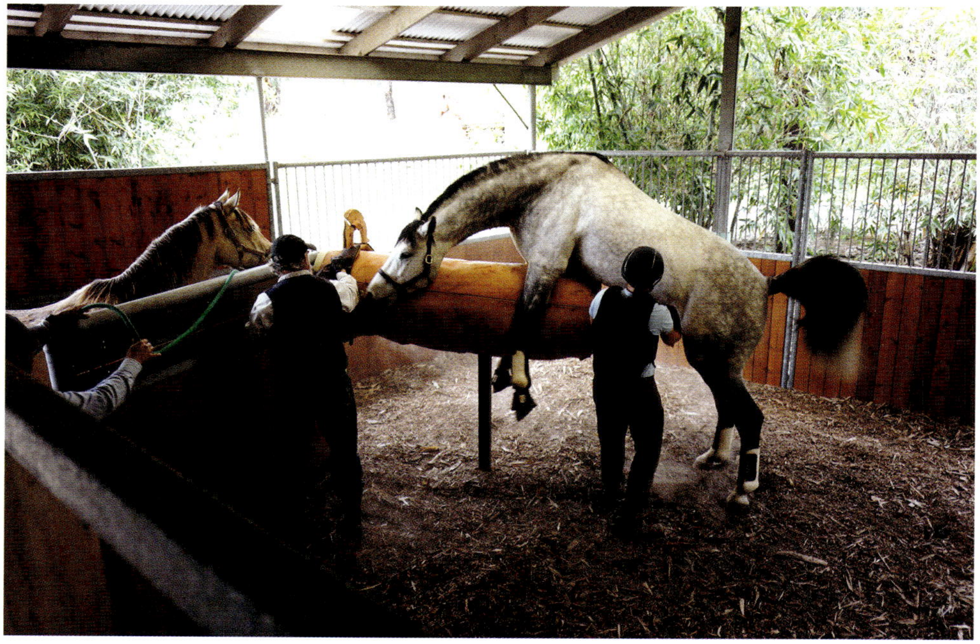

imported a number of Percheron stallions and bred them to the heaviest mares on the ranch, the colts being broke to harness early and put to work at producing the corn necessary for their own development and that of their future offspring. The experiment proved a complete success, and while a tempting market was ready to absorb all the resulting offspring, only the male animals were disposed of. About four years ago the fully developed half-bred and three-quarter blood Percheron mares were bred to some of the best jacks imported from Kentucky, Tennessee and California, and the young mules, now maturing, promise to equal the best Missouri and California bred mules ever imported here. The foresight and courage exhibited by Mr. Carter in this undertaking will undoubtedly prove of immense importance to the Territory, entirely aside from the financial advantages to accrue from it, since the great European war is bound to deplete the mule market of the United States to an extent that will send prices soaring.

Besides Percherons, the Parker Ranch also has imported a number of full blood, standard bred and German Coach stallions. Probably the most famous polo pony in the world, "Carry the News," having been bred and raised on that ranch, together with many others just as good, though less famed. This is the class of horses especially desired for the cavalry—the half or three-quarter full blood cross with the stocky native mares—while the artillery requires a somewhat heavier animal, as for instance a cross with the German Coach or Hannoverian. An officer's

{ 8.26 } *Superior draft and pack mules bred by Parker Ranch were sought after by military, plantation, and farm/ranch buyers. This draft mule stands 16 hands tall at John Purdy Stables near ranch headquarters.*

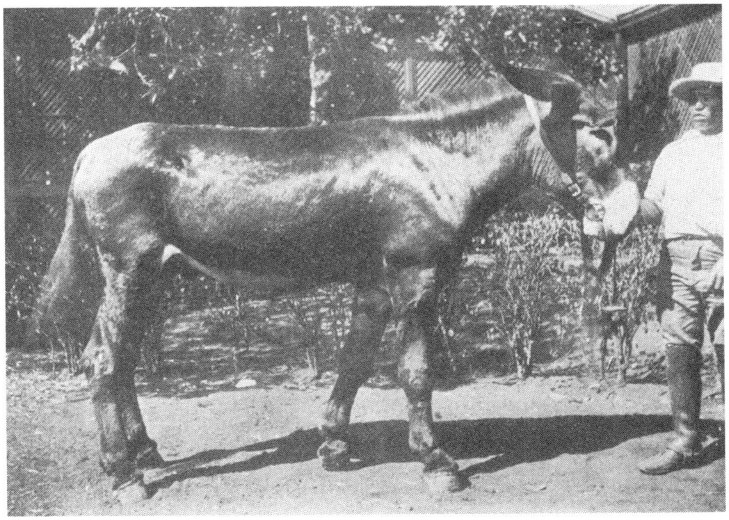

{ 8.27 } *This jack was imported by the Wight family for their Puakea Ranch Company, which was later acquired by Parker Ranch. J. Karimoto is the man at halter wearing leather leggings.*

> mount however must now be at least part thoroughbred, and especial attention is called to the efforts of Dr. FitzGerald, the Deputy Territorial Veterinarian on Maui, to encourage the breeding of this class of animals in the Territory.
>
> That mules can be raised here equal to, if not better than, any place else in the world was well demonstrated by the entries of Hawaiian breds at the Hilo County Fair. This industry is now in full swing, the Parker Ranch alone having 250 large mares in foal to imported Jacks, and in a few years the ranches here should be able to supply the entire local demand for mules. (Norgaard 1915)

FitzGerald's Observations on Tropical Degeneracy

FitzGerald offered suggestions for keeping up the momentum for upgrading horseflesh. First, he said, the territory should establish a breeding depot for the US government. His wish came true, as the US Remount Service established five throughout the Islands: F. F. Baldwin on Maui, William Hyde Rice on Kaua'i, Dillingham Ranch on O'ahu, and both Parker and Kapāpala Ranches on the Big Island were designated. Second, he envisioned organization of a territory-wide horse improvement society, and finally, annual livestock fairs on each island to showcase sires, broodmares, and their progeny.

FitzGerald was not only a visionary but a very astute observer of conditions affecting horse health and welfare. He coined the term "tropical degeneracy," a phenomenon that exists today. In essence, the question was: Why in livestock was a mainland cohort (like a twin or sibling of identical parenthood) of the same age larger in frame and condition? Put another way, a Nevada Quarter Horse yearling was similiar in size to the Hawaiian sibling that was already two years old. FitzGerald aptly pointed out that under tropical conditions, forage tends to be high in moisture (washy) and low in protein, carbohydrates, and fiber. Tropical soils are notoriously imbalanced in minerals—especially calcium, phosphorous, and magnesium. His recommendation of supplementing growing colts with bone meal (mineral sources) and alfalfa hay (protein, minerals, and fiber) matched the better dietary intake of mainland conditions; hence the Hawaiian yearling would match in size and condition his mainland cohort instead of requiring another year of growth. It is interesting that FitzGerald's observations ring true today, more than a century later. Here he describes "tropical degeneracy," while providing evidence-based recommendations:

> It must of course be admitted that climatic influences in the tropics are such that there is a tendency to diminution in size and bone. This is illustrated by the native horses of all tropical countries being small boned, wiry animals (as in Arabia and India); but from observations made by the writer on the thoroughbred stud farm of Mr. H.A. Baldwin of Hāmākua Poko, as well as with mares of his own, he is of the opinion that climatic conditions play only

a small part, and that the lack of a sufficient and balanced ration is almost solely responsible for any degeneracy occurring.

From experiments, made by the writer through the courtesy of Mr. H.A. Baldwin and Mr. F.F. Baldwin, in the feeding and raising of young stock, he confirmed the opinion that with proper care and feeding, (even less than is necessary in other countries), colts can be raised here with the same bone, and substance, as in any other country, provided the natural deficiencies of the country are supplied artificially, via:—bonemeal, and substituting alfalfa for *manienie* grass in part. (FitzGerald 1913)

Norgaard's Reflections

In summary, the foregoing chronicling of the supportive role of both territorial and federal government services in improving all aspects of the equine species reflects a remarkable combination of good business, foresight, patriotism, and outreach. In 1910, Norgaard reflected prophetically in a global context:

Horse and mule breeding has taken an immense upward swing during the past few years, and it is highly satisfactory to report that the past period has demonstrated the absolute fitness or rather superiority, of locally raised horses for all the branches of the military service stationed here. About three years ago the cavalry began experimenting with Parker Ranch horses, first as polo ponies and then as regular mounts and officers' chargers, since which time about 200 head of horses have been purchased on various ranches in Hawaii and are giving great satisfaction. It may therefore be safely predicted that no more horses will be sent here for military purposes, but that the future needs of the regiments stationed here will be supplied by the local horse breeders. The only possible objection to such an arrangement might be the price asked for Island-bred horses, as there remain but few of the cheap cow-ponies of common-breed stock. All the larger breeders now use only pedigreed stallions of high class, and the colts and young animals are no longer left to care for themselves on the ranges at all times of the year, but are fed, broken and handled and, in fact, looked after and cared for, selected and classified until they can hardly be called range horses any longer; and, as a steadily increasing percentage shows all the qualities and marks of high breeding seen in the blue grass regions of the States, it is obvious that they cannot be sold at the figures which prevailed five to ten years ago.

While no radical changes have been made, progress in this very important industry is noticeable everywhere; however, there is still ample scope for improvement, more especially in the class of draft animals being raised. Too much stress cannot be laid upon the necessity of this Territory becoming self-supporting in horse flesh, particularly draft stock, as there is little doubt that the shortage of horse flesh in the United States, created by the demands of the warring governments for remounts and artillery horses, will be felt in the islands.

> The abnormal demand created by the tremendous orders from Europe in America can better be judged when cognizance is taken of recent statistics which show that the life of the average horse in action is five days; that the cavalry and artillery are proving the most effective branches of the service; and that agents of foreign countries are daily travelling through the horse breeding states purchasing everything available and at all suitable for remounts and artillery purposes. This drain upon a once great industry, already crippled by anti-racing laws is already being deplored by the leading authorities in the horse-breeding world and army world of the United States, who see the gravity of the situation. Under the circumstances it would seem advisable for horse breeders of the Territory to take such steps as will, to some extent at least, enable the industry to supply the draft animals required by the plantations, at the same time assuring themselves of a goodly profit which would otherwise go to the breeders on the mainland. There is no greater stimulus to the horse breeding industry, especially among small owners, than an opportunity to select from a number of high class stallions a sire suited to their mares. (Norgaard 1910)

Norgaard's prophecy was realized as the drumbeat of World War I resonated to the shores of the Hawaiian Islands.

CHAPTER 9

THE WORLD WARS IMPROVE HORSE QUALITY

War is a terrible way to bring about change, especially when it is not for the better. Conversely, when war brings change that is for the better, we must conscientiously examine these improvements, balancing them against the horrific price that was paid. In America we owe our freedom to our willingness to engage in war to protect life, liberty, and justice. Yet, other benefits brought about by the sacrifice of life and limb, when taken as a whole, are largely economic and scientific in nature, far beyond the joys of freedom.

Hawaiʻi, despite its profound and damaging blow from the attack on Pearl Harbor, reaped significant and genuine benefits of war before World War II and even before World War I. One of these areas of benefit came in the form of vastly improved horse quality. Aside from the war, no other single political or social event did more to improve horse quality in America. Hawaiʻi, first a kingdom, then a U.S. territory (and eventually a state), likely benefited as much as any regional area in what became the fifty United States of America. But it did not start off this way.

Lessons of the Civil War

The Civil War depleted horse resources on both sides. The responsibility fell to the restored Union and eventually the US Cavalry to remount troops in due haste. This meant orders from the War Department approved as an interim measure and the purchase of horses of substandard conformation and breeding, even to include the acquisition of mustang-bred mounts for the cavalry. The book *War Horse* (Livingston and Roberts 2003) aptly describes the situation, quoting

Horses and Horsemanship through the Ages (Gianoli 1969):

> Developing a dependable source of remounts has plagued man ever since he began to ride horseback thousands of years ago. As a hunter and warrior, he was only as good as the horse under him. That meant that he must be riding one with strength, stamina and the conformation to stay sound in spite of hard use. Without such a mount, the rider would soon be afoot. There also had to be a constant supply of similar animals to replace those ridden down, crippled or killed. Rather than depending upon horses captured from the wild herds, man began to raise his own. He learned that breeding the best to the best produced a superior mount. The need for more effective horses also gave rise to improved training techniques and the development of stronger, more comfortable riding equipment. A supply of horses was always critical for any army. Some of the first written communications between military men that have been discovered document the remount problem.

Working out of Washington, DC, and Front Royal, Virginia, purchasing boards traveled extensively to gathering sites, usually at military forts, to review candidate mounts offered by private treaty farmers, horse breeders, and ranchers. By 1873, the average price for a cavalry mount was $142—very good money. The purchasing boards consisted of a quartermaster, a pair of regimental officers, and a veterinary surgeon.

Selection was limited to geldings between five and eight years of age and of sound conformation, ranging between fourteen and sixteen hands, and weighing anywhere from 700 to 1,100 pounds.

For camouflage purposes and availability, the cavalry preferred solid color mounts of bay, chestnut, sorrel, and black horses. In the heyday of the US Remount campaign, entire companies could be made up of a single coat color—a sorrel company, a chestnut company, a bay company, or a black company. Grays and roans were usually reserved for officer's mounts, while the pintos, buckskins, and palominos were relegated to the M company, often called the Brindles or Calico Company.

Teddy Roosevelt, in his observations in preparing for and executing the invasion of Cuba in the Spanish American War in 1897, expressed genuine frustration with the lack of horse quality, transportation protocol, and general care of the animals. While serving as a colonel of the First United States Volunteer Cavalry, Roosevelt was blunt in his assessment:

> Meanwhile we were purchasing horses. Judging from what I saw I do not think that we got heavy enough animals, and of those purchased certainly a half were nearly unbroken. It was no easy matter to handle them on the picket-lines, and to provide for feeding and watering; and the efforts to shoe and ride them were at first productive of much vigorous excitement. Of course, those that were wild from the range had to be thrown and tied down before they

> could be shod. Half the horses of the regiment bucked, or possessed some other of the amiable weaknesses incident to horse life on the great ranches; but we had abundance of men who were utterly unmoved by any antic a horse might commit. Every animal was speedily mastered, though a large number remained to the end mounts upon which an ordinary rider would have felt very uncomfortable. (Roosevelt 1902)

Roosevelt was equally earnest in his assessment of training protocol of both the men and their mounts:

> When we put them on horseback, there was, of course, trouble with the horses; but the horsemanship of the riders was consummate. In fact, the men were immensely interested in making their horses perform each evolution with the utmost speed and accuracy, and in forcing each unquiet, vicious brute to get into line and stay in line, whether he would or not. The guidon-bearers held their plunging steeds true to the line, no matter what they tried to do; and each wild rider brought his wild horse into his proper place with a dash and ease which showed the natural cavalryman. (Roosevelt 1902)

In the final days of shipment of horses, pack mules, and personnel out of Tampa Bay, the colonel took the chaotic process and gave it organization from the standpoint of food, feed, and housing of his charges in harbor facilities that were rudimentary. At minimum, however, the harbor was deep draft, and gangway loading of the animals, personnel, and provisions was an orderly process.

This was not true, however, after they anchored off Cuba's shores, waiting for the end of naval bombardment. At disembarkation, chaos returned. Roosevelt was saddened by what he witnessed: "While I was superintending the landing at the ruined dock, with Bucky O'Neill, a boatful of colored infantry soldiers capsized, and two of the men went to the bottom; Bucky O'Neill plunging in, in full uniform, to save them, but in vain" (Roosevelt 1902).

No doubt Roosevelt's experiences in Cuba regarding the handling of horses and mules in war played a major role in the ensuing decade, as America prepared for World War I with the birth of the US Remount Service and its allied organizations.

US Remount Service, 1907–1947

As military support became a dire need in the Western frontier, the quartermaster general expanded the Remount Service to go beyond the Front Royal, Virginia, station to include similar facilities in Oklahoma (Fort Reno), Nebraska (Fort Robinson), Montana (Fort Keough), and California (Pomona Quartermaster Remount Depot).

A dozen major military campaigns were waged in the West between 1866 and 1891 in which ten US Cavalry regiments battled Indian uprisings. Each of the ten regiments was made up of ten companies. A company was made up of approximately seventy soldiers. Each company was supplied with a farrier and farrier's helper. Caring for an average of seventy mounts, the blacksmith chores called for monthly reshoeing. Including officers and support staff, the Indian campaign enlisted around ten thousand military personnel.

During these stages of military history, the Kingdom of Hawai'i had little use for cavalry forces aside from royal mounted guards. In 1893, however, the monarchy was overthrown, and in 1898 the Islands were annexed by the United States.

In the ninety-five-year period between the arrival of the horse in the Islands in 1803 and the establishment of the Territory of Hawai'i as a US entity, the majority of the horses imported were destined for ranching or plantation work, commercial draying, and the landed gentry. Ranches across the island chain were concentrating on domesticating feral cattle, horses, goats, and sheep in an effort to commercialize ranching toward beef production, and common cow horses were all they required.

The term "remount" is defined as a fresh horse to replace a lost or disabled one. This term became universal in the horse circles of the US military in a historic context. For more than a century, the American horse industry benefited greatly from the formal Remount Service and the Horse Breeding Program of the US Army.

The US Remount Service began well before World War I as a means of acquiring horses and mules for immediate military transportation. The market was insufficiently equipped to fill this need; hence the US Army Horse Breeding Program was instituted, using mares owned by civilian breeders covered by government-owned stallions.

Ranchers across the West, already equipped with bands of broodmares, took advantage of the government program, offering of some of America's finest Thoroughbreds, Standardbreds, American Saddlebreds, Morgans, and Arabian stallions to sire their foal crops. These offspring were then availed to the military as coming four-year-old started mounts, with the balance becoming the property of the rancher. Prudent ranchers appreciated the upgrade in quality of their cow horses as much as the grateful cowhands that were now mounted on superior steeds. The general horse market was enhanced by the availability of good saddle, polo, pleasure, and police mounts. Hawaiian ranchers were poised to become profound beneficiaries of the US Remount Service.

American Remount Service Association: An Allied Support Group

An American Remount Association flyer dated 1922 announced, "Good ancestry coupled with good environment, including ample feed, are the requisites for producing high class stock." The association was clear in its purpose:

> The production of the high class riding horse is of paramount importance at the present time on account of the dearth of such horses in this country. If an emergency

> should arise necessitating the purchase of a large number of this class of animals with which to mount the Army, the problem of obtaining them would be one of the most serious problems confronting the purchasing officers. Agents are continually scouring the country for saddle hoses for park and show ring use, for cross country work and for polo mounts. The cattle ranchers are having serious difficulty to find suitable horses for their cowboys.

The association went further, stating the basic principles governing the production and supply of animals for the army in an emergency:

> The value of the horse and mule in modern warfare is only fully appreciated by those who know that the proportion of animals to soldiers is practically the same now as in the Civil War.
>
> The study of the supply *in emergency* is not only necessary, but the horse and mule industry *in time of peace* also requires attention, particularly because of the fact that [of] all the essential supplies of an Army, the animal takes the longest time to produce—*at least seven years for a mature one that will stand campaign.*

Stallion Enrollment

Hawai'i scored more than a dozen of the nation's finest sires, with Hawai'i, Maui, Lāna'i, Moloka'i, O'ahu, and Kaua'i serving as their tropical homes. Dowsetts and Dillinghams on O'ahu; Parkers, Shipmans, C. Brewer (Kapāpala), Kūka'iau Ranch Ltd., Hinds, and Greenwells on the Big Island; Baldwins and Rices on Maui; Cookes on Moloka'i; and William Hyde Rice on Kaua'i and Lāna'i Ranch began to recognize the need for superior horseflesh. By the turn of the century and with the advent of World War I around the corner, these major ranches became the venue of interest for the US quartermaster general's remount program, and horse quality was about to take a quantum leap forward.

Six Hawaiian ranches, noted for quality broodmare bands, were appointed by the War Department as remount stations as part of the National US Remount Service. Dillingham Ranch on O'ahu, F. F. Baldwin Ranch on Maui, Parker and Kapāpala Ranches on Hawai'i Island, Kīlauea Sugar Company on Kaua'i, and Moloka'i Ranch were selected to receive top-flight stallions of Thoroughbred and Standardbred breeding to mate with their respective broodmare bands. At a later point in time, the military selection committee passed through the outfits, topping off prospects for US Cavalry use.

During the mid-1930s, the average number of mares bred throughout the United States and its territories was seventeen thousand dams producing an average of ten thousand foals per year, approaching a 60 percent production rate, somewhat typical of the equine species.

Percherons by far led in draft horse popularity, with 5,901 sires available throughout the states and territories. The Belgian stallion was also popular, listed at 4,055 head in 1938. Shire, Clydesdale,

French draft, and German Coach sires were used in smaller numbers. When total US horse importation is taken into consideration, it is not surprising that the greatest increases in new stallions occurred within the draft breeds, accounting for 80 percent of imports.

A brief history of Fort Robinson in Nebraska illustrates the efficiency of the remount program.

The Fort Robinson Story

Of all the remount stations, Fort Robinson in western Nebraska emerged as the most significant in the history of the US Cavalry and its success. Remarkably, the fort nearly lost its status as a regular troop station before the War Department decided to establish a quartermaster remount depot there. Some background is in order.

Major General James B. Aleshire, the quartermaster general, established the Remount Service in 1907. This decision placed the responsibility for purchasing and issuing horses for the army under the jurisdiction of the Quartermaster Corps. Besides procurement and issue functions, a breeding program was established. Riding horses, draft horses, and mules would now be processed and economically produced and maintained under strict supervision and standards.

The plan was designed by region. The Fort Reno, Oklahoma, depot was established in 1908 to serve military needs of the southwest. In 1909, Fort Keogh, Montana, was established to serve the northwest, and Front Royal, Virginia, was designated as the procurement center for the eastern United States in 1911. By this time, the Quartermaster General's Office designated the Remount Division as a distinct entity.

In 1919, Fort Robinson was converted from a troop station to a quartermaster remount depot due to its natural comparative advantages, which were numerous. Fort Robinson provided all of the following amenities:

- Adequate housing with permanent barracks, officers' quarters, and support facilities
- Expansive acreage of ideal terrain
- Bountiful water resources, as Soldier Creek and White River ran through it
- Abundant resources of prairie hay
- Bottomlands suitable for farming
- Good railroad connection for shipments in and out of animals, personnel, and freight

By June of that year, forty-nine enlisted men arrived to form the first detachment. Within days, nine hundred mules arrived from Fort Dodge, Iowa, and Camp Pike, Arkansas. By summer's end, the first shipment of twenty horses arrived, by which time remount officers purchased nearly two hundred mounts from area ranchers known for their excellent equine production resources. Fort Robinson was underway as America's premium military horse center by converting an aged cavalry post into the country's largest remount station.

By 1931, the facility had received and processed more than ten thousand animals, 65 percent horses of riding and draft usage.

The remaining 35 percent were mules, of which two-thirds were draft animals and the rest pack animals. The majority of these animals were bought for remount service by purchasing agents.

Most of the horses were of Thoroughbred breeding, standing fifteen hands and one inch high and straight gaited. Browns, blacks, and dark bays were the common colors. With horses going at an average price of $165 per head, the remount service naturally expected better than average cavalry mounts, and disappointment was unfortunately not uncommon. It became necessary to reassess acquisition methods. At this point, agents were attended by a remount committee that imposed detailed screening of candidate animals. The committee was comprised of cavalry veterinarians and officers of utmost qualifications, and the purchasing system was thus perfected.

Purchased horses and mules were subjected to forty-eight-hour isolation in remote corrals holding about fifty head. From this point, the animals were moved to a branding chute where each received a hot Preston brand on the left side of the neck. The brand was a combination of one letter and three numerals, establishing permanent individual serial numbers to each animal. Each animal was given an intradermal mallein test for glanders, vaccinated for encephalomyelitis, and run through a medicated dipping vat for ringworm and external parasite control. These animals were further quarantined for more than eighty days, during which time respiratory diseases could be dealt with under controlled circumstances. The logic of this practice was based on the risk of outbreaks of the highly contagious streptococcal infection strangles, a common sequel in the comingling of Equidae. During quarantine, the disease would run its course and not put the entire population in jeopardy later.

The training process began with roaching manes and clipping the fetlocks of both horses and mules. Riding horses were bridled, saddled, and ridden for the first time. Oblong breaking pens of thirty-by-sixty-foot dimensions with flared (outward leaning) walls were installed to prevent injuries of both riders and mounts. Before issue, a horse needed to be ridden under saddle and snaffle bit at three gaits and gentle enough for a handler to pick up each foot without the mount needing additional restraint. Fractious horses would be retained as "re-rides" until they were gentle enough to pass inspection.

In 1923, the first lots of three-year-olds were issued to the cavalry school at Fort Riley, Kansas. While Fort Robinson remounts went largely to posts in the central and western United States, overseas shipments were not uncommon to areas that included Hawaiʻi, the Philippines, the Canal Zone, and Alaska. Establishing an efficient and productive breeding program was central to the mission of this fort. Taking several years to develop, the breeding stock of mostly Thoroughbred stallions and mares initially averaged about thirty-five foals a year, destined to be issued or sold as three- or four-year-olds once trained. Half would go to cavalry schools,

{ 9.1 } *Meeting at the Parker Ranch Race Track Stables, the Remount Committee sifted through dozens of Thoroughbred geldings, topping off the best to go to Schofield Barracks on O'ahu after training. (Theodore Vredenburg at halter; A. W. Carter in suit with arms folded.)*

{ 9.2 } *After final negotiations for military acquisition of 36 geldings, the Remount Committee posed for photographs on the steps of Parker Ranch offices. (A. W. Carter in suit and tie; Theodore Vredenburg in* palaka *jacket.)*

a quarter to artillery schools, and the balance made available for officer purchase.

The depot stallions were often the finest available in the nation. In 1933, Dr. Joseph Hylton of Douglas, Wyoming, made his stallion Sir Barton available to Fort Robinson. Sir Barton was America's first Triple Crown winner (1919).

Throughout the remount system, many depot stallions were loaned out to civilian breeders who "passed muster" by the judgment committee. Hawai'i was a grateful beneficiary of this system, with stallions stationed on all major islands.

In one remount area of the continental United States, more than one hundred depot stallions were issued to civilian breeders, who could receive a $10 breeding fee for each mare covered. Offspring of superior quality were of course made available to the remount service, while the balance of the colts greatly enhanced the breeders' quality of horseflesh. Fort Robinson was enthusiastic in recruiting civilian breeders, as noted in the following quote:

> Remount officers were always seeking to attract new interest in horse breeding. Explanations of remount breeding operations were published in the local papers to inform the public. Stallion and mare exhibits were sent to county fairs to "attract the attention of private owners to breeding privilege offered at remount depots." Interested civilian breeders were encouraged to visit the depot, where quartermaster personnel received them hospitably. In this era of increasing mechanization, the success of army breeding programs depended heavily on gaining and keeping the interest of civilian agents. During the 1930s the depot held frequent open houses, where jumping competitions and horse exhibits were common. (Buecker 2004)

In 1927, the army conducted a study of the cost-effectiveness of its remount depots. In comparing boarding cost per day, Front Royal Depot required twenty-six cents per day, Fort Reno (Oklahoma) twenty cents per day, while Fort Robinson kept mounts at a mere cost of seven cents per day. The Quartermaster Corps took great satisfaction in its 1919 decision to convert Fort Robinson from a troop station to a remount depot, an institution that stood as a unique instance of government economy and efficiency. Moreover, Fort Robinson was exemplary in its advancement of the quality of the American horse.

A. W. Carter's Role

Carter was an early petitioner for remount status. As early as 1908, he petitioned Washington, DC, for the US Army to consider Parker Ranch as a Remount Station for the cavalry.

In 1910, Carter shipped twenty remounts on the SS *Waialeale* to the Fifth Cavalry stationed at Schofield Barracks on O'ahu. Later, ranch-trained officer's mounts were predominately offspring of Frolic, a Governor Stanford (California) Thoroughbred that had been acquired by Parker Ranch in the acquisition of Humu'ula Sheep Station Company. In the interim, the US Remount Service

{ 9.3 } *Considered by all to be the "Dean of Hawai'i Cattlemen," A. W. Carter was also the "Dean of Hawai'i Horse Breeders." No single individual was more influential in shaping the Hawai'i cattle and horse industry than Carter.*

had forwarded Parker Ranch the noted stallions Harvester, Gold Oak, Rodgers, Ormesby, and Overall.

Carter matched the army's vigorous presentation of top-quality stallions by importing more than a hundred registered Thoroughbred mares for breeding purposes. By this point in time, Parker Ranch had developed a highly profitable Thoroughbred breeding program, supplying beyond military needs to serve the markets of polo and horse racing enthusiasm. Plantations also sought top-flight mounts for their managers and *luna* personnel.

Role of the US Army Veterinary Corps

In 2016, the United States Army Veterinary Corps will celebrate its centennial milestone. The role of this corps in military horse health and the Remount Service is epic.

Although the Veterinary Corps was formally established by an act of Congress on June 3, 1916, the need for veterinary expertise was acknowledged as early as 1776 when General Washington directed that a "regiment of horses with a farrier" be raised. While not veterinarians, farriers during that period were called upon to treat horse ailments.

During the Civil War, the War Department provided a veterinary surgeon for each cavalry regiment. The veterinarian held the rank of regimental sergeant major and was paid $75 per month. After the war ended, the need for veterinarians was even more apparent. Unlike their cavalry counterparts, the artillery units were authorized by Congress in 1875 to receive medicines and dressings for horses, but no veterinarians. Four years later, Congress passed a resolution requiring all applicants for cavalry veterinary positions to be graduates of a recognized veterinary college.

Veterinarians were also being sought in 1890 to inspect meat, poultry, and dairy products intended for frontier-post destinations. Veterinarians were ideally suited for ensuring food safety and wholesomeness, given their academic strength in microbiology, epidemiology, pathology, and public health. Lack of adequate quality assurance practices for maintaining the health of animals and soldiers that led to tremendous loss of life during the Spanish-American War was pivotal in the establishment of the Veterinary Corps.

With an aim toward prevention, the American Veterinary Medical Association and other like-minded allied groups actively supported legislation for the establishment of the Army Veterinary Corps. Commissioning of veterinary officers was the direct result of the passage of the National Defense Act on June 3, 1916, which allowed the army surgeon general to begin organizing this new corps within the regular army. When war was declared in April 1917, fifty-seven veterinarians were already working for the army in the area of equine surgery and medicine.

{9.4} *Twenty-three Parker Ranch–bred polo mounts stand as testimony to A. W. Carter's judgment in advancing horse quality for a market far beyond Parker Ranch.*

Corps numbers swelled to 2,313 officers within an eighteen-month period.

Since World War I, the Veterinary Corps has served in all conflicts, playing a significant role in maintaining the health and well-being of soldiers and animals. The highly technical education required of veterinarians has allowed them to meet the requirements for their changing mission for nearly one hundred years (Poppe 2006).

Influence of US Armed Forces on Equestrian Activities

On January 12, 1909, the USS *Virginia* disembarked at Pearl Harbor in Honolulu five hundred of the finest US Cavalry mounts for service in the Territory of Hawai'i. A day later, the USS *Thomas* docked, delivering 473 officers and men of the Fifth Cavalry for assignment at Schofield Barracks.

The high levels of esprit de corps displayed at Schofield Barracks in the early 1900s can be traced back and connected directly to their livestock—primarily the horses and mules. Schofield's Fifth Cavalry wasted no time in establishing their presence and military might by hosting exhibitions and tournaments.

Located on the plains of Leilehua, O'ahu, the military outpost had precontact significance as a training ground on that island. The outpost was formally

{9.5} *A Schofield Barracks cavalry mount bearing both Parker Ranch brand and US Cavalry identification, referred to as a Preston brand.*

christened Schofield Barracks in honor of Lt. General John McAlister Schofield, who distinguished himself in Civil War battles. Rising to commander of the US Army in later years, his name proudly represents one of America's most strategic military posts, as well as one of Hawai'i's best-known army bases.

Within a year of arrival, the Fifth Cavalry presented Hawai'i's first mounted band, consisting of more than thirty men on horseback, complete with a mounted maestro. Crowds gathered in due respect for the disciplined and composed sorrel-colored mounts, with musicians of premiere musical talent astride, marching in cadence to the melodic beat.

In 1913, the Fifth Cavalry and artillery units trekked the course with infantrymen in a spirit that sparked pioneering courage in the wives and families of the men by their presence at the final campsite, where the band and cook wagons had prepared a welcoming reception for the trail-weary men. Dancing, beach games, food, and merriment kept esprit de corps at high levels despite the remoteness of the distant military outpost.

In 1915, Schofield sponsored its first four-day Equestrian Tournament in Kapi'olani Park, Honolulu. They showcased their military might and the role of horses in defense of America. O'ahu's citizens were enamored as they watched horse-drawn escort wagons expertly coordinating passes at the intersections of figure-eight patterns and pack trains of dozens of sturdy mules bearing pannier

{9.6} *Cavalry officers played a significant role in horse show success at Schofield Barracks, often mounted on Hawai'i-bred mounts.*

packs (large, basketlike side bags) loaded with ammunition. An impressive succession of horse races, games, and exhibitions was featured at Kapi'olani Park for many years before evolving into an annual Schofield Barracks Horse Show.

In early 1919, the Hawaiian regiments were demobilized and the infantrymen distributed among other outposts. Months later, however, the Seventeenth Cavalry arrived at Schofield Barracks, followed a year later by the Fourth Cavalry. The strength of cavalry and horsemanship in general was further enhanced by the arrival of army major, Dr. Clarence Fronk in 1922.

Running parallel to the formal military exhibitions was the realization of the value of horses and horse programs as a beneficial form of recreation and relaxation for military members and their families. The Schofield Riding Club was organized in February 1925 for officers, ladies, and children. The club sponsored post-riding classes, gymkhanas (games on horseback), and treasure hunts, while also participating in the annual Horse and Transportation Horse Shows throughout the 1930s. The Hawaiian Division Polo Association was organized by the Schofield Officers in April 1931 after the 11th Field Artillery Team took permanent possession of the T. H. Davies Cup upon winning the annual tournament for three years in a row. Members of the Schofield Barracks Polo Association played on three polo fields on post. The largest was the Benson Memorial Polo Field, which was considered to be world-class.

Dr. Clarence Fronk

Assigned as chief of surgical services at the Tripler General Hospital, Dr. Fronk came with considerable respect as a horseman and polo player. Leaving military service to establish the Fronk-Wynn Clinic in Honolulu, Dr. Fronk turned his horse interest toward support of the youth equestrian opportunities, utilizing his own horses stabled at Town and Country Stables at Kapi'olani Park. A rider, breeder, and trainer of fine horses, Dr. Fronk's influence on the image and role of the Arabian horse breed is notable. On a national front, he served with distinction as regional director and vice president of the American Horse Shows Association, retiring as an honorary life member. Neighbor Islands welcomed the avid bird and game hunter, while Parker Ranch benefited from the surgeon's generous lease of his prized Arabian stallion during the management era of Richard "Dick" Penhallow. Dr. Fronk's presence greatly enhanced Hawai'i's horse circles, and the opportunity would never have been realized without the military assignment of this stellar surgeon.

{9.7} *On loan to Parker Ranch for cross-breeding purposes, the Arabian stallion from Dr. Fronk in Honolulu drew minimal appreciation despite the ranch's need for distance horses. (Groom Kanakanui Iokepa at halter.)*

As military bases and personnel were greatly expanded in numbers as World War II loomed, riding clubs sprung forth, affording not only enlisted men but their wives and families a means of retaining contact with their companion animal of choice. Military-based riding clubs served as a vestige of the cavalry era, as the armed forces turned to mechanization via jeeps, trucks, tanks, and aircraft.

Such private clubs, whether the Pony Club, 4-H, or rodeos, required formal and official approval of the base commander if they were to enjoy any support, growth, or longevity. These clubs were established under Military Regulation 210-1 as private clubs open to military families and Department of Defense civilians stabling their horses on the host base. Serving as recreational and social outlets for families, informal horse shows, training clinics, and play days were occasionally open to the public, further necessitating high-level administrative approval. Gymkhana, a fairly safe category of mounted games, was the most common form of horse club activities, while polo and rodeo enjoyed a different venue and nature of membership. The term "gymkhana" traces its roots to the early Middle Ages. By the 1800s, the term was in common use by British soldiers serving in Asia where the Anglo/Indian term was used to mean "a field day on horseback." Simply a "play day" in present-day lingo, it can be enjoyed by a variety of participants in age and competence.

In the last three decades of the previous millennium, some of these clubs enjoyed phenomenal success. While the Wheeler Air Force Base has had a shorter lifespan than that of Schofield Barracks, by the mid-1950s its weekend events attracted more than two thousand attendees. Schofield Barracks Boots and Saddle Club was granted its sanction in 1968 and allowed the use of a sizeable parcel of land for their activities, including a large ring, practice arena, bleachers, and a cross country-course with eighteen jumps.

Valerie van der Veer, an equine and military historian on O'ahu, has done extensive research regarding the military influence on horse activities in the State of Hawai'i. Here she shares her perspective on the role of the armed forces in Hawaiian rodeo.

THE ARMED FORCES AND RODEO

Valerie van der Veer

In the mid-1930s, as the Second World War approached, interest in horse shows, both civilian and military, rose in fervor within O'ahu circles. However, a new sport involving cowboys started making its presence known. Military officers created the foundation for equestrian programs with their military exhibitions, polo, and horse shows, but it was the enlisted troops who would take O'ahu's horse world to the next level with the introduction of rodeos.

During the 1930s, 1940s, and 1950s, O'ahu's military presence was ripe with enlistees from the Midwest and many rural areas of the continental United States looking for something to do while serving their country. The influx of top-notch military cowboys and hardworking volunteers blended perfectly with O'ahu's traditional *paniolo*, and the world of rodeo exploded onto the O'ahu scene not only as a form of recreation but also as a spectator sport. With crowds attending in the thousands, it was a surefire way for organizations to raise funds and for businessmen to make money.

The 1932 "Aloha Rodeo" is said to be one of the first rodeos on O'ahu to include military personnel. Stationed at Schofield Barracks in 1932, Don G. Sikes recalled his experience at the rodeo in an article he wrote in 1978 for *Real West Magazine:*

> Apparently some promoters decided to try to put on a rodeo in Honolulu with riders from the Army service companies and from the Parker Ranch on the Big Island of Hawai'i. Someone had secured the use of an army personnel carrier to haul the riders from Schofield. The rodeo grounds were in a small valley three or four miles northwest of Honolulu, near 'Aiea. The promoters had scraped the algarroba bushes and cactus off of an area large enough to set up an arena, bleacher seats, a couple of saddling chutes, and a small parking lot. The bucking horses were all from the Parker Ranch, and the riding bulls were only Hereford steers. (Sikes 1978)

The Honolulu Stadium served as the hub for O'ahu's rodeos in the 1940s. As early as 1942, the Army and Navy Relief Funds and the Red Cross benefited from portions

THE ARMED FORCES AND RODEO

(continued from previous page)

of proceeds generated by the rodeos held at the stadium and sponsored by Mid-Pacific Rodeo. The Mid-Pacific Stampede and Rodeos were generally two- or three-day events involving roping, bull riding, best cowboy awards, and equestrian demonstrations complete with parades and *pāʻū* riders.

Both the Honolulu Junior Chamber of Commerce and the Hawaiian Civic Club sponsored rodeos at the Honolulu Stadium. The chamber sponsored the Tom Boyd Rodeos, which featured "Dusty" Rhodes the Rodeo Clown, and the Hawaiian Civic Club sponsored their Kanaka Series Rodeos. Elsewhere, members of the armed forces and members of the Hawaiian Rodeo and Roping Club participated in island rodeos sponsored by the Koʻolaupoko Hawaiian Civic Club and hosted at the Heʻeia Rodeo grounds in Kāneʻohe. The gallantry continued with parades, floats, costume contests, calf roping, bareback and saddle bronc riding, and barrel racing. A December 1953 rodeo featured Kekaulike Kawananakoa, granddaughter of Princess Abigail Kawananakoa, as the rodeo queen. At the time, she was the only woman polo player in Hawaiʻi and was considered an expert at riding and roping.

Two Game Changers

During this era, there were two significant events from which all future military rodeo and military horse programs on Oʻahu would evolve and flourish. The first took place in 1936 in Fort Riley, Kansas, when avid roper and bronc rider Dee Benjamin Gibson enlisted in the US Cavalry. He was just shy of his eighteenth birthday and was assigned to Schofield Barracks. After a three-year stint, he remained on Oʻahu working at the Pearl Harbor dry docks. By 1947, Dee and his father, Hank, were importing dairy heifers to Oʻahu and had started the Koko Head Dairy. Importing the heifers gave birth to Dee's lifetime career of transporting livestock between California and Hawaiʻi. His unique background with rodeo, his access to cattle and transport, his experience and connections with the military, and his hard work and dedication jettisoned him onto a path from which all military programs on Oʻahu would evolve. Oʻahu's horse world was both amazed and impressed, as Dee Gibson evolved into the single most significant player in Oʻahu's rodeo world. He left his stamp on everything he touched, which was just about every military horse program on Oʻahu.

Second, behind the scenes and seemingly unrelated to the horse world, Marine Corps Air Station (MCAS) ʻEwa, home to marine aviation in the Pacific during World War II, was shutting down. The base, airstrip, and land dotted with dome-shaped concrete aircraft revetments was absorbed by the US Navy and became part of Naval Air Station (NAS) Barbers Point. By June 1952, MCAS ʻEwa was no more, and

THE ARMED FORCES AND RODEO

(continued from previous page)

the marines who had previously been stationed and tucked away at the remote base now found themselves stationed at Kāneʻohe MCAS—in the middle of Hawaiʻi's rodeo community. This subtle shift of personnel within the military set the stage for all future horse programs on Oʻahu. From this almost unnoticed event, all of Oʻahu's military stables and riding clubs (with the exception of Schofield) were born, and they would flourish on Oʻahu during the 1970s and 1980s.

Kāneʻohe: The Beginning

Finding themselves in the heart in rodeo country, with Lt. Col. Fraser "Poke" West, USMC, in their midst, and partnered with Dee Gibson, the marines set about planning the first permanent rodeo facility to be built on a military installation on Oʻahu. Along the water, on the northeastern side of Kāneʻohe Marine Corps Air Station, the marines found a perfect location for their own rodeo arena. "Poke" West was the self-proclaimed "daddy of service rodeos and horse-show exhibiting," and he led the charge in developing plans for the facility, which included an arena with bucking chutes overlooking the beautiful Pacific Ocean. Officially labeled Building 1554, the facility was called Truan Arena. It was dedicated on October 26, 1956, by Brig. Gen. George R. E. Shell in honor of Sgt. Fritz Truan. Their first rodeo, sponsored by the First Marine Brigade, took place October 26 and 27, 1956, and drew nearly ten thousand spectators on day one. Attendance on day two was even higher when a parade through Kailua kicked off the day's events and the doors were open to the public.

{9.8} *World War II hero Fritz Truan with Brigadier General LeRoy P. Hunt, USMC Kāneʻohe Bay, Hawaiʻi, Marine Air Station Rodeo, 1944.*

The Fritz Truan Story

California born and raised, Fritz Truan found rodeo a challenge of choice, especially in rough stock events. Able to ride "anything with hair," he excelled at saddle bronc riding in the early 1930s rodeo circles across the nation.

Truan was declared a world champion upon winning the saddle bronc event at Madison Square Garden in 1939. A year

THE ARMED FORCES AND RODEO

(continued from previous page)

later he rose to World All Around and Saddle Bronc Champion by winning in other rough stock events. In 1941, with World War II raging, he won the Sam Jackson Championship Trophy at the Pendleton Round-Up in Oregon. He proudly enlisted in the US Marine Corps on December 7, 1942, the first anniversary of the bombing of Pearl Harbor. By this time in American rodeo history, he was already revered as the "King of the Cowboys."

Truan was sent to Hawai'i, where he continued his rodeo successes under a "leatherneck" banner at the Marine Corps Air Station at 'Ewa Field, where he starred in major rodeos. Throughout this period, he readily befriended local *paniolo* before heading for the bloody battle of Iwo Jima.

Ever the fearless marine, Truan led an assault on the slopes of Mount Suribachi, where he was killed in a hail of enemy gunfire on February 28, 1945. Sadly, America lost an icon in both the US Marine and rodeo world during the final months of the war. In a postwar (1947) Hawaiian rodeo at the Honolulu Stadium, taps was played in honor of the fallen marine and revered King of the Cowboys.

Truan's memory lived on in Hawai'i, where he was honored in several ways. The Marine Corps Air Station Kāne'ohe rodeo arena, as noted, was named in his honor. When that facility was retired, his name was immortalized in the blessing of the Barbers Point Arena, dedicated to the Cowboy King, Fritz Truan.

Legendary actor John Wayne, who befriended Truan over many years of cowboy films, was inspired by Truan's sacrifice to film *Sands of Iwo Jima,* in which he stars in a re-enactment of the battle that claimed Truan's life.

Lt. Col. West was incredibly active in O'ahu's rodeo community during his time on O'ahu (1954–1957). In addition to designing the Fritz Truan Arena and being a roper and bull rider himself, he organized rodeos at the marine base and spent a good deal of time coordinating the Navy Relief Fundraising Rodeos near Pearl Harbor. The 1957 O'ahu Championship Rodeo was a four-day Wild West contest, raising over $20,000 and drawing more than nineteen thousand spectators to Furlong Field near Pearl Harbor.

Wheeler Field

Moving full speed ahead, rodeo fever continued into the next decade. In 1960, as the Valley Cattle Company announced plans for the development of the $250,000 Saddle City in the civilian community of Waimānalo, the founders Dee Gibson and Grover Godfry simultaneously teamed up with the military for the development of the rodeo grounds on Wheeler Air Field in Wahiawā. Wheeler Field would become the second permanent rodeo facility to be built on a military installation on O'ahu. When

THE ARMED FORCES AND RODEO

(continued from previous page)

Wheeler Field's Rodeo Arena first opened its doors for the Wheeler-Wahiawā Stampede in April 1960, it boasted a ten-thousand-seat amphitheater and parking for twenty thousand cars.

Barbers Point

About the same time that Wheeler Field's Rodeo Arena came to fruition, Lt. Cmdr. Winfield Junk, USN, was assigned to NAS Barbers Point in the remote area of ʻEwa. In addition to being a naval aviator and World War II hero and now special services commander, Junk was a horseman. He paid particular attention to the portion of the base that had formerly been occupied by the US Marine Corps and previously known as MCAS ʻEwa. As the new special services commander, he was responsible for overseeing the facilities and personnel responsible for the morale, welfare, and recreation of military members and their families. He noticed horses tethered to trees on the portion of the grounds of the former MCAS ʻEwa, while equipment was stored in and under the abandoned revetments. Acting upon the recommendation of his new friend, Dee Gibson, Junk flip-flopped the design. He built paddocks in and around the revetments and used the large concrete revetments as barns to shelter the horses.

In his role as special services commander and with his connections to cowboys on the mainland, Junk orchestrated the 1962 Barbers Point Rodeo. This rodeo was quite a production, and it will forever be remembered by the old-timers of Oʻahu. The Special

{9.9} *Revetments such as these at ʻEwa served as protective hangars for fighter planes during World War II.*

THE ARMED FORCES AND RODEO

(continued from previous page)

Services Division of NAS Barbers Point (Junk), in conjunction with the Hawai'i Stock Contractors (Dee Gibson), pulled off a coup when they flew in five of the world's top cowboys from the mainland—including headline trick rider Lee Hendricks and his famous horse Golden Star—and then added a horse show with gaited horses and jumping into the mix. And even better, the naval air station opened its doors to the public so all members of the community could attend.

Junk moved fast and furiously to establish Barbers Point as another option for rodeos. Along with his passion for rodeos, he introduced trail rides, riding lessons, and horse boarding into his recreational plan. It didn't take long for him to become known as the "Cowboy Commander," While it would be another ten years and another set of hands before rodeos reached their peak at NAS Barber Point, the facility was established as the third permanent rodeo facility to be built on a military installation on O'ahu.

{ 9.10 } *In subsequent years of peace, horse clubs converted the revetments to stalling barns.*

THE ARMED FORCES AND RODEO

(continued from previous page)

Lt. Cmdr. Winfield Junk

Prior to receiving his military assignment to Hawai'i and establishing Barbers Point Stables, Winfield Junk was a World War II military aviator and hero. He earned many military honors for his heroism, including the Navy Cross, the Distinguished Flying Cross, and several air medals. He was the 118th navy aviator to fly a jet and the first navy jet pilot to enter the air force's Test Pilot Program in Mojave, California.

After retiring from the navy, Junk relocated to the Windward side of O'ahu, where he spent many years training, showing, judging, and managing barns. He was vice president of the Hawai'i Quarter Horse Association and played a significant role in introducing Quarter Horses to Hawai'i rodeo and horse show worlds.

In 1978, the Hawai'i Horse Show Association established a perpetual trophy in his honor. Today, this trophy is awarded to the Western Performance Horse scoring the most points in Open Trail, Open Western Riding, and Open Stock Horse.

His Navy Cross citation reads as follows:

> JUNK, WINFIELD HIGDON LT USNR
> For distinguishing himself by extraordinary heroism in operations against the enemy while participating in aerial flights as a pilot of a carrier based torpedo plane. On 19 October 1944 he participated in a bombing attack in the vicinity of the Central Philippines, which resulted in serious damage to a large tanker and a medium cargo ship. On 25 October 1944 he participated in a torpedo attack against an enemy carrier task group in the vicinity of the Philippine Sea. Dropping his torpedo at low altitude and close range he scored a direct and damaging hit on an enemy aircraft fire. His skill and courage were at all times in keeping with the highest traditions of the United States Naval Service.

The Shift

The 1970s brought a turnabout for the military horse community and an increased awareness of horses as a form of recreation for everyone. Because machines replaced the need for horses and a network of roads for automobiles was established, there were many idle, well-trained horses on the island. Horse boarding, leasing, riding lessons, trail riding, 4-H, and other horse programs sprang up under the shadows of the military. They found their foothold in the former military horse facilities once used for polo, military regalia, and rodeo events. Because these new boarding stables and riding programs operated on military Installations, the fees were affordable to the military families stationed on O'ahu.

THE ARMED FORCES AND RODEO

(continued from previous page)

Camp Smith

Located high atop Hālawa Heights, Camp Smith was home to a military horse stable for over fifty years. Marines utilized mounted patrols to rescue hikers and to assist with security forces. Their programs progressed into offering lessons and rental trail horses for military families. When their barn doors closed about 1999, the stables boasted four instructors and seventeen government-owned school horses.

Later Years

In 1968, Schofield Barracks formed the Boots and Saddle Club and successfully transitioned their facility into a boarding stable for military families and their privately owned horses. The club members found themselves on solid ground through the 1970s, as they sponsored hunter paces, cross-county events, and horse shows. However, as the army's mission expanded in the 1980s, leadership considered shuttering the stables. The Boots and Saddle Club made a run at protecting their stable by hosting an All-Armed Forces Invitational Rodeo in 1985, but their tenacity and efforts were in vain. Leadership had made the decision. Despite eminent closure, the Boots and Saddle Club staged a Buffalo Soldiers Pageant with African American soldiers in full traditional cavalry regalia, honoring the twelve thousand Afro-American horsemen who served the US Army Cavalry during the Indian Wars of 1866–1891. In 1986 the army closed the stables and bulldozed the entire historic facility.

Rodeos and horse shows continued through the 1960s in the Truan Arena. In addition to the rodeo facility, military families were provided with a venue for boarding their privately owned horses, taking lessons, and enjoying trail rides. Dave Moniz, who had previously worked under Frank Carvajal at Saddle City (created by Dee Gibson), ran the military horse programs for Kāneʻohe's Special Services for years.

Unfortunately, by 1972 the combination of salty sea air and termites had taken its toll on the rodeo facility, and at the same time the US Marine military mission was expanding and looking for land for additional housing. Kāneʻohe's horse programs and rodeo grounds were the first of the military stables to feel the effects of change in their horse programs. In 1972, Dave Moniz relocated the horses, equipment, personnel, all stable operations, and his good friend *paniolo* George Kaeo Jr. from Kāneʻohe to another military installation—NAS Barbers Point. Kāneʻohe's private boarding pastures would survive another couple of years before being completely bulldozed in 1976.

Wheeler Stables, under the leadership of Col. Henry "Hank" English, thrived in the 1970s and 1980s. English held the reins at Wheeler's stable for years after his retirement

THE ARMED FORCES AND RODEO

(continued from previous page)

from the air force. As the rodeo era faded, he successfully transitioned Wheeler's military stable into a full-scale boarding facility with lesson programs, horse shows, and gymkhanas. Col. English's impact on Oʻahu's horse world went well beyond the military families who crossed paths with him at Wheeler. He was the leader of Oʻahu's Leeward Hawaiʻi Air Corps (LEEHAC) horse programs, which sponsored 4-H and a horse show circuit on the Leeward side of the island. He coordinated the talent and expertise of Oʻahu's horse community in order to provide horse shows that were affordable and open to many military and civilian families on the ʻEwa Plain and Leeward Coast.

Wheeler's wooden rodeo arena and facilities had been modeled after Kāneʻohe's rodeo facility, and as time went on, the wooden structures fought the same foes of weather and termites as Kāneʻohe's. Wheeler Air Force Base was traded to the army in 1991 (as part of a deal involving the trading of Fort Kamehameha, located on Hickam Air Force Base, to the US Air Force). Once again, the army decided to make room for their expanded modern-day mission and bulldozed the historic, albeit deteriorated, rodeo facility.

While the original historic Wheeler Stables and Rodeo grounds no longer exist, a smaller area was re-created to continue providing military families with affordable horse boarding while stationed in Hawaiʻi. Operating under the auspices of the US Army's Morale Welfare and Recreation (MWR), the army ran the stables until approximately 2011. At that time, the Wheeler Stables and Saddle Club began operating as a command-sponsored "private organization" recognized by the US Army. Today, the club provides horse boarding for privately owned horses and the occasional horse show, gymkhana, or clinic.

By 1972, Dave Moniz had relocated the horse programs from Kāneʻohe to Barbers Point. Along with George Keao Jr., Sam Kaula, many of his island *paniolo* friends, and numerous off-duty military cowboys stationed on island, he set about repairing and revitalizing the Barbers Point Rodeo facility established by Lt. Cmdr. Winfield Junk. They had witnessed the deterioration at Kāneʻohe's Truan Arena firsthand and were posturing the Barbers Point facility to succeed for the long haul. Using welded pipe, they built fencing, chutes, and additional arenas as a means of protection against termites and deterioration. A grand reopening for the stables was held during the summer of 1972, and by 1974 Dave and Kay Moniz had completely expanded the boarding facilities, lesson programs, summer fun programs, and trail rides while operating shoulder to shoulder with Col. English of Wheeler, Pam Tongg of Tongg Ranch, and all the *paniolo* in Dave's hometown of Waiʻanae.

While rodeos were defunct at the closed Kāneʻohe Facility and at a standstill at Wheeler, Barbers Point Stables stepped into the spotlight with its updated facility.

THE ARMED FORCES AND RODEO

(continued from previous page)

In January 1974, Dave Moniz and Buddy Gibson (son of Dee Gibson) sponsored and managed a hugely successful two-day Jackpot Rodeo at Barbers Point. The success of the rodeo and the enthusiasm generated at the remote Barbers Point put the almost forgotten facility back on the map. Its future was set in motion with a series of horse shows, junior rodeos, and gymkhanas.

George "Keoki" Kaeo Jr.

> **COIN DECIDES OVERALL RODEO CHAMP**
>
> A flip of the coin broke a tie and made George Kaeo, Jr of Campos Ranch in Kaneohe winner of the All Around Cowboy Award at the four day Oahu Championship Rodeo sponsored by the Navy Relief Society .
>
> The four day wild west contest drew a total of 19,000 spectators to Furlong Field near Pearl Harbor and put put about $20,000 into the Navy Relief Society coffers.
>
> Mr. Kaeo was tied with Marine Col. Fraser West for top honors in the rodeo when the judges toted up the composite scores for each of the four days. The flip of the coin favored Mr. Kaeo.
>
> —*Honolulu Advertiser,* July 8, 1957

George "Keoki" Kaeo Jr. was always connected to rodeo and the military. In December 1973, the *Paniolo Press* paid tribute to Mr. Kaeo: "He was born in Hanalei, Kauai. George worked at Parker Ranch under Mr. Carter and accompanied race horses from Parker Ranch to Bay Meadows on the mainland, played polo with Walter Dillingham and was a friend of Ikua Purdy." In the late 1960s "Keoki" joined Dave Moniz at Kāneʻohe's military stable and then shifted to Barbers Point's military stable in the 1970s when the operation relocated. He is best remembered and loved for his kind spirit and his willingness to assist military families from all walks of life.

Barbers Point Stables

The future would bring two key pivot points. The first occurred in 1999 when NAS Barbers was closed as part of the government's Base Realignment and Closure (BRAC) process. Fortunately, despite the closure of the base, the stables continued to operate.

THE ARMED FORCES AND RODEO

(continued from previous page)

The navy retained the majority of the former MCAS ʻEwa, which housed the NAS Barbers Point Golf Course, the very historic ʻEwa Field Battlefield, and the adjacent World War II Revetment District—home to Barbers Point Stables.

The second pivot occurred in 2010 when the Barbers Point Riding Club was given notice that their lease would not be renewed and the stables would be closing. While a good number of families relocated their horses in accordance with the mandate, a more proactive group began taking steps toward revitalizing the dilapidating facility, connecting themselves to federal agencies responsible for preservation and pleading their case at all levels within the military.

Today, Historic Barbers Point Stables continues to operate under the guidance of the Barbers Point Riding Club, a "private organization" recognized by the US Navy. A partnership of protection and preservation with the navy has emerged, and while the riding club remains focused on providing affordable horse boarding and share boarding for military families, they have added stewardship of the facility to their mission. Volunteers work around the clock to protect, preserve, and revitalize this historic stable.

Barbers Point Stables is one of the best examples of "adaptive reuse" in the Hawaiian Islands. The stable is nestled among a series of Historic World War II revetments with original streets and markings that tie directly to the December 7, 1941, attack on ʻEwa Field and Pearl Harbor. The navy has acknowledged that this historic stable located within the World War II Revetment District is eligible for the national registry.

Boots and Saddle Club

The Boots and Saddle Club boldly staged an All Armed Forces Invitational Rodeo in 1985, preceded only by a similar Barbers Point event in 1962.

While military polo activities are chronicled in another section on Hawaiian polo history, it would not be premature to state that the influence of the US armed forces on the history of performance horse activities in the Islands has been profoundly positive.

Some of the continued efforts to preserve equestrian activities on Oʻahu's military bases appropriately use patriotism as a central theme. John Bond, from the organization Save ʻEwa Field and Barbers Point ʻEwa Stables, wisely themed his heroic efforts around the rodeo great, Fritz Truan.

While the armed forces provided significant benefits to all of Hawai'i's horse circles, business and social circles were busy celebrating equestrian performance activities.

Since the days of the Kingdom of Hawai'i, the use of horses in performance has enriched the beauty, environment, culture, heritage, and mystique of the Islands. By definition, in this text the term "performance horse" reflects its use in competition. While *pā'ū* riders are often rated competitively in parades and festivals, there are no stand-alone *pā'ū* venues, save for the elegant horses and riders' roles as part of a larger event such as the Kamehameha Day Parades and celebrations held on all islands (see plate 2).

Old Hawai'i on Horseback, originally staged at Anna Ranch by Anna Lindsey Perry-Fiske, has been a fine venue of proper *pā'ū* horsemanship. Barbara Nobriga of Mahealani Ranch in Kona, Pudding Lassiter of Pu'umoi Ranch in Hilo, DeeDee Keakealani-Bertelmann of Parker Ranch, and Queenie Dowsett of Waimea have assumed authoritative roles in Hawaiian horsewomanship in the old Hawaiian ways, while Patricia Bergin's efforts have kept Old Hawai'i on Horseback itself as a periodic gala festival.

Horse racing in Hawai'i, although lacking in pari-mutuel gaming support, nevertheless holds its place as the Islands' oldest equine sporting event, followed by polo. Rodeo, of course, has endured a two-century span as a formidable force due to its huge image in national championships and affordable nature. Thanks to rodeo and ranch work, the Hawai'i horse population has shifted to the predominance of Quarter Horses since the late 1950s. Along with this popularity came Quarter Horse shows, which are not an uncommon occurrence in Hawai'i horse circles. A. Morgan Brown, formerly of Waimea on the Island of Hawai'i, single-handedly promoted the Quarter Horse's popularity in all horse circles of the state, with enduring results (see plate 3).

The value of the Thoroughbred remount sires in the racing industry was equally profound in several western states. Comparatively, Hawai'i's thirteen remount sires stood well alongside other states. Leading up to World War II, significant progress was made in the distribution of remount sires and dams, including the draft breeds. In the period between 1908 and 1948, the Remount Service stationed more than seven hundred stallions per year (all breeds) on America's farms and ranches, including several noted outfits in the Territory of Hawai'i. In 1938, the distribution of remount sires among qualified states and territories numbered 587 stallions of Thoroughbred breeding. Texas led with 122, and the Rocky Mountain states were well represented: Wyoming (41), Colorado (33), and Montana (32). Oklahoma was home to 34, and California stood 27 stallions. The value of remount bloodstock to America's horse industry continues to be heralded to the present day.

The American Quarter Horse Association (AQHA) in 2014 recognized the historic contributions the Remount Service sires made in founding some of the finest products of the Quarter Horse breed. A long-standing exhibit, "War Horses: Bred to Serve," stood in testimony at the Amarillo headquarters, housed in the American Quarter Horse Hall of Fame and Museum.

Recognizing that the majority of the remount sires were of Thoroughbred breeding, their female offspring became the founding mothers of the American Quarter Horse. By 2014, sixty-nine of the ninety-nine equine members of the AQHA Hall of Fame are direct descendants of remount stallions (Phares and Clanahan 2014).

Thoroughbred, warmblood, and to a lesser degree Morgan horses dominate the show circles for dressage and hunter/jumper competitions. Amy Rich on O'ahu and Haku Baldwin on Maui are the peerless icons of these activities in Hawai'i's horse history. No doubt, however, the Thoroughbred horse was the common denominator in most performance events, especially racing.

CHAPTER 10

HORSE RACING

Horse numbers were well established in the Islands within the first two decades of the 1800s. Human nature now is no different than it was then—people love to see horses run, and wagering, while informal, is an added value.

Matched racing on roadways was common in the early years (1840s and 1850s) of the Hawaiian Kingdom. This was the case on all islands except Kahoʻolawe. Soon "bush tracks" added formality and measured distances to the sport of kings.

The first formally judged horse races were staged on Oʻahu on June 11, 1872. The Hawaiian Jockey Club was founded that year by King Kalākaua. It boasted board members of significant influence in Hawaiian history: Governor John Dominis, Samuel Parker Sr., A. S. Cleghorn, and Major Cornwell.

In the following decade, Kapiʻolani Park Racetrack was built as a one-mile oval that could be viewed from a grandstand and clubhouse. This track became the focal point of social activity in Waikīkī, with its signature event, the Rosita Cup Races, held on King Kamehameha Day (June 11) of each year. In 1914, the track was demolished.

Birth, Growth, and Maturity of Kapiʻolani Park

Kapiʻolani Park has an extraordinary sense of place that holds great meaning to countless individuals from all walks of life in Hawaiʻi's capital city, Honolulu. Whether for a history buff, a cultural enthusiast, a family in need of a picnic venue, an earnest jogger in pursuit of an aerobic experience, or a solo wanderer seeking solace and quietude, Kapiʻolani Park, with its broad, open spaces amidst clusters of shade trees, provides comfort and function for all. Preserving the park's

serenity is the mission of the Kapi‘olani Park Preservation Society and its leader, Jack Gillmar. Thanks to this organization and its 2002 publication, *Kapiolani Park: A History,* individuals with a passion for preserving the history of events, in this case equestrian activities, are gifted with a definitive documentary resource from which to garner factual insight into "the way it was" in our chosen genre. Author Robert R. Weyeneth and illustrator MacKinnon Simpson are credited with producing this great work.

The histories of Kapi‘olani Park on O‘ahu and Ho‘olulu Park on the Big Island reveal close parallels between the two, as well as genuine differences. One thing is certain: love and enthusiasm for horse racing moved both venues to the forefront as they gained in popularity. Both entities had the Hawaiian Republic as early sponsors. Both parks witnessed the growing pressure

{ **10.1** } *Horse races were common at Kapi‘olani Park, attracting the largest crowds.*

of baseball enthusiasts competing with waning promotion of horse racing.

Yet there were different outcomes. While Act 66 of the Hawaiian Legislative Session (1886) called for a seaside park where Ho'olulu Park was born in 1900, it was an inland venue of fifty-five acres. Kapi'olani Park, via Act 53 of the Republic of Hawai'i (1896), on the other hand, maintained significant shoreline space. Ho'olulu Park was built on sturdy flatlands of ancient *pāhoehoe* (smooth, flat lava). Kapi'olani Park started as sandy marshlands in part, but lying in the shadow of Diamond Head and flanked by the Waikīkī coast, no one could argue with the superior venue of O'ahu's offering. Kapi'olani Park stands today as it always has, in a rich landscape of Honolulu. The demise of Ho'olulu Park in 1971 came in the form of conversion to a vibrant multicomplex of badly needed sports and community facilities such as the Walter Victor Baseball Stadium, the Edith Kanakaole Tennis Stadium, the Sparky Kawamoto Swimming Pool, the Ah Fook Chinen Civic Auditorium, and Aunty Sally's Lū'au House; all named after men and women who once enjoyed festivities in the "old Ho'olulu Park days."

Gillmar is clear and candid in the book's preface that Kapi'olani Park is Honolulu's equivalent of New York City's Central Park. Never purchased by the City of Honolulu, the park property was made available by King Kalākaua from Crown Lands and continues to be regulated as a charitable trust under the original Act 53 of 1896.

Archibald Scott Cleghorn, an early designer of the park, envisioned a setting of peaceful pastoral scenery and a venue for leisurely recreation, such as carriage riding, casual strolling, and, of course, horse racing.

King Kalākaua's appointees were often partners in business or relatives of the king through marriage. These men shared the king's love for good horses and his passion for horse racing, yet their support for the development of Kapi'olani Park was underscored by broad public spirit.

Kapi'olani Park Association assumed control of the park in late 1876. It could hardly be described as a park, as the undeveloped land varied from sandy plains to swampy wetlands. Early work was limited to dredging and drainage, road building, and tree planting. By 1884, the racetrack, grandstand, and stables were turned over to the Hawaiian Jockey Club for management and maintenance under a mutual agreement. In 1896, the Honolulu Park Commission (HPC) assumed management of Kapi'olani Park. The HPC was a public agency tasked with the legislative mandate to operate the park as recreational grounds for all of O'ahu's citizenry. In 1913, the City and County of Honolulu assumed jurisdiction over Kapi'olani Park and manages the facility to the present day.

The Kapi'olani Park Association succeeded admirably in developing a first-class one-mile racetrack, the crowning piece in the design of the entire park. Within the racing oval was the massive outdoor polo field that was virtually

{ **10.2** } *An unidentified polo team awaits competition at Kapi'olani Park. Note the Native Hawaiian player second from left.*

lined—first with carriages and later cars—on tournament days. More than adequate stabling and jockey/trainer cottages provided support to both the racing and polo interests.

There was a dark decade in the history of the park, when the military chose to bivouac inside the racing oval. Shortly after the United States annexed Hawai'i (1898), members of the First New York Voluntary Infantry Regiment set up "temporary" encampment at the site, which became known as Camp McKinley. Heavy trafficking of drills, cavalry, supply wagons, and wheeled artillery soon reduced the finely turfed landscape of the area to rutted pathways. Seeking permanent quarters, the military command was rebuffed and evicted by the commission instead. To the credit of the commission, the army was held responsible for restoring the park landscape, including the racetrack turf, after nearly a decade of abuse.

In 1901, the Honolulu Polo Association leased the polo field, and a year later industrialist Walter F. Dillingham arranged for an interisland polo match after forming the Hawai'i Polo and Racing Club. By 1916, Dillingham's influence replaced horse racing with polo as the primary equestrian sport. In 1926, the racetrack was closed and polo served as the sport of the elite, with baseball pressure mounting by the year. The old stables, once leased by the veterinary brothers Leonard and Lloyd Case as the Kapi'olani Park Riding Stables, soon became the Town and Country Stables, operated by O'ahu's premiere horsewoman, Amy Patton Wight Rich.

{ 10.3 } *Considered an anomaly, Ho'olulu Park boasted one of the few circular half-mile race-tracks in America. Running in a constantly turning gait, coupled with muddy track conditions, made jockeying at this track for the brave and hearty.*

Hoʻolulu Park

In 1900, the Hoʻolulu Park racetrack in Hilo was planned as a circular full-mile course. Established by a territorial executive order, the track served as a colorful venue for seventy-one years. Like Kapiʻolani Park and because of its unique and historic nature, the Hoʻolulu Park facility deserves a detailed background.

Act 66 of the Hawaiian Legislative Session of 1886 authorized the minister of the interior to acquire all shore side land between the Wailuku River and Waiākea (beach side) in Hilo for park purposes.

In 1887, a private group proposed a recreational park in Hilo called Seaside Park. Two to three hundred acres were identified in Waiākea, including present-day Coconut Island (Mokuola), Wailoa Park, Reeds Bay, Liliʻuokalani Gardens, and Hoʻolulu Park. More than fifty-five acres of the land were set aside for a racetrack, baseball field, and bicycle path, as well as support buildings such as restrooms, pavilions, horse stalls, and judges' stands.

Without a formal race course, the April 2, 1897, races took place on a sandy straightaway along the shores of Hilo Bay between the Crescent City Cracker Company and Waiākea Bridge.

The half-mile dash was won by Joaquin Carvalho's racer, Dolly, while Jiro Inada, a *luna* (plantation overseer) at Honomū Sugar Company, placed second on his red mare. The purse was $100.

Impatient for government progress on this proposal (Act 66), a group of Hilo businessmen led by Jack R. Wilson in 1899 formed an organization called the Hawaiian Racing Association. Wilson was general manager of the Volcano Stables and Transportation Company, a livery business he had established in 1883.

Wilson selected a 55.36-acre tract of land in Waiākea that was part of the Crown Lands leased by Waiākea Mill Company managed by a good friend, C. C. Kennedy. Wilson optimistically announced that the racetrack and attendant facilities would be ready in time for the 1900 Fourth of July festivities.

Although the final plan called only for a half-mile circular track, Wilson's foresight envisioned a full-mile oval course surrounding the circle, with both finish lines located in front of the grandstands. In failing health, Wilson never completed the oval mile track, but the circular half-mile course may well be a historic one of a kind in the United States.

{ 10.4 } *Unidentified* paniolo *at Hoʻolulu Racetrack.*

{ 10.5 } *Without the support of C. C. Kennedy, Hoʻolulu Park Racetrack would never have become a reality.*

Wilson loved Hawaiʻi and was thoughtful in naming the racetrack in keeping with Hawaiian tradition. A close friend, George C. Beckley, was a purser on board a steamship of the Wilder Steamship Lines who provided the means for convenient overnight voyages to Hilo during racing season. Hoʻolulu was the name of Beckley's son, and Wilson sought the purser's consent to name the place Hoʻolulu Park. Beckley agreed, and the name lasted over a century. In Hawaiian tradition, Hoʻolulu was the name of one of two men entrusted to inter the remains of Kamehameha I, committed to keeping its location secret by sacrificing their own lives in the process.

The grand opening of Hoʻolulu Park in 1900 marked the beginning of a seventy-one year history of horse racing, polo, and rodeo at this historic location. The park served the community of the Big Island in a broader spectrum as home to baseball, football, golf, boxing, soccer, auto and motorcycle racing, demolition derbies, and military drills.

In 1902, Hoʻolulu Park featured its first polo match, which was held between horse races. The Blue Team of Prouty, Gerard, Grace, and Robinson outplayed the Pinks manned by W. Baldwin, R. Balding, Scott, and Kennedy.

1903 brought the Grand Congress of Cowboys, Hoʻolulu Park's first genuine rodeo, with steer roping and bronc riding. A Maui roper named Mahi took the roping honors with a 49.5-second run.

The rules below, published for the bronc-riding event, were uniquely Hawaiian in nature, but more importantly they reflected the seriousness of competition and the need for regulation:

> a. The riding shall be done with a clean saddle to be furnished by the rider. Said saddle shall be without roll, bucking straps, knee pads or other fittings to hold the rider in place.
>
> b. No tying of stirrups will be allowed, either by the Hawaiian "Kaulahele" or otherwise.
>
> c. No bridle or bits are to be used on the horses. Hackamore or punuku may be used, provided it is not arranged so as to shut off the wind of the horse.
>
> d. In passing judgment on the skill of the various riders, the judges will consider adversely[:]
>
> - Taking hold of the saddle in any way.
> - Holding on by the spurs.
> - Aggressive or harsh treatment of the horse. If a horse will not buck without harsh treatment, another will be furnished. (Subica 2008, 155)

Interestingly, the terms *kaula hele* and *pūnuku* are symbolic of the influence of the *ʻōlelo kanaka* on *paniolo* life. While Bob Pestana of Kapāpala Ranch and Levi Kaiako of Molokaʻi Ranch were finalists, the former bronc rider's exceptional final ride declared him champion Bronc Buster of the Territory of Hawaiʻi and winner of the $100 purse.

The judges for the rodeo were listed as Prince Cupid (David Kalākaua), Robert Horner (Kūkaʻiau Ranch), and Frank Woods (Kahuā Ranch).

A special feature of the July 4, 1907, races was moving the prized Primo Cup Trophy from Honolulu's Kapiʻolani Park raceway to Hoʻolulu Park. To further spur competition, the Hawaiian Jockey Club put up a $1,000 purse for a single race.

The featured race was the mile-and-a-quarter Hilo Merchant's Stake, in which George Richardson's Lazell won the purse. The mile-and-a-half Free for All Race was won by a horse named Fidia, owned by J. T. Moir, who took home the Primo Cup and $150 in cash.

On July 30 of the same year, a genuine grudge match occurred that was dubbed the Pepper Race. Ikeda, proprietor of Hilo Shoyu Factory, challenged Suefuji to a half-mile race, granting the latter a fifty-four-foot lead at the starting line. Over $400 was at stake when the flag dropped. Charlie was the Ikeda jockey and Nakamura rode for Suefuji. As the Ikeda horse neared the one-eighth mile post, Nakamura thrust a handkerchief of paprika in the face of Charlie and his horse causing them to retreat, but only momentarily, when they were "peppered" again. The Suefuji mount won the race under severe protest. Suefuji and Nakamura were arrested and charged with malicious injury. Nakamura claimed the "red powder" was used for his "back pain" and no harm was intended. He was fined $100.

While steer-roping competition was held on other islands, Eben Low's efforts to promote full rodeo (roping and riding) competition in the territory were heroic. In 1905 and 1907, he promoted Wild West rodeo shows on O'ahu. His seminal rodeo campaign trip to Cheyenne, Wyoming, in 1907 cemented his place in Hawai'i's history as the "Father of Early Rodeo." It was after the Cheyenne trip that same year that he produced the Honolulu rodeo venue, inviting his Wyoming counterpart Angus McPhee to enter Hawaiian competition, sealing a brotherly bond between the two territories that has passed a century mark in history.

In February 1908, Low rented Ho'olulu Park for a day and produced the first Wild West Show for Big Island fans.

{ 10.6 } *Despite being one armed, Eben Low enjoyed competing in steer roping.*

{ 10.7 } *Angus McPhee, befriended by Eben Low leading up to the 1907 Cheyenne Frontier Days, came to the Islands as part of the O'ahu Wild West Show, and later the following year he made Hawai'i his home.*

{ 10.8 } *A revered cattleman, Joe Correia's way with horses was equally remarkable. Even in his senior years as foreman of Kūka'iau Ranch, obstinate broncs were turned over to him for schooling. His gentle manner salvaged many good horses for a lifetime of work.*

Low featured rodeo entrants Johnny Winters and Angus McPhee, past world champions of the Cheyenne Frontier Days Rodeo, "the Daddy of 'em All." Competing alongside local rodeo hands, the Cheyenne cowboys enjoyed the event schedule, which included steer roping, bronco busting, fancy trick roping, a stagecoach holdup, barrel racing, a maverick branding contest, a wild horse race, and wild steer riding, with horse racing between each feature.

In a press interview after the February show, Angus McPhee made an interesting comparison of rodeo stock: "The Wyoming steer isn't in it with the Hawaiian breed as the Hawaiian steer is a tough customer to throw and keep down after he is thrown. The Hawaiian steer is capable of climbing trees and [they] were quick on their feet as cats and even when thrown would bounce up again like a rubber ball."

On the Fourth of July weekend of the same year, the Hawaiian Jockey Club sponsored a Wild *Paniolo* Show at Hoʻolulu Park that drew twenty-seven steer ropers. While entries came from top ropers such as Ikua Purdy, Archie Kaaua, Joe Correia (Kūkaʻiau Ranch), and Billy Spencer, first place went to fifteen-year-old Kahuā Ranch cowboy William Paul Mahinauli Akau, followed by James Umaumakea Stevens of Kūkaʻiau Ranch and Maikaʻi Kailikini of Kahoʻolawe Ranch.

By 1909, Hilo had gained territory-wide acclaim as the center of horse racing. Key leaders were John O'Rourke and Felix Brughelli. Trotting matches became common. A stallion named Frolic, owned by O'Rourke (later owned by Sam Parker Sr.), was eventually purchased by Parker Ranch. Under the guidance of A. W. Carter in producing fine Thoroughbreds, Frolic became a noted sire of military remount and polo horses during World War I.

In 1911, Al Ruddle became the preeminent Ford dealer on the Big Island as owner of Ruddle Sales and Service, but during his early years he was employed by Volcano Stables and Transportation Company. On February 11, 1911, Ruddle promoted an automobile and motorcycle race day. Of interest was the third event, challenging his Buick against Ollie Shipman's horse, "JT." Shipman's mount was off to an early lead but lost to Ruddle in the half-mile race in a photo-finish. Ruddle took home the trophy and a lot of pride.

By 1912, purses paid out at Hoʻolulu Park peaked at $2,000. This growth came about due to the skilled private party management of the park as well as the racing administration. Furthermore, races were featured to attract interest from different ethnic groups and careers. At the July 4, 1912, event, races were broken down into Japanese-owned, Portuguese-owned, *luna*-owned, and even Hawaiian-bred (*kanaka*) horses.

The 1912 races marked the end of great horse racing at Hoʻolulu Park, as management was turned over to the County of Hawaiʻi. The 55.36-acre lease of Crown Land making up Hoʻolulu Park was also turned over to the county. In 1913, the facilities were torn down. In the ensuing seven years, Hoʻolulu Park became overgrown with weeds, sparking community interest in cleaning up the facility.

On July 4, 1919, horse racing returned to a limited degree. Without privately raised purse money, only local horses showed their stuff. By 1920, things reached comedic proportions when the county offered fifty-pound bags of rice as purses: two bags for first place and one for second place at the New Year's Day races.

Often, other racing associations incorporated racing to add to the color of Hoʻolulu Park activities. In 1929, the Hilo Racing Association arranged a New Year's Day meet that combined eight horse races, four foot races, and one bicycle race. The latter course started at the Olaʻa Courthouse and ran on into Hilo, finishing with two laps around the Hoʻolulu Circle. George Menino passed Wing Kong Chong in a final sprint of a four-lap footrace.

The featured horse race of the day was the four-man relay heat on a two-lap course. Winning the race was the Kūkaʻiau team, made up of borrowed riders, mostly Hilo boys: Henry Vasconcellos, John Vincent, Antone Pacheco, and Fred Branco (Laupāhoehoe).

In the early 1930s, women riders entered the scene, prompted by a Ladies Race sponsored by the Hilo Jockey Club. On New Year's Day, 1931, Mrs. Henry Lai Hipp (later known as Anna Perry-Fiske) won the race on a horse named Kaʻala. Another celebrity jockey was none other than Ouida Hill, wife of William Doc Hill, who later became a prominent territorial senator and was an early proponent of horse racing at Hoʻolulu Park.

As a Hilo resident during these early years, Anna established a riding academy at Hoʻolulu Park open to all interested riders, including youngsters. Her role, however, was somewhat reflective of Hilo high society, and her horses were classic, well-mannered mounts purchased from Parker Ranch.

By 1934, women began serving in administrative capacities. Mrs. Winifred McKaig and Mrs. A. G. Correa served as secretary and treasurer, respectively, of

{ 10.9 } *Fannie "Pane" Purdy Stevens. Without the fanfare of other contenders, she was one of the finest Native Hawaiian horsewomen that Hawai'i ever produced.*

the Ho'olulu Jockey Club. Other women jockeys such as Rhoda J. Carvalho joined Anna in winning races over their male counterparts. A noted lady jockey of Waimea, Fanny Purdy Stevens, was a genuine threat in open races on or off the track.

Emerging as a major force in restoring horse racing to a paying basis for owners, trainers, grooms, and jockeys was a tall, flamboyant high school principal, William J. "Bill" Nobriga.

By 1936, Nobriga had established the Big Island Jockey Club on a sound and geographically inclusive basis. This attracted horse enthusiasts from Ka'ū, Hāmākua, Waimea, and Kohala. Succeeding him in a leadership role was Ronald von Holt of Kahuā Ranch, who often sponsored cowboy relay races featuring legendary Kohala horsemen such as William Akau, Peter Kainoa, John Iokepa, and Henry Rafael.

Bill Nobriga is credited with placing *pā'ū* riding (parade riding in long, flowing skirts representative of each island and its colors) on a competitive basis. While Anna won the contest featured at the 1937 Kamehameha Day races at the park, Nobriga's stunningly beautiful wife, Mercedes, placed a close second. Judges for the *pā'ū* riders were Princess Kekau Kawananakoa (O'ahu), Herbert Shipman (Hilo), and Harold F. Rice (Maui). To Nobriga's credit, the family tradition of *pā'ū* riding has carried on well into the new millennium and often features his granddaughters and great-granddaughters in classic regalia.

Another prominent name that emerged from Ho'olulu Park history is DeSilva. John DeSilva gained popularity as the perennial jockey, trainer, and riding instructor, and he actually lived in a stall at Ho'olulu Park. His older brother Frank was not only a fine horseman of equal stature but sired several sons with like skills, including Frank Jr., Ernest, and James Richard "Casey" DeSilva. Frank senior was also a dapper figure among the ladies, developing the nickname "The Sheik," which was readily given an Azorean twist to "Sheiking."

The outbreak of World War II put a damper on horse racing. In February 1946, the Big Island Jockey Club scheduled a fourteen-heat race card, half

{ 10.10 } *Anna Perry-Fiske in full* pāʻū *regalia passes before the judge's stand at Hoʻolulu Park.*

of which were canceled due to heavy rains causing sloppy track conditions. The race of the day was won by a Carl Meyer–owned Parker Ranch–bred race horse named Mamao, garnering a $1,000 cash prize.

The April 1, 1946, tsunami, while devastating Hilo Bay and most of Waiākea, spared Hoʻolulu Park altogether. With the presence of former military housing on site, Hoʻolulu Park provided emergency housing for hundreds of homeless families whose lives were spared from the tsunami, in which 150 lives were lost.

Other Racetracks

In the 1880s, formal races were staged on Maui, at the Koko o na Moku (Bloodlines of the Islands) Racetrack at Kaʻanapali Beach near Lahaina. The track stretched from the present-day Kaʻanapali Beach Hotel to the Westin Maui Resort. Also around 1880, the Kahului Fairgrounds Racetrack was built. While the Koko o na Moku Racetrack was closed after its final races on July 4, 1918, the Kahului Fairgrounds Racetrack enjoyed action into the 1980s.

{ 10.11 } *Although built and rebuilt four times, Parker Ranch's century-old racetrack is a lasting symbol of the ranch's historic leadership in production of fine horses. Taken in 1960, this aerial view shows the breeding facility in the foreground adjacent to the racetrack.*

Parker Ranch's traditional "bush track" was located on Heihei Flats, just a mile west of Pu'u Holoholokū. Through the middle to late 1800s, it was used for breezing (intensive, controlled running) mounts and informal cowboy races. In 1904, Parker Ranch trustee A. W. Carter built a half-mile oval track that was eventually rebuilt of redwood in 1934. In the mid-1960s, at the insistence of owner Richard Smart, the rails were replaced with new materials, requiring frequent repainting in white, which became the norm. Twenty-five years later, livestock manager Robby Hind overhauled the equestrian complex (Paniolo Park) with a new and expansive grandstand, officials stand, and rodeo arena. The race course now sported a quarter-mile straightaway, starting from the southwest corner of the oval and finishing at a line in front of the grandstand. In 1989, the track was again rebuilt, utilizing bright white PVC tubing for the rails

{ 10.12 } *Winning a silver platter for racing honors, a young Donnie DeSilva is mounted on a Parker Ranch Thoroughbred.*

{ 10.13 } *Gold Bryan, a frequent winner at Ho'olulu Park, started on the tracks of Hawai'i before leaving for a successful West Coast career.*

{ 10.14 } *The crowding alley was used for processing mares brought in from the range for hand breeding at the Parker Ranch Race Track and Stables (1960).*

and risers, providing a maintenance-free advantage. With more than thirty years of use, the improved equestrian complex has weathered well and still looks new.

1939 was a banner year for O'ahu racing interests. The O'ahu Jockey Club was incorporated and a new racetrack was built in Kailua in Windward O'ahu. It was used frequently for a decade, especially during World War II for military entertainment. Located between Oneawa and Kainalu Avenues, it was referred to as the "Pineapple Derby." Situated near the present-day location of Kainalu Elementary School, the midfield of the track was used by Japanese watermelon farmers. Hopes were that the O'ahu Jockey Club would rebuild the track into a mile-long course with covered bleachers and a clubhouse, but the war and pressing economic factors dashed the plan.

Pari-Mutuel Betting Fails to Pass

One aspect of horse racing that we believe would have a positive effect on horse activities in the Islands is legalized gambling. Gambling on horse racing is a universal aspect that, when legalized, brings along a profoundly positive economic impact. To some it also brings social corruption and grief, which is the war cry of opponents. Hawai'i is no different than other states where traditionally conservative legislators are strongly influenced by opposing bodies. However, the long history of legalization efforts, coupled with a faltering economy with little in the way of light at the end of the tunnel, keeps the legalization question alive.

{ 10.15 } *The O'ahu Jockey Club scheduled a race meet on Labor Day, 1946, hoping to establish an annual event for the town of Kailua.*

In the 1937 Territorial Legislature, Senator David K. Trask introduced a bill to develop legalized pari-mutuel betting on horse racing. The Trask plan called for seventy-four race meets, the bulk of which would be scheduled at the Kailua Racetrack on O'ahu, with fourteen divided

{ 10.16 } *Plantation life throughout the Hawaiian Islands often included horse racing, as in this July 4, 1950, race meet in Kahuku, Oʻahu.*

between Hawaiʻi, Maui, and Kauaʻi islands. He proposed a racing board to regulate licensing of owners, trainers, jockey exercise boys, grooms, agents, stewards, judges, timers, and starters. With pari-mutuel wagering, the odds would be established according to the amounts bet on each horse. Trask's bill died a fiery death at the hands of well-organized but somewhat hysterical opposition parties.

In 1951, Representative Manuel Henriques of Kauaʻi submitted another bill to legalize horse race betting on a "County Option" basis. This bill featured a forty-day race meet with a county-appointed race commission that would have regulatory authority, much like the Trask bill. Although the Kauaʻi bill never got far, it would have provided a "trial basis" for pari-mutuel gambling for the rest of the territory to get a feel for it—good or bad.

Not to be ignored, Hilo's own Representative Raymond Kobayashi introduced a bill to legalize betting on horse racing and cockfights. It was a gutsy gamble on Kobayashi's part, given that the 1953 legislature began his first term in office. Unfortunately, it was also his last term, largely explained by his bold initiative.

In 1959, another legislative bill to allow pari-mutuel horse racing on Maui failed in the House of Representatives.

In 1997, Senators Malama Solomon and Joe Tanaka sponsored a bill to have pari-mutuel betting on horse racing become a reality. Targeting neighbor island racetrack venues, their logic was to generate a new economic engine to neutralize the closing of sugar plantations. In 1999, Senate Legislative Bill SB-476 again proposed pari-mutuel horse betting, followed by a 2000 version, SB-2335, that put a five-year trial cap. All three senate bills were set aside, but we have not seen the last of this initiative.

Recent Interest in Horse Racing

In 2012, horse enthusiast Joe Kemple wrote a two-part article published in *Mālama Lio* entitled "Horse Racing in Hawaii—Why Not? The Argument for Bringing the Sport of Kings Back to the Islands."

Horse racing never left the islands, thanks to racetracks like Parker Ranch that spanned an active life over more than a century. The Annual July 4th Race and Rodeo sponsored by the ranch itself is not the only time the racetrack is used for racing. Periodic rodeos also feature matched lengths of quarter and half mile, as well as three-man relay heats.

Gambling at horse races is no more legal than doing so at cockfights, although the latter sport is illegal according to animal protection statutes. Wagering, however, is commonplace at both venues. While cockfights are closely monitored by law enforcement agencies, gaming at the horse racing facility in Waimea suffered only one "bust" by police in its 110-year-old history. Some of Hawai'i Island's most prominent figures were charged with gambling, creating quite a stir in political circles. Charges rendered in a 1980s bust that received media attention named well-known attorneys, former police commissioners, and prominent businessmen and ranchers. Police Chief Guy Paul gained little support for the bust as most folks were comfortable with the innocuous nature of a century-old tradition of friendly wagering of a few bucks on the rare occasions of horse racing in Hawai'i. Paul's efforts to subdue cockfighting gambling, on the contrary, gained him significant support over concerns of underworld involvement.

Kemple's articles took on a more formal and businesslike approach, as the core of his argument was legalized pari-mutuel wagering presented hypothetically within the framework of sustaining Hawai'i's economy. He clearly framed his argument within the published *Hawai'i 2050 Sustainability Plan* and its repetitive call for diversification of the state's economy. Kemple stressed that attracting outside and foreign as well as local investment in the horse industry (agricultural diversification) would generate job training and competitive employment.

Clearly, to attract a racing enthusiast/angel investor of the magnitude necessary to rebuild tracks on O'ahu and Maui, coupled with in-shipment of horses, personnel, and supporting materials such as feed, it would be necessary to legalize pari-mutuel wagering. An effective and informed economic observer would likely conclude that the horse racing industry could help Hawai'i achieve desired sustainability. Achieving legislative support, however, for any formal gambling presents a huge challenge due to strong conservative opposition in Hawai'i. Senators Solomon and Tanaka can certainly attest to this.

With the death of senior Senator Daniel K. Inouye, many leaders, including former governor Ben Cayetano, foresee significant loss of federal funding to the Aloha State. He opined recently that the mood of the legislature may soften on the subject of gambling. Time will tell.

Although Senator Malama Solomon has left the legislature, she is not one to quit. Behind her now is a very bleak state economy with little in the way of innovative thrust for improving it. Senator Solomon, a rancher, continues to be a powerful voice for agriculture, including the sport of rodeo and preservation of *paniolo* culture. No doubt she will go down in Hawai'i's ranching history as an enduring advocate.

Other Hawai'i women left their mark decades ago, earning a place in Hawai'i's horse history for their lasting contributions to Hawai'i's horse programs. The next chapter tells their story.

CHAPTER 11

LEGENDARY HORSEWOMEN

The Amy Rich Story

The story of Amy Rich blends several distinct components: Green Banks of old Hawai'i, early childhood challenges, primary education in Honoka'a, premonition of deaths of loved ones, secondary and tertiary training in England, a nursing career in Southampton and the British Royal Navy, and lastly, after several periodic trips to the Islands, a final home in Hawai'i.

Green Banks

Amy Rich's most cherished memories start with her childhood home at Green Banks in Hālawa, North Kohala. It was there that she rode her first horse, instilling in her a lifelong passion to remain on the back of a fine mount, a species she loved as much as the students she molded into fine horsewomen and horsemen.

Amy was born to Florence Wight (Patton), daughter of Dr. James Wight and Jane Tomkins, in 1890 at Green Banks, a Victorian estate on land that once accommodated a significantly sacred *heiau* (ancient Hawaiian temple). Amy's father, William Henry Patton, a Nebraska native, was related to George S. Patton, who in later history became a noted US Army general and fine horseman. A second daughter was Cara, who together with Amy as Patton siblings provided mutual comfort as tragedy prevailed unmercifully upon the second generation of Wight family members. One such incident occurred in the still of the night, when Amy awoke Cara sharing a dream that their father had succumbed to tuberculosis, away in Nebraska, where their mother had taken him to rest in his native land. The two girls, living with relatives in Honoka'a, learned in the coming days that their father indeed was gone:

Amy's dream had proven prophetic. Amy and Cara returned to live at Green Banks for a few years until their mother moved the family to England.

Interestingly, the death of their grandfather, James Wight, in 1905 at the age of ninety-one, occurred a few years later in a circumstance eerily similar to their own father's death. As with her father's death, Amy foresaw their grandfather's passing and told Cara about it days before the actual word of his passing reached Green Banks, thousands of miles away.

During the years they spent in England, the girls were enrolled in private girls' schools, all the while longing to return to Green Banks. When this finally happened in 1917, Amy was shocked and saddened to witness the seemingly haunted, weathered buildings that were once an elegant Victorian estate.

Native Hawaiian people believe that catastrophic tragedy will befall anyone who disrespects sacred property and the deceased. The elder Wight, while successful in his endeavors, committed grievous missteps in his quest for wealth. In acquiring landholdings, he was not above adverse possession or pressuring indebted *maka'āinana* (commoners) to hand over their land titles at a fraction of their real value. Despite advice to the contrary, Wight coveted, acquired, and altered sacred land that held *heiau* (pre-Christian places of worship), boldly disrespecting native tradition. Even his own family suffered from his driving ambition, and at one point he disowned one of his sons for marrying a Native Hawaiian woman; later, he disowned a son-in-law for the simple act of trimming a hibiscus hedge without his explicit permission.

Familial Premonitions—General Patton's Death

Mortal premonitions seem to be an inherent Patton family trait. Ruth Ellen, second daughter of General Patton, in her memoirs, *The Button Box: A Daughter's Loving Memoir of Mrs. George S. Patton,* wrote that at the moment of her father's death, she awoke in a dream with her father in plain view, fully uniformed at the foot of her bed, flashing a sweet smile. Elder sister Beatrice, when called by Ruth Ellen, described an eerily similar experience. She was awakened from a sound sleep by a ringing bedside telephone in the middle of the night. Despite a static-riddled connection, she heard her father's voice asking, "Little Bee, are you alright?" When she anxiously called the overseas operator to reconnect, she was informed that no such call had been made to her number. (Trotten 2005)

Akua Nānā

Akua nānā, a Hawaiian expression meaning that the gods are watching, became a common reference to Wight's way of life. Some *maka'āinana* say that he sired thirteen children, while others refer to a dozen. In either case, six of these children did not live beyond childhood. The only two sons (with ten sisters) born of this union were also forsaken—one by death in a horse accident and the other by disinheritance.

Sheltered from this heinous disrespect of Hawaiian cultural beliefs, Amy grew up dutifully proud of her grandfather and was unaware that the final disposition of her beloved home, Green Banks, was by adverse possession by the federal government. While a Wight descendant had purchased the estate and sold it for a modest profit, it later became a central focus for drug trafficking, and the land was forfeited. Hopefully, the tragedy surrounding Green Banks has finally run its course.

Fortunately for Amy, Green Banks instilled warm memories of happy times, and it provided her first introduction to a life with horses that she cherished for her entire lifetime. Her mother's insistence that she receive a professional education also significantly impacted the course Amy's life would take. Both her love of horses and a professional education served Amy well. Educated in England and Germany, Amy became a registered nurse after attending Royal S Hands School of Nursing in Southampton, and she later served as a nurse in the British Royal Navy. Married in Bournemouth in 1915 to army officer and British banker John Rich, Amy continued her nursing career while still managing periodic trips home to Honolulu. On one of these treks home in 1931, she learned of the death of her husband—this time with no premonition or warning of his pending demise.

Amy remained in England for a few years, continuing to train show horses and young hunter mounts in her own ring. By 1936, however, the foreboding war clouds over Britain beckoned her home to the Islands. Between 1937 and 1938, she found time to exercise the many polo ponies of the Hawai'i Polo and Racing Club at Kapi'olani Park, all the while yearning for an opportunity to teach horsemanship. Fortuitously, she was in the right place at the right time, when her keen eye witnessed a schooling session underway at the Town and Country Stables across from Kapi'olani Park. Amy observed young horsemanship students of an exasperated Dr. Lloyd Case bawling in disarray and offered to help Case teach his young charges. She probably knew in her heart that she was now home for good.

In addition to assuming teaching chores, Amy lent a skilled hand managing the stables, first as a partner to Case, then eventually owner when the horse practitioner moved back to the East Coast. By 1939, her caseload of anxious young riders filled the afternoon and summer schedules, rewarding Amy with deep satisfaction that her place in life was finally found: caring for horses she cherished and nurturing youths toward a lifetime of appreciation for God's noble creature. Her student clientele spanned seven to seventeen years of age, with skill levels ranging from fearful novice to polished show rider.

By 1941, the war years became an overwhelming force, affecting the lives of

{ 11.1 } *A highly disciplined horsewoman, Amy Rich dedicated her life's career to teaching generations of young O'ahu riders from novice to senior status.*

Town & Country Stables

TWELFTH ANNUAL HORSE SHOW

MRS. A. W. RICH
MRS. ALICE HOLBROOK

JUDGES:
LIEUTENANT-COLONEL PAUL L. JOLLEY, G.S.C.
COLONEL MILES SUMNER, U. S. Army, Ret.

1:00 P.M. Saturday, May 28, 1949
POLO FIELD • KAPIOLANI PARK
HONOLULU, T. H.

• • •

Aloha! to Alice Holbrook who is leaving us in June

{ 11.2 } *Town and Country Stables 12th Annual Horse Show (1949), an Amy Rich show honoring Mrs. Alice Holbrook and judged by military officers.*

everyone in Hawai'i, especially O'ahu's populace. Recreational and organized sports activities were rare or nonexistent, as the available parks and fields now served the military.

Many of these servicemen were seasoned horsemen, ranging from East Coast polo players to Rocky Mountain ranch hands. Regardless of the persuasion, to a man they found comfort among the spacious breezeways and shed rows of the Town and Country Stables, managed by a horsewoman who was sensitive to the servicemen's need to be among horses they loved just as dearly. Although much of their conduct was astride a horse, the servicemen's desire to serve the stables in performing various chores such as grooming, shoeing, and doctoring brought reciprocal benefit to Amy, who was struggling to keep her stable operation a going concern during those troubled times. Some of her cherished mementoes of the war years and the appreciative soldiers became part of her daily apparel, such as a carved leather belt and a silver horse shoenail keeper for her four-in-hand necktie.

By war's end, she estimated that approximately 85,000 servicemen enjoyed the riding pleasure of her large stable of mounts. Besides her own horses, several clients boarded horses with Amy, as did some of the military's strings. All of them enjoyed her special care with patriotic fervor. As is common practice at war's end, military mounts of no further use were put down, and Amy understandably mourned their demise.

With the war years behind her, she rebuilt the riding school curriculum of the Town and Country Stables with renewed zest. Serving as many as 120 summer students and 140 regular school year students, she depended on a battery of sound mounts that at times numbered over a hundred when boarders' horses were included. A core of twenty-four to thirty horses provided the mainstay core of lesson horses that brought many a child from novice to expert levels of horsemanship.

Amy had a pair of dependable and skilled horsewomen—Mary Frances Evans and Blanche Saure—who served as her able assistants over the years. Breezer Bush and Freddy Gouveia, familiar names in Honolulu circles, served loyally as trainers and farriers. Too numerous to mention are the dozens of support people Amy enjoyed over her thirty-six-year tenure of helping others through horses.

{11.3} *Doggedly persistent in elevating a student's level of horsemanship, Amy Rich was genuine in acknowledging success among her subjects. Here she awards Diana Damon, who later married Antony Smart, son of the owner of Parker Ranch.*

With a weekly schedule of at least six classes and a host of private pupils requiring tutorage, Amy's teaching posture was that of strict martinet in a disciplined environment with a mission of achieving sportsmanship, humane appreciation for animals, and pride in one's ability to master the mount. Learning to mount lightly and quietly in the flat saddle was the early lesson, followed by balancing and control of the horse. A pupil was expected to become adept at walking the horse forward, halting, turning, and backing before cantering was attempted. Students were expected to learn to gait, walk, and trot, as well as bearing the rein. For the novice to learn the mastery of his or her mount was the central theme of her beginners' curriculum, and hundreds of O'ahu youths owed a debt of gratitude to this dedicated lady of the saddle.

In the final years of her tenure at Town and Country Stables, Amy sensed the tenuous nature of her stable location. The City and County of Honolulu had been eying her facility as an ideal venue for expansion of the parking facilities serving Kapi'olani Park.

By 1950, she sold the facility as she looked to Waimānalo to become the home of the New Town and Country Stables, a name she incorporated in partnership with Frances Gibson. The twenty-acre lease has served the facility since 1965, affording a commanding view of the emerald-green Olomana Golf Course and the deep blue ocean beyond. Tucked up against the verdant foothills, the facility expanded to include a complete rodeo facility, the dream location of Bud and Katie Gibson. While English horsemanship and dressage prevail in honor of Amy Rich, so does a wide array of Western riding events, Quarter Horse shows, and, of course, full-blown rodeo activity. To Mrs. Rich's likely delight, the latter events draw the servicemen and women who defend our country with the same patriotic fervor for which she stood more than seventy years ago.

In a fitting tribute, Mrs. Amy Rich was treated to a surprise eightieth birthday gathering at the stables in 1970. By that juncture, she was overseeing instruction for the third generation of her first pupils of the late 1930s era. In former students alone, more than two hundred of them welcomed her arrival with leis, songs, and hearty tribute to the woman who enhanced their lives via the noble steed. Amy Rich died in New Zealand in 1974 while visiting her sister, Mrs. Cara Morgan of Christchurch.

Harriet "Haku" Baldwin

Another great woman of Hawai'i horse circles was "Haku" Baldwin. Born in 1913 to Henry Damon and Gertrude McKinnan, Harriet was the last of four children conceived of that union. Her siblings included Frances, Joan, and Henry. The family homestead was called Pu'ukapu and was located on a ridge of that same name near Fort Shafter, O'ahu. There were two main houses on the estate, one of which was for family, with additional rooms added when a new child was born. Her grandparents, the Samuel Mills Damons, lived on a nearby ridge called Pu'u o Maui. Both ridges overlook Moanalua Valley, and Harriet's early childhood jaunts on horseback covered the countryside, including Red Hill and Pearl Harbor.

A more than decent student at Punahou, Harriet's abiding love of horses made her yearn for the outdoors, sprawling landscapes, and verdant hills. On occasional trips to Maui with the Castle family, Harriet was able to enjoy Maui summers, where life on horseback was more appealing. Upon completion of her education at Punahou and later at Dominican College in California, the debutante returned home, retaining her nickname, "Haku," which originated during her stays on Maui. Because of teasing schoolmates altering her Hawaiianized name "Haleaka" (Hawaiian for Harriet) to "Haleliʻiliʻi" (outhouse), she took the name given her by Chu Baldwin: "Halehaku," a gulch on the road to Hāna that abounds with ancient legends. Within days, the name was reduced to Haku, which she kept throughout her adolescent and adult life. Fittingly, the colloquial use of the word *haku* means "lord," christening a young lady to become an overlord of Maui's prominent horse history. And an overlord she became.

On her summer trips to Maui, much of the time was spent in the Upcountry visiting relatives and friends that were horse enthusiasts. One of her schoolmate friends was her distant cousin Barbara "Ba" Baldwin. Together with the Castles of Olinda, Haku and her Baldwin cousins enjoyed cattle drives, brandings, and *nānāʻāina* (looking over the ranch lands) rides with the cowhands mounted on "haole horses" (gentle mounts reserved for guests). Being around the Baldwin brothers Edward, Chu, and Asa gave Haku a further sense that the family as a whole shared her sense of comfort around horses, the outdoors, and Maui as a home place.

During this era, a teenaged Baldwin "cowboy gang" consisting of Manduke, Chu, Squeak, and Dwight enjoyed the excitement of frequent wild cattle hunts, riding and roping alongside the great ranch hands of that period, led by Ikua Purdy, the legendary world champion steer roper of 1908.

Haku's husband, Richard Holbron "Manduke" Baldwin, was born in 1911 to Samuel A. and Katherine Smith Baldwin, one of five children of the union. Early on, Manduke acquired his nickname in reference to an involuntary introduction to the art of swimming (with tongue-in-cheek reference to famed swimmer Duke Kahanamoku), a moniker that he enjoyed over a long, exciting, and successful life. Just as challenging was his introduction to a life aboard a good horse, which entailed long treks alongside his caring and observant father. Barely seven years of age, Manduke rode through the expansive meadow of Pā Kauhi mounted on his horse Peanuts. Trips through the crater as well as around the ridges of Haleakalā gave him a lasting appreciation for the stamina and surefootedness of ranch horses.

While Baldwin cousins and brothers formed a close-knit core of the future's top polo players, cowboys, ranch managers, and sportsmen in general, Harold Frederick "Oskie" Rice was a pivotal figure in the adventures of talented Maui boys in relationships that endured human tragedy, world wars, and the great depression. Many of these young men were educated at Punahou, Cornell, and Yale and chose to return home for their love of the Islands and rugged ranch life.

Manduke returned from Cornell in the early 1930s to manage the Haleakalā Ranch beef operation and, most significantly, to wed Haku. This union in many

{ 11.4 } *Haku Baldwin dedicated her life's work to the betterment of society through the horse. Her broad array of equine expertise spanned racing, polo, dressage, vaulting, breeding, and training.*

ways was blessed with synergism of the finest order. Their innate and combined spirits, intellectual prowess, physical strengths, athletic natures, and philanthropic dispositions would place the couple clearly above all wedded couples of the territory and state in terms of exemplary progress in the sport horse genre, as well as in the advancement of agricultural and ranching techniques. This would unfold over the coming half century of their matrimonial bond. While this book celebrates Haku for her broad role in advancing horsemanship, it can be said that Hawai'i would likely never have enjoyed the fruits of her work had she not been wholeheartedly supported, counseled, and gently steered by her legendary spouse, Manduke. Like her, he never sought recognition, credit, or notoriety for their synergistic mission of making Hawai'i—Maui, the territory, and the state—better for both man and animal.

Hawai'i's horse history is not without a litany of great men and women over the more than two hundred years of the presence of the noble species. What makes Haku unique is the latitude of disciplines in which she excelled: seven in all, including cowboying, racing, polo, horse breeding, dressage, vaulting, and therapeutic horsemanship.

Cowboy Life

Early in her marriage, Haku readily adapted to the rigors of work on the Haleakalā Ranch. Whether it was cattle drives, brandings, or shipping days, the crew would set out long before daybreak, having already wrangled and saddled horses that were fit for the day's chores. Haku's role on cattle-working days was a participatory, meaningful one; certainly not as a tagalong "boss's wife." Brandings brought about a little more camaraderie over a hearty lunch and short interludes of friendly exchange. Some of the more senior cowboys napped beneath their slickers, while the more energetic engaged in a game of *kamau* (also *keiki lua*), a card game similar to trumps. Haku, on the other hand, preferred to visit about the horses, cattle, calves, or bulls. In light of the ranch's sloping landscape from the mountain to the shore, stamina of the horses was a key element not to be lost from her keen observation. With frequent exposure to cattle work, especially the long and often uphill strain on the horses before reaching the work site, Haku conceived the idea to bring in Arab breeding to restore stamina.

She imported a well-bred Arab stud, Kinohi ("elegant"), to cross on the ranch mares, which provided a genuine boost in cow horse productivity in terms of travel to high-elevation work stations. While the process took seven to eight years for fruition, the half-Arab mounts traveled with greater ease to work and home, but they failed to adapt to corral work due to their fidgety and easily distracted nature. More than likely, however, some of the half-breds enjoyed life on the polo field.

Hot, dirty, and arduous aptly describes shipping days, when the fat cattle were driven down to Kahului for a trip to Honolulu aboard the SS *Humu'ula* or the SS *Hawai'i*. Leaving the ranch about 3 a.m., the market cattle arrived in Kahului before daybreak to await the docking vessel. As boarding time neared, the herd was moved to corrals near Kanahā Pond, while cowboys were treated to Pākē (Chinese) food at Ah Fook Restaurant, a highlight of the day. Kahului Harbor was already deeply drafted, so there was no need to rope, lead, and swim each steer out to a longboat and belly-sling them onto the steamship.

Instead, Maui cattle were loaded out on a sided, wood-cleated ramp that serviced the top deck of the vessel. Following a well-mounted senior cowhand, the cattle, once started, filed aboard the ship for their one-way trip to Honolulu and the Hawai'i Meat Company plant. Almost as much as the Pākē lunch, the men enjoyed the clatter of their horses' shod hooves on the pavement as they started back to their Upcountry home, where the mounts received a cool washdown and vigorous roll over their well-used backs. No doubt Haku' s keen eye sought horse breeding suitable for all purposes, including the heated surroundings of coastal cattle work.

Horse Racing

Haku enjoyed a passion for the speed horse and its place in Hawai'i's horse circles, whether it was Kahului Fairgrounds, Ho'olulu Park, Kapi'olani Park, or the Kailua Racetrack. She was gifted with three values: first was her innate ability to bring out the best in a racehorse without harming it; second was surrounding herself with men who represented the best speed-horse talent in the territory, whether trainers, jockeys, or farriers; and third was her visual assessment of the anatomical features of a horse, enabling her to determine its speed with ease, which endowed her with the seasoned judgment of a Kentucky breeder.

From the Blue Grass State of Kentucky she brought Benny Rollins, a wisp of a man who came with breeding stallions for the Dillinghams, for whom he was to work as a jockey. Haku lured Rollins over to the Valley Isle, where he was blessed with son Benji Rollins, who developed the jockey qualities of his father. Rollins was outfitted with his own stables and bush track for training. Haku already had Harold Amoral on staff, who developed a long-standing, multifaceted career as a training jockey, trainer, conditioner and boss of grooming and feeding. Along with a youthful George Manoa, polo enhanced the value of the men Haku kept at her side.

Racehorses Haku worked were in some cases Haleakalā Ranch owned or the two Parker Ranch speed horses that she and Manduke owned. Eight Parker Ranch broodmares were in the core of Haku's horse-breeding operation that fortunately served the polo cause equally well. The mares were sired by Parker Ranch's best, which speaks to the close relationship of the Baldwins and A. W. Carter and his son Hartwell. Some of the sires were Remount Service stallions, including Harvester, Overall, Ormesby, Rodgers, and Gold Oak. In addition to the mares, the two two-year-old colts (fillies) were purchased for training at the tracks. Blue ribbon breeding of the two speed horses included Herodiones, Moanalua, Opua, and Advanced Guard on sire and distaff sides.

Haku's racing colors were powder blue silk with a rainbow sash, while Haleakalā Ranch's colors were white with blue polka dots. Clarence (Brother) Sakamoto was first line jockey, and by this time young Benji Rollins was the able backup rider. The Maui County Fair in November and the July 4th Races were the top island venues, but Kailua and Kapiʻolani Park tracks often were the turf tracks of Maui's victory horses. By the end of the 1940s, Maui's Kahului facility was abandoned and demolished, leaving polo as a sport of choice for Haku's energies.

Haku and Polo

Intimately aware of her husband's prowess on the polo field, Haku took the supportive role for his favorite pastime by managing his string of horses and guiding the breeding program to produce prospects. The setup could not have been better, with ample stabling, great staffing, an exercise track, a small polo field, and spacious, rolling hills for aerobic exercise for the polo ponies. Much of the preparation was for the Honolulu polo tournaments, which from early on were played at the Kapiʻolani Park field.

A young Johnny Sakamoto took Manduke's polo horses on Saturdays to the Pukalani polo field, which was the venue for weekend tournaments leading up to the Oʻahu fields where Hawaiʻi's greatest went into head-to-head combat on the field. Francis Iʻi Brown, Harold K. Castle, Walter F. Dillingham, Walter MacFarland, Arthur H. Rice, and Harold F. Rice filled the rosters of the Oʻahu and Maui teams in the early years.

Another generation (the second) of Maui players gained legendary notoriety as Oskie Rice, Gordon von Tempsky, and Manduke Baldwin stormed the Oʻahu polo fields during annual tournaments and the Shriners Maui/Mexico games at the end of the season. Harold Amoral (pers. comm.) shared that Haku shipped him and his crew to Oʻahu for tournaments, along with seventeen horses for boarding at the Kapiʻolani Park Stables, for seventeen consecutive years. Over a given season, Amoral and George Manoa camped on site in jockey cottages while they managed, under Haku's watchful eye, the feeding, grooming, doctoring, shoeing, and training of the mounts. For the Friday evening tournaments, they ponied the mounts to the Honolulu Stadium in Mo'ili'ili and back to the stables at the end of the games. Short one player in one match, Manduke suited up Amoral, and the Maui cowboys won again.

Haku loved teaching horsemanship, and her polo curriculum was especially designed for the youth. With deserving pride, this brought forth a third generation of both Rice and Baldwin boys to achieve polo honors in college and national polo alike. Harold F. "Freddy" Rice Jr. and Peter Baldwin were merciless in field competition. Along with Peter's brother Ben and another Haku polo product, Stanley Woolaway, the Maui boys under the Cornell banner in 1959 won the National Intercollegiate Championship as well as the National 12 Goal Championships, both staged at the Armory in New York City. Just as significant was Haku's teaching polo to many a young man of the Valley Isle: Sam and Mike Lyons, George "Sonny Boy" Manoa, Allen Sakamoto, and a score of others too numerous to mention.

Son Peter continued to bring polo pride to the Baldwin name into the 1980s in Hawai'i, the mainland, and the down under countries of New Zealand and Australia. Nineteen eighty-seven was a banner year for Haku's son, when the Maui Team won the Pacific Coast Open, the Americas Cup, and the US Handicap, garnering Peter Baldwin the United States Polo Association's "Amateur Player of the Year" award. Haku and Manduke had a lot to be proud of.

Dressage

Just as Haku approached racing and polo with the gusto of the field commander Patton, the highly refined and polished horsewoman methodically emerged as a force in the classical art of horsemanship—dressage.

An underlying principle of dressage, a term derived from the French verb *dresser,* meaning "to train," is based on kindness in making horses safe and pleasurable to ride, a theme dear to Haku's heart.

Developed as part of the education of noblemen, schooling in equitation (horseback riding) was commonplace through the royal courts Europe, including France, Germany, Sweden, Spain, and the Netherlands. As the military influence on dressage developed as a means of competition, Hawai'i was treated to such exposure before, during, and after World War I. Undoubtedly, Haku was a very youthful but observant horse enthusiast who enjoyed the events at Kapi'olani Park when both army officers and their wives and daughters took part in the artful competition of dressage.

With interest waning in horse racing, Haku was able to turn her attention to other genres of horsemanship, and dressage and, later on, vaulting grew to become lasting alternative uses for the fine line of Baldwin horses.

No doubt the Baldwin stables, training spaces, and feed and tack rooms had all the basic elements for gradual conversion from a racing and polo center to a facility for the refined, genteel, disciplined art of dressage. Clearly envisioning a standalone equestrian center, however, Haku set out to locate property that had the amenities of convenient access, appropriate topography and drainage, and moderate rainfall while appealing to the eye. Starting with a twenty-two-acre verdant hollow in Makawao in 1967, Haku set out to convert the former chicken-processing plant and horse farm of Dennis DeCoite into the remarkably popular Maui Horse Center. But it didn't happen overnight.

Always aware of the need for access to veterinary services, Haku invited newly established veterinary practitioner Ted Cleghorn to become part of the equestrian complex. By 1972, Cleghorn had converted the sturdily built but utilitarian chicken plant into an attractive veterinary hospital serving both small and large animal patients. Over the past four decades, Makawao Veterinary Clinic has led the island of Maui's quest for top-flight veterinary services, with unabashed appreciation of Haku's foresight expressed by the congenial founder, Dr. Ted Cleghorn.

Armed with convenient animal health services, Haku converted outbuildings for utility use while building state-of-the-art prefabricated horse barns. An existing home was partially converted to a temporary office, while permanent business headquarters were furnished at the *makai* end of a large horse barn.

Horse paddocks and runs sprang up surrounding the headquarters. A large dressage field was graded and turfed in an area that was remote from main traffic and conveniently placed within the bounds of an existing rectangle of an old stand of trees that gave the appearance of long-term existence. The field was nestled beneath the footing of a significant ridge named Kalama Hill, affording protection from the trade winds. Given the periodic deluge of Kona rainstorms, the property was afforded appropriate grading to accommodate heavy drainage while safeguarding the topographic landscape.

Riding lessons became the mainstay in the afternoon and weekends. Full-day summer camps were increasingly dependent on a core of ably trained volunteers, as the novice riders gradually approached dressage training standards. While some of the horses were privately owned, Haku maintained a string of lesson horses that safely launched many youths toward a career in professional horsemanship.

A turning point in Haku's attention to dressage came in 1972, when she attended the Equestrian Olympics in Munich, Germany. Germany was emerging as the "Vatican of Dressage" for its supreme domination of the sport through its system of riding, training, and breeding of their mounts. Accompanying Haku was Tom Poulin, a seasoned authority in the world of dressage. Poulin's influence on Haku's development of the sport at the Maui Horse Center (MHC) was matched by another noted rider and former Olympian, Inez Propfe-Credo. Over the ensuing four decades, spending alternative months at the MHC, Poulin and Propfe-Credo helped Haku propel the Maui institution to become the premiere dressage center of the Pacific.

Haku Baldwin as a Veterinary Client

In 1967, a young veterinarian arrived on the Maui scene. Skilled in both small and large animals, Dr. Ted Cleghorn, an O'ahu native, was welcomed on the Valley Isle for his skills, especially in horse medicine and surgery, competence that had been sorely missed on Maui since Dr. J. C. FitzGerald retired from practice thirty years before.

About the time Dr. Cleghorn was actively looking for an appropriate location for a veterinary facility, Haku had already acquired Makawao property for her planned horse center. Maui's animal care of the finest order was born when Haku offered him a venue for his practice, which led to the establishment of the Makawao Veterinary Clinic.

The synergy of a highly qualified, broadly trained practitioner and a prominent horsewoman whose life's mission was the betterment of mankind through her beloved species, the horse, generated profound enhancement of the Valley Isle as a special place to live on multiple levels: a great place to live and work, raise a family, care for animals, steward the land, and cherish the landscape.

In a 2012 interview, Dr. Cleghorn shared his memories of what made Haku a special client in addition to being a great lady. First was her practical nature, in which therapy for her horses was based on reasonable care, expenditure, and after care, seeking a healing outcome. There were many examples that he cited, but two stood out. When enthusiastic therapy yielded minimal results, she would defer to "Dr. Green," which was her way of suggesting that the horse be turned out on good pasture for extended rest and let nature take its own course and time. Her other grasp of practical care was her willingness to put down (euthanize) a horse when the quality of life and prognosis was dismal. Her willingness to bid farewell to some of her most beloved mounts took courage and was an expression of love and humane care for her animals in its purest sense.

Client compliance with a recommended regimen of treatment has great bearing on the outcome. Dr. Cleghorn prescribed protocols of treatment for a plethora of conditions over the span of more than three decades. With utmost confidence in her veterinarian, Haku followed his recommendations in exacting detail. Despite the knowledgeable and influential position she held in the highest horse circles, she never tried to second-guess Dr. Cleghorn's judgment or try to impose her ideas or knowledge upon him. Instead, she set her mind in dedicated attention to what were sometimes highly complicated regimens that in turn yielded consistently productive outcomes. The strength of this mutually respectful and long-standing relationship reaped rewards for the patient, the owner, and her veterinarian. To this day, Dr. Cleghorn speaks highly of his special client-cherishing memories of the times they worked together.

Haku, the Good Sport

The equestrian component of the 1972 World Olympics set the golden standard for equestrian competition, a fact evident today, more than forty years later.

Haku's quest to elevate Hawai'i's dressage events to as high a level as was practical led her to attend this premier global event. She was accompanied by Tom Poulin; Terry Tugman, an O'ahu equestrienne; and Dr. Billy Linfoot, a noted California veterinarian and polo enthusiast. While most performances were open to the public, the final performance was by invitation for a select few. Poulin and Linfoot, both nationally recognized, were among the invitees on the short list. Aware of how disappointed Haku would be to miss the finals after coming all this way, Linfoot executed a plan. Borrowing plaster of Paris from a colleague, he fashioned a lower body cast for her and commandeered a wheelchair for the venerable horsewoman, wheeling her through entry gates without incident. Once inside, personnel showered her with sympathy and attention for her recuperation from a "severe horse accident," even providing the trio with a front-row box seat to review the Olympic equestrian finals.

After the event, Linfoot deftly removed the two-part body cast, snugly held together with bands of vet-wrap, while Haku selected fashionable attire for a gala evening dinner. The threesome cherished their memory of the Olympic finals, made possible by a resourceful veterinarian and friend.

{11.5} *Harold Amoral (left), Haku's right-hand man, confers with Dr. Billy Linfoot, internationally known veterinarian and polo player. Both men were close associates of Haku Baldwin.*

Poulin was drawn to dressage through his appreciation of classical art, fascinated by the ability of a horse and rider in composing an art form in motion. With early training in Canada in the mode of Spanish dressage technique, he went on to become associated with the American Dressage Institute (ADI) at Skidmore College in Saratoga Springs, New York. Haku soon became a member of the ADI under the mentorship of Poulin, who described her as "a horsewoman who never lost her love for learning, while being a quiet enduring visionary with the life mission of exposing Maui's youth to horses" (pers. comm.).

Inez Propfe-Credo also came to MHC with excellent credentials, one of which was coaching the Brazil Dressage Team in the Pan American Games.

The onsite cottage at MHC provided convenient housing, as Poulin and Propfe-Credo alternated training months. For the student horsewomen, the mildly contrasting teaching styles of the pair of instructors served to broaden their riding horizons and not conflict with them.

Haku loved her own special mounts—an Illinois warmblood gelding, Sir Charles, and a mare named Indigo. Later through Poulin she acquired another warmblood, Talisman, whose registered name was Bacchus (the god of wine). Talisman was the final mount of her life. She built a new indoor arena and named the building Talisman Hall in his honor.

Schooling shows alternated with formal dressage competition, with teaching being the mission of the former and judging of the latter for the pair of mainland dressage authorities.

The unique theme of the MHC dressage program is continuity of advancement. While the most basic dressage riders could have remained at a comfortable level of competence, achieving advancement seemed to be nearly uniform among the core of participants. This progressive attitude was largely due to the repetitive monthlong alternative sessions provided by Poulin and Propfe-Credo, underwritten by Haku. Riders could move beyond basic-level testing to freestyle tests, where they could develop their own ground pattern that included all the required movements of that level to achieve marking by the judges. In the freestyle to music test, additional marks could be gained by artistic interpretation, choreography, and choice of musical accompaniment.

While riders were able to show their mounts in a variety of paces, it was the rhythm and regularity of paces that the authorities looked for. A variety of movements, including lateral work, flying changes, pirouettes, the passage, and the piaffe were components of the Grand Prix and the Grand Prix Special Tests. The progressive nature of the MHC program became evident in the performance of Nicki Weber-Wales and Susan Brookover in one of these events. Weber-Wales rode Haku's mount Sir Charles, receiving a 60.73 percent rating for her ride, followed by Brookover riding Belle Goddess, who earned a 57.7 score for their efforts.

Despite advancing age keeping her from being on horseback, Haku's devotion to developing dressage as a horse sport never waned through her twilight years. While the mentor Propfe-Credo is sorely missed, Poulin has continued the periodic MHC trips through the years, keeping the spirit of Haku alive and well.

Vaulting

Simply described, vaulting is essentially gymnastics on horseback. Like dressage, the sport originated in European cavalry schools. However, the modern version of the sporting event was not recognized as an international sport until the early 1980s. In Hawaiʻi equestrian circles, the event was readily acknowledged as complementary to dressage due to Haku's influence. She believed that both vaulting and dressage developed a rider's sense of balance and increased confidence while aboard a horse.

Vaulting was successfully established in American horse circles through horse clubs that supported this event, along with other equestrian activities like dressage. The Maui Horse Center provided a natural setting where, under Haku's guidance, excellent facilities, personnel, and access to appropriate horses were available.

Haku knew that there were specific qualities and characteristics that made a good vaulting horse. Not many fit the bill for conformation, attitude, gait, and training features; she selected only the top equine candidates from her broad array of horses. Finding horses that stood between fifteen and seventeen hands was a mild challenge compared to finding desirable qualities such as long backs that were strong and broad and croups that were wide and flat—all uncommon conformations among Maui horses. Vaulting horses needed good flesh cover, which was never an issue at the Maui Horse Center. More than adequate flesh cover made an otherwise bony back into a comfortable "exercise mat" for both the vaulter and the horse.

Breeding and purchasing ideal vaulting mounts were well-used alternatives for finding steeds of the right conformation and temperament. While vaulting prospects can be found in any breed, horses six years or older are preferred as social maturity is usually well established by this age. Geldings are preferred over mares, while stallions are out of bounds for obvious reasons.

Because most vaulters are youthful, Haku selected "bombproof" horses that exhibited consistently good character, especially around children. These horses need to be comfortable while being extensively longed—cantering in a thirty- to fifty-foot circle around a longeur. The longeur is the attendant with a flat, nylon longe line attached to the mount's snaffle bit that controls the horse. A vaulting horse needs to be comfortable with one, two, and sometimes three riders on his back doing acrobatics to musical accompaniment while the horse canters in cadence. A steady rhythmic, balanced canter was another characteristic Haku sought in selecting vaulting mounts.

Haku, together with her circle of horse enthusiasts and capable, experienced volunteers, soon had a vaulting

{11.6} *With encouragement and support from Haku, Jan Marrack brought dressage and vaulting to the Big Island. She is pictured with her Hawai'i Preparatory Academy charges in Waimea along with Dona Singlehurst, certified tester. Front row left to right: Dona Singlehurst, Julie Marrack, Jenny Hewitt, Sheena Rice, Celesty Levy. Back row: Chris O'Kieffe, Cara Cadwallader, Katie Robertson, Jan Marrack.*

program up and running. Vaulting events require a lot of qualified hands to assist the longeur, who controls the longe line while using verbal commands to control the mount.

Haku's inspiration in developing dressage and vaulting was not limited to the island of Maui. In Hilo, Hawai'i, she found a very enthusiastic protégé in Big Island horsewoman Jan Marrack.

Residing in Hilo in the 1970s, Marrack staged much of her horse activities at Pana'ewa Equestrian Center. Her work with aspiring young horsewomen included daughters Lisa and Julie, who brought aboard their horse-loving friends Dawn Dawrs, Kristi Lundborg, Jan Willocks, and Christy Lassiter.

Haku Baldwin was influential in reaffirming Marrack's life interest in dressage, inspiring her to pass this experience on to the next generation. Marrack was fortunate to have not only the right facility and appropriately mannered horses but a cadre of attentive, athletic, and dedicated young ladies.

Barely underway with a dressage regime, Marrack hosted another visit from Haku. This time Haku handed her a vaulting surcingle and a firm command: "Get going with vaulting, Jan!"

By 1977, Marrack and her equestrian maidens blessed Hilo with both forms of advanced horsewomanship, providing tutorship to a broad circle of interested parties. The Orchid Isle Vaulting Club (OIVC) was born.

Marrack's desire to offer more expertise and coaching technique to club members led her to England and Germany in 1977. With the enhanced techniques she acquired, she took the Hilo team to advanced performance levels, using graduated standards of improvement. Her exposure to German horsemanship paid added dividends when in 1978, ten young vaulters from Germany accompanied by their coach Paul Lorenz paid an extended visit to the Orchid Isle and its vaulting club. Hosted by Haku Baldwin on both the Big Island and Maui, members of the distinguished Stuttgart Riding Club (SRC) were treated to vaulting experiences as well as camping with Orchid Isle Vaulting Club members at scenic Kahuku Ranch on the southern coast of the island of Hawai'i. This was a memorable experience cherished by the team from Germany. Members of the OIVC were also rewarded by being exposed to excellent dressage and vaulting techniques. The Stuttgart Team had been Germany's acclaimed National Champion Vaulting Team for the previous five years.

{11.7} *Haku Baldwin's Maui Animal Aloha Center logo aptly reflects the effective role of animals large and small bringing joy to those in need. No other horseman or horsewoman in Hawai'i has left a more lasting legacy as a humanitarian through her multiple resources and expertise as well as her genuine love and care for horses and children.*

Marrack's dressage and vaulting efforts were enduring, as three decades later the Pana'ewa Equestrian Center has continued to be the venue for such events. In 2013, the Hawai'i Dressage and Eventing Association conducted a successful Hunter Schooling Show and Fun Day. Haku would be proud of her inspired protégé Jan Marrack's lasting influence on Hawai'i's youth.

Haku went out of her way in extending Hawaiian hospitality to the SRC, as her Maui vaulting team had successfully competed in Munich the year before. Ever the advocate, she arranged for a Honolulu visit before the SRC returned home. As their official host, Mayor Frank Fasi declared their O'ahu visit "Hawai'i Vaulter's Day" to honor the German equestrian guests. Haku knew how to do it right!

Maui Animal Aloha Center

The pinnacle of Haku's career with horses was founding the Maui Animal Aloha Center (MAAC) on the campus of the Maui Horse Center in 1992.

With the support of a dedicated circle of advisors and volunteers, Haku established the center to provide special-needs children and adults a broad range of physical as well as psychological benefits through therapeutic activities and educational programs via direct interaction with the horse.

Many authorities in the field of therapy for challenged individuals have produced evidence that dressage plays a vital role. Recognized as an effective tool in assisting physical therapists in the treatment of human neurological disorders, the horse's movement in dressage patterns provides part of the kinetic input, while the precise pattern of the rider's pelvis mimics the hip movement during a normal walking gait of a human. By its nature and function, the horse lends itself to multisensory therapy just as the rider does.

To the challenged child aboard one of the center's special mounts, sensory input of horse and rider during the riding session improves body awareness and spatial orientation. This input converts to significant psychological benefits that are vital to rehabilitation.

The therapeutic riding sessions grew to become a highlight of the MAAC's list of more than successful programs. Riders that were sometimes challenged from the effects of cerebral palsy, autism, multiple sclerosis, paraplegia, and stroke not only found improvement in their general well-being but also a warm sense of bonding with the kindly horses.

This program was a logical context in which the Special Olympics format was developed. For the Olympians, the sight, smell, touch, and mass movement of the horse brought on warm interaction. Softly pinching the fuzzy muzzle of the gentle mounts evoked a feeling of trust. Being part of the grooming and saddle process evoked a feeling of accomplishment and self-worth in the participants, whose facial expressions moved from awe to appreciation.

I Saw a Child

I saw a child who couldn't walk,
sit on a horse, laugh and talk.
Then ride it through a field of
daisies
and yet he could not walk unaided.
I saw a child, no legs below, sit on
a horse,
and make it go through woods of
green and
places he had never been to sit
and stare,
except from a chair.
I saw a child who could only crawl,
mount a horse and sit up tall.
Put it through degrees of paces
and laugh at the wonder in
our faces.
I saw a child born into strife,
take up and hold the reins of life.
and that same child was heard
to say,
thank God for showing me
the way . . .

JOHN ANTHONY DAVIS

In the gathering to celebrate the first anniversary of the center's existence, more than 700 volunteer hours had been logged and 275 therapeutic riding sessions had been sponsored, according to Haku's year-end message. Never resting on her laurels nor expecting due credit, Haku turned to enhancing the MAAC mission to further develop an outreach program for those in need.

Animal-Assisted Therapy

The Animal-Assisted Therapy (AAT) program was an extension of therapeutic support of the MAAC to the hospitals, care homes, and infirmaries, as well as the elderly and shut-ins in their respective homes. It was Lisa DeCoit, a name synonymous with animal-assisted therapy on Maui, who carried out this mission to fruition.

Beginning with taking minihorses on a rickety wooden trailer up to Kula Hospital and up elevators to a ward of appreciative patients to placing on the laps of homebound shut-ins a purring ball of a kitten, the AAT program reached into the hearts and pockets of Maui communities as the program evolved into one of pride and success. Today the AAT program enjoys its own facility on the MHC campus in quiet testimony to Haku's broad vision of helping the people of the Valley Isle through sharing all of God's creatures great and small. Haku left this world in a quiet ride into the Maui sunset. Shortly after her passing, the MHC was rechristened the Haku Baldwin Center in tribute to her iconic and lasting role.

Other islands also had key players who followed their passion for pursuing and establishing horse venues and activities. While not with as broad a scope or influence as Amy Rich and Haku Baldwin, these individuals nonetheless effectively achieved what they set out to do.

CHAPTER 12

RODEO

Where there are cattle and horses, there will undoubtedly be friendly competitions in the sport of rodeo. Those unfamiliar with the large ranching industry of Hawai'i may not realize the extent to which rodeo competitions have become an established institution across the state. Even as early as 1905, Eben Low produced the Congress of Rodeos in Honolulu, which included mainland and local contestants. This chapter details the evolution of various clubs throughout the Islands.

Na'alehu Rodeo: Fourth of July since 1949

To most Big Island folks, Na'alehu is not just another dusty former plantation town. Actually, the town is central to the ranch heritage of Ka'ū District, stretching from South Point at Kahuku Ranch to the Volcano community near Keauhou Ranch.

There were many small ranchers that made up the litany of livestock operators long before C. Brewer merged Ka'alu'alu, Kapāpala, and Keauhou Ranches into the Hawaiian Ranch Company in the late 1950s. Names such as Princess Ruth, Campbell, Vredenburg, Macomber, Brown, Reed, Richardson, Hayselden, Monsarrat, Searle, Hanoa, and Shipman reflect the array of livestock operators in the late 1800 and early 1900s.

Following World War II, rodeo activity became dormant for several years. After the 1944 Marine Rodeo of Parker Ranch, many a cowboy longed for the return of competition with roping and rough stock events. Leadership at C. Brewer's Hutchinson Sugar Company (HSC) in Na'alehu and its subsidiary outfit, Ka'alu'alu Ranch Company (KRC), recognized the need for a community festival centered on the *paniolo* sport of rodeo. Through the combined leadership of

{ 12.1 } *Early ranchmen of Naʻalehu and Waiohinu. Pictured are (left to right) A. P. Ah Fong, Howard Kupahu, Ben Kamoku, Joe Macomber, Will Mokiao, and Henry Kaʻapana. A great-grandson of Henry Kaʻapana, Ralph Kaʻapana has emerged as Naʻalehu Rodeo's consistent advocate.*

Roy Replogle (HSC) and Fred Schattauer (KRC), they sponsored the first rodeo in 1949 with their respective company resources, knowledgeable personnel, suitable land, and rodeo livestock.

Cowboy life was not new to Kaʻū, as the region's ranchers boasted legendary roping skills among their cowboys. Names such as Beck (Peke Bob), Kaʻapana, Kanakaole, Ke, and Mokiao are notable. With ensuing generations, a natural, iconic figure emerged in John Wellington Peiper Sr. Peiper and his crew were key figures in making Naʻalehu Rodeo a success.

The first arena was built a short distance from where it exists today, immediately south of Naʻalehu Community Park. It was a temporary facility erected with hog wire and wood posts and measured more than 450 feet long and 200 feet wide. The only relatively permanent parts of the facility were the bucking chutes, roping chute, and attendant boxes.

The rodeo was an invitational ranch rodeo limited to major outfits on the Big Island. In the 1980s, the rodeo opened up to smaller ranches and rodeo clubs. Until the rodeo went beyond invitational to a more public forum, the Naʻalehu Rodeo was noted for its unique hospitality: each invited ranch was served a large cardboard box of hot *laulau* (steamed, ti-leaf-wrapped package of pork, beef, fish, and taro leaves) fresh from the spacious wooden steamer located at the slaughterhouse adjacent to the Kaʻaluʻalu cowboy saddle house.

Adjacent to the arena was a Japanese hotel named Shimizu, a barbershop owned by Agapito Sumarnap called Pete's Barber Shop, a Buddhist church, and eventually the Naʻalehu Coffee Shop, owned by the Toguchi brothers, Tom and Roy.

{ 12.2 } *The historic Naʻalehu Rodeo offered combined attractions with its carnival and beer garden activities.*

{ 12.3 } *Successes at Naʻalehu Rodeo were consistent largely through grassroots efforts of the Kaʻaluʻalu Ranch cowboys, led by Johnny Pieper. On the fence are (left to right) George Beck, Leighton Beck, Hanoa Paaluhi, and Tom Kaniho. On the ground are (left to right) Aula Ke, Johnny Peiper, and Sam Ah Yee.*

Another unique feature of the Naʻalehu Rodeo was the beer garden, a tentlike extension of the "Civic Center" building that served as clubhouse. The beer garden had two features, one very positive and the other less favorable. On a positive, cultural note was the presence of Freddy Punahoa Konanui, a slack key master whose musical talent was known throughout the Big Island. Although his ancestral home was Kalapana, Kaʻū was where many of his relatives lived and worked, often on neighboring ranches such as Kapāpala. In fact, on several fronts, the connection to the village of Kalapana was bound by centuries of familial interrelationships. Accompanying

Konanui was his brother-in-law George Ka'apana, another slack key stalwart of the day.

Unfortunately, the beer garden in the wee hours often was host to brawls involving multigenerational rival factions of families from South Kona and Ka'ū. Eventually, the beer garden went by the wayside as sponsorship shifted from plantation to the Ka'ū Roping Club, headed by respected horseman Johnny Peiper. Contractor Tommy Ishimaru and restaurant owner Tommy Toguchi were vital supporters.

The Na'alehu Rodeo featured a unique reining event called the *huli pōkole* (short turn) race. Competitors lined up at the starting point and, at the signal of a blank pistol shot, charged forward about a hundred feet, passed a second line, pivoted their mounts, and raced back to the starting point (now the finishing line) where a flag judge determined first- through third-place winners. A favorite grudge match (pronounced "grouch" match) pitted Carl "Buster" Enos on a half-Belgian gelding against Reed Glover of Kahuku Ranch on a top polo mount. The crowd roared when Enos, appearing to gallop in slow motion, would beat Glover. Winning was more often a measure of horsemanship. Enos was a splendid reinsman, capable of executing rapid pivoting while astride a 1,300-pound ranch-bred, half-draft mount. The Na'alehu Rodeo is recorded as the first venue to feature the *po'owai'ū* event, won by Leighton Beck in 1949.

As the Hawaiian Ranch grew into a leadership role in the industry, thanks largely to the influence of Fred Schattauer, some interesting consequences affected the quality of the rodeo. Hawaiian Ranch horses were Belgian/Appaloosa crosses, adding enhanced cow sense, while having Brahma bulls service the cowherds of the coastal plains of Wai 'Ahukini produced half-bred steers that served as genuinely rank bucking stock each July 4th rodeo. A young Billy Bergin, riding for Pu'u'Ō'ō Ranch, won the steer-riding event in 1957.

A new arena was built on the highway across from the Mormon Church, but this venue was not a lasting one due to its inconvenient location. Eventually, the Ka'ū Roping Club built an arena on adjacent lands abandoned by the Buddhist church and Shimizu Hotel. Jimmy Miranda, who was then a cattle supervisor at the Hawaiian Ranch, headed up the project in 1974. The plantation continued to be supportive, and the ranch also supported the Ka'ū Roping Club's efforts in the ensuing years.

Falling into disrepair, the arena suffered waning rodeo support and interest until the club, with the leadership of Peiper and William Ahia, resurfaced with renewed vigor. By this juncture, leadership was courting the younger generation of rodeo enthusiasts, such as Wally Andrade.

When Parker Ranch established its Ka'ū Division in 1976, its superintendent, Charley Kimura, developed an enthusiastic role in support of the facility. In addition to the July 4th rodeo, Kimura encouraged play days and jackpot roping throughout the years Parker Ranch spent in Ka'ū. Much of the support included physical improvements, fence materials, welding, and heavy equipment availability. With the closure of the plantation and Parker Ranch's Ka'ū Division, the organizational fabric of the rodeo club was compromised by lack of "sugar daddy" sponsorships or resources of any magnitude. This was weaning time for the Ka'ū Roping Club, and the future looked bleak.

John Cross, a C. Brewer executive who managed the phasing out of Ka'ū Sugar Company (the combined Hutchison Sugar Company of Na'alehu with the Hawaiian Agricultural Company of Pāhala) approached the club regarding an opportunity to buy the fee simple land beneath the arena. Leadership of the club at this time belonged to the Ka'apana and Malicki families, who entered into negotiation with C. Brewer Properties pending successful acquisition of nonprofit 501(c)(3) status. Negotiations were protracted but successful.

Under private club ownership, the arena facility hosted its first formal event in 2010, approximately sixty years after the first Na'alehu Rodeo was staged.

Maui Independence Day Rodeos: Makawao Rodeo

As early as 1949, the County Fair at Kahului Fairgrounds combined rodeo activities with its well-attended horse races. Steer roping, bronc riding and steer riding were standard events. A young Ikua (Martin) Purdy, son of the legendary world champion, won the steer-riding event in 1954.

With the burgeoning business growth of the Kahului/Wailuku districts, it wasn't long before the fairgrounds lost its venues. This affected rodeo and racing, while polo had other Upcountry venues such as Pukalani Polo Grounds.

By the early fifties, the need for a permanent home for rodeo activities became apparent when young stars such as Freddy Rice and his cousins Ben and Peter Baldwin returned home from college and military service armed with fervent enthusiasm. Makawao is to Maui's rodeo cowboy scene as Honoka'a is to the Big Island landscape. Both venues exist today with the enduring image of America's native sport.

Harold F. "Oskie" Rice headed up the family ranch, Ka'ono'ulu, and was a top cowboy in his own right in the context of ranching. So was Manduke Baldwin of Haleakalā Ranch, whose sons Peter and Ben were serious rodeo contenders, as was their cousin Freddy, son of Oskie.

A spacious plateau was an obvious choice, with access, power, and water amenities in a relatively central Maui location. The man behind the scene who secured the rodeo venue was Oskie Rice; hence the newly built arena appropriately bears his name today.

Independence Day was the traditional date of Maui's main rodeo, carried over from the days of the Kahului Fairgrounds to its present permanent home in Makawao. Coincidentally, the Na'alehu Rodeo, also established in 1949, has perennially held its rodeo on Independence Day. Beyond this coincidence, few parallels exist, given the country-style image of

{ 12.4 } *Hawai'i Saddle Club founding directors. In the back row are (left to right) Ethel Andrade, John Waihee Sr., Billy Mainaaupo, and television's Sheriff Ken. In the front row are (left to right) Jack Ramos, William Nakoa, Morgan Brown, and Willy Andrade.*

Na'alehu's relaxed community celebration as opposed to the intense competition of the Maui Rodeo.

Peter Baldwin showed leadership skill in how the Makawao rodeo was framed. While the rodeo is historically planned and managed by committee, Baldwin established a high standard of stock quality, rules of engagement, and high purses and payoffs, while drawing on broad community and business support.

Along with Clem Andrade, Freddy Rice, and Albert Silva, Baldwin was a founding force in establishing the Hawai'i Rodeo Association (HRA) and its subsequent publication of a rule book that remains the gold standard of conduct in rodeo scenes throughout the state. This set of rules, carefully adhered to, gave the Makawao Rodeo an exceptional leg up in the minds of rodeo contestants, as the playing field was as level as it could get.

A young Brendan Balthazar gradually emerged as the leader of the Makawao Rodeo scene and took performance to an even higher level. As team ropers demanded horned steers, Balthazar stepped forth with a start-up herd of steers that he offered for use at the Makawao venue, as well as to the Maui District High School Rodeo Association's frequent performances headed up by John FitzGerald and others.

As with most organizations, leadership moves on, making way for another generation. Maui has no shortage of rodeo leaders, and soon others emerged as the new leaders.

Hawai'i Saddle Club: Honoka'a Rodeo

The Hawai'i Saddle Club was formed in 1954 by an enthusiastic circle of Honoka'a, Āhualoa, and Pa'auilo residents, although Waimea supplied much of the early and critical leadership.

Dr. Edwin "Buzz" Willett, a community physician and horse enthusiast, was a central and genuinely cohesive force in the birth of the organization. From its inception to the present, the Hawai'i Saddle Club and its flagship event, the Honoka'a Rodeo, has had close ties to the Andrade family of Honoka'a.

One of Hawai'i's oldest rodeo clubs was born when like-minded Willett and William "Willy" Andrade dedicated themselves to the mission of establishing a permanent arena facility in Honoka'a on the Big Island. Honoka'a in 1954 was a cow town and plantation village already known for producing top ranch and rodeo hands. The town, however, lacked a rodeo facility to call its own.

Willett and Andrade were inspired to change this after traveling to O'ahu to attend the wedding of Willett's brother. After the wedding party, the pair retired to a Kailua bar. a favorite watering hole for military personnel owned by horse enthusiast J. D. Souza. Many of these military folks were rodeo hands. To accommodate his unique clientele, Souza built a rough-stock arena adjacent to the bar—literally at his back door. The Honoka'a horsemen were impressed with the arena, complete with bucking and stripping chutes and pens for bucking bulls and ornery broncs, and they were also in awe of the countless number of marines eager to ride the wildest and the woolliest.

Returning to Honoka'a as devout pioneers in a quest of a full-on roping and rough-stock arena, Willett and Andrade convened a like-minded board of directors while serving as president and vice president, respectively. Ethel Andrade held the secretary position and John Teves served as treasurer. Other original board members included John Solomon, William Nakoa, Morgan Brown, John Waihee Sr., Billy Mainaaupo, and Jack Ramos. The club colors were red with gold (yellow) trim. The club logo remains the same: an original image of the Big Island with the silhouette of a saddle within. A star is placed at the approximate location of Honoka'a town.

Dr. Edwin "Buzz" Willett and William "Willy" Andrade were a cohesive

{ 12.5 } *A product of Maui, Dr. Edwin "Buzz" Willett enjoyed a career as a family physician but was well known as the founding force in developing the Honoka'a Rodeo and Hawai'i Saddle Club.*

leadership team. Maui-born horseman Willett established a successful medical practice in North Hawai'i. He was proud of his half-Azorean heritage, and it was as much a function of Willett's popularity in Honoka'a as was his bedside manner and diagnostic prowess. Interestingly, his initial desire for a career in veterinary medicine was redirected to human medicine when he received a full-ride scholarship to medical school. He was affectionately called "Doc" or "Buzz" by his close friends. Willy Andrade and Willett were inseparable buddies. A handsome and likeable scion, Willy came from a long line of ranchers in scattered communities of Hāmākua and surrounding areas.

It took this highly energetic, likeable, and collaborative pair of men to secure the property and gather a huge volunteer workforce to design and build

{ 12.6 } *The leadership of Hawai'i Saddle Club in 1964 consisted of (left to right) Buddy Maertens, Willy Miranda, Jack Ramos, George DeSilva, Fran Andrade, Johnny Correia, and John Teves.*

{ 12.7 } *A vintage photo of Willy Andrade about the time he cofounded the Hawai'i Saddle Club with Dr. Buzz Willett (1958).*

{12.8} *A spacious arena built of eucalyptus siding and bleachers lined with heavy hog wire served the sport well.*

a state-of–the-art facility, which remains a focus of pride for Hawai'i's premier rodeo town, Honoka'a.

The primary issue confronting the newly organized Hawai'i Saddle Club was not how to build a rodeo arena but where to get land that was relatively flat and well graded. The property had to be easily accessible, with close proximity to town, and have a leasehold agreement of reasonable duration and affordable terms. Enter Willy's mother, Rose (Mrs. Dan Correia), a rancher and saloon keeper whose heart, without a doubt, was a hundred percent behind the project. Rose offered one of her properties that met all the criteria for use by the Saddle Club.

While volunteer bulldozer operators landscaped the site, just a few hundred feet above the brand new Māmalahoa Highway, dozens of committee members went to upland forests armed with chainsaws to harvest post, rail, and boarding materials. Neighboring ranches donated

{ 12.9 } *Pictured are (left to right) George Kaeo, Heine Arruda, and Bobby Komine.*

wire, steel, and personnel wherever it was needed. Before long, the arena took shape as a 250-by-300-foot facility boasting five stout bucking chutes, stock pens, loading chute, and return alley, all in clear view of a spacious judges' stand. Six-tiered bleachers of hard eucalyptus boarding spanned both the *mauka* and *makai* flanks of the arena. Ample parking and concessionaire spaces rounded out the arena complex.

Within a year, a former cow pasture became the permanent site for one of the state's most highly attended rodeo venues. Willett and Andrade got it done, an idea that began in a chance visit to the saloon of J. D. Souza on O'ahu.

On March 19, 2014, the Hawai'i Saddle Club celebrated its sixtieth anniversary by dedicating the new Rose Andrade Correia Rodeo Stadium. The $3.5-million-dollar county facility was built through the County of Hawai'i Parks and Recreation Division, with Mayor Billy Kenoi and Councilwoman Valerie Poindexter as lead proponents. The naming of a municipal facility after Rose was a milestone, and it was an appropriate tribute to a woman whose foresight and generosity guaranteed a permanent home not just for the Hawai'i Saddle Club but a facility for Quarter Horse shows, dressage events, training clinics, and 4-H activities.

Hawai'i Paniolo Club

The Hawai'i Paniolo Club (HPC) was founded in 1958 by Joseph Serrao, who had the diplomatic skills to bring together diverse, deeply cliqued groups of horsemen. The DeLima family—Thomas, his son Bobby, and his brother Ernest—served on the board of directors. Tony Phillips, William Kamau, and Peter Mehau were among racing enthusiasts and played more honorary roles. The DeSilva family was represented by Frank "Sheiking" and his sons Ernest and Richard "Casey." Frank's brother John DeSilva, as noted earlier, actually lived in a stall at Ho'olulu Park and was a consummate jockey/trainer. A Hawaiian named

{ 12.10 } *Hawai'i Saddle Club 1971 Rodeo Champions. Kneeling are (left to right) Bazie Brandt, LaVerne Souza, Hugh Hill, Herman "Brother" Teves, Anna Perry-Fiske (sponsor), Jack Ramos (sponsor), and Jesse Medeiros. Standing are (left to right) Benji Rollins, Warren Miura (holding son Michael), Joey Schutte, Bud Gibson, David Caires, Dingy Joseph, Bert Miranda, and Brendan Balthazar.*

Charley Macomber also lived in a stall and kept horses there. Mako Imaizumi, a dairyman from Kūkūau, was an early member.

Earl "Pinhead" DeSilva, brother-in-law of the senior DeLima brothers (he married Nora DeLima, who owned the Pink Elephant Bar in old Waiākea Town), was a horse enthusiast too. Early main jockeys were Bobby DeLima, Bobby DeMattos, Joe Perreira, Casey DeSilva, Billy Bergin, Clarence "Bow" Mattos, John DeSilva, Ernest Mattos, and "Tuna" Sampaio.

While horse racing was the anchor event of the Hawai'i Paniolo Club, rodeo staging was the primary mission of the fledgling club. Prior to club formation, a loosely knit group sponsored the first rodeo, held in 1958 in a makeshift arena formed by blocking both ends (three hundred feet apart) of the circular half-mile track in the section fronting the massive wooden grandstand. Dunnage lumber from Hilo Wharf was appropriated from members such as Yoichi Nagata and Ernest "Hoof" Watson, who worked for the Hawai'i Transportation and Terminal Company at the wharf.

In the roping events, ropers had to approach the steer "on the bend" (to the left), because the arena reflected the curvature of the circular racetrack. Clarence "Bow" Mattos won the bronc riding using a Hawaiian tree saddle with a burlap bag bucking roll and no rear cinch strap.

Mako Imaizumi roped in shorts and rubber boots, drawing loud applause from the crowd. Arthur Lorenzo, fresh out of the armed services, roped on a small palomino that barely caught up with the steer, when it leaped over the inside rail with the mounted roper in pursuit. The crowd rooted for the steer as it drew farther and farther away from Lorenzo, crossing the midfield and into the anxious loops of rescue ropers.

The Hawai'i Paniolo Club rebuilt the arena in reverse, with chutes aimed in a Puna direction with no grandstand exposure. During this era, Bobby DeLima and Casey DeSilva emerged as top-flight bull and bronc riders. Clem Andrade entered statewide prominence as a champion calf and team roper, while moving rodeo management to a more professional level. Despite Serrao's diplomatic and cohesive role, HPC faded into oblivion as a result of disruptive factions.

Parker Ranch July 4th Rodeo and Races: Paka Paniolo Horseman's Association

In the vision of A. W. Carter and his son, Hartwell, who together led Parker Ranch from 1899 to 1960, the need for a racetrack, first built in 1910, was essential to the Thoroughbred horse program, in which training racing prospects for export became a national requirement. Such activities blended well with the Remount Program as well as the sport of polo.

When forward-thinking Dick Penhallow succeeded Hartwell Carter's management in 1960, he immediately established a "Western stock horse" vision in terms of breeding, training, and showing of Parker

Ranch horses. This meant building a roping arena to serve ranch hands interested in progressive training techniques.

Penhallow also changed the scenery of the annual July 4th races, intact since the 1920s, to add calf roping, team roping and wild cow milking. It was an employee-only roster, and the community came out in force to support Parker Ranch *paniolo* in racing and rodeo events. The ranch dubbed their organization Paka Paniolo (Parker Cowboy) Horsemen's Association and elected officers to lead the charge. Working closely with management, the organization flourished for a decade, after which interest among the men waned.

Despite the decline of the Paka Paniolo Horseman's Association, Parker Ranch continued the July 4th races and rodeo tradition as a company function for the entire community, with no admission charged. After the event, Parker Ranch owner Richard Smart hosted an invitation-only July 4th celebration luncheon at his Pu'u 'Ōpelo home that was quite a gala affair, with a genuine *paniolo* flavor.

Over the last decade of the last millennium, the July 4th Rodeo and Races began to lose popularity, and the image was eroding. As the new millennium arrived, the ranch wisely opened up events to neighboring ranches, and the popularity of the event sky rocketed. In 2014, car parking literally carpeted the entire equestrian complex and adjoining highways.

Following in the footsteps of Smart tradition, an invitation-only celebratory luncheon is held at the ranch's support complex to the rear (south) of the racetrack and arena for participants and families, Parker Ranch employees, retirees, and guests. And the show goes on.

Hawai'i Rodeo Association

In 1962, Hawai'i's rodeo circles took the initiative to formally organize a body to regulate rules for the sport in uniform codes. This was the birth of the Hawai'i Rodeo Association (HRA), with its guiding principles setting the foundation for organization and management of rodeo in the State of Hawai'i for many years to come.

Hawai'i Rodeo Association founders were Freddy Rice, Clement Andrade, Peter Baldwin, and Albert Silva, with Sally Rice serving as secretary. A rules committee was formed, and by the time the first statewide HRA finals were scheduled, a published set of guidelines for competition was provided for all contestants. Attorney and horseman Bob Bethea authored the rule book. Members of the HRA were required to belong to other rodeo clubs, such as the Hawai'i Saddle Club, Hilo Paniolo Club, Maui Roping Club, Saddle City, Na'alehu Roping Club, or the Kona-Kā'u Roping and Polo Club, plus an array of military organizations for armed forces personnel.

The first HRA state finals were held at Ho'olulu Park Arena in June 1964. Two of the HRA founders won their respective competitions: Clem Andrade for team roping and Freddy Rice for calf roping. Willy Gomes won the steer wrestling, and Bobby Komine won the bull riding. Casey DeSilva won the saddle bronc

{ 12.11 } *First HRA State Finals Rodeo (1964) at Hoʻolulu Park in Hilo. In the front row are (left to right) Casey DeSilva, saddle bronc riding; Dingy Joseph, All-Around Cowboy; Fern White, barrel racing. In the back row are (left to right) Clem Andrade, team roping; Freddy Rice, calf roping; Willy Gomes, steer wrestling; Bobby Komine, bull riding. These were the first State Rodeo champions.*

riding, and Fern White the barrel racing. Stanley Joseph captured the All-Around Cowboy title.

The organization enjoyed broad success over the next two decades, when it became formally known as the Hawaiʻi Rodeo Cowboys Association (HRCA), as the original acronym was already associated with a car-racing organization.

The HRCA eventually weakened due to perceived overregulation and the discord it wrought between clubs that eschewed the encumbrances. Increased costs of interisland transportation of contestants and mounts over the past decade have dealt a heavy blow to statewide competition. In addition, the advent of organized team-roping series such as the United States Team Roping Competition (USTRC) and the American Cowboys Team Roping Association (ACTRA), with their sizable purse offerings, brought greater professionalism and financial return to the sport.

Kona-Kaʻū Roping and Polo Club

Aptly named, this organization served an area of intensive ranching interests from South Point through South Kona. Until the birth of this club, Kona proper never had an organized body of horse enthusiasts, and the Naʻalehu rodeo activities seem to be led as an adjunct to Kaʻaluʻalu Ranch and Hutchison Sugar Company societal functions.

Two key individuals were instrumental in joining the districts of Kaʻū and South Kona. Freddy and Sally Rice brought the districts together as they settled into life at Kahuku Ranch in 1958. Freddy's love for both rodeo and polo and Sally's penchant for organized activities provided the vision, drive, and commonsense enthusiasm to gather like-minded ranch folks to form a committee with the task of establishing a club to serve the combined districts.

With the leadership (and coaching) of the couple, whole families convened at convenient locations such as Hoʻokena School, where members of the Basque, Henriques, Deniz, Rapoza, Medeiros, Onaka, Thompson, Wall, Freitas, Hedemann, Manoa, Ackerman, Mitchell, and Loando families came forth with enthusiasm and great ideas.

One of the major decisions centered on location, and the former grounds of Honaunau School could not have been a better choice, with its safe, paved access, running water, spacious parking, and broad grounds for an arena of large proportions. Surrounded by a canopy of monkeypod trees, the chosen site boasted all the amenities a budding club could want.

The Rices skillfully guided the committee toward leadership from within, while the Loando and Medeiros brothers stepped forth with their wives as secretarial support. Thompson and Henriques men stepped in with building plans and materials for an arena 275 feet in length and 150 feet in width. Bucking chutes, holding pens, and a judge's stand went up almost simultaneously, while the organization was logically christened the Kona-Kaʻū Roping and Polo Club in mid-March 1964. Fifty years later, the club celebrated its golden anniversary.

Within the span of a half century, the arena was rebuilt three times, and the presidency was first occupied by Auggy Loando, then Alfred Medeiros, and later by Mark Loando.

We note that Billy served as arena director annually from 1970 to 1990, witnessing club activities with deep appreciation for the membership, especially the distaff side, where Loke (Clarence) Medeiros and Mabel (Alfred) Medeiros ran the judges' stand with admirable, professional conduct from start to finish. Jaye Jose, daughter of founders Alfred and Mabel Medeiros, currently runs the judges' stand for the new generation of leaders.

Through those years, the club came to represent all of Kona, from Puʻu Waʻawaʻa Ranch cowhands through the ranches of Jimmy Stewart's own Hoʻomau Ranch, where championship heeler Manuel Medeiros starred as the herdsman of Hawaiʻi's finest Angus purebred herd.

By the early 1990s, under the leadership of Alfred Medeiros, the club sought to assure a permanent future for the arena. The facility was officially turned over to the County Parks and Recreation

Department with the agreement that the County of Hawai'i would assume responsibility for all maintenance and improvements. With this accomplished, the executive committee, consisting of George Gouveia, Manuel Medeiros, Kimo Medeiros, and Jimmy Freitas, wholeheartedly supported President Alfred Medeiros "passing the torch" to the next generation, led by Mark Loando and his team of Sally Inkster, Roy Loando, Lino Kamakau, and others.

On the fiftieth anniversary of the club's inception in 2014, the Kona-Ka'ū Roping and Polo Club again passed the torch to a new generation of leadership under Shane Jose (grandson of Alfred Medeiros), Tony Loando, and Aki Smith, as well as Sally Inkster, who agreed to continue service as secretary to preserve continuity.

Thanks to the seeds planted by Freddy and Sally Rice, rodeo has a future in Kona. A new Honaunau Rodeo Stadium was dedicated by Mayor Billy Kenoi and Councilwoman Maile Medeiros-David on October 28, 2016.

The Gibson Story: New Town and Country Stables Rodeo

Since John Palmer Parker I and his sons, A. W. Carter and his son Hartwell, and H. P. Baldwin and his son Manduke put Hawaiian ranching on the world map, few father-and-son teams can boast greater contributions to the modern livestock industry than Dee Gibson and his son, Bud. Their collective contribution to the sport of rodeo eclipses even their stellar careers as ranchmen. Their relentless drive for excellence was built on familial synergy that combined the values of hard work, Western spirit, business acumen, and an innate ability to challenge diversity.

Kansas-born and bred, Dee Gibson entered the US Cavalry in 1936 just a month shy of his eighteenth birthday. Fort Riley, Kansas, home the "Big Red One," was a foremost cavalry outpost only forty miles north from his home in Reading, a small town in Lyon County in the heart of the Flint Hills, the location of some of America's finest ranch country. The Flint Hills are also the ancestral home of some of America's world champion rodeo hands, such as the Roberts brothers of Strong City, Kansas. After a three-year stint, Dee left the army to work in the naval shipyards of San Diego and Pearl Harbor. While on O'ahu, he married Frances Morris, whose roots trace to the Moraes family of Hilo.

While still working at the Pearl Harbor dry docks, Dee and his father, Hank, started the Koko Head Dairy in 1947. Importing dairy heifers gave birth to Dee's life career in livestock transport between California and Hawai'i. After short stints of managing dairies for other O'ahu interests, Dee started Valley Dairy in 1952 with a state-of-the-art milking parlor complete with artificial insemination services. Expanding to Kaua'i in 1957, Dee opened Seaside Ranch, which included dairy and feedlot services, and Wailua Ranch, which included alfalfa and hog operations. But rodeo production was in his heart, calling him back to O'ahu.

An avid team and calf roper as well as a bronc rider, Dee had expertise in rodeo arena design and construction. In 1957 he built the portable arena used at the old Honolulu Stadium. Kāneʻohe Marine Corps Air Base, Barbers Point, and Wheeler Air Force Base were sites of Dee-built rodeo arenas. He even produced the rodeos as well as served as stock contractor at a variety of arenas, including Kahului Fairgrounds on Maui.

Dee's crowning achievement was establishing Saddle City in Waimānalo, Oʻahu, in 1959, where he produced weekly rodeos and horse shows. For premium rough stock, Dee imported Bob Barmby bulls and Christenson Brothers' broncs, which represented premium-quality bucking stock from the mainland United States.

Dee's choice of top bucking stock had a twofold value in that local riders could compete on bulls and broncs of mainland caliber, while professional riders from the mainland were attracted to Hawaiʻi's rodeos where they might draw a bucker that would match their championship abilities. In fact, there existed a third benefit in that novice local riders were rubbing elbows with world champions, men who valued the opportunity to attract new riders into the sport as well as serve as mentors.

The first semiprofessional venue for such interaction in Hawaiʻi was the 1960 Rodeo Cowboys Association (RCA), forerunners of the Professional Rodeo Cowboys Association (PRCA) Rodeo that Dee produced, drawing such notables as bull rider Ronnie Rossen, bronc riders Casey Tibbs, Harry Thomkins, and Jim Shoulders, and finally Benny Reynolds, World Champion All-Around Cowboy, who worked four events: bulls, broncs, barebacks, and steer wrestling. Local rodeo hands of that generation still speak highly today of those national figures and their willingness to share their experiences. The rodeo was staged in Barbers Point, using portable chutes and panels, and at Saddle City's arena.

{ 12.12 } *Dee Gibson was proud of his Western heritage, which was reflected in his regular cowboy attire, consisting of a felt hat and long-sleeved Western shirt.*

Beckoned to California in 1966, Dee worked out of Chowchilla, just south of Merced in the San Joaquin Valley, as an auctioneer, a trusted buyer, and consultant for many large dairies on the mainland, Hawaiʻi, and internationally for the US Department of Agriculture, staging shipments of quality cattle to the Islands. The bulk of his order-buying was for several dairy operators on Oʻahu, which drew his

{ 12.13 } *In a partnership that gave birth to the New Town and Country Stables, Frances Gibson (left) and Amy Rich provided expertise and property, respectively.*

mechanical skills into producing Hawai'i's first self-contained livestock shipping containers for mainland transport.

One can safely imagine that a little Bud Gibson was everywhere his father went except for his years of boarding school at Hawai'i Preparatory Academy on the Big Island and University of Hawai'i college terms. Handling stock and people in the livestock industry is an art that requires a deep background and dealing in utmost good faith. Mutual respect is the core of cowboy values—earning it and showing it comes from the heart. Bud was born into this life and was afforded a great teacher in his dad. Bud summed it up poignantly: "Dee along with his partner and wife Frances Gibson's main purpose in everything they did was to improve on the quality of the livestock and the education of the people involved, which allowed local people to become equal with their mainland counterparts in the beef, dairy, rodeo, and horse industry" (pers. comm.). That constitutes parental respect, earned and given.

Armed with a college education and youthful but thorough life experiences, Bud set out in 1972 to bring full-scale rodeos to the New Town and Country Stables, a Waimānalo equestrian center established by his mother Frances in partnership with Amy Wight Rich, O'ahu's premier horsewoman. The New Town and Country Stables is still in operation, celebrating its fifty years of performances in February 2014. Bud and Katy Gibson have run it since 1971. Amy retired in 1972 and passed away in 1974, and Bud's mother, Frances, retired in 1976.

Bud is unabashed in his appreciation for the role of three ladies in his quest for success in the horse world: his mother, Frances, for her strength of character; Amy Rich for the foundation she provided him in English horsemanship; and his life partner, Katy, who not only supports his career but enhances their joint mission in bettering Hawai'i's sense of place, with the equine as its centerpiece.

Bud's achievements in horse-related activities started early, with showmanship success as early as ten years of age. By his thirteenth year, he became the youngest member of the Rodeo Cowboys Association as a genuine cardholder. He remains a current member of the Professional Rodeo Cowboys Association. His exposure to livestock activities spanned all of the Hawaiian Islands (save for Ni'ihau), with hog and dairy operations on Kaua'i, rodeo and polo on Maui and Hawai'i Island, and horse and cattle ventures on Moloka'i.

His rodeo career is far beyond activities around the Waimānalo rodeo facility at New Town and Country Stables. He reigned as state champion bull and bronc rider of the Hawai'i (Rodeo) Cowboys Association in 1967, 1968, and 1971. His expertise in rodeo arena design and construction extends beyond the Hawaiian Islands into the Pacific Basin.

In his ranching operations, Bud has utilized the best of the Brahma breed, not only in commercial beef production by cross-breeding but in producing nationally ranked bucking bulls for competitions of the Professional Rodeo Cowboys Association, the National Finals Rodeo, and the Professional Bull Riders. As a resource for semen for artificial insemination, his now-famous bucking bull Rocky has sired many offspring bulls that have starred in professional rodeo circles (see plate 4).

Bud's love for the Thoroughbred horse goes far beyond dressage, vaulting, and hunter/jumper classes and deep into pari-mutuel racing and polo. An avid polo player since boyhood, Bud achieved a three-goal rating early on in both Hawai'i and California circles. His three-goal rating took him to New Zealand polo competitions, where his aggressive style and keen horsemanship brought considerable respect from his peers. Through his design and building talents, Bud oversaw the rebuilding of both the Hawai'i Polo Club (Mokulē'ia) and the Honolulu Polo Club (Waimānalo) after storm and flood devastation.

Astride a top snaffle bit prospect, Bud is in his element as he continues to train cutting, cow horse, and reining prospects for the West Coast horse circles. In 1992, he won the $10,000 Pro Limited Division of the World Championship Snaffle Bit Futurity in Reno, Nevada.

As an accomplished horseman in every respect, Bud Gibson has brought honor to Hawai'i as an iconic example of success through lifetime dedication to the equine species, underscored with pride in his family and native land.

Parker Ranch Round-Up Club

Founded in 1974 by the employees of the ranch, the Labor Day Rodeo has passed its thirtieth anniversary. Two factors brought about renewed interest in forming a rodeo club: a new facility and a cause célèbre—youth scholarships. Under the leadership of Walter Slater, livestock manager, an old wire-and-post roping arena was rebuilt into a state-of-the-art pipe facility that included bucking chutes, a return alley, a battery of sorting pens, and a heeler's box. A dozen years later, Robby Hind rebuilt the entire facility with galvanized panels and added a spacious covered grandstand, Hawai'i's first in rodeo venues.

By this juncture, ranch employees had enrolled their children in private institutions—notably Parker School, Hawai'i Preparatory Academy, and Kamehameha Schools—and the burden of tuition was real. Through the grace of Parker Ranch, the Round-Up Club was provided the arena and stock gratis for producing annual rodeos as a fund-raising engine for the children's scholarships.

In recent years, the ranch has partnered with the employees as support grew to include advertising, concessions, and security. The grounds are kept in immaculate condition, including lawn irrigation and repair and maintenance year-round.

The Parker Ranch rodeo facility has been home to the Hawai'i High School Rodeo Association for six annual rodeos, as well as the district and state finals for more than twenty-five years with unflinching support.

Leadership of the Round-Up Club has always been sound, with early officers including Louie Akuna, John Kainoa, Lucky Puhi, and Clayton Bertelmann. Sadly, only Puhi lives on today, managing Waiki'i Ranch, savoring the progressive growth of the organization.

Parker Ranch's history of hosting rodeos comes with some well-established rules relative to the humane treatment of rodeo stock. Most salient is the "knock down" rule disqualifying ropers when the steer falls due to excessive handling.

Ranch wives who played strong roles in how the rodeos were handled, as well as scholarship distribution, were Paula DeSilva, Keikilani Kainoa (deceased), Lehua Hoopai (now at Palani Ranch), and Sherrie Kalaniopio. Leadership today is in the hands of DeeDee Keakealani-Bertelmann, Livestock Division inventory specialist. Broadly experienced, she has elevated rodeo management to a new and higher level.

Great Waikoloa Rodeo: Waikoloa Stables

Early in 1971, the budding community of Waikoloa Village launched recreational development plans by building Waikoloa Stables, an equestrian center that included nine stalls, a tack room, feed room, and lounge.

Designed by premiere architect Vladimir N. Ossipoff and built by Morrison-Knudsen, the center was a three-winged facility built of redwood and cedar topped with an attractive shake roofline. Two of the flanks housed the stalls, ventilated with spacious windows and Dutch doors that were serviced by lanai-type shed rows. The two stall rows formed a crescent shape that unfortunately trapped the fierce *makani kama'āina* (trade winds) that blew across a dusty, dry lot used for turn-out space for the horses. The third leg of the complex led to a two-story structure providing an ideal location for a judge's stand serving the soon-to-be-built Waikoloa Rodeo Arena.

For eye appeal and wind protection, the four acres surrounding the complex were irrigated and landscaped with turf and trees. A significant amenity was access to horseback trails in the surrounding ten thousand acres owned by the development.

Countryside Stables at Waikoloa Village was its formal name, but the community commonly referred to it as the Waikoloa Stables or Waikoloa Arena, the latter consisting of a board-fenced oval 250 feet long and 150 feet wide.

Dr. Max B. Smith, an O'ahu veterinarian who operated Paniolo Park on Parker Ranch in Waimea, was brought in to oversee the stables operation. Waimea rancher and horseman Morgan Brown was managing day-to-day operations with the stable help of Tommy Goo and able horse training skills of Ellen Cockey, who was trained in both English and Western riding instruction.

Early on, the complex was utilized primarily as a venue for Quarter Horse shows sponsored by the Hawai'i Quarter Horse Association, an organization largely fostered by the respected horseman Morgan Brown. The venue attracted horse owners from Maui, O'ahu, Kaua'i, and even Moloka'i, but Big Island Quarter Horse enthusiasts were the mainstay.

When the Smith contract was over a couple of years later, a profoundly successful plan for Waikoloa Stables was ushered in by Maui hotel industry executive, Bob Hoffman. Gregarious by nature, Hoffman not only had the appearance of Teddy Roosevelt, but he had the drive, foresight, and perseverance of the cavalry colonel who stormed San Juan Hill.

Visionary by nature, Hoffman quickly seized the opportunity to take advantage of the region's *paniolo* genre by staging rodeos, rope-a-thons, horse races, and polo matches while maintaining the striking architectural ambience of the Waikoloa Stables. He wisely circled himself with a staff to move plans forward. Sportscaster Carlos Rivas played a key public relations role along with professional announcing of all events.

Leroy Lindsey, George Purdy Jr., Herman Keala, Ken Silva, and later, Warren Miura all served Hoffman's initiatives well. Peripherally, he enjoyed an advisory circle of rodeo leaders that gave the events professional endorsement. Clem Andrade, Bob Bethea, and Freddy Rice blended their input with that of a large following of contestants who legitimized Hoffman's plans to move equestrian activities forward.

An exception to formality was the Great Waikoloa Horse Races, a twelve-heat event that was more comedic than intense in competition. On February 18, 1974,

Hawaii Quarter Horse Association

5th Annual

QUARTER HORSE SHOW

July 17, 1971
Parker Ranch Race Track

{ 12.14 } *Quarter Horse Show held at Parker Ranch Race Track, which in later years was called Paniolo Park.*

{ 12.15 } *Skilled in public relations, especially in the sports world, Carlos Rivas put Waikoloa Village development on the map as an equestrian community through rodeo, polo, racing, and showing. Renowned artist Herb Kane captured the image of the Irish-Spanish sportsman.*

the first meet was held, using a 440-yard straightaway that paralleled Waikoloa Road near the stables entryway. In keeping with the fun-filled informality, the "bush track" fit the event to a tee, with flagged starters and finishers attending limed lines. Cowboy races matched Hoffman against Ken Silva, George Purdy Jr. versus Herman Keala, and Ed Hoffman (son of Bob and Shirley) running past Fred Stevens Jr. Entertainer/polo enthusiast Al Lopaka outflanked Leroy Lindsey, while Freddy Rice outdistanced Parker Ranch livestock manager, Walter Slater. In the kid's race, Holi Bergin edged past Jock Agorastos, while the ladies' race pitted Linda Levi against Marcia Reynolds, both of Hilo. The race that captured the hearts of all matched hotelier Angus Coombs against golf pro Jackie Pung. Coombs, in Scottish kilt and mounted on a less than fleet steed named Aunty Maude, pulled up his mount at the finish line to let Pung trot on by, while the noble Scot doffed his cap. The packed crowd roared its approval throughout the complex. This was vintage Bob Hoffman, giving the village of Waikoloa broad exposure as a budding second city of South Kohala, an honor that was duly acclaimed by the new millennium.

The roping, rodeo, and polo events differed in that serious competition ruled the days (see plate 5). Converting the spacious oval show arena to accommodate bucking and roping chutes, catch pens, and return alleys prepared the former riding area for full-on rodeo action. Ample parking for cars, trucks, and trailers was landscaped and convenient. Food concessionaires enjoyed protected enclosure in the roomy space beneath the two-story judges' booth. A portable loading/unloading chute was placed for semitrailer loads of roping calves and steers and robust bucking bulls.

In the ensuing years, the Great Waikoloa Rodeo, held in February, kicked off the Hawai'i Rodeo Cowboys Association's circuit of sanctioned rodeos that would be followed by the Kona Stampede (March), Bud Gibson's New Town and Country Rodeo (June), Makawao (July 4th), and the Parker Ranch Round-Up (September). Hoffman's insistence on abiding by the HRCA sanctioning enhanced the professional standards of all Waikoloa equestrian activities in attracting Hawai'i's finest competitors.

In 1975, Hoffman established the rope-a-thon series of calf and steer roping events over four performances spread over a year's time. At the series culmination, event winners were awarded quality Ozark brand saddles, an award system that replaced the ubiquitous trophy buckle with a premium quality, leather-tooled saddle. In 1975, the Top Header award went to Jimmy Freitas, and the Top Heeler award was won by his partner and close friend, Manuel Medeiros, both of Kona. Dingy Joseph of O'ahu won the calf roping, seconded by Freddy Rice. While Marie Bethea of Hilo won the barrel racing, she barely edged out Carol Knight (Brown) of Kona by a few dollars.

The management of the Waikoloa Stables and the rodeo were greatly enhanced with the naming of Warren Miura as manager. Eventually Warren and

{ 12.16 } *Waikoloa Rope-a-Thon winners in 1975 (left to right): Manuel Medeiros, Marie Bethea, Stanley Joseph, and Jimmy Freitas. Freitas and Medeiros won in team roping, Joseph in calf roping, and Bethea in barrel racing.*

his wife, Marilyn, assumed the business as an operation of their own. The Miuras came with wide respect in horse circles throughout the state.

In wrapping up their tenure at Waikoloa Stables, the Miuras went into the construction business while raising their children, Michael and Liz, both of whom excelled as student athletes at Hawai'i Preparatory Academy before moving on to mainland colleges and careers. Upon retiring, the Miuras sold their Waikoloa home and moved to enjoy their lives in Washington State.

Horseman Charles Stevens eventually acquired the lease of the facility and expanded stall space by adding a twenty-four-stall facility in the former trailer parking lot. The facility was not oriented to public use, as Steven's forte was always training reining and cutting horses. The stables remained minimally active while Stevens moved his headquarters to California for a decade or so. Upon returning home, he gave up his Waikoloa operation to purchase Dutch Schumann's SC Ranch in Pa'auilo in 2011.

The Waikoloa Village Association is considering an offer to lease the facility to interested horse enthusiasts. It is gratifying to see an Ossipof-designed stable and newly renovated arena back in full use. The Big Island can always use another viable venue for horse activities.

Kaua'i Stampede: CJM Stables

Nestled shoreside in sunny Kōloa, Kaua'i, sits a rodeo facility built from the ground up by Jimmy and Joyce Miranda, who chose Kaua'i as their permanent home and place of business. Both Jimmy and Joyce attended Colorado State University and both came from rodeo and ranching backgrounds. The strong attraction of the Islands, coupled with Jimmy's Kūka'iau Ranch roots, likely drew them to return to the land of his birth.

Clifton James Miranda was the second son of Willy and Dorothy Miranda in the village of 'Umikoa, home of Kūka'iau Ranch, Ltd. Father Willy was an epic cowboy and horseman and effectively passed on his love for ranch life to his children.

At age fifteen, young Jimmy hosted a youth rodeo at the arena next to their home. A year later in 1958, his father partnered with Willy Andrade and produced an islandwide youth rodeo, possibly the first in the history of Hawaiian rodeo. The venue was the Hawai'i Saddle Club arena at Honoka'a.

Upon returning home from college, the young Miranda couple moved to Na'alehu, where Jimmy became the cattle superintendent for C. Brewer's Hawaiian Ranch Company. It was Jimmy's rodeo leadership that relocated and rebuilt the Na'alehu Rodeo Arena. While the facility has been rebuilt and renovated several times since then, the layout remains constant, a reflection of his wisdom and experience.

The move to Kaua'i was a bold, pioneering venture for the young couple, especially as they began to expand their family circle with the arrival of their daughter, Marty, and son, Russell. No one doubted that Jimmy would succeed in a venture that was centered on riding stables to serve the burgeoning tourist development of west Kaua'i.

While it was built in the image of an equestrian center, the centerpiece of his vision was a regulation-sized and fully equipped rodeo arena. Most unique in structure were the walls of the rodeo arena, built with horizontally placed utility poles laid one length upon the other to a height of nearly six feet. Attractively featuring a "log cabin" appearance, the structural soundness was formidable even in the mind of a mad Brahma bull.

An avid contestant, Jimmy readily abided by HRCA standards, bringing the Kaua'i Stampede to the forefront in the rodeo circuit of the State of Hawai'i.

Impact of the Quarter Horse on Hawaiian Rodeo

No single factor improved rodeo performance more than the Quarter Horse. The advent of the breed to the Hawaiian Islands was a game-changing transition. In 1945, Hartwell Carter imported the territory's first registered Quarter Horse, a palomino stallion named Sappho P-376. This stallion went on to produce more than two hundred foals, two of which were retained as band sires in their own right: Contra Costa and Roper. Sappho unfortunately passed on to his offspring a broncky streak, Roman noses, and brittle hooves.

Carter more than redeemed himself when he obtained a direct son of Lucky Blanton, a stallion named Lucky Tom, a great sire of both ranch and performance horses.

In 1947, Harold W. Rice, owner/manager of Ka'ono'ulu Ranch on Maui, imported the second American Quarter Horse Association stallion from Del Rio, Texas, named Jimmy S. While the Maui horse sired a lot of cow horse prospects throughout the territory, he became a noted producer of top rodeo mounts, especially when relocated to the Big Island, where he stood at Kahuku Ranch in Ka'ū. Managed by H. F. "Freddy" Rice, grandson of H. W., Jimmy S colts were sought after by team ropers.

Increasing popularity of Quarter Horses led to the formation in 1960 of the Hawai'i State Quarter Horse Association, led by Robert L. "Bob" Brown, a horseman responsible for enduring importation of top Quarter Horses. In O'ahu horse circles, he was referred to as the "father" of Quarter Horse importation to the Hawaiian Islands. Two noted broodmares he imported included a direct daughter of Lucky Blanton and a Clabber-bred mare, Slippers.

Brown's most significant import, however, was the stallion Flying Joe, a Hancock and Waggoner–bred gray that was shared between McCandless, Pu'u Wa'awa'a, and Parker ranches. Flying Joe developed a broad reputation as a consistent sire of sound, sensible colts with deeply embedded cow sense. They were routinely as good in the rodeo arena as they were in the rough ranch country of the Big Island.

Hawai'i, however, was still short of quality rodeo horses, as evidenced by the accurate assessment of Dr. Max Smith, a prominent horseman who relocated from Arizona's Driftwood country to the state of Hawai'i. Smith (1966) wrote,

> An example of the need for more good horses is that at the recent RCA rodeo in Honolulu in November 1965, 15 of the 18 bulldoggers were riding the same Quarter Horse. This was a fine bay gelding Wyn Junk imported from Jim Shoulders. He has had several offers to sell this horse for a good price since the rodeo. In the calf roping at the same rodeo, seven cowboys were mounted on Bobbie Komine's good palomino gelding, Top Nick. Also, six of the team ropers were mounted on the same horse. To top it off, Rex Allen borrowed him to ride in his act at the end of the performance.

In the ensuing decade, the role of the Quarter Horse in Hawai'i grew tremendously thanks to several individuals and ranches, including Smith, Peter Baldwin, Bob Brown, Morgan Brown, Freddy Rice, Parker Ranch, Kūka'iau Ranch, Pu'u Wa'awa'a Ranch, G. E. "Dutch" Schuman, and Wyn Junk, to name a few.

By 1975, the grand majority of Hawai'i's ranch, show, and rodeo horses were of Quarter Horse breeding, with a minority of them registered. By the new millennium, the pendulum had swung toward registered mounts being the grand majority.

HAWAI'I HIGH SCHOOL RODEO

Dr. Billy Bergin

Over the fifteen years that I served as national director of the National High School Rodeo Association (NHSRA), I chose to chronicle each year's progress with a snapshot summary of the National Finals Rodeo (NHSRF). Over the last decade since retiring from that position, I have had frequent inquiries from families of participants for information on past performances. I hope that by recounting the fifteen-year span of youth rodeo successes in this text, the values gained by participants, their families, and most importantly their children and grandchildren will be remembered for many generations to come.

In 1958, a momentous, historic rodeo event took place at the original Honoka'a Rodeo Arena when the Hawai'i Saddle Club produced a junior rodeo. There was a full array of events, and the participants and winners have evolved into prominent members of modern Hawai'i communities. These include names such as Miranda, Spence, Correia, Johansen, Branco, Boteilho, and Kainoa. It was organized by Willy Miranda and Willy Andrade. Stanley Boteilho, age ten, won the calf riding.

Five years later, another junior rodeo was arranged by the same pair of men. It was held at the same arena in August 1963. Earl Spence and Waltham Johansen won the team roping, Juni and Kealoha Medeiros came out of South Kona to win the ribbon roping, and Melvin Miranda captured the steer riding. Junior rodeos also occurred on Maui occasionally. In the ribbon roping during the 1965 Hawai'i Saddle Club rodeo, Alvin Baptiste and Manfred Branco took first place honors, a feat that they repeated in the following year's rodeo.

To the best of my memory, research, and experience, the first purely high school rodeo was organized by young Jimmy Miranda in 1966 at Kūka'iau. The All-Around High School Cowboy at that event was none other than Franklin Boteilho, current manager of Hualālai Ranch in Kona. Other serious junior cowboys participating in that event included Stanley Boteilho, Manfred Branco, Waltham Johansen, Reynolds Botelho, Harry Medeiros, and Johnny Andrade Jr.

A decade passed before interest returned to providing rodeo activities dedicated to our youth. In 1974, Bob Hoffman, as project manager of Waikoloa, and the late George Purdy Jr., Waikoloa Stables manager, organized a Keiki Rodeo that was well attended. It was held at the Waikoloa arena, and one of the more prominent winners included Keoni Lindsey, son of Gabriel and Annabelle Lindsey of Waimea. All age groups, from toddlers to high schoolers, were represented in the schedule of events.

In 1979, a young boy named Holi (my son) decided that it was high time for another youth rodeo. At age nine, Holi organized what he called a Little Britches Rodeo at Paniolo Park. His entry blank was written with a pencil on plain paper. The entry blank named his mother as rodeo secretary, and the arena director was listed as Holi Bergin.

Winners of the team roping were brothers Nolan and David Hao. Nolan later went on to musical fame as a member of the group Hoʻaikāne, which produced several winning recordings. David also developed into an accomplished slack key artist in his own right.

In 1980, a group of parents gathered at the Warren Matsumoto arena to form the Keiki Hawaiʻi Rodeo Association, a family- and community-based organization. In the beginning, much of the organization was done by the Bergin, Miranda, and White families, but several other names became major players in terms of support. The Kainoa, Aguiar, and FitzGerald families on the Big Island, who were firmly committed to supporting and promoting youth rodeo, joined forces with Bill White, Jim Miller, myself, and Parker Ranch.

While other neighbor islands began to show interest in sponsoring youth rodeos, the Big Island families successfully produced four to five Keiki Rodeos per year over an eight-year period, eventually moving up to six scheduled rodeos per year. Events were bracketed into four age groups to even out the competition: 8 and under, 9–10, 11–13, and high school. Events included barrel racing, pole bending, musical tires, calf scrambling, calf roping and mugging, and team roping. At a 1986 Hawaiʻi Rodeo Association rodeo in Hilo, Stemo Lindsey introduced the special event of high school team roping as part of the total show.

While 1987 proved to be an active year of rodeo performances for the Keiki Hawaiʻi Rodeo Association (KHRA), it was also a pivotal time, as the importance of exposure to junior rodeos was recognized on a national level. Scott Lynch's son Chris and his classmate Jay Kubler had completed their Montana State High School Rodeo Finals in Pueblo, Colorado, in July. The Lynch family wintered in Hawaiʻi, working on fencing contracts and participating in rodeo competitions. It was Scott Lynch and Bill White's persistence that provided the impetus to gather a formal committee to follow up on forming a Hawaiʻi High School Rodeo Association (HHSRA) and to apply for membership with the National High School Rodeo Association. A board of directors was formed on which I served as president, Gene Aguiar as first vice president, Mel Miranda as second vice president, Phyllis Aguiar as treasurer, and Jaye Jose as secretary. Billy Gomes served as the Big Island director, and Glen Medeiros, Bob Farias Sr., and Roy Teves served similar positions for the island counties of Maui, Kauaʻi, and Oʻahu, respectively. Pudding Lassiter and Bill White served as directors at large, and Pat FitzGerald was the Queen's Contest director. My son Holi served as the association's first student president, with Ryan White as vice president and DeeDee Keakealani as secretary.

Leejay Lindsey, a charter member of the Hawaiʻi High School Rodeo Association and a junior at Konawaena High School, represented the sixth generation of that cowboy family dynasty.

HAWAIʻI HIGH SCHOOL RODEO

(continued from previous page)

{12.17} *At age nine, Holi Bergin organized a youth rodeo at Paniolo Park. He called it Little Britches Rodeo and named himself arena director and his mother, Pat, as rodeo secretary.*

HAWAI'I HIGH SCHOOL RODEO

(continued from previous page)

Another family deeply involved in support of youth rodeo is reflected in the children of Sally and Freddy Rice. Of special note is Morag Rice, who started with Keiki Rodeo winnings, moved on to Hawai'i Rodeo Association championships, and reigned as Miss Rodeo Hawai'i. She represented Hawai'i at the National Finals Rodeo in Las Vegas, Nevada, in December of 1988. The grandchildren, sons of Mcgrew Rice, Kaulike, and Oskie, were also active participants in Keiki Rodeo events. Today, Rice grandchildren and great-grandchildren continue this legacy through active support and participation in *keiki* and high school rodeo events (see plate 7).

In early 1988, Hawai'i was admitted to the National High School Rodeo Association, giving Hawai'i's youth a chance to compete on a national level. This change came about by transformation of the Keiki Hawai'i Rodeo Association into a nonprofit corporation called the Hawai'i High School Rodeo Association (see plate 6). The constitution and by-laws mandated that events servicing the three younger brackets continue.

Under NHSRA and HHSRA rules, membership and participation required that students have passing grades that by national (NHSRA) rules means passing better than half of the courses if four or more courses are taken. If a contender is enrolled in less than four courses, passing grades are required in all courses to compete. In the 1994–1995 season, the HHSRA general membership voted to move up to a 2.0 minimum GPA, similar to that of Hawai'i interscholastic leagues on each island—such as the OIA, ILH, BIIF, MIL, and KIF—for participation in high school athletics.

{ 12.18 } *An influential advocate for the sport of rodeo in Hawai'i for more than forty years, Bill White is shown receiving a plaque from HHSRA president Gene Aguiar in appreciation of his services.*

On a national level, HHSRA trekked to Pueblo, Colorado, in July 1988 for its first National Finals Rodeo. Twelve contestants, together with an entourage of family and friends, descended upon the southern Colorado town with gusto, and although no event go-rounds or places were won, Hawai'i managed to handily win the volleyball tournament under the able coaching of Bill White (father of qualifier Ryan) and Sonny Keakealani (father of qualifier DeeDee).

A return to Pueblo in 1989 was highlighted by Billy Benevides Jr. qualifying in the coveted third go-round in bull riding. While Billy was not able to place in the final top ten, he nevertheless put Hawai'i on the National High School Rodeo map, especially in bull riding. Billy went on to serve youth rodeo as a bullfighter in the Hawai'i District

HAWAI'I HIGH SCHOOL RODEO

(continued from previous page)

{ 12.19 } *Clad in team colors and lei* papale, *the 1988 Hawai'i High School Rodeo Association team launched a long-standing relationship with national competition. Seated in the top row are (left to right) Monty Miranda, Billy Benevides, Shawn Aguiar, Chris Lopes, and Peter Andrade. Standing are (left to right) DeeDee Keakealani, Leejay Lindsey, Holi Bergin, Shay Van Zandt, Ryan White, Craig Diego, Toni Ann Gomes, and Dr. Billy Bergin, national director.*

HAWAIʻI HIGH SCHOOL RODEO

(continued from previous page)

and the State Finals, as well as being a frequent competitor in state rodeo competitions.

In 1990, the National High School Finals Rodeo (NHSFR) was moved to Shawnee, Oklahoma, for a three-year stint. Here we found new friends, new horses, and a beautiful, brand-new rodeo facility. Hawaiʻi redeemed its bull-riding skill when Ollie White won second in the nationals. Renee Gouveia (Rosario) in 1991 and my son Brady in 1992 placed in cutting-horse competition nationally. Also, in volleyball, after a five-year vacuum, the Hawaiian team took home the coveted trophy in Shawnee in 1992.

By 1993, the National High School Rodeo Finals moved to Gillette, Wyoming, and Hawaiʻi's team had grown from a first-year team of twelve qualifiers to twenty-seven contenders, with all five rodeo islands represented. Again, Gillette presented a rodeo

{ 12.20 } *High school freshman Brady Bergin in a 1992 photo. As a high school graduate from Hawaiʻi Preparatory Academy in 1995, Brady garnered third place in boy's cutting at the National High School Finals Rodeo in Gillette, Wyoming.*

HAWAI'I HIGH SCHOOL RODEO

(continued from previous page)

complex called Camplex that proved to be a facility of the finest order, where 49,838 people watched 1,445 contestants compete in thirteen rodeo performances. Gillette provided an exhilarating variety of weather conditions: nearly record low temperatures, wind, rain, hail, and finally, nearly record high temperatures. Facilities at Camplex easily housed over 1,430 horses and 650 trailers. Housing was a great improvement, with the Hawai'i team able to turn back two of its allotted eighteen rooms.

In rodeo competition, the first go-round was highlighted by Damien Flores placing ninth in bull riding, following the standard set earlier by Billy Benevides Jr. in 1989 and Ollie White in 1990. Although the Hawai'i team typically lands two or three contestants in the top twenty final go-round in bull riding and girls' cutting, 1993 was not our year. Nonetheless, this did not faze the Hawai'i competitors when it came to enthusiasm, sportsmanship, and aloha. Queen Mary Wilson was truly an Ambassador of Aloha, elegantly representing our state in rodeo and queen competitions alike. The entire team was a credit to our Aloha State throughout the stay, and no one could have been prouder than Janey Harris, who evolved as the official host mother of HHSRA in Wyoming.

As the team trekked to Gillette, Wyoming, in 1994, Hawai'i was led by a strong queen candidate in Julie Miranda, who brought Hawai'i to the forefront by successfully placing in the horsemanship class of the queen's contest, narrowly missing a buckle. Although not our best rodeo year, the team represented our state in fine fashion.

At the NHSRF 1993 competition in Gillette, Wyoming, Hawai'i's team established a new record in the near half century of National High School Rodeo. Hano Naehu and Bruddah Kaiama won the second go-round of team roping with a 5.84-second run, winning a beautiful plaque for their efforts. More importantly, since NHSRA's beginning in 1949, these Hawaiian team ropers established a new record fast time in National Finals history. Although their first go-round carried a broken barrier penalty, the team still made the top-twenty cut for a spot in the prestigious third and final go-round.

Hawai'i continued to remain in the spotlight during the weeklong rodeo in hospitable Gillette. As a whole, the team climbed nearly halfway up the ladder of national competition in twenty-fourth place behind its strength in multiple events, in addition to the team-roping event. Maui's Leo Caires and the Big Island's Nicky Rapoza were tough in bull riding. Leo's efforts garnered a third place as the 1995 NHSRF Rookie of the Year. Rapoza made the third and final go-round, going in at seventeenth place and emerging eleventh in the nation when all was said and done. In boys' cutting, my son Brady had a great year, placing fourth in the first go, third in the second go, and second in the third go. His efforts generated substantial points for the team, an AQHA college scholarship, and a shiny buckle naming him third in the nation at the 1995 National Finals.

HAWAI'I HIGH SCHOOL RODEO

(continued from previous page)

On the subject of scholarships, by the tenth year of national affiliation Hawai'i had earned at least one, and more often two, $500 college scholarships each year. The highest scholarship achievement, a $1,000 Wrangler Merit Scholarship award, went to Karla Tadio of Honoka'a awarded in Shawnee, Oklahoma.

The 1996 NHSRF was reminiscent for many, returning to Pueblo, Colorado, where Hawai'i first established a National Finals presence in 1988. The team was thirty strong, but competition was tough. Despite a rough couple of bull rides, Keone DeSilva served as the bull riding event director in the rough-stock arena for the second and final goes. Galvin Rita showed remarkable strength in overcoming the loss of his team-roping mount, which expired from colic nearly right out from under him. The highlight for the team was Queen Adrienne Knuppel, who garnered more points in all categories of the queen's contest than any of Hawai'i's candidates of previous years.

In 1997, genuine honors were received by the team from the Aloha State. Bruddah Kelekoma scored third in the second go bull riding and twenty-fourth overall. He got down to business with his team-roping partner, B. J. Delima, to win tenth in the nation in team roping. The combined points boosted Bruddah into ninth place in the nation in All-Around Cowboy standings and B. J. into eleventh place for Cowboy Rookie of the Year. Buckles and scholarships were duly awarded to these fine competitors.

Entering its first finals competition in Springfield, Illinois, HHSRA celebrated its twelfth anniversary of national competition and reflected on the record of many of its members who prevailed in the National Intercollegiate Rodeo Association, Professional Rodeo Cowboys Association, Bull Riders Only, Professional Bull Riders, and United States Team Roping Competition associations.

In prominent rodeo circles, the Hawai'i High School Rodeo Association is proud to recall continued success of Ryan White (1988), Monty and Dusty Miranda (1992, 1993), Wayne Tasaka (1993), Burton James (1993) Melanie DeMattos (1993), Mary Wilson (1993, 1994), Scott Miller (1995), Damien Flores (1993), Ross Farias (1993), and most prominently, Myron Duarte of National Finals Rodeo (NFR) fame.

Hawai'i returned to Gillette, Wyoming, in 1998. While volleyball didn't work out, nothing dampened the enthusiasm for rodeo and other related fun, such as the successful entry of a Hawaiian float in the NHSRA 50th Anniversary celebration parade. Contestants' parents pitched in to make this event a truly memorable one. This enthusiasm carried over to our student competitors, who gave it their all in their respective events. Kalia Goo turned in respectable performances in cutting, and B. J. DeLima made Hawai'i look good in calf and team roping with Nick Rodrigues. Despite pulling a sorry bull in his first go, Nick returned to win second in the second go-round. Between Nick and B. J.,

HAWAI'I HIGH SCHOOL RODEO

(continued from previous page)

Hawai'i kept in the race, coming in twenty-second overall in bull riding, just missing the third and final short go. Nick also placed twenty-second in bull riding. Watching others ride the rank bulls and getting bucked off caused any observer to marvel at Nick's ability to remain astride these monstrous animals. Dominic Barretto won the Determination Award for his fierce devotion to rodeo.

Hawai'i returned to Gillette for the second year and last rotation in 1999. After a two-year venue in Springfield, Illinois, the competition moved to Farmington, New Mexico, for two years and then again to Gillette, Wyoming, for another two-year period. This two-year rotation cycle repeats itself unless changed by national directors in the future.

The year 1999 was special for Hawai'i, with some significant firsts in rodeo competition and an overwhelming volleyball victory for the third time in a dozen years. It was a pleasurable experience to be in Gillette with twenty-one enthusiastic contestants and their supportive families and friends. The team conducted themselves with great sportsmanship, rodeo performances, and mutual support for one another. Across all events, it was gratifying to see consistency as the theme: tying down two calves by J. C. Cabral, two breakaway calves by Tanya Deluz, and two downed steers by Dominc Barretto. Standout performances were credited to Chelsea Branco in Girl's Breakaway roping with her 3.5-second run in the first go-round and a cool 3.3-second run in the second go that placed her in fourth place in the national average on two. While she drew a sorry calf on her final go-round, she made the best of it and turned in a stellar performance.

Not to be outdone, Melissa DeMattos was right on top of things with her second go-round pole-bending run that placed her in the top ten of the full second go-round action, marking another first in that event on the national level. Jesse Dowsett set the pace in the boys' cutting first go with a 143, and although the second cut didn't work out as well, the entire team was proud of his achievement. Both performances were quite an achievement for a pair of high school freshmen setting the standard as they did. Serving graciously as Hawai'i's representative, queen contestant Maria Estocado garnered many compliments from her fellow competitors as well as from long-standing chairperson James Higginbotham.

Getting serious outside the arena, Hawai'i took home its third volleyball win in eleven years, with "Goat" Dudoit as coach. Other festivities included a parade and float complete with ali'i and hula dancers, as well as a Cowboy Prom with Hawai'i's own Chinky Hubbard and Mona Lisa Prito unanimously elected prom king and queen by prom attendees.

HAWAI'I HIGH SCHOOL RODEO

(continued from previous page)

With my election as president of the National High School Rodeo Association in 1999, parent leaders stepped in to help in whatever way they could to ensure that the Hawai'i team would continue without a hitch. Among these capable and willing leaders were the likes of Paul Deluz, Bobby DeMattos, Pat FitzGerald, Andrea Adrian, and Sally Inkster. These individuals deserve full credit for the success of the State and National Finals during this period. Through their efforts, a team of top hands returned for a second trip to the Springfield, Illinois, competition, dealing with distance, travel, and roller-coaster weather of 100-degree heat and drenching thunderstorms. Though the competitors were valiant in their efforts, the environment took its toll in the arena, but it did not dampen their enthusiasm for fun and excitement in the Land of Lincoln. As always, the team spirit made for a memorable visit to Illinois, and they looked forward to the following year's National Finals in Farmington, New Mexico.

An air of excitement prevailed as the team prepared for the 2002 finals in Farmington, the first venue in the southwest for the team. Nestled in the northwestern corner of New Mexico, Farmington offered a vivid contrast from the Midwestern farm feeling of Springfield, Illinois, the high mesa of Gillette, Wyoming, the plains of Shawnee, Oklahoma, and the rolling hills of the Colorado Rockies in Pueblo. The largest team of qualifiers in our fourteen-year history signed on for the finals that year, with thirty-four qualifiers participating. By rodeo time, the number dropped to twenty-nine, still a significant number for Hawai'i. This team had the added benefit of being one of the closest teams of parents and contestants in our history. To top it off, it was one of the most productive finals for Hawai'i. This was particularly evident in calf roping, all four competitors tying down their calves in the first go, with Ziggy Jewell leading the pack with a 12.88 run. Both he and Colby Costa had successful ties in the second go, Ziggy scoring 29.57 on two, almost qualifying him for the final go. In Girls' Breakaway, Krystle Estocado turned in a hot 3.59 run on the first go and roping tough on the second.

Cutting performances were off the charts, with Queen Nahe Nobriga scoring 206 on two for a total score of 412. Her brother Kala'i turned in outstanding times in his cutting competitions, with a fifth-place first go with a 277, a first-place win in the second go with a 220, and an outstanding performance of second place in both go-rounds in the finals go-round, bringing him to third in the nation after three full go-rounds. These winners gave Hawai'i a twenty-ninth-place berth out of forty-five states, provinces, and countries.

This event marked the fifteenth year that I served as High School Rodeo director for the State of Hawai'i. I announced my retirement and turned the reins of the organization over to the capable hands of Patrick FitzGerald, parent and longtime supporter of

HAWAIʻI HIGH SCHOOL RODEO

(continued from previous page)

HHSRA. I did so with a deep sense of satisfaction, for the time I spent with high school rodeo brought some of the greatest joys of my lifetime.

Youth rodeo has come a long way since it first began in 1958 with Willy Andrade and Willy Miranda. Two decades later, the Keiki Hawaiʻi Rodeo Association was formally chartered by the Miranda, White, Aguiar, and Bergin families and became a statewide venue for organized youth rodeo. A decade later in 1988, KHRA, under the same leadership, was converted into a nationally recognized entity as the Hawaiʻi High School Rodeo Association under the auspices of the National High School Rodeo Association.

Over that fifteen year-span, Hawaiʻi contestants achieved world championship ranking: Oliver White, second in bull riding, Shawnee 1992; Brady Bergin in 1995 and Kalaʻi Nobriga in 2002, both placing third in the world in high school boy's cutting competition at the NHSRF.

Even more profound than placing in national championships is the hard work and determination that these young men and women endured to become state qualifiers. They surfaced as leading contenders in both their district and state competitions, while maintaining a 2.0 or better GPA consistent with academic requirements of all Hawaiʻi high school interscholastic sports activities. Underscoring these academic successes was the greater impact of keeping the borderline high school student in high school through graduation. In some instances, high school rodeo was the only thing that provided the incentive to stay in school to graduate. Inspired by this confidence, some of these men and women went on to college when they became aware through their exposure to national high school competitions that there was a whole world of opportunities for college attendance through rodeo scholarships. Many of them combined their college years with intercollegiate rodeo. Some of these individuals include Heidi Ho, Dusty Miranda, Monty Miranda, Ryan White, Wayne Tasaka, Burton James, Melanie DeMattos, Mary Wilson, Josh FitzGerald, Keone DeSilva, Scott Miller, Leo Baptiste, Kevin Hill, Galvin Rita, Kelli-ann Rita, Ross Farias, and most prominently, Myron Duarte of NFR and PBR fame. Scott Miller went on to the professional ranks in saddle bronc riding.

Today, new competitors join the ranks of the Hawaiʻi youth rodeo organization. These are the grandchildren and great-grandchildren of Willy Andrade and Willy Miranda, the children of *keiki* rodeo participants such as Shane Jose, DeeDee Keakealani-Bertelmann, Morag Rice Miranda, and a host of second- and third-generation competitors, as their *paniolo* family legacy lives on.

REFLECTIONS OF THE HAWAI'I NATIONAL DIRECTOR 1988–2002

Dr. Billy Bergin

In reflecting on these years of service, two distinct components emerge: the role of state leadership and the function of the national director.

In a statewide context, there was immediate (1988) establishment of island district boards: Hawai'i, O'ahu, Kaua'i, and Maui. Moloka'i was granted separate district standing, as its values were distinct from that of the county seat, Maui. Paralleling these efforts was the election of a full slate of state officers, who in turn formally nominated me as Hawai'i national director. Formal adoption of this nomination is a function of the full national board, occurring in January 1988 in Douglas, Wyoming.

Each district was mandated to produce six rodeos beginning in August and culminating with district finals in April of each year. The state's role was to host the state finals in Kamuela annually. All district qualifiers were eligible to enter the state finals provided they maintained a C or better average in their grades. During this term, 222 rodeos were conducted, in accordance with NHSRA rules, and more than 1,500 Hawai'i youths participated.

Challenges

Adopting the mandatory 2.0 grade point rule was not easy, especially for the boys, because rodeo enthusiasts rarely participated in other state sports activities that required the C or better average. Furthermore, on a national scale, only the California HSRA had a 2.0 rule, so the precedent was very narrow, garnering skepticism from the broad majority of other states and provinces. But Hawai'i stayed the course for the betterment of our youth, thanks to the persistence of Vice President Pat FitzGerald. The 2.0 rule positively affected our young participants, who used this leverage to pursue college careers.

A less pleasant aspect of any organized sport is the desire of parents to unduly influence their child's position or standing in the competition. High school rodeo experienced similar challenges in which special interest groups selectively used the rule book to qualify their children for a performance or used the same handbook to disqualify other participants. This was a great disappointment for all to witness. To curtail this activity, parents were reminded that they are not judges in high school rodeo; the students are empowered to self-regulate through serving as event directors, rodeo officials, and arena directors. Such parental interference was not unique to Hawai'i or unique to youth rodeo; it happens across the land.

Observations of Dr. Billy Bergin

REFLECTIONS OF THE HAWAI'I NATIONAL DIRECTOR 1988–2002

(continued from previous page)

My role on the national board was a period of intense learning for me, both from my colleagues with in-depth rodeo experience and also from full immersion into the arena action itself during the world's largest rodeo. Typically, a National High School Rodeo Finals has 1,500 entries over a seven-day period, with both morning and evening performances that culminate in a final go-round in a singular Sunday event. Originally assigned as an "aide-de-camp" in the rough-stock arena, I was eventually assigned duties of arena director managing the cutting arena, a role that combined critical pressure with patience and diplomacy.

Perhaps my greatest contribution over the course of fifteen years was chairing the Humane Relations Committee, which required oversight in each of the thirteen performances regarding the welfare of rough stock, performance horses, and all classes of rodeo cattle and goats. Given my penchant for statistical analysis, I was able to compile accident, injury, and death losses of stock in all performances over the fifteen-year period. The incidence of injury was only 0.002 percent, and the loss of life for all stock was a minuscule 0.0003 percent. The NHSRA should be given due credit for its humane care of all rodeo stock, from the premium roping horse to the flighty goat.

As national president in 1999–2000, my main objectives were twofold: to move the NHSRF to an eastern venue and to complete a comprehensive 20/20 Vision Plan. NHSRF moved to Springfield, Illinois, in 2000, giving the eastern states along the Atlantic seaboard greater access to the finals, thereby generating significant membership growth. The Illinois venue had its downside, as it is the hotbed of anti-rodeo and animal rights activism. Armed with a huge database of information on animal care, such challenges were readily diffused in direct discussions with Alex Pacheco, then president of People for the Ethical Treatment of Animals (PETA).

The NHSRA 20/20 Vision Plan was a mission inspired by the 1985 community development plan drawn up by Richard Smart as to how the village of Kamuela should prepare itself for the envisioned exponential growth into a regional center of north Hawai'i, Waimea Town, by the year 2020. The NHSRA 20/20 Vision Plan used the same time frame but produced a road map for organizational growth over the decades approaching the twentieth year of the new millennium—2020.

✢ National High School Rodeo Association ✢ 20/20 Vision Plan

The mission of the 20/20 Vision Plan is to develop collective foresight in charting the course of the NHSRA over the ensuing two decades. Input from a variety of present and past national directors, NHSR Foundation directors, student officers, and office staff and management provided the basis for the 20/20 Vision Plan. The goals must be practical, but set high, bordering on achievable. It is a plan that remains forever in motion, requiring periodic review, upgrading, and fine tuning. This is our collective plan, and it must be collectively embraced.

The components of the 20/20 Vision Plan are based on summary review of the six years of planning and steering committee recommendations, goals set forth in workshops of the full board, and objectives cited in student officers' scoping sessions. Components called for include membership development, attendance generation, public relations/marketing, scholarship enhancement, NHSFR approval, and office development.

In retrospect, all desire for success was centered on student athletes and their progress both academically and in performances. In observing youth rodeo in Hawai'i today, there is a new generation of children of the original student athletes who currently enjoy successful experiences in school and rodeo while perpetuating the values of the American West, just as their predecessors did.

There were special people worthy of merit and acknowledgment during my tenure, beginning with my wife, Pat, and my family. Andrea Adrian, John and Patrick FitzGerald, Bobby DeMattos, Sally Inkster, Pat Kelekoma, Clifford Ornellas, and Calvin Rita played key roles in the success of the HHSRA over my fifteen-year involvement. In addition, Parker Ranch deserves enduring credit for its support in supplying livestock and facilities throughout Hawai'i's broad history of rodeo.

CHAPTER 13

POLO

The first reported polo matches in Hawai'i were played during the reign of King Kalākaua at Pālama near Honolulu in 1880, but in a global context the sport was centuries old by then.

Persians are credited with inventing the sport, albeit in a crude fashion, as early as 500 BCE. While a polo ball was to come later, the Persians started the sport using severed human heads of enemy warriors with contemptuous vigor. As the game caught on among several tribal circles, a polo ball was produced by rounding off a gnarly knot of willow wood called *pulu*—hence the term "polo" for the sport itself.

Spreading in popularity to China, India, and Tibet, the sport approached sophistication, save for the mounted Mongols, who batted about sheep carcasses or parts thereof. British officers returning from India introduced polo to the Western world in the form that exists today: a highly refined team game on horseback.

Evolution of Polo

Like horse racing, polo is commonly referred to as the "sport of kings." The fact that two different sports use this appellation is indeed a tribute to fine horses. There is little doubt that, in centuries past, when equine sports were born, both pastimes were available only to the ruling class, which had the time and resources to practice them. Polo began in Persia as a cavalry training game involving the elite mounted guards.

In time, polo grew to become a national sport, with male and female players of the noble Persian class. In medieval times, polo spread to the Byzantines and eventually to the Indian subcontinent and China, where the Tang dynasty celebrated the sport in art and sculpture.

British military officers stationed in India recognized polo as a horse sport that deserved celebration throughout the

Western world, founding the first polo club in Assam, India, in 1834. In that same year, the Tenth Hussars of Aldershot, Hants, England, introduced polo to Britain. Modern polo had its beginnings at the Imphal Polo Ground in Manipur State, India. By 1862, the Calcutta Polo Club was established by British officers Captain Robert Stewart and Major General Joe Shearer. Shearer, considered the father of modern-day polo, led the British campaign in spreading polo worldwide in the nineteenth and early twentieth centuries. Codification of the rules of the sport by the governing body, Hurlingham Polo Association, was formalized in an international context, some of which still exists today (*Hurlingham Polo Magazine* 2013).

Argentine Connection

David Shennan, a British settler in the Pampas of Argentina, organized the country's first polo match in 1875. Horse-savvy and skillful riders, the gauchos readily adopted the sport, and several clubs opened up in subsequent years throughout the land. In 1892, the River Plate Polo Association was established as the formal national governing body. By 1924, Argentina qualified for the Olympics in Paris, garnering a gold medal victory for the team. This success was repeated in the 1936 Berlin Olympics, establishing Argentina as the world's "Mecca of polo." Today Argentina can boast having the largest number of 10-handicap players of any country. At one point (1975), Argentina assembled four 10-handicap players, forming a 40-handicap team. By 2011, Argentina hosted the World Polo Championship at the Estancia Grande Polo Club in the province of San Luis.

If Germany has emerged as the "Vatican of Dressage," then Argentina is recognized globally as the "Cathedral of Polo," according to Lord Patrick Beresford in the spring 2013 issue of *Hurlingham Polo Magazine*.

In terms of facilities, within thirty-five miles of Buenos Aires lies the home of the world's greatest polo ground, Palermo. Within a few square miles, there are more polo grounds than in the entire British Isles.

While grooms still wear the gaucho apparel of beret and *bombachas* (baggy trousers), gone are the heavy-headed criollo (creole) polo ponies of yesteryear, now replaced by gallant Thoroughbred mounts. Gone are the heavy-handed gaucho training methods, instead replaced by the gentle and thoughtful approaches of Monty Roberts and others.

The value of Argentine polo ponies from leading breeders is phenomenal. At the November 2012 Ellerstina auction, twenty-one yearling fillies were offered, twenty of which sold for an average of $95,000.

Why polo prospects are preferably fillies needs research, but gender-guaranteed embryos were sold at the same auction, sixteen of such were sold. The first three lots went for $100,000, $90,000, and $55,000 respectively. There is little doubt that Argentina is the Cathedral of Polo and Palermo its High Altar.

Birth of United States Polo

The first polo match in the United States took place at Dickels Riding Academy on May 6, 1876, organized by James Gordon Bennett Jr. English players in Texas, however, argued that Bennett's New York Polo match was second to their May 2, 1876, game in Denison, Texas. A challenge was published in the June 2, 1876, *Galveston Daily News,* which included a grudge match to establish Texas as the true birthplace of American polo. Not to be outdone, Boerne, Texas, jumped into the melee when the owner of Balcones Ranch, retired British captain Glynn Turquand, claimed that polo was played at his outfit "before James Gordon Bennett ever picked up a polo mallet."

Bennett seems to have restored legitimacy, however, in bringing polo to the United States when he partnered with August Belmont and H. L. Herbert in financing the New York Polo Grounds, establishing a home base at the Westchester Polo Club. Belmont's name and money brought inarguable testimony that New York was indeed the birthplace of American polo.

By the early 1900s, Harry Payne Whitney emerged as a major force of change in American polo, moving away from the British game of short passes to fast-breaking, long passes far downfield to waiting teammates.

Basic Polo Safety

Polo is a sport known for its speed, beauty, and danger. Whether the game is played indoors or out, certain basic rules apply to avoid accidents while promoting fair play. A "bump" refers to a player being permitted to ride into an opponent's horse to spoil the player's shot or remove him from play. Angles of collision cannot exceed 45 degrees. The greater the velocity of play, the smaller the angle can be. "Riding off" is an extension of a "bump," as the opponent continues horse-to-horse contact, edging the opponent out of play.

The "line of the ball" refers to the imaginary pathway at which a struck ball is traveling, allowing a right-of-way for the last player striking the ball. Crossing the line by others can put players at risk and is the most common foul. Polo must be played right-handed.

A "hook" refers to a player spoiling another's shot by placing his mallet in the way of the striking player's mallet. While a legal and effective form of play, improper use of hooking can put both players at risk. A notable example occurred when Lt. Col. George S. Patton hooked the reins of Manduke Baldwin during a World War II polo match on O'ahu. In the melee, Patton was thrown beneath his own horse, narrowly escaping injury. However, his upbraiding of the umpire in streams of obscenities cost him not only a foul but ejection from the game and loss of his US Army team captaincy. Unscathed, Manduke finished the chukker (period) in fine fashion. The tragic death of entertainer Al Lopaka at a Mokulē'ia match in 1985 likely involved a rule infraction, an aspect of the incident that was eventually clarified by officials as a simple unfortunate accident.

Al Lopaka

Born Alton J. Lopez on the island of Lāna'i, Al Lopaka was destined for glory in the entertainment arena and on the polo field. A mentor prominent in both circles was Tommy Campos, the revered O'ahu horseman, whose skill as a polo player and trainer was matched by his role as protector of prominent entertainers such as Don Ho and Lopaka.

Al couldn't have asked for a better, more disciplined, or devoted mentor than Tommy Campos. Al's meteoric polo career from novice to star status (5-goal) was also due to his natural athleticism, love for horses, and deep commitment to achieving excellence.

On the fateful day of June 23, 1985, Al competed in his last polo match, a celebrity game with prominent players of the game. Mounted on his favorite horse, Heidi, Al's close proximity to an opponent caused their horses' limbs to become entangled, creating a high-speed tumble. The headfirst plummet provided no opportunity for Al to break the fall with his forearms. After a weeklong coma, he died peacefully at the age of forty-two, fulfilling his prophecy of dying with a smile after a bout of polo.

The Polo Field

An outdoor polo field is 300 by 160 yards, or the area of nine football fields. Ample peripheral runoff space makes for safer play. Kapi'olani Park, Benson Field, Schofield Barracks, and the Moanalua Field were early venues. Dillingham's Mokulē'ia Field and Waimānalo Field followed with outdoor grounds.

Over the past century, indoor polo has become commonplace, supplying faster and more vivid action while reducing players from four to three. These changes made polo more affordable for both developer (field owner) and players. Playtime remains at seven minutes per chukker and up to thirty seconds for overtime. The typical dimensions of an indoor polo field are 300 by 150 feet. The minimum size is 150 by 75 feet.

The Polo Pony

As mounts of bygone eras were small in stature, averaging fourteen hands, the term "polo pony" was quite applicable. With early British influence, the Thoroughbred breed became the mainstay resource for taller and faster mounts. For the last century, the average polo pony has rarely stood less than fifteen hands, yet the moniker "pony" remains, reflecting the historic equine forebears of small stature. In local circles, polo ponies are often registered Quarter Horses, a breed that lends itself to all equestrian sporting activities. Modern-day polo ponies of sixteen hands are not uncommon. The traditional Thoroughbred, however, still rules the greater polo fields of the world, confirming the sage words of the late great enthusiast Ed Hedemann.

Trained to be reined by single-handed riders, responding to the leg and weight cues for moving forward, stopping, or turning, a good polo mount can account for 60 to 75 percent of the player's skill and net worth of his team.

In reality, what changed the size from a fourteen-hand polo "pony" to a robust sixteen-hand mount was the ruling in recent years that allowed a player to "ride off" his opponent as he attempts to strike the ball. Riding off, as noted earlier, is a process in which a player comes up alongside the opponent, bumping him out of his pathway to the ball. An eleven-hundred-pound mount can readily bulldoze a nine-hundred-pound polo pony. The bigger horse has the ability to ride off a mount of his size, while a smaller polo pony is compromised in its efforts to ride off a horse of significantly greater mass. Riding off was previously referred to as the "off-side rule" before it was abandoned in the early 1900s. Hawaiian polo players moved to bigger horses early on, and they attribute their success to this paradigm.

A 1914 article by Herbert Reed describes this change in the game:

> The Hawaiians and the newcomers from Southern California are fair samples of what the demand has come to since the abandonment of the off-side rule and the consequent emphasis on ruggedness and tremendous pace. They are bigger and stronger than many of the famous mounts of the old days. There can be no doubt that the small ponies were far easier to ride than the powerful mounts of today, for their stride was probably considerably smoother, but they could hardly be expected to stand the terrific shocks of the modern game. (Reed 2012)

Americans led the change to bigger mounts owing to the fact that they were bigger men, needing horses that could stand up under the heaviest form of shock action while packing a player of greater mass.

Reed in his 1914 article was unabashed in his praise of this Parker Ranch–bred mount: "Carry the News undoubtedly will be the star of the American string, as Harry Payne Whitney has said that his light chestnut gelding with the white face and the white stockings is one of the best polo ponies he has ever ridden."

Polo Comes to Hawaiʻi

The November 3, 1880, Pālama polo match between British naval officers of the HMS *Gannett* and Oʻahu players is reflective of the influence of the military in spreading the popularity of the sport. Louis von Tempsky, the father of Hawaiian polo, was introduced to the sport by British Major Haley of the Tenth Hussars as the officer enjoyed lengthy Hawaiian hospitality on his way back to England from war. As a young adult, Glasgow-born

{ 13.1 } *Credited with bringing polo to the Hawaiian Islands, Louis von Tempsky staged his first match in Hāwī, Kohala District.*

von Tempsky left his native land for New Zealand, where his skills as a stockman were further honed. Settling in the Hawaiian Islands, the Scotsman readily fit into equestrian and ranching circles. On December 25, 1886, von Tempsky first took the sport of polo to Hāwī on Hawai'i Island, where he engaged a "dozen sporting youngbloods" to put on a game under his tutelage (Cowan-Smith and Stone 1988).

While the Big Island had the potential for expansive popularity of the sport, it was von Tempsky's settling in Maui that gave birth to a nucleus of ranching families—the Baldwins and Rices—that sealed forever the place of polo in Hawaiian history. On Christmas Day a year later, at Haleakalā Ranch, von Tempsky introduced polo to the Baldwin brothers, Harry, Arthur, Fred, and Frank, beginning a polo dynasty that is evident even today.

In 1897, another polo field sprang up on Maui in Sunnyside, near Pā'ia and Haikū, and it had a large player turnout.

It took a Hawai'i team in 1899 to roust a British team out of India. Hawai'i's attraction for international polo matches has never waned, as indicated over the ensuing century of entries from Argentina, Australia, Canada, Chile, England, Germany, Hong Kong, Ireland, Italy, Manila, New Zealand, and El Salvador.

In 1900, polo was established by S. E. Damon at Moanalua as the O'ahu Polo Club, with Walter F. Dillingham taking the cue. O'ahu's most prominent businessman of that era, Dillingham took the sport seriously, especially when challenged by the Maui families. The Dillinghams were noted for breeding top mounts for polo, having stood the renowned Thoroughbred stallion Skymore for more than a decade. Stabled alongside Skymore was Aloha Moon, a stud that combined success on the polo field and the breeding barn. Skylark, a direct son of Skymore, carried on through the 1970s, producing polo ponies and cow horses for Parker Ranch and Pu'u Wa'awa'a Ranch. The latter outfit was jointly owned by Dillingham and Carlsmith interests.

Dillingham organized O'ahu's first teams and matches at his Crowbar Ranch in Mokulē'ia, while helping Damon further develop the polo fields at Moanalua and the O'ahu Polo Club (OPC) organizations. He captained the OPC team.

In 1901, Hawai'i's first interisland tournament was featured at the Moanalua Field, with O'ahu outscoring Maui 9 to 3.

Riding for OPC were Ned Damon, J. Fleming, and C. S. and Albert Judd, who clearly upset the favored Maui team of Louis von Tempsky and three Baldwin brothers. A rematch on Maui at the Makawao Polo Grounds was more disastrous, with an 11 to 0 shutout of the native sons. But Maui players in the coming years more than made up for the shutout of 1901.

Baldwin, Dillingham, Rice, and von Tempsky all produced several generations of polo-playing horsemen whose upbringing was on the field, with secondary education at Punahou and New Mexico Military Academy, climaxing with college at Cornell University. Not surprisingly, college polo was their forte at the latter two institutions, yielding remarkable reputations that remain today.

Another parallel among these families is the universal mission of bringing superior horse stock to Hawai'i, especially that of Thoroughbred breeding. It is no fluke that their ranches were named as remount stations by the US Remount Service in recognition of their established wisdom in producing fine mounts.

Hawai'i was consistent in producing strong island teams on Maui and O'ahu, while Kaua'i and especially the Big Island were marginal in this regard. In 1902, polo was introduced to Kaua'i through the efforts of the Spalding family, who organized matches at Waipouli and Kapa'a. To their credit, the Rice family of Kaua'i also remained steady in polo support, as did Parker Ranch on the island of Hawai'i, producing grand polo ponies on a large, nearly global scale.

In 1913, when the neighbor island teams joined forces with O'ahu, polo history was made. When Frank and Sam Baldwin of Maui joined with Arthur Rice of Kaua'i and hooked up with Walter F. Dillingham and Harold Castle of O'ahu, a formidable team was born. Shocking elite California polo circles by winning the coveted Bourne Cup in San Mateo, the Hawai'i team solidified the reputation of the territory as a resource of top players and exceptional horses.

In 1914, the Parker Ranch–bred polo mount Carry the News gained international recognition for exemplary performance in several matches between American and British teams in New Jersey and English venues. Owner Dr. Will Baldwin turned down a $16,000 cash offer from Jock Whitney for the horse, described as "probably the most famous polo pony in the world today" in a 1915 article that appeared in the *Maui News.* Aware that the Parker Ranch–bred mount was a key to victory for the US polo team over England, Will Baldwin tore the check in half and gave the horse to Whitney for the sake of the US team's hopeful victory. The US team prevailed in later weeks.

Hawai'i's polo history is not without tragedy. In 1925 a fire broke out in a new barn at the Maui Polo Grounds in Kahului, trapping fourteen top mounts, half of which had arrived from the mainland via the steamship *Manulani* and been placed in their new stalls only two hours earlier. The other seven were the finest polo ponies Maui could offer at the time. Unknown causes still haunt the memory of the barn's demise.

The architects of the territorial team, Walter F. Dillingham and Frank Baldwin, sustained Hawai'i's place in the national annals of polo competition over the ensuing three decades leading up to World War II. By 1935, the two were referred to as "America's Polo Maestros of the Mid-Pacific," honors that they truly deserved (Cowan-Smith and Stone 1988). The extent of their influence became evident before World War II when they reinstated Lt. Col. George S. Patton as the US Army team captain and player. During this era, Maui's Edward Baldwin earned a 7-goal from the United States Polo Association. Pukalani Polo Field (Maui), Kapi'olani Park (O'ahu), and Benson Field (Schofield Barracks) were the prime sites for polo action.

Military Polo

The military's involvement in Hawai'i polo is no less intensive. Polo was most popular among officers, and joining the Schofield Barracks Polo Association became the avenue for active play over the seven-month season for the Hawai'i Department of the Military. Through twice-weekly intramural meets, officers enjoyed playing on one of three regulation-size polo fields between May and November annually. One of the fields, the Benson Memorial Polo Field, named in honor of Lt. Guy Benson of the Eleventh Field Artillery, enjoyed an international reputation as one of the best-turfed, full-sized fields in the world at that time, rivaling New York's famed Meadowbrook Polo Field. Of course, all of Hawai'i polo fields had the advantage of year-round, all-weather usage, given the ideal climatic conditions.

Military polo was increasingly dependent on locally supplied mounts. By 1934, a third of the ninety polo mounts at Schofield Barracks were the property of the respective officers who enjoyed the privilege of stabling on the base with fields nearby. Long-standing relationships developed between the officers and the ranchers who produced large crops of cavalry prospects, among which were horses suitable for polo and available for private purchase.

Such a relationship blossomed between Lt. Col. George S. Patton and A. W. Carter, trustee and manager of Parker Ranch on the Big Island while Patton served in Hawai'i. Patton's daughter Ruth Ellen was delighted to be gifted a fine sorrel gelding, Ho'okupu, son of the famed Parker Ranch stallion Gold Oak, which was shown successfully in hunter/jumper classes in Virginia and Maryland.

If Patton had had his way, the US military today would still boast a mounted cavalry, along with an army polo team. He viewed the cavalry as shock troops in a purely offensive military context. In designing a cavalry saber, he considered the mounted trooper as a projectile with the saber its point, smashing open gaps in enemy lines, harassing their flanks, while disrupting supply lines in the rear, causing psychological terror. This attitude explains Patton's view of polo as an effective system for instilling the values for shock cavalry in real war.

Patton was sincere but bellicose in his belief that the intrinsic value of the sport of polo was its warlike quest for victory at all costs, an attribute that was embedded in the hearts of charging cavalry officers in the heat of battle. Polo experience, he believed, gives the officer the ability to think fast under the most excitable circumstances. Using an aggressive riding style, the officer attacks at ferocious speed while setting aside his natural instinct for safety. Mounted cavalry officers—even in the face of mortal enemies manned with artillery—provide shock and awe, disabling opponents with bold flair. While his belligerent attitude served the US Army well, in Hawai'i's polo circles, it brought him disdain. His "wings were clipped" by Walter F. Dillingham and Frank Baldwin.

Patton, later promoted to general and serving as commander of army divisions in World War II, was an avid polo player noted for his fine horsemanship and superb stick work while he served in the army. On the polo field, he was ruthless in an aggressive technique that was accompanied by loud obscenities. Officials at the 1934 US Army vs. Maui match at Kapi'olani Park, as noted earlier, chose to expel him from the match for reasons of unsportsmanlike conduct (obscenity), relieving him as team captain and relegating his role to the sidelines for observations. Patton was further frustrated over the army's loss to Maui by a score of 8 to 5. Appealing for reinstatement for subsequent match play, Patton was granted a pardon from Walter F. Dillingham and Frank Baldwin on firm conditions, one of which was acknowledging defeat from the "Maui Cowboys," a moniker he created with disdain while the Valley Isle *paniolo* savored their victory.

With the pressure of World War II on manpower and resources, polo activities became dormant. For the military officers' mounts, their usefulness declined dramatically. While the stables at Schofield Barracks remained standing after the cavalry was disbanded, it would be thirty

{ 13.2 } *George S. Patton benefited from his relationship with A. W. Carter when Patton's daughter Ruth Ellen was gifted with a son of the US Remount sire Gold Oak, a mount she put to very good use. Here she is astride Ho'okupu, whose name means "gift" in Hawaiian.*

{ 13.3 } *Visiting the Pattons at their Maryland estate, A. W. Carter was elated with the long-standing friendship that cemented the relationship between Parker Ranch and the US Remount movement.*

years before private club horses would again be housed on the premises. Eventually demolished in 1986, the demise of the stables erased the image of the heyday of military horse activities of years gone by.

Polo Reborn

Just when it looked like polo would die the quiet death of military horse activities, a reorganized Hawaiʻi Polo and Racing Club rose from the ashes and in 1950 staged indoor matches in the "Old Stadium," also called the "Termite Palace" in the Mōʻiliʻili section of downtown Honolulu. This rekindled interest in polo players and the attendant social crowd.

Kapiʻolani Stables provided a convenient home for the mounts used at Honolulu Stadium, where indoor polo was played using three players instead of four and using a smaller field that created an action-packed flavor to the game. At this venue, Maui ruled without mercy via the team of Richard "Manduke" Baldwin, Gordon von Tempsky, and Harold "Oskie" Rice, which plundered Oʻahu, mainland, and Mexican teams. It was during this era that the nationally rated 9-goal polo phenom Peter Perkins moved to Hawaiʻi in 1952, becoming the Islands' highest-rated resident player.

But true revival followed in a few years, when hotelier Fred Dailey and his wife Murph formed the Waikīkī Polo Club in 1957.

Dailey was well backgrounded in the sport, having played with the Black Horse Troop in Chicago before settling permanently and prominently in Hawaiʻi's hotel industry. Through his connections with Honolulu's wealthier residents, he was able to secure an indoor field in Kapiʻolani Park. Without a doubt, Fred Dailey became the modern-day "Maestro of Polo in the Mid-Pacific," and his efforts had just begun. In 1963, the City and County of Honolulu assumed control of the field and stables at Kapiʻolani Park, at which time Daily moved operations to Mokulēʻia on Dillingham lands. Dailey renovated the property by uprooting and relocating forty trees and returfing the field with a cutting-edge variety of Bermuda grass that was more trauma and drought resistant and rapid in regrowth and recovery. In honor of the Dillingham role in polo's history, the facility was dedicated as the Walter F. Dillingham Field.

In the following decade, Fred Dailey gave life to polo not only on Oʻahu but the neighbor islands, where players, trainers, and horse breeders sought a venue for their beloved sport. During this period, several prominent multigoal players throughout the state showed skill and passion in executing top-flight stick work and horsemanship. Some of these included Tommy Campos, Fred Dailey, Ed Hedemann, Peter Baldwin, George Manoa, Peter Perkins, Eddie and Freddy Rice, "Tuna" Sampaio, and the Tongg brothers, Ronny and Tenney. Many of these players were featured in the 1963 Aloha Week Polo Tournament, the last of the major events before the City and County of Honolulu demolished Kapiʻolani Park stables. This serious blow to the game of polo was neutralized when Dailey gave it new life and longevity at Dillingham Polo Field.

{ 13.4 } *Gordon von Tempsky, flanked by Hawaiʻi's foremost polo players, Manduke Baldwin and Oskie Rice. Von Tempsky's polo skills brought pride to his father, Louis, who introduced the sport to the Islands.*

{ 13.5 } *Peter Perkins. Though not a native of Hawaiʻi, the 10-goal polo player spent much of his adult life in the Islands, raising the caliber of play to even higher levels.*

{ 13.6 } *Ed Hedeman always came across as a playboy at heart, but his serious attention to the game of polo, and especially the mounts, was a foremost aspect of his personality. Playing polo in the old Honaunau School grounds are (left to right) George Manoa, Freddy Rice, Dick Solmssen, and Ed Hedemann.*

More than five thousand spectators covered the periphery of the polo grounds to witness the first official game at the newly renovated field on January 10, 1965. In a reversal of the outcome fifty-two years earlier, the California team returned home with the coveted Bourne Cup, the trophy garnered by the Hawai'i team in 1913 at the San Mateo Tournament.

Daily went further in his support for polo from both a spectator and player perspective. Classy musical entertainment was a given at the Mokulē'ia venue, and there was even an occasional landing by a parachutist midfield, between chukkers, to add a flair to the event. While Dailey used his skills in spectator entertainment, he also made very significant efforts to make the sport more affordable.

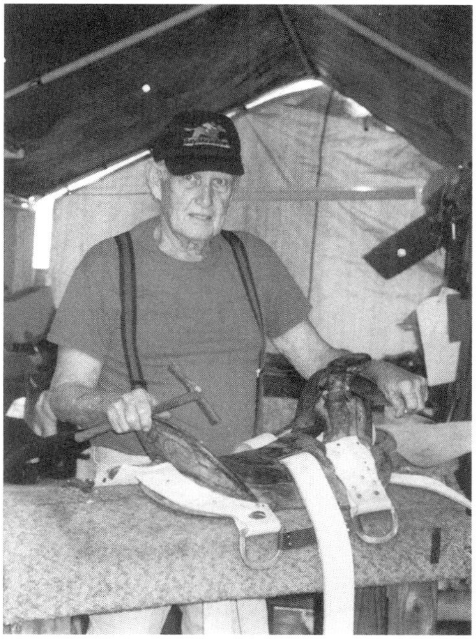

{ 13.7 } *In his twilight years, Ed Hedemann kept busy repairing and making saddles.*

{ 13.8 } *One of Hawai'i's most prominent sportsmen, Peter Baldwin enjoyed rodeo as much as polo. His enduring support of equestrian activities carries forth a long-standing family tradition.*

{ 13.9 } *Mokulē'ia, O'ahu, polo matches attracted local, national, and international competitors. Five local regulars in the 1960s included these men (left to right): Gary Aiko, Eric Kirkhoff, Jim Rewald, Al Lopaka, and Lester Maruoka.*

Annual dues were reduced to a tenth of typical mainland clubs, while polo string numbers were reduced to lower cost of ownership, conditioning, and housing. His fostering role in polo earned him the moniker "Mr. Polo."

The 1960s were banner years for other reasons, one of which was the homegrown talent in both genders. In 1962 at age seventeen, Ronnie Tongg became the world's youngest player to win the US Open in polo. In 1962 and 1965, Tongg rode on the winning teams at the National Open Polo Championships. He was the only player born and raised in Hawai'i to compete on an international level, with victories in Argentina, England, France, New Zealand, and the Philippines. In titles won, Tongg was awarded seven Hawaiian, ten national, and sixteen international acclamations. In Hawai'i's polo history, no single individual has come close to matching the fame, technique, athleticism, and sportsmanship of Ronnie Tongg of Honolulu, Hawai'i.

Born in 1945, Ronnie was introduced to polo at Kapi'olani Park. He learned to ride and play in a singular effort, largely mentored by his father, Ruddy Fah Tongg. Ronnie was exposed early on to the dynastic polo families of Baldwin, Castle, Dillingham, Rice, and von Tempsky. However, it was Peter Perkins who directly influenced him and helped him gain a firm foundation of the basics of the game. A true guiding force for Tongg's life in polo was Dr. Billy Linfoot, a California veterinarian and stellar player and mentor.

The informative biography *The Golden Mallet* (Layton 2003) celebrates Tongg's national and international successes in detail, along with meaningful glimpses into his personal life that include family, religion, and the professional standards by which he led his life.

In the heart of the text, Tongg credits the gaucho, whose horse-training expertise became a major factor in Argentina's evolving reputation as the source of the world's top polo ponies and players. He also acknowledges the American cowboy for revolutionizing the selection and training of US polo ponies by applying Western stock-horse standards and the comparative advantages of confirmation, agility, temperament, and breaking speed that come with it.

The same analogy extends to Hawai'i's territorial polo history: the *paniolo* of Maui and Hawai'i islands were on-ranch trainers of some of the finest polo mounts the Islands have produced. A. W. Carter recognized this advantage when he assigned four Lindsey brothers to train a band of polo prospects from Parker Ranch's crop of three-year-old geldings. Carry the News was one of the Lindsey brother products. The "Polo Field" on the ranch remains an iconic reminder of days gone by. Though still lined by a rectangle of weathered and leaning eucalyptus trees, the rubble and irregular turf are barely suitable for steer roping, let alone polo.

For the next two decades, polo flourished on O'ahu due to the support and generosity of Fred Dailey, despite a serious error in judgment in 1981. What began as a noble gesture on his part to increase the assets of the polo club instead turned into a catastrophic loss. Dailey, with the support of his board of directors but without due diligence, transferred all the assets of the Hawai'i Polo Club Foundation over to shell scam artist Ronald Rewald, head of a front business called Bishop, Baldwin, Rewald, and O'Connor, no doubt taken in by the flamboyant financier. Like others who were duped by Rewald, the board failed to recognize that this was a Ponzi scheme carefully orchestrated by the con artist. Assets invested with Rewald survived only months before his entire shell organization collapsed, sending O'ahu's business community spiraling downward in a frenzy of denial, distancing, shock, and crushing disappointment.

In true Dailey tradition, the polo operation was rescued, this time by Michael Dailey, Fred's son, who became the managing director of the foundation established for the perpetuation of the sport of polo and its heritage. Meanwhile, a trio of businessmen—Bob McGregor, Mike Sheehan, and Enrique Zobel—established the Honolulu Polo Club in 1986 on leased land in Waimānalo.

Women have always had a place in Hawai'i's polo scene. Haku Baldwin holds a special place in Hawai'i polo annals in managing and training some of the Islands' top mounts in the 1930 to 1960 era. In 1981, the US Polo Association's Women's Polo Team outscored the Hawai'i men's team 8 to 4.

On June 24, 2012, Mokulē'ia was the venue for the US Polo Association

Women's Challenge polo matches. The all-women matches were followed by international competition with US teams (including Hawai'i) versus the best of China, India, Mexico, and New Zealand.

Waikoloa Polo

Unlike rodeo, racing and polo matches, while starting off with vigor, failed to survive historic tenure. In the case of polo on the Big Island, enthusiasm wanes for a few years, then resurfaces when the clubs reorganize. In all cases, however, when it's hot it's hot, as in the case of the Waikoloa Polo Club, which at its outset in 1976 was one of only two registered polo clubs in the state. Polo season opened in October and ran for two months.

Facing serious competition at the Mokulē'ia Polo Grounds on O'ahu, the Waikoloa Club took an early 3-0 lead in the first match with the great stick work of Jimmy Greenwell, Dick Ednie, Dick Solmssen, and Freddy Rice. The Mokulē'ia team rebounded and outflanked Waikoloa in a 6-4 victory. Again taking an early 3-1 lead in the second match, the stick work of young George Hedemann of Kona enhanced the play of his mates, Greenwell, Solmssen, and Rice. Alas, team Mokulē'ia was reborn and came away as 7-4 match champions.

In the third annual Waikoloa Inter-Island Tournament, genuine participation of Hawai'i's polo elite was evident. Sam Delgado, Ronnie Tongg, and Winston Mirikitani trumped the Maui team of Ben Baldwin, Jimmy Greenwell, and Bim Wilson.

In a subsequent all-star game, Peter Baldwin's squad, with effective stick work of Robby Hind, outscored the team of Baldwin's cousin Freddy Rice. The Huggo's Restaurant team of Kona in later play showed excellent skill in the performance of three natives of the district, George Hedemann, Robby Hind, and Alfred Medeiros Sr.

Waiki'i Ranch Polo

As Kohala Ranch was developed in the early 1980s, efforts to include a polo field and clubhouse were minimal in terms of site preparation and facility construction. The field was uneven and the turf of minimal quality from lack of subsoil preparation, further challenged by little or no irrigation.

A polo team was nonetheless put together, and it did give Kohala Ranch's facility some legitimacy despite the substandard turf conditions. Stalwarts of that club were Dick Ednie, daughters Erin and Fiona, and later son Jed. Lee Beerman was a strong force for the team, which they dubbed Mauna Kea. Over the coming decade, the Waiki'i Ranch Polo Field became the mainstay venue for a variety of teams and a plethora of players who crossed over between teams to make competition viable.

In the mid-1980s, Waiki'i Ranch was developed by Gerald Kremkow, a mainland architect turned developer. Utilizing a 3,000-acre Parker Ranch parcel that once headquartered the Waiki'i Section of cattle grazing, corn production, fruit orchards, and hog and turkey farming, Kremkow with financial backing envisioned a gated community of small ranch lots of 10-, 20-, and 40-acre increments. Central to the theme was cattle grazing via shared easements that webbed throughout the project. Several amenities appeared to ensure success of the venture, as an upscale clubhouse, athletic club, roping and cutting arenas, as well as polo grounds were built.

All of the amenities were built with good taste and architectural protocol, but Kremkow's imposition of inflexible conditions, covenants, and restrictions brought sales progress to an impractically low level. Although the project was taken over by the financiers—a New Zealand consortium that staged a "fire sale" to jump-start the rescue efforts—the one consistent draw that remained was the aura and splendor generated by the polo field and attendant matches held at Waikiʻi.

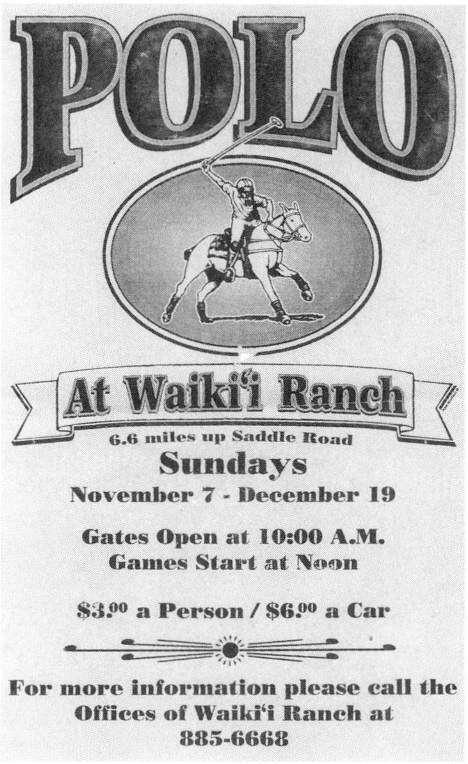

{13.10} *Credit goes to Waikiʻi Ranch and its polo facility for enduring the up and down interest in the sport. Waikiʻi polo matches add special ambience to the sport not found in other Big Island facilities.*

{13.11} *Mauna Kea Polo Club leveraged as a significant group that eventually found their home in the verdant polo field of Waikiʻi Ranch. Enjoying their win after a challenging polo match are (left to right) Paula Beamer, Lester Maruoka, Dick Ednie, Nolan George, and Herbie Ching, with children and young fans.*

The Waikiʻi Polo Field site was logically chosen by Kremkow on a somewhat natural flat lying in the southeastern base of Puʻu Kahekili, immediately approached from the upper of the two Waikiʻi gated entryways. Expertly graded into a rectangle roughly 1,000 by 750 feet, the field was readily covered with an emerald mat of kikuyu grass of durable quality. Although the adjacently placed 3,600-square-foot pavilion had more of an open-air canoe house feel, the attractive hipped roofline reflected the style that soon became standard in the development. The pavilion served well for judging and announcing purposes during competition and as a food service area afterwards. Since the birth of Waikiʻi Ranch, the polo field is kept in pristine condition despite moderately heavy use, largely from frequent mowing and irrigation. In fact, the entire Waikiʻi Ranch is a very well maintained development thanks to the work of its manager, Lucky Puhi, and his able assistant Yaku Kotaki.

Polo Action

As the Mauna Kea Polo Club was wrapping up its venue at the Kohala facility in 1993, Waikiʻi provided a convenient alternative. The Sherman Memorial Cup was won by the Hoʻomau Feeds team of Herbie Ching, Lee Beerman, and George Hedemann. The Sherman Cup award started a decade-long series of cup awards that have given the Waikiʻi venue a colorful history. Other cup awards that followed included the Floral Cup, "Da Winery" Cup, Christmas Cup (donated by Bert and Joann Wong), Gene Turchi Memorial Cup, Thanksgiving Cup (donated by Ernest Nakahara), and the SC Ranch Cup (donated by Dutch and Kerry Schuman).

Sponsorship

If any individual deserves credit for keeping polo alive on the Big Island, the honor goes to Herbie Ching, who spent countless hours keeping the clubs together and leveling the playing field through his experience and judgment. There is no polo field on Hawaiʻi Island that he has not competed on, umpired, announced at, or managed. Ching successfully hustled a wide array of polo sponsors, including his own farm supply outfit, Hoʻomau Feeds of Kona. Other sponsors included Noh Foods (Oʻahu), Kona Jewelers, C&H Properties, Island Shells, Huggo's Restaurant, Pacific Rim Collection, and No Ka Oe Florals.

Some of these sponsors also produced polo club teams during the active decade of Waikiʻi polo matches. Crossover of players among the teams was commonplace, related more to balancing competition than team loyalty. Oʻahu teams included Honolulu, Mapu Lane, and High Flyers polo clubs. Over the years, several of Maui's top players enjoyed the Waikiʻi field, including Herman Louie DeCoite, Peter Baldwin, and Kimo Huddleston.

Besides the mainstay teams of Waikiʻi Ranch, Mauna Kea, and Hoʻomau Feeds, other consistently playing polo clubs have included SC Ranch, Waikoloa Stables, Ihu

Nui, Huggo's, KC Supply, Kona Sports, Island Shells, and Pacific Rim.

The permanent move to the Big Island of many O'ahu players enhanced activity at the Waiki'i Field, not just in play time but in sponsorship and organizational skill. Besides Beerman, others include Paula (Gorecki) Beamer, Lester Maruoka, Kawika Tahere, Skip and Alex Schuman, Tara Gallison, Lani Nakachi, and Penny Bradley. Waiki'i Ranch property owners also formed a major force in polo competition in their home field. These include Bill and Lori Bergin, Tony (deceased) and Lee Mullins, Dick Solmssen, Kenny Shamel, and the Child family men, Woody and sons Woody II and Trevor.

Polo at Waiki'i Ranch flourished over the decade leading up to the new millennium. The final game of Mauna Kea Polo Club's polo season (at its adoptive Waiki'i home) was played on December 10, 2000. A large turnout of players resulted in a round-robin format. The Mauna Kea Club roster included Ashley and George Hedemann, Herbie Ching, and Dick

{13.12} *Mauna Kea Polo Club members. In the back row are (left to right) Bill George, Dick Solmssen, Alex Penovaroff, Lee Beerman, Dick Ednie, Eric von Platen, Paula Beamer, Bruce Cholupca, Ronnie Tong, Lani Nakachi, and Waysen Vanatta. In the front row are (left to right) Bill Bergin, Herbie Ching, George Hedemann with Daniel and Ashley, Bob Miller and son, Charles Stevens, Megan Matson, and Kenny Shamel.*

{ **13.13** } *On Veterans Day, 2012, the Waiki'i Polo Club honored the military stationed at Pōhakuloa Training Camp.*

Ednie, who beat a Waiki'i Ranch team of Charles Stevens, Lee and Tony Mullins, and Kenny Shamel. The Waiki'i Ranch team fared no better when matched against the Kona Sports Club, made up of Iwalani Ka'au'a, Kawika Tahere, Bruce Chaloupka, and Ronnie Tongg.

A decade of polo quietude chilled the hills of Waiki'i Ranch until 2011, when the polo club was revitalized.

Mauna Kea Polo Club formalized its existence by forming a limited liability corporation (LLC) with an annual individual membership fee of $50. President Jed Ednie, Vice President Jason Lau, Secretary Lori Bergin, and Treasurer Bob Barnes are officers. Active members include Paula Beamer, Woody Childs and sons Woody Childs II and Trevor Childs, Nolan George, Richard Kaniho, Tom Richmond, and Kenny Shamel. These individuals are long-standing polo enthusiasts, and the Mauna Kea Polo Club has an optimistic future.

Overpopulation of horses and donkeys is an issue confronting states all across America. Hawai'i is no exception, as the next chapter explains.

CHAPTER 14

OVERPOPULATION ISSUES

Feral Horse Management: "Wild Horse Annie"

In the early 1950s, a Nevada horsewoman named Velma B. Johnston, better known as "Wild Horse Annie," brought national attention to the plight of the dwindling and exploited wild horse population of the West. She is credited with the passage through Congress of the Wild Horse Annie Act of 1959. A dozen years later, Congress passed the Wild Free-Roaming Horses and Burros Act of 1971. While the original act made it illegal to hunt wild horses and burros on public lands, the latter act provided controlled adoption of America's feral equines. In 2005, the Burns Amendment was passed, allowing wild horses to be sold or slaughtered. In recent years, Congress created legislation to disallow all slaughter of horses in the United States, a move that created a major backward leap in the progress of horse welfare in our country. The unintended consequences have had a profoundly negative impact. In mustang numbers alone, which reached over 37,000 on Bureau of Land Management (BLM) lands in 2012 and grow at a rate of 20 percent per year, total head counts can double in size in four years. By simple geometric progression, BLM is faced with an increasingly unmanageable crisis.

Fortunately, Hawai'i's statute allows for the humane depopulation of all livestock. As for adoption of feral equines, the first public occurrence was when a band of wild donkeys (known as Kona Nightingales) from the Waikoloa development area was offered for disposal. The animals

Bureau of Land Management Challenges

Long-term problems for free-ranging horses and burros are far more pressing on mainland BLM lands than those of Waipiʻo Valley and the lands of Waikoloa, where overpopulation has been brought under control before ecological damage and die-off occurred.

The BLM is assuming responsibility to manage, protect, and control the Equidae in accordance to the Wild Horse and Burro Act of 1971, likely never envisioning that it was a no-win mission. Today, more than forty years later, adoption numbers are declining, averaging only four thousand head per year coupled with annual gathers of about ten thousand. As a result, pressure on short-term housing (feedlot) and long-term pasturage has become severe.

By 2012, short- and long-term facilities held nearly fifty thousand head at a cost to the program of 60 percent of its $78 million dollar budget, according to Dr. Boyd M. Spratling, cochair of the National BLM Wild Horse and Burro Advisory Board. Preparing a prospective adoptee for adoption costs the board $2,000, compared to $11,000 per head for long-term lifetime holding. These costs are likely to escalate unless relieved by reducing reproductive capacity, approval and restoration of slaughtering facilities, and accepting the unfortunate but effective route of humane euthanasia. (Spratling 2012)

were confined in the Puʻu Pāpapa Corral for several days, and despite extensive advertising, few people took up the offer to take home a Nightingale. The sixty head of wild donkeys were then turned out into Boise Paddock below the Keʻāmuku stretch of the Hawaiʻi Belt Road. In 2000, Parker Ranch performed another gathering of donkeys, and these were offered up again at the Puʻu Pāpapa Corral. Rancher Buddy Azevedo kindly loaded out several dozen of these, providing a sanctuary for them on his Kaʻū ranch lands.

A middle ground between absolute depopulation is the sanctuary approach, where willing landowners take the oversupply from private lands or public domain such as Bureau of Land Management ranges. For the BLM, oversupply meant finding ranchers with sufficient carrying capacity for several thousand refugee mustangs. In 1989, a Bartlesville, Oklahoma, rancher was the first to provide long-term pasturage. Near Cassoday, a pair of neighboring ranchers from the Kansas Flint Hills named Bob Buford and Sterling Varner won such a contract after passing rigorous review by BLM staff.

The Flint Hills of Kansas rival the Sand Hills of Nebraska as America's finest grazing lands. Billy notes that after a decade of living in Manhattan, Kansas, during his college years, it instilled a deep appreciation for the Flint Hills that began south of his Midwestern home. There the highly fertile soils grow some of the finest tall prairie grasses, a high-percentage calf crop producing stout 600 pound weaners. In the context of preservation of history and heritage, it is exemplary that the pair of Cassoday, Kansas, ranchers followed swiftly by reserving more than thirty thousand acres of some of America's finest grazing land to house 4,487 wild horses for the remainder of their natural lives. Kept on a healthy regimen of appropriate vaccinations and deworming, mares and geldings graze separately on a combined operation (Buford and Varner) called the Shadow 7 Ranch. With our Congress blindly moving toward outlawing all forms of commercial marketing of horseflesh for foreign trade, the demand for housing and feeding an additional eighty to ninety thousand horses per year is likely to wreak havoc with programs such as Shadow 7, as the pressure for willing operators will become severe. By 2012, BLM's long-term holding pasturage housed more than thirty-one thousand horses located on privately owned ranch lands in Oklahoma, South Dakota, Iowa, and Kansas. The average cost per head of long-term pasturage is $1.30 per day, according to BLM staff.

The Wild Free-Roaming Horses and Burros Act, with all its noble intentions, in effect tripled the population of wild horses in America. To manage this soaring population, the Bureau of Land Management, the agency whose lands are home to the majority of these feral horses, created the Adopt-a-Horse program to find homes for the burgeoning numbers. The system, while costly, seemed to work for a few years. Adoptability was enhanced when BLM limited candidate horses to under six years of age, and the long-range pasturage was developed and became home for the aged ones.

The Adopt-a-Horse program eventually ran out of legitimate adopters, and some feared that illegitimate buyers were out there snapping up carloads of mustangs to go to the few remaining slaughter facilities in the United States, a process that absorbed the majority of the nation's annual oversupply of the horse population. This option was shut out when Congress outlawed horse slaughter in the country.

Despite Congress lifting the ban on horse slaughter in the United States in mid-December 2011, horse processing will not resume in the immediate future largely due to the need for obtaining a federal grant of inspection to conduct a hazard analysis. No funding requests for such requirements were filed with Congress in 2012.

Youth Mustang Adoption Program

Interestingly, a group of transplanted Hawaiʻi horsemen developed a successful youth version of the Adopt-a-Horse program. The father and son team of Pat and Josh FitzGerald and Josh's wife, Erica, have been instrumental in launching the Teens and Oregon Mustangs (TAOMs) program. Pat and Josh are the grandson and great-grandson respectively of renowned Hawai'i veterinarian Dr. J. C. FitzGerald, whose mission of improving horse quality in the Islands was nothing short of heroic.

Teens and Oregon Mustangs was formed in 2009 by a group of mustang horse lovers, with the goal of helping the Bureau of Land Management adopt out yearling Oregon mustangs and providing youth opportunities for competition and learning. In 2009, fifteen youths participated and competed in the event, all with great success. All of the horses were tamed, ground-trained, and ready for adoption at the end of ninety-eight days with their youth trainers. All fifteen horses were adopted at the end of the event. This event was part of the 2009 National Adopt a Wild Horse Day (NAWHD) of Oregon, and the youth trainers were justly proud of their achievement.

This program is modeled similarly to the Mustang Heritage Foundation's (MHF) Extreme Mustang Makeover® events (www.extrememustangmakeover.com). Teens and Oregon Mustangs have MHF's support for the event, which helps with funding and trainer incentive money for the youth. However, the Oregon group is an independent organization, with members designing and operating the program themselves, and they are not directly affiliated with the national program. The FitzGerald team, together with behind-the-scenes workers Robin Burns and Keith Morey, works closely with the Oregon BLM Office out of Burns/Hines, Oregon, to get the horses, manage their paperwork, and monitor the horses' well-being during the ninety-eight-day program. Both have been supportive of the event and were instrumental in making it happen in 2009. Another major sponsor in 2009 was FitzGerald Farms, which donated use of their equipment and facilities to support the effort.

Teens and Oregon Mustangs have continued their program through 2014, expanding the age group to ten to eighteen years for the youth participants and increasing the number of participants to twenty. It is their vision to continue this growth in the ensuing years, making it an annual event. The Bureau of Land Management has now engaged the FitzGeralds to expand the TAOMs program beyond Oregon to government lands in neighboring states.

Consumption of Mule Meat

Consumption of mule meat was not uncommon in Hawai'i in rural areas as recently as the 1940s. In his 1990 *Hawaiian Journal of History* article, "My Boyhood in Pa'auilo," Robert Campbell Stewart, a Scottish Hawaiian native of Hāmākua, shares some history:

> There were times that mules, which pulled the train cars, would get very badly hurt because their cars became runaway cars. Then the camp policemen would come around and let everyone know when a mule was to be killed. This was done—the announcing—so that we villagers would be there to

ENLIGHTENMENT

Dr. Billy Bergin

Historically, the United States Department of Agriculture (USDA) has overseen legitimate, federally inspected facilities for slaughtering horses for shipment to other countries as a source of protein.

Despite America's disdain for consuming horsemeat, many of our forefathers serving in the War of 1812, the Spanish-American War, the Civil War, and the First World War consumed horsemeat in the absence of beef, pork, mutton, and goat meat to survive. While the diet of soldiers has normalized over the years, one cannot deny the historic fact that horsemeat saw the military through the most trying times.

Many of our ancestors left European roots to become Americans by choice for a better life, while never losing sight of and holding on to many traditions of their motherland, including language, music, dress, faith, and diets. In present-day France, Belgium, Germany, and Scandinavia, horsemeat is routinely offered as a menu item in many restaurants. In years past, much of the nation's federally inspected horsemeat shipped abroad for consumption came from packing houses of America's heartland, such as Rockford, Illinois, and Topeka, Kansas.

As a veterinary student, I had extensive exposure to the horse-slaughtering industry via routine visits (two to four days weekly for two years) to the Hill Packing Company operation of Topeka, Kansas. There were early morning wet lab experiences (4 to 7 a.m.) through the courtesy and support of the packing company management and mentoring oversight of the federal veterinary inspector, Dr. V. Y. Druley, who had spent the bulk of his early military career attached to the US Cavalry Veterinary Corps.

Eighty horses daily were inspected antemortem, washed down, humanely slaughtered, chilled, and shrouded for shipment to European communities abroad for restaurant use. Opportunities abounded for students interested in equine practice to preexamine a vast array of conditions and anatomical systems prior to the detailed postmortem examination by Dr. Druley, who shared insight as the activities, normal or otherwise, of the neurological, anatomical, reproductive, respiratory, digestive, and cardiovascular systems of the horses. Many of these horses were draft types of the north-central states, and there was an array of average but no

{ 14.1 } *An Irish newspaper poster. Ireland is one of the greatest horse-loving countries of the world, having tremendous respect for the animal. Yet the industry, government, and people of Ireland accept the fact that human consumption of horse meat is a practical end use for the "no longer wanted" horse.*

ENLIGHTENMENT

(continued from previous page)

longer productive or valuable mounts. Normally they were horses in good condition, and they were always ambulatory.

There were seven members of my Kansas State University veterinary class of 1967 who took up careers in equine practice, and many credit Dr. Druley's mentorship and the Hill Packing Company accommodation as a profound educational foundation upon which we dedicated our professional careers over the ensuing decades.

On our last day at the plant, shortly before graduation, Dr. Druley, a small but very tidy gentleman, invited the students to join him in his USDA office upstairs. As a token of appreciation for allowing him to share his knowledge about the health of the noble horse with budding practitioners, he presented the students with a gift of a carefully wrapped horse loin.

Gingerly, but gratefully, the gift was accepted with lots of handshaking and words of appreciation, before piling into the school van and heading back to campus. En route, the conversation was somewhat serious: savoring the many early mornings of mentoring, the hands-on palpation opportunities followed within minutes of direct postmortem examination of ovarian changes, cryptorchidism, laminitis, and so on. Would any of us eat meat of the noble and cherished horse? Not only no, but *hell no!*

Somehow, the loin wound up in the refrigerator of my home. With finals behind us, the seven gathered at the Bergin home licking wounds from rigorous finals, state board, and accreditation examinations. Libation flowed freely, as did stories of joint escapades over the past four years. As the night progressed, appetites signaled the need for food and with nothing open at the late hour, our attention turned to the loin. Just maybe, Dr. Druley had a point: horsemeat could be a delight to the palate. Following the cooking instructions Dr. Druley provided, we newly minted veterinarians sat down to partake of a meal prepared with the loin as protein. While some of us had previously consumed donkey flesh prepared as jerky in home environments, this would be a first for all to try horsemeat. The meat was found to be appetizing and delicious, and the group could now understand why it continued to be a source of protein for many European diets. Furthermore, all were in agreement that converting the horse to wholesome nourishment is a dignified end to the life of an equine, when compared to an ill-conceived ban on such disposition because as Americans we find the mere thought distasteful. One could well argue whether it is more or less humane to allow the noble steed to end its life in overcrowded, uncontrolled environments detrimental to both health and spirit.

receive the free mule meat. If the mule to be killed was a sick mule, it would be taken to a wooden chute, after it was killed, and pushed down through it to the ocean. The mule meat we did get, though, was dried and eaten as jerk meat. (Stewart 1990)

Unintended Consequences of Equine Slaughter Ban

Since 2006, Congress has prohibited funding inspection of horses destined for food. This legislation forced the closure of the only two equine slaughter plants in America. Congress yielded to animal welfare pressure, ignoring testimony from major veterinary organizations such as the American Veterinary Medical Association and the American Association of Equine Practitioners (AAEP) and equine organizations such as the American Quarter Horse Association warning that such legislation would in fact worsen equine welfare efforts.

Then president of the AAEP, Dr. William A. Moyer put it succinctly in a retrospective statement on June 27, 2011: "If Congress pursues the option of banning the processing of U.S. horses without the appropriate funding and infrastructure in place to appropriately care for these animals, this action may only amplify the negative welfare implications for this highly vulnerable population of horses" (Moyer 2011).

Things got worse pronto. Horses that would have been slaughtered at plants in the United States were now trucked in greater numbers to Canada and Mexico. In 2010, nearly 138,000 horses left the United States for these two countries, compared to 105,000 horses slaughtered in U.S. plants in 2006, the last year domestic marketing was allowed. Eighty percent of Mexican-slaughtered horses are of U.S. origin, 10 to 15 percent of which come from racetracks.

Furthermore, ceasing domestic slaughter resulted in lowering U.S. horse prices between 8 and 21 percent. Exacerbated by

Tainted Horseflesh

Canadian authorities in 2012 reported alarming findings of drug residues of both phenylbutazone (Phenylbutazolidin) and clenbuterol (Ventipulmin) in the flesh of U.S. racehorses. Already, European food safety officials had begun to discourage the import of any horsemeat of U.S. racehorses based on concerns that USDA's oversight was lax in mandating a six-month drug-free requirement on horses shipped out of the country for slaughter.

Some Canadian horse-slaughter plants have turned away all U.S. horses in response to European market fears, while other plant operators refuse only those horses with a racing history and accept only those shipments accompanied by confirmed drug-free affidavits. In the interim, USDA has responded by reinforcing the existing law requiring that slaughter horses bound for Mexico or Canada must be free of specific drugs for six months or more before shipping certificates can be issued that include confirming affidavits.

The US horse racing industry has struggled to overcome its image of drug abuse and overuse of therapeutic regimes based on concerns for the well-being of the mounts as well as cheating. Now the European market is voicing legitimate concerns for the health of people consuming the flesh of racehorses.

the poor U.S. economy, marginal horse owners were turning in (to rescue groups) or turning out (nonpermissible release on government and private lands) by trailer loads.

Meanwhile, county and animal welfare groups bore the cost of collecting and caring for these abandoned horses, operating on budgets with increasing constraints. County and state governments have become burdened with surges of animal neglect investigations, while operating short on staff and funding.

Horse rescue operations have not been immune to animal neglect investigations, as many are operating beyond maximum capacity. Increasing budget constraints have forced some rescue operations to close their doors altogether.

More recently, the *Journal of American Veterinary Medicine* reported a major setback in legalized horse slaughter in the United States when the government took action to prohibit the use of tax dollars to inspect the facilities, reinstating a ban on domestic horse slaughter for fiscal year 2014 (JAVMA 2014). This action reaffirmed the government's 2006 posture.

There is no lack of enthusiasm to resume horse-slaughter operations in the Illinois and Texas facilities. Other states are offering to build or provide plant facilities in South Dakota, North Dakota, Nebraska, Missouri, and Wyoming.

With federal funding in need for inspection services and hazard analysis yet to be conducted, major obstacles remain. From the state perspective, however, mobilization of actual processing services is less than ninety days away from execution. In the meantime, the nation's ability to deal with the loss of this avenue of disposition of unwanted horses, mules, and donkeys has been severely hindered by three other factors: slow recession recovery, drought in Texas and the southwest, and conversion of farmland from hay production to corn and soybean farming (biofuel).

The extremely low rainfall cycles affecting Texas and the southwest in 2010, 2011, and 2012 have crippled the cattle industry. Despite expedited sales through slaughter and sale barns, the remaining livestock, including horses, requires shipment of hay and grain from surrounding states that are already short in production due in part to conversion to crops for biofuel (ethanol). This pressure has driven hay prices to record levels across the nation.

In Texas alone, ranchers have lost more than $750 million in drought-ruined hay. Hay prices more than doubled in 2010, going from $120 per ton to as much as $275 per ton. In California and Arizona, high hay prices have been barely affordable by the dairy industry, leaving other livestock operators out of the competition. To the horse owners, decisions had to be made to shut down, destock by sale, or in the worst cases, turn their horses, donkeys, and mules loose.

The drought and wildfires that ravaged crops in Texas have increased demand for West Coast hay, where more bales are being sent to China and Japan via the ports of Los Angeles and Long Beach.

Animal shelters across the West, including California and Hawai'i, are at their wits' end, with the rise in sanctuary facilities operating virtually "hand to mouth," growing numbers of rescued animals, and ever-increasing costs.

California and Oregon families of once proudly owned Arabians, Paints, Quarter Horses, and Thoroughbreds are increasingly cutting loose of these no-longer-affordable luxuries, with double-digit unemployment and home foreclosures becoming commonplace. With depressed horse values, and with euthanasia not a pleasant or affordable alternative to consider, turning "Dobbins" out in government or private rangelands offers a more amenable pathway.

Placed into this admixture, the disposition of 138,000 American horses that were annually exported to Mexico and Canada in 2010 and 2011 and the severity of America's unwanted horse disposal have combined to create a crisis of historic proportions in the nation's once proud legacy of world leadership in humane animal care.

Hawai'i is not immune to the impact of the poor economy, horse oversupply, and drought conditions. While the state no longer has facilities for horse slaughter (supplying zoos with meat for lions, etc.), a limited number of horses go to Tongan and Samoan groups for consumption, a custom in their culture and allowable in Hawai'i law.

Hawai'i has conducted only a handful of horse rescue operations. These vary from informal adoption in small numbers to those parties willing to house twenty to thirty head at any given time.

In 2013, the National Cattlemen's Beef Association took an official stand in support of reestablishing horse-slaughter facilities in its proposed amendment to Horse Harvesting and Processing:

> WHEREAS, the method of euthanasia employed by processing facilities that harvest horses is a humane end of life, and
>
> WHEREAS, there is a continued need for the humane harvest of horses to prevent the inhumane treatment of horses that would suffer from neglect and abandonment, and
>
> WHEREAS, there exists an extremely insufficient infrastructure and no funding mechanism to support the humane existence of unwanted horses, and
>
> WHEREAS, unwanted horses are processed into products that are consumed by humans in overseas markets, and
>
> WHEREAS, the value of unwanted horses as a food animal dictates they not be abused, lest this value be diminished, and
>
> WHEREAS, the cattle industry depends upon an economically healthy horse industry and systems to offer a humane end of life for unwanted horses,
>
> THEREFORE BE IT RESOLVED, NCBA opposes any horse harvesting and/or processing prevention act and any such legislation that would prohibit the harvest of horses for human consumption.
>
> BE IT FURTHER RESOLVED, NCBA supports federal inspection of horse processing facilities.

Adopt-a-Horse Fizzles

When the Adopt-a-Horse program of the Bureau of Land Management ran out of adopters, the agency moved to "warehousing" unwanted horses in confinement similar to feedlots. At a cost of more than $23 million dollars to taxpayers of America, more than thirty-one thousand of these horses languish in dry lots. Practical government measures such as the federal Burns Amendment (humane slaughter of aged horses) and BLM's proposal of simple euthanasia as a means of population control were readily shot down by well-meaning but naïve public outcry.

Jay F. Kirkpatrick, a noted reproductive physiologist, is the director of the Science and Conservation Center in Billings, Montana, and in our view he provides the most realistic overview of the overpopulation problems facing America's wild horse population. While birth control (oral contraception) took humanity by a storm, few people, save for Dr. Kirkpatrick, have come forward with practical alternatives for the horse. He opines that "controlling populations with removals, adoptions, warehousing, slaughter, or euthanasia while reproduction continues, is akin to treating brain cancer with aspirin" (Kirkpatrick 2008).

Largely due to Kirkpatrick's research, a contraceptive vaccine for horses was developed more than two decades ago and applied very effectively by the National Park Service along the eastern seaboard in such locations as Assateague Island National Seashore, Cape Lookout National Seashores, Carrot Island, and the Rachel Carson National Estuarine Reserve. Using a darting process, immunoconceptive vaccination with porcine zona pellucida (PZP) causes the mare's ovum to become resistant to sperm penetration. Having no significant side effects, annual vaccination of bands of feral mares brings reproduction under control at a cost of $28 per dose, as opposed to a projected cost of $100,000 to permanently depopulate a herd of forty mustangs.

In 2012, the Environmental Protection Agency (EPA) granted the Humane Society of the United States (HSUS) registration of the injectable PZP product Zona Stat-H as a restricted-use pesticide in controlling populations of wild horses and donkeys (Cima 2012). HSUS's intent is to work with Bureau of Land Management programs by lessening the frequency of herd roundups as conception rates fall to a level that eventually produces animal numbers that match adoption levels. BLM is already using a hand-injected pelleted product, PZP-22, that provides two years of efficacy. Zona Stat-H offers the advantage of requiring much less "hands-on" application by being administered by a jab stick or syringe dart.

On a local scale, the Big Island's Waipiʻo Valley, the last holdout of feral horses, could be at significant risk of losing its historic band of wild mounts. In late 2006, a disgruntled taro farmer took it upon himself to destroy by gunshot horses that allegedly grazed among his paddies. By the time sufficient attention and action was brought to bear, eight head were killed—likely 25 percent of the full band that roams freely on the seaward valley floor. While old-timers of the valley speak of again as many feral horses roaming in the deeper reaches where the valleys of Waipiʻo and Waimanu converge, such a small total number of these feral animals remains at risk.

The Waipi'o horse inhabits an environment similar to the white horses of the Camargue that inhabit the marshy delta of the Rhone River in the south of France. The mistral winds of this region are just as salt-ridden as the *'ehu kai* (sea breeze) buffeting the shores of Waipi'o and Waimanu Valleys, stunting the vegetation of the coastal marshes. Another commonality of the two environments is the use of drained marshes for growing rice, a commodity replaced by taro in the valleys of Hāmākua. And finally, the people of Polynesia as well as the French swamplands are uncompromisingly independent, proud of their heritage of converting flood lands to productive agricultural endeavors. The horses of Waipi'o, however, remain at risk of extinction despite increased community involvement.

One horse rancher of Waiki'i, Hawai'i, has stepped forth and offered, if the need arises due to incessant killing of the Waipi'o horses, to buy sufficient land on the valley floor to create an appropriately designed, well-managed sanctuary for these treasured mounts. We may never have to take up this generous offer, but at least it is there.

Michael Olival, owner of the Waipi'o on Horseback trail riding outfit, has maintained a large band of Waipi'o horses on his adjacent Kukuihaele Ranch lands. With his program came the problem of oversupply, and in 2011 he offered for public sale mares, geldings, and yearlings at $300 apiece or $250 per head for buyers of ten or more horses. Sales were not brisk. By 2014, valley horse numbers had more than tripled and taro field invasion was again reaching a critical point.

Oversupply issues are not limited to horses. Brady shares insight into similar problems with donkeys. He begins with a brief history of the coffee industry and the critical role donkeys served in the industry.

THE NIGHTINGALES

Dr. Brady Bergin

Coffee plants were first introduced to the islands (O'ahu) in 1813 by a visiting Spaniard named Francisco de Paula y Marin, but it is not known whether or not these plants thrived. Shortly after the donkey's arrival in 1825, John Wilkinson, an English agriculturalist, arrived in O'ahu with coffee plants from Brazil. These plants were cultivated by Wilkinson at the Mānoa Valley estate of the island's governor, Kamauleule, who was more commonly known as Boki. These plants did not thrive despite Wilkinson's care up until his death in 1827. The first coffee planted in the Kona region of the Big Island were clippings from the estate of Boki brought over by Reverend Samuel Ruggles in 1828. These plants, which were cultivated by Reverend Ruggles, were slow to become established, but they eventually thrived and proved to be one of the most successful early attempts at growing coffee in Hawai'i.

From that point on, the success of Kona coffee continued. Soon coffee growers learned that the combination of soils and temperature found at the higher elevations of

THE NIGHTINGALES

(continued from previous page)

Hualālai allowed the plants to flourish, giving it the signature Kona coffee flavor. By the mid-1830s, small quantities of Kona coffee were being commercially grown in the Kingdom of Hawai'i well before any commercial coffee production occurred in the United States. Planting and growing coffee along the rugged, steep slopes of Hualālai was no easy feat, however. There were no roads, and the trails were sparse along the mountainside, making transportation of equipment and supplies not only difficult but very inefficient. It was at this point in time that donkeys were truly recognized for their ability as pack animals, and they quickly became the primary source of transportation for the coffee industry. These donkeys inhabiting the Kona region became affectionately referred to as the "Kona Nightingales," named for their incessant melodious braying throughout all hours of the day.

Given the steep, rocky terrain of the Kona Coast, coffee farming was hard, tedious work. The primary role of the donkey was to carry the bags of handpicked coffee cherries down the mountain, following narrow and steep lava-rock trails to drying and roasting facilities in various upland communities such as Hōlualoa and Keauhou. Donkeys were also depended upon to transport a variety of market produce to shipping points along the Kona Coast from Nāpōʻopoʻo to Kīholo. On return trips they carried merchandise, fish, salt, and other supplies back up to the farm country. These beasts of burden provided the power needed to transport the heavily laden burlap bags full of coffee cherries, thus freeing human personnel from the backbreaking task of carrying single bags upon their backs, as would be required of this difficult farming operation. Some say that Kona coffee wouldn't be what it is today if it weren't for the reliable and hardworking donkeys.

Donkeys are noted for their sociable disposition, for being adaptable, and for forming strong attachments to other animals of their own or with other species, which is why they make great guardians for flocks. Perhaps due to their sociable nature, they work better in pairs rather than solo. They are also known for being territorial, even more so than horses, which leads them to be more aggressive even in domestic settings.

The donkey's natural characteristics of being hardy, loyal, sure footed, and heat tolerant and requiring low-maintenance care made it an indispensable partner for the Kona coffee farmer. Just as the miners of America discovered, their sociable disposition and their ability to adapt to human companionship allowed coffee farmers to lead them without ropes and, on some occasions, send them along the trails on their own. However, there were a number of additional reasons why the donkey made the ideal coffee farming implement.

Originating in north Africa, the donkey's gastrointestinal system adapted to digesting and processing the sparse, low-quality forage often found in arid areas, which

THE NIGHTINGALES

(continued from previous page)

allowed them to thrive under challenging environmental conditions. Their grazing behavior has been described as selective browsing or trickle feeding, meaning that they function best when small amounts of fiber are consumed continuously throughout the day. Donkeys will often spend fourteen to sixteen hours a day grazing and will travel more than a dozen miles in search of appropriate forage when conditions are dire. In comparison to the horse, donkeys require more fiber and less protein. Donkeys also eat coarse herbage that horses usually won't eat. Feeding them the higher-quality and higher-calorie commercial equine feeds commonly causes obesity in the domestic donkey and predisposes them to laminitis. The basic nutritional needs for donkeys are adequately met through consumption of pasture grass or hay. The amount needed depends on climate conditions, workload, and metabolism.

Fresh, clean water is an essential nutrient for all species, but donkeys have a lower water requirement than most other domestic species (with the exception of the camel), which enables them to tolerate a greater degree of dehydration without physiological detriment. Donkeys can withstand up to a 30 percent daily weight loss from dehydration, yet they can restore this deficiency within minutes of water consumption. It has been reported that most donkeys are capable of going without water for three days without it causing them any harm.

Aptly described as a beast of burden, the donkey is truly a remarkable species. It has the carrying capacity nearly twice that of a horse, as it is able to carry 30 percent of its own body weight, whereas a horse is more comfortable carrying 15 to 20 percent. Smaller in stature, the donkey likely can carry the same amount as a larger horse and is able to carry loads at lower net energy consumption than man. Smaller hooves that are tougher, more elastic, more upright, and rarely, if at all, need hoof care combine to make them easy keepers. More upright pastern angles may allow for steadier hoof placement, resulting in less slipping when crossing rocks and steep terrain, making them a more sure-footed and safer mode of transport in rugged landscape. Taken all together, then, donkeys are more efficient and ecofriendly transporters.

Other interesting and little-known facts about the donkey include the purpose of their long ears, which aid in cooling the body from the fanning motion they create. Like the Arabian horse, donkeys lack the fifth lumbar vertebra in the spinal column. By comparison, the donkey possesses fewer chromosomes (62) than a horse (64) or mule (63) and has a life expectancy of twenty-seven years or more. Under the right conditions, they have been known to live beyond forty years of age.

On the other hand, donkeys are stoic when it comes to showing outward signs of pain, which can be good or bad, as caretakers often don't realize how serious the situation is until it is too late. While notably characterized as stubborn, it is somewhat of a

THE NIGHTINGALES

(continued from previous page)

misnomer. Donkeys possess an innate attribute for self-preservation and will methodically evaluate novel situations and not rush into anything new. This trait is often misinterpreted as being stubborn or intractable by human beings. Whereas a horse relies more on its "flight response," immediately removing itself from danger, donkeys sustain fewer lacerations because they don't run through or get stuck in fences. A product of their evolution, donkeys tend to fight, while the immediate response of a horse is flight, frequently endangering itself in the process. It is no wonder the donkey was the preferred choice for easing the daily burdens of the coffee farmer.

{ 14.2 } *Placement of signage along highways and Waikoloa Village Road was necessary precaution to warn motorists of danger created by donkeys grazing along roadways or crossing them.*

Donkey Problems of the Past

The laborious duties of the donkey continued up until around the end of World War II. By this time some basic roads were built and mule-drawn wagons were more efficient than single donkeys for the long trips to the coast. However, the donkey still proved to be valuable for a short time longer, providing transportation from fields to roads. Subsequently, as with many industries, something better comes along; thus donkeys were phased out when mining became more mechanized. The miners' donkeys were eventually turned loose into the American desert, where many descendants still roam today.

The Kona Nightingales suffered a similar fate as those mining donkeys, when after over a hundred years of service and labor their time had come. In the late 1940s, a number of US Army jeeps became available as war surplus and soon displaced the donkeys as a more efficient means of transportation. Over the years, many of these working donkeys were released into the wilderness to fend for themselves, which they were more than capable of doing in the lush tropical environment. The feral donkey was already established by 1882. C. E Dutton, a geologist attached to the US Army Ordinance Corps, conducted a geological tour in the Hawaiian Islands on behalf of the newly established United States Geological

THE NIGHTINGALES

(continued from previous page)

Survey Division. He reported that in exploring the summit of Mauna Loa through ʻAinapō Camp of Kapāpala, he came upon wild horses, donkeys, and occasionally wild mules (Maly 2005).

In his 1918 annual report of Kapāpala Ranch Ltd., Manager Julian Monsarrat complained of the large burden created by approximately 550 head of wild donkeys. Annual efforts to reduce this burden yielded a disposal rate of only 150 head, according to the frustrated rancher. Neighboring Keauhou Ranch was home to a feral band that occupied a grassy meadow aptly called Kīpuka Kēkake (Donkey Canyon). Known herds were also scattered throughout the districts of North and South Kona and as far south as Kahuku.

The post–World War II advent of the jeep further exacerbated the problem. Some of the feral herds of Kona were able to migrate from the mountain areas of McCandless Ranch and Huʻehuʻe Ranch to the ocean areas of Kaʻūpūlehu. Some speculate that the construction of the Queen Kaʻahumanu Highway in 1975 divided the grazing grounds *mauka* from the lower freshwater ponds and salt licks near the ocean thus leaving a separate herd along Kona's "Gold Coast." In fact, there are still warning signs of donkey crossings along the Queen Kaʻahumanu Highway today, despite the lack of a current herd along the coast. While there were earlier attempts at depopulation through organized efforts to eradicate the herds, such as occurred in Kaʻū, as well as consumption by the local populace for food, the feral population continued to exist.

Waikoloa Donkey History

An intriguing question worthy of exploration is: How did the donkeys end up nearly forty-five miles away in the Waikoloa area?

Waikoloa is a vast *ahupuaʻa* (land division extending from mountains to the ocean) of roughly 100,000 acres that arches *makai* in a westerly direction from the elevation of the present-day Pōhakuloa Training Area Bob Cat Trail. Early shepherds (about 1875) Akuna and Nahulu camped at Puʻu Kekeʻe (Pōhakuloa) and Puʻu Hīnaʻi (a cinder cone across from Waikoloa Village) respectively and worked their flocks on foot, each using a donkey to secure their provisions from the central camp in Keʻāmuku. Later, when the Puʻu Loa Sheep and Grazing Company was established, mules were used to a limited extent.

As Parker Ranch acquired the lands of Waikoloa from Lucy Peabody in 1914, there were some wild goats, sheep, and cattle, but no horses or donkeys. In the late 1960s, Waikoloa Village was being designed and built as a Western community that would be equipped with its own rodeo arena and riding stables, but even up until 1974 no donkeys

THE NIGHTINGALES

(continued from previous page)

roamed the wilds of this *ahupuaʻa*. However, in that year, thirty head of donkeys were purchased from Huʻehuʻe Ranch by the Waikoloa Development Company through their project manager, Bob Hoffman, for the purpose of developing a sort of Western ambiance for this newly established community. Hoffman is worthy of praise for developing the image of Waikoloa as a *paniolo*-friendly community. Hoffman loved the Hawaiian cowboy culture and was instrumental in instituting the Great Waikoloa Rodeo and Horse Races, along with veteran publicist and well-known broadcaster, Carlos Rivas, an employee and Waikoloa resident. Rodeo enthusiasts throughout the state welcomed the new venue.

This new environment suited the donkeys very well. The dry, rocky terrain scattered with *kiawe* (algaroba) trees and copious amounts of fountain grass provided the most ideal conditions and their most natural habitat. The population steadily grew, and their grazing migration expanded over thousands of acres, well beyond the Waikoloa Village Association land and into neighboring ranches such as Parker Ranch. Without proper management, it wasn't long before the population was deemed out of control.

{ 14.3 } *With a small band of donkeys in the foreground, a large herd on the ridge above meanders toward a water source.*

Donkey Dispersals

THE NIGHTINGALES

(continued from previous page)

Warren Miura and his wife, Marilyn, top rodeo hands, operated and managed the Waikoloa Stables rodeos, play days, stables, horse shows, and trail rides from 1976 to 1988. During Miura's tenure, the thirty head of donkeys thrived in the dry, grassy hills of Waikoloa far beyond Hoffman's dreams. Miura had early concerns that the propagation rate and lack of herd management of these feral donkeys would eventually lead to an overpopulation problem. Other neighboring ranchers shared the same concern, which prompted a drive of approximately sixty head up to Parker Ranch's Puʻu Pāpapa Corral, just *mauka* of Highway 190 at the east end of the Keʻāmuku stretch. Very few donkeys were claimed, despite advertising them for adoption at no cost; unfortunately, with no available alternatives in sight, the donkeys were released back into Waikoloa properties *makai*. Other attempts were made in the 1980s and 1990s to round up the herd and give away as many as possible to thin out the population, but the success was minuscule.

During the first decade of 2000, the Waikoloa donkey nuisance emerged as a significant issue. By this time the vast herds were now encroaching deep into the Parker Ranch paddocks known as Range II and Range III. To address this already serious donkey overpopulation, Parker Ranch, under the management of R. L. "Robby" Hind, took the initiative in 2000 to hold another drive using the same Puʻu Pāpapa Corral. This roundup was slightly more successful, as the ranch was able to dispose of forty head that were adopted by Kaʻū rancher Buddy Azevedo, but even this had a very small effect on the overall numbers. It is speculated that this eventual vast herd of donkeys was not founded with only thirty head.

A Second Coming

The expansion of resorts along Kona's "Gold Coast" began encroaching on the donkey herds in that area, and it wasn't long before they became a nuisance to human beings. Unfortunately, early attempts to control the population in this particular area were done by the easiest and most effective means, which included eradication and slaughter for human consumption. At about the same period of time, Kona Village Hotel and Resort general manager Fred Duerr was frustrated by donkey nuisances that included traffic risks on Highway 19, as well as on the resort's own roadways. In addition, the Four Seasons Hualālai Resort was under tremendous pressure, as the profusion of donkey droppings on their award-winning golf course had become intolerable, traffic issues notwithstanding. Duerr had no objection to keeping a few head in a paddock at Kona Village Resort, but beyond that accommodation, the donkeys were no longer welcome.

THE NIGHTINGALES

(continued from previous page)

He gathered a consortium of neighboring landowners/developers of Hualālai and Kūki'ō Resorts, who recommended gathering large numbers of these donkeys and moving them to Waikoloa. An independent consultant had the donkeys rounded up by cowboys and trucked several trailer loads of them from Ka'ūpūlehu trapping pens to large, privately owned parcels *mauka* in Waikoloa Village. It is interesting to note that Hu'ehu'e Ranch, Hualālai Resort, and their independent consultant deemed Parker Ranch and Waikoloa development as new homes for feral donkeys. It is reasonable to assume that both receiving entities were involved in the decision to transfer the livestock onto their properties.

The decision may have seemed a logical solution to the Ka'ūpūlehu Donkey Consortium, as the habitat on these large parcels suited the donkeys well, but what was possibly overlooked was the lack of water sources and perimeter fencing on these properties. This oversight allowed this newly relocated herd to migrate over thousands of acres, finding their way onto neighboring ranches and comingling with the lower herd residing near Waikoloa Village. These donkeys from Ka'ūpūlehu seemed to have settled in these *mauka* paddocks and gained a lot of attention, as their favorite lounging area was a large, open flat immediately across Highway 190 and Pu'u Nohonaohae Nui, where the former Military Tank Road crosses at a metal cattle guard and fence gate. The quiet nature of this relocation was effective, because Parker Ranch manager "Robby" Hind and cattle superintendents Alan "Blue" Coleman and Godfrey Kainoa, as well as their respective foremen Gordon Kalaniopio and Mark Yamaguchi, were all unaware of the intrusion aside from the noticeable rapid expansion of donkey herd sizes in their cattle-grazing paddocks.

There were several pivotal individuals involved who were close to Ka'ūpūlehu interests, Waikoloa's development, and Parker Ranch's administration: planner Sidney Fuke, development consultant Roger Harris, and Carl A. Carlson Jr., then trustee of the Parker Ranch. Roger Harris shed some light on the background of the "second coming" of donkeys to Waikoloa.

While the Ka'ūpūlehu Donkey Consortium succeeded in a thorough gather of the donkeys in the area, disposal came in two forms. About half of the gather was disposed of immediately by local parties, leaving around thirty head of adults in need of repopulation. According to Harris, permission was granted by Michael A. "Corky" Bryan, vice president of marketing for Parker Ranch at the time, to deliver twenty-seven head to the Waikoloa property that adjoined Parker Ranch under lease.

By 2006, Parker Ranch ceased to lease the Waikoloa parcels, and rancher Stanley Boteilho entered into a grazing permit relationship with Waikoloa Village Association.

THE NIGHTINGALES

(continued from previous page)

The association was rightfully desirous of keeping adjacent lands free of fire fuel since an August 2006 range fire swept across thirty thousand acres of pasture from Lālāmilo to the Village of Waikoloa, threatening to destroy homes.

In the wake of the fire, fences were breached to allow heavy equipment in to help extinguish the fire and cut firebreaks to prevent it from moving forward. Unfortunately, these fences were never repaired, which allowed the donkeys to roam farther and pose a higher risk of getting out on the highways.

Drought and Brushfire Impact

Depending on the amount of rainfall and the availability of forage, these herds, now called Waikoloa Nightingales, roamed several thousands of acres from the perimeter of Waikoloa Village, on lands predominantly owned by the Waikoloa Village Association (WVA), to the previously mentioned privately owned lands to the north and east (*mauka*). Many of these parcels were primarily used for grazing cattle, but some were now more heavily populated with donkeys, making them less productive to ranchers. The WVA's land, for example, while leased by Parker Ranch, was only used periodically in times when their bordering parcels were low on feed. What made this area even less desirable was the fact that it was in the midst of one of the worst droughts the island had seen in decades. Waikoloa's naturally arid climatic conditions, coupled with the lack of significant rainfall over the years, compounded the problem, leaving little opportunity to replenish the grass and trees without the necessary moisture for regrowth and recovery. More importantly, it left the donkeys without any natural sources of water (ponds, streams, etc.). This made survival for these herds much more challenging and forced them to migrate in search of food and water (see plate 8).

Waikoloa Nightingales

By 2009, the population of feral donkeys in the Waikoloa areas expanded to include two major bands. The *makai* (lower elevation) band calls Waikoloa Village its home territory and creates a nuisance, damaging yards and landscaping, even venturing onto the golf course. The *mauka* (upper elevation) band frequents the Highway 19 area from the Saddle Road Junction to the east end of Keʻāmuku stretch. Both bands have ventured onto highways and have created a safety hazard. Waikoloa resident Anika Glass actively campaigned for the control of these donkeys, forming a group called Mālama Waikoloa Nightingales.

THE NIGHTINGALES

(continued from previous page)

Growing up in the San Joaquin Valley of California, the daughter of a meat market owner, Glass had a general understanding and appreciation of cattle, ranching, farming, and the dairy business. She moved to Waikoloa in August 2004 and learned early on that fences are not maintained unless the tract of land is actively used for grazing cattle. Nor are they likely to be repaired following an automobile accident that may take out large sections of fencing, nor is any attempt made to contact the owner, as it is assumed that owners maintain their fences. To add further complications to the matter, the owner will most likely want to determine the responsible party if they want any form of recompense.

With barren wastelands devoid of food, breaks in the fencing made it easier for donkeys to access Waikoloa Village proper. Homes with lush, irrigated lawns and decorative features were ready targets. Even more tempting was the Waikoloa Village Golf Course, with its manicured greens, sand traps (for salt supplementation), and large water hazards, which must have seemed like an oasis for these weary donkeys. This encroachment obviously created major concerns for residents of Waikoloa Village. The once beloved Waikoloa Nightingales were quickly becoming a nuisance by destroying fences, lawns, and gardens.

{ 14.4 } *As the sun sets in Waikoloa, a herd of feral donkeys presents their collective ears in a signal of curiosity.*

THE NIGHTINGALES

(continued from previous page)

They also put pets on high alert. There were numerous reports of dogs being chased or threatened by trespassing donkeys, which makes sense as canines are the donkey's natural enemy. It's not hard to imagine a dog out for a walk with its master coming across a grazing donkey and proceeding to bark at it, which would then induce a defensive charge from the donkey. To my knowledge, however, there were no confirmed pet injuries or deaths as a result of a donkey attack.

At one point, the Hawai'i Civil Defense was called in to investigate a complaint that these feral donkeys were chasing children at Waikoloa Elementary and Middle School, forcing teachers to keep children in during recess due to the risk of being attacked. Thankfully, it turned out to be a rumor, as the only confirmed sighting of any donkeys on school grounds was by custodial staff during the twilight hours of the morning. The more common clue of their presence was the occasional piles of manure being stumbled upon on the sports fields, which brought forth minimal complaints. In fact, students and teachers loved the donkeys so much that they were considering making them the school's mascot.

Contrarily, numerous Waikoloa residents didn't share that same love for the donkeys. Many took their complaints to Jim Whillock, president of the Waikoloa Village Association, as the WVA owned the land that the donkeys currently called their home. Unfortunately, following consultation with their legal advisors, the WVA chose not to claim any responsibility for the donkeys for liability purposes. According to Whillock, the donkeys were the responsibility of whoever was leasing the land from the WVA at the given time. Requests by home and property owners for perimeter fencing to help prevent the donkeys from entering the village were declined, despite the fact that they proceeded with fencing off certain parts of the Waikoloa Village Golf Course for that same reason. Some residents asked if the WVA could provide a designated area with water access for the donkeys, but that too was declined.

The WVA did attempt to resolve the problem by contacting various agencies, but Whillock discovered that no county, state, or federal agency was willing to provide any form of relief. The reason given was that this particular feral species does not fall within the purview of responsibility according to county ordinance. These animals, being feral, have no formal ownership and thus are not classified as pets, nor are they considered livestock as are feral goats, sheep, and pigs. The entire migration area for the donkeys was owned by several different individuals, which also complicated matters.

The county did, however, engage the services of their risk management officer, Scott Knowles, to walk the roadway fence line and organize a voluntary group to mend the fences on the southeast side of Waikoloa Road. County officials even considered rounding up and corralling the errant donkeys in hopes of offering them up for adoption, likely working through the Hawai'i Island Humane Society (HIHS). Although equipped with

THE NIGHTINGALES

(continued from previous page)

knowledge and leadership, HIHS lacked the space, equipment, and financial resources to become involved. Many frustrated and concerned residents logically contacted the Hawai'i Island Humane Society to remove the "loose" donkeys in the village and along the roadways, but the HIHS contract with the county clearly stated that they were not responsible for any feral species. It is important to note that the Hawai'i County Police Department went out of their way to respond to complaints or reports of donkeys on the Waikoloa Road and consistently tried to contact the ranchers in the area to move them back behind fences. They deserve credit for stepping up to assist in whatever way they could to ameliorate the situation.

The State Department of Land and Natural Resources (DLNR) was also contacted, but they reasoned that their involvement would be beyond their purview as well, since the donkeys were predominantly located on private land and were not classified the same as other feral species. The DLNR, with limited funding and resources, did offer lethal eradications to depopulate or reduce the feral donkey population, which became the leading solution despite strong opposition from some Waikoloa residents and groups such as Mālama Waikoloa Nightingales.

In determining responsibility for the donkey overpopulation, Whillock singled out other landowners in the area and leaseholders who were leasing these parcels from WVA at that given time. As mentioned previously, Parker Ranch leased the WVA land up until 2007 and used it sparingly for their cattle.

Concerned Waikoloa resident and Mālama Waikoloa Nightingales founder, Anika Glass, worked with the South Kohala Traffic Safety Committee, the County of Hawai'i, and the Humane Societies of the Big Island and the Humane Society of United States (HSUS) to address the issue. Glass persistently involved the WVA and its manager Jim Whillock, serving as community liaison—organizing and planning meetings and maintaining communications to keep all parties informed.

Mālama Waikoloa Nightingales (MWN), made up entirely of volunteers, was founded in February 2009, with support of the South Kohala Traffic Safety Committee. It is not supported with any funding. While the organization may or may not facilitate improvements in the safety of roadways, MWN is not responsible for the safety of Waikoloa Road or where the donkeys are at any given time.

Mālama Waikoloa Nightingales is dedicated to keeping feral donkeys off Waikoloa Road. They work tirelessly to ensure that as many donkeys as possible have been fenced off the road and are concerned about the safety of both people and donkeys. The volunteers strongly support humane management of Waikoloa donkey herds and believe that rehoming and fertility control are essential for long-term success. Humane management of the entire herd drives them to achieve their objectives.

THE NIGHTINGALES

(continued from previous page)

While many volunteers and agencies came forward to work on the problem, Glass was instrumental in bringing the Humane Society of the United States on board to assist with the Waikoloa donkey issue. In 2009 Glass reached out to the HSUS, seeking their involvement and assistance. Her role was to keep the community on board, as HSUS does not become involved in efforts that create local outrage and resistance. She accomplished this through community meetings, e-mails, and blogs. She was also instrumental in securing the support of my practice, ʻĀina Hou Animal Hospital; our team was able to donate time, services, and energy to help resolve the donkey overpopulation issues. Glass is commended for her efforts, as no single individual did more to temper the situation than she did.

A New Lease

After the fire of 2006, WVA wanted someone to graze and manage their land regularly to help reduce the brush fire risk surrounding Waikoloa Village in the future. Retired electrician and lifelong rancher Stanley Boteilho opted to lease the property. With a long history of ranching in his family, Boteilho understood the vast challenge facing him when signing up for this responsibility. Foremost among these were miles of fence repair along Waikoloa Road and internal cross-fencing between neighboring properties. In addition, he also assumed responsibility for the estimated four to six hundred feral donkeys freely roaming the area. Finally, there was someone willing to take the initiative to address the problem. Boteilho was genuinely concerned not only for the welfare of the donkeys that were dying of starvation and dehydation but, more importantly, the need for diligence in ensuring the safety of motorists. On previous occasions, drivers had accidently hit these animals when they chose to cross the highways, typically between dusk and dawn, when visibility is at its lowest.

Boteilho came with the right credentials as one of several sons of Edward Boteilho and his wife, Josephine, who reared their children as responsible and knowledgeable animal husbandry men and women. However, for him the issue was "purely business," as his small herd of cattle was not only competing for forage with numerous donkeys, but his water bill was profoundly impacted from consumption by "someone else's donkeys."

The feral donkey population continued to thrive and finally reached a breaking point during the summer of 2009 in the midst of some of the most severe and persistent drought conditions the Big Island has ever faced. That summer, I was approached by Boteilho for some advice. At the time he was aware of the DLNR's offer to eradicate, but he wasn't satisfied with that option and knew these animals deserved a better fate. He was unequivocal in his stance: "Somebody told me that I could shoot them since they

Former Parker Ranch livestock manager Walter Slater waxed poetic about the lowly donkey that helped settle a broncky horse named Stinger.

{ 14.5 } *The horse depicted adds an appropriate "kick" to Walter Slater's poem.*

Stinger Was His Name

This little SOB disliked me from the start
Hated the hackamore and refused to lead
He liked me better when I wasn't around
Tied to a snubbing post with a foot tied up
Flaring nostrils with ears laid back
Bloodshot eyes showing lots of white
Damn he would really like to kick and bite
Kicking and striking his best defense
Dogs and cats learned their distance to keep
Necked to an old burro learning to lead
Setting back like a borrowed dog he wasn't too bright
Old Happy the burro had a neat little trick
After a few tugs and pulls and if that didn't work
Old Happy would kick him in the belly so fast you lost count
He finally learned to lead and is getting wiser
His scrapes and bruises are starting to heal
Time for the saddle and weight on his back
All humped up looks like a camel carrying a pack
Never untracked just waiting to unwind
I knew the explosion was coming soon
He was planning to get even for all that I'd done
Jumping straight up and landing on his back
I got out of the way and was lucky not to be hurt
While he was down I tied all four feet to let him sweat a bit
A couple hours passed and still in a nasty mood
This time he moved out and started to buck
Making the stirrups pop over his back
I hobbled my stirrups an advantage I needed
To my surprise he just trotted away and never looked back
From that day on we got along fine
Dutch oven biscuits were a treat he liked
He whispered in my ear I'll never be a cutter, just your friend
For that, I'll never use you on long cold drives
Almost a true story by

Walter Slater

THE NIGHTINGALES

(continued from previous page)

were on my lease, but I didn't feel that was the right way to go. I felt sorry for them. I had a couple of donkeys as pets myself when I was a kid."

Growing up on the Big Island, I was already familiar with the Waikoloa Nightingales, but I had no idea how big the problem was until Boteilho described the conditions. It was difficult to comprehend the seriousness and magnitude of the problem until Boteilho led me on an ATV tour of the area. The sheer numbers of donkeys were staggering, as they were observed flowing across a hillside in the distance (see plate 9). Also very much in evidence were the many donkey bones and carcasses scattered in the barren vicinity of their only water source, Boteilho's water trough. The weak and injured likely stayed near the water source until they died. During that tour, Boteilho took me to an injured donkey he had been monitoring. The donkey was quite thin and appeared old, but what was most alarming was that he was walking on the exposed cannon bone of his left forelimb and in obvious pain. There was no hoof or any other anatomical structures left distal to the cannon bone. It appeared he had sustained a severe degloving injury to that limb some time ago, as what flesh remained just below his carpus had already granulated around the exposed bone. He was humanely euthanized that day.

{ 14.6 } *A glimpse at the depth and extent of environmental degradation of the land due to donkey overpopulation and eventual death of the animals, exacerbated by a decade of drought.*

THE NIGHTINGALES

(continued from previous page)

The impact of what I had witnessed struck me to the very core of my animal husbandry upbringing. I knew that I could not simply walk away. Following are the events that changed the course of my life and the lives of others committed to preserving a feral herd of donkeys.

Practical Solution

I wasn't sure what I could do at the time and never imagined getting to the point where we are today. I started by introducing myself to Anika, who was the only person with an organized effort to help the donkeys. I offered to help in any way I could. Around the same time, Anika made contact with Inga Gibson, our local representative for the Humane Society of the United States. The HSUS was unwavering in its support for this effort, as their organization is committed to protecting wildlife and working with local communities to solve wildlife conflicts in a humane and sustainable way, especially one that avoids lethal eradication. Support from HSUS was financial through the generosity of their donors and on the ground through HSUS's State Affairs and Equine Protection Departments teaming up with community volunteers and veterinary professionals. When HSUS is called in to rescue animals in crisis, they typically coordinate with their Emergency Services Placement Partners to take in animals from these rescues and facilitate placement in loving homes. Their support has been invaluable.

{ 14.7 } *An orphan donkey adopted by ʻĀina Hou Animal Hospital, Daisy gained celebrity status during the Waikoloa Nightingale campaign alongside her friend, Dr. Brady Bergin.*

This was the starting point of this project and the development of our plan. Our primary goals were simple: stop the population growth and reduce the herd population by adopting them out to appropriate new "homes." The primary means of controlling the population was through surgical castration of the jacks, which was no easy task. HSUS offered to provide PZP immunization for temporary sterilization of the jennies, but we declined as our hope was to no longer have any jennies exposed to intact jacks.

Rescue and Rehoming

Our first rescue was Daisy, a young orphan with an umbilical hernia that I adopted. She currently resides at ʻĀina Hou Animal Hospital (AHAH),

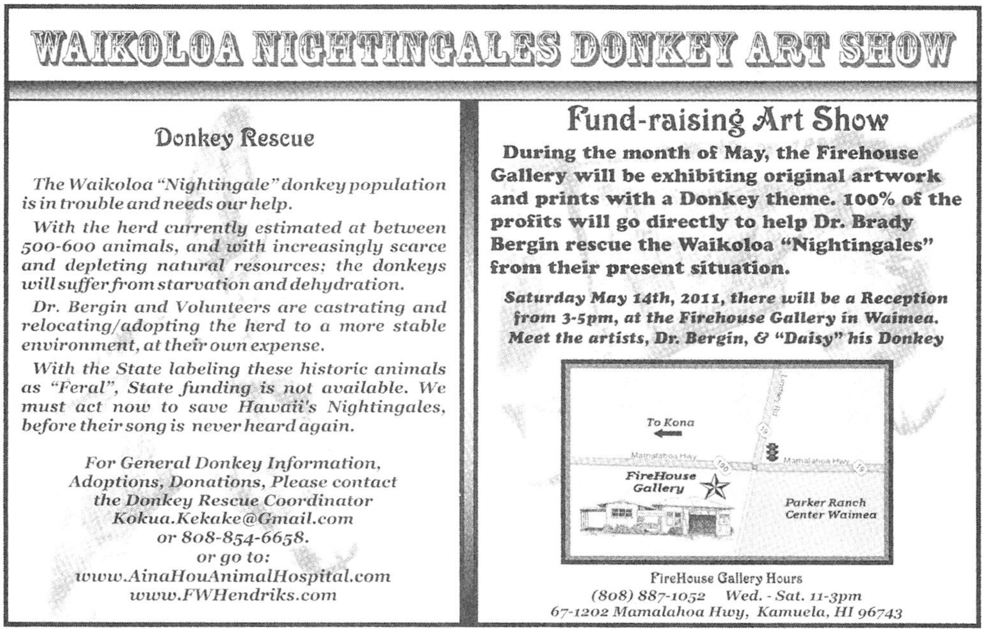

THE NIGHTINGALES

(continued from previous page)

{ 14.8 } *The community rallied to raise financial support for the donkey rehoming rescue project. A local art show was such an example.*

THE NIGHTINGALES

(continued from previous page)

where she serves as resident mascot and constant companion to Salt Point, an imported Thoroughbred stallion from Lexington, Kentucky, and great-grandson of Secretariat.

Without our having fiscal resources to support the project, a Fundraiser Art Show at the Firehouse Gallery in Waimea was organized by F. W. Hendriks, which was well attended (even Daisy was in attendance).

The Waikoloa Donkey Rescue and Rehoming Project officially got off the ground in November 2010 when Boteilho put out food and water and humanely trapped the donkeys, then delivered seventy head to AHAH within a two-day period. This was the beginning of what would become the largest capture and rehoming of donkeys in Hawaiʻi, in which hundreds of donkeys were trapped and delivered by rancher Boteilho. "It's a lot of work, but I feel good about it," Boteilho said of his efforts in an HSUS article by Julie Hauserman (2011). "My friends help me, my father-in-law helps me, so that makes it interesting. I like helping the animals so it's all a plus. And the way it's turning out, it couldn't be better for the donkeys," he continued. The tremendous community support and so many people willing to adopt the donkeys was nothing short of phenomenal.

{ 14.9 } *A watered corral/trap used for gathering feral donkeys in the Waikoloa rangeland. What started as a 30-head novelty band in 1974 grew to more than 600 feral donkeys that roamed the hills of Waikoloa in 2010.*

As an example, Hōkūkano Ranch from Kealakekua, Kona, took a large number of donkeys to return them to the area they were from originally. The transport of these animals was orchestrated by Bronson Branco, nephew of Boteilho.

From the onset, I committed my services and the services of AHAH support staff and our veterinary hospital. Processing of the animals required coordination, lots of manpower, and proper equipment for castrating, deworming, ear-tagging, and vaccinating the animals. We were clear on how we wanted the work to progress—castrations would be done humanely and there would be no shortcuts (see plate 10). All donkeys would be held on site until they were adopted. AHAH staff was responsible for the care, feeding, and watering of all donkeys. Adopters were required to sign a contract indicating that the adopted animals were not to be used for human consumption or for reproduction purposes.

A single individual who did more for this entire project and remained with it from beginning to conclusion was former Parker Ranch superintendent Sonny Keakealani. Sonny was with us every step of the way, not only helping with processing the donkeys

THE NIGHTINGALES

(continued from previous page)

{ **14.10** } *Outdoor stalls of 'Āina Hou Animal Hospital served more than 72 donkeys as temporary shelter prior to processing and distribution to permanent homes.*

THE NIGHTINGALES

(continued from previous page)

but also, perhaps more importantly, keeping a keen eye out for our personal safety and protecting us from any errant donkey by simply placing himself between donkeys and working personnel. His confident, self-assured manner made all of us comfortable knowing that he was capable of handling any and all crises that might arise. I am forever grateful for his skill, expertise, and presence during this project (see plate 11).

People in the local community went out of their way to provide support, especially in finding appropriate homes for the donkeys. Bird McIver, founder of the nonprofit CB Horse Rescue, was invaluable in finding suitable homes on the east side of the island. Her professional credentials in agriculture and animal science coupled with her years of rescue experience fully complemented the efforts of the project. She was tireless in her mission, making frequent trips from across the island, filling her trailer with adoptable donkeys for Puna residents. Once there, she fed and cared for them through adoption and educated new owners in appropriate care, also ensuring that there was sufficient grass, water, and fencing at the new locations. Bird was without question one of our most reliable volunteers. Incredibly, through her dedicated efforts, she was able to rehome well over a hundred donkeys on the east side of the island.

With backgrounds in animal husbandry, Mark and Cassie Richter of Kamuela spent countless hours fostering younger donkeys at their farm, domesticating and exposing them to haltering, leading, and hoof care, as well as co-inhabiting with other farm animals. They were able to rehome seventy donkeys to people who sought them for family pets or livestock guardians, two of which were adopted by the Honolulu Zoo. Like Bird, Mark and Cassie spent time working with the adopters to ensure they understood the responsibilities associated with caring for these creatures.

Betina Tacoronte of Equine 808 Horse Rescue on Oʻahu played an important role in the rescue. A former rodeo contender from Colorado and a military wife, Betina learned of the plight of the donkeys in her work with Inga Gibson of HSUS. She first became interested in horse rescue when she offered to help a nurse at a military stable with a horse that was emaciated and in poor condition. She set out searching for help but found no program to help people with their horses. There were no horse rescues. The more she searched, the more she realized how many horses needed help. The Humane Society did not have funding or facilities, so she ended up rescuing that first of six horses on her own in 2007 before the organization started after realizing the need for this service. Her work has grown bigger than she ever imagined, and now as director she works with other rescue organizations. Her goal was to establish a minimum standard of care for horses and to provide appropriate education to people. Thus far, Betina has accepted twenty-two donkeys, keeping the first two that were shipped in 2013 to her new rescue facility in Colorado.

THE NIGHTINGALES

(continued from previous page)

Shipping animals to neighboring islands is costly, but she teamed up with Young Brothers interisland shipping company and arranged to get the donkeys to O'ahu. On June 1, 2011, Equine 808 obtained one of these donkeys, naming him Marty after the zebra in the *Madagascar* cartoon feature. He became the ambassador for the mission to do whatever they could to find loving homes for these displaced donkeys. The mission of Equine 808 closely aligns with that of the donkey rescue mission: "As horses are not indigenous to Hawai'i and having great love of horses, we feel it is our civic duty to provide a sanctuary for injured, abused, neglected, and unwanted horses by offering emergency relief, refuge, medical care, rehabilitation and adoption services and to provide education in the arenas of proper horse ownership, responsibility, health and care and to provide a community connection to all."

Extending the Reach

As the population of gelded jacks and jennies increased and local homing sources were saturated, the Hawai'i team looked to mainland venues for their donkeys. Such an effort required a well-coordinated and orchestrated plan. This transport, the largest phase of the project in terms of planning and resources involved, took many months to organize. A project of this magnitude required gathering, transferring, treating, castrating, and shipping a planeload of donkeys to California. Throughout the donkey rehoming project, the team was in contact with Mark Meyers, head of Peaceful Valley Donkey Rescue in California, a sanctuary with proven success in donkey placement (see plate 12). When contacted regarding the proposal, he readily agreed to assist.

Keith Dane, director of Equine Protection for HSUS, and Inga Gibson, HSUS's Hawai'i state director, are credited with providing the necessary resources to bring this project to fruition.

Inga Gibson, while located on O'ahu, spent considerable time on site and offered HSUS involvement provided the males were castrated and adoption done by responsible parties. The HSUS became involved in 2007, describing the donkeys as "iconic symbols of Hawai'i's history." Gibson interfaced with all parties and despite an unfortunate memorandum inferring civil liability on the part of WCA, which then withdrew from any involvement, Gibson took affirmative action to secure funding for feed and castrating. She also scheduled an aerial survey of the affected area for Keith Dane and myself that provided a meaningful, factual perspective on the magnitude of the problem.

Dane took the time to visit the Big Island to review the situation and galvanized his organization into action. He describes the procedure in a mahalo letter posted on the Mālama Waikoloa Nightingale Web site:

THE NIGHTINGALES

(continued from previous page)

The first step, passively gathering wild donkeys, proved to be the biggest hurdle. Previous gatherings were done during drought conditions, thus luring the donkeys with food and drink was relatively easy. The first attempt in February proved to be challenging because the winter rains had come, and ample sustenance was now available to the donkeys in the wild. Plans for the castration clinic were then put on hold. Undeterred, the Hawai'i team continued to monitor the situation, setting and checking traps when there was the slightest dry spell, then gathering, castrating, treating, and rehoming occasional groups of donkeys. With the assistance of HSUS and other financial backers, Dr. Brady Bergin worked to find a secure holding area where the donkeys would be secure until enough were accumulated to justify the veterinary clinic and subsequent airlift. He was also successful in securing a favorable rate with Pacific Airlift to provide an entire specially equipped 747 to transport the stock to California.

As summer approached the team targeted mid-August for the clinic and airlift to occur. Plans were set in motion to prepare for the clinic which involved the coordination of many local volunteers, and a team of equine veterinarians and technicians from Steinbeck Veterinary Clinic in Salinas, California, organized by HSUS. Volunteers even included Hawai'i State Senator Clayton Hee, a horseman currently residing on O'ahu.

{ **14.11** } *Using a Powder River squeeze chute, each donkey was carefully restrained for haltering, then cast for anesthesia, deworming, vaccination, castration, and hoof trimming. Dr. Brady Bergin administers a sedative under the watchful eye of Blue Coleman.*

{ **14.12** } *Waiki'i Ranch served a heroic role in providing temporary pasturage and corral facilities while neutering, processing, and rehoming brought overpopulation under control.*

THE NIGHTINGALES

(continued from previous page)

Waiki'i Ranch was key to the procedure offering its cattle chutes and space for the mission. The homeowner's association not only allowed us to use their corrals for processing, they allowed nearly 200 donkeys to be temporarily pastured there. Manager and support staff, Lucky Puhi and Yaku Kotaki, made the extra effort to repair and repaint the corral.

Ensuring that it was safe and in top shape for our use, Dr. Lisa Wood of Veterinary Associates Inc., along with HSUS veterinarians and technicians joined forces with Dr. Brady Bergin, local cowboys and other volunteers in getting the job done.

Within two days in late August, 165 donkeys were processed. It included 98 castrated jacks and 67 jennies. All were treated for parasites, checked for health concerns and those bound for California micro chipped and blood drawn for a Coggins test, a state of California entry requirement. Given the large number of volunteers, the clinic went smoothly. After two weeks of recovery, 119 donkeys (77 jacks and 47 jennies) were on their way.

{ 14.13 } *Processing donkeys for airlift took many hands to accomplish. The volunteers pictured are credited for making it happen. In the back row sitting on the truck are (left to right) Alika Miyasato, Ashley Borsum, and Kalysa Hamilton. Standing are (left to right) Keith Dane, Bill Bergin, Michelle Surbeck, Dr. Wade Tenney, Dr. Lisa Wood, Dr. Malia Lyons, Rico Rosario, Bob Hamilton, Liz Hendriks, Renee Rosario, La'akea Bertelmann, Mark Richter, Kassie Rogers, Lori Bergin, Dr. Jonathan Hirsh, and Dr. Brady Bergin. Kneeling are (left to right) Bryson DeSilva, Julie Phipps, and Giga Cullen. Volunteers not pictured are F. W. Hendriks, Inga Gibson, Senator Clayton Hee, Sonny Keakealani, Blue Coleman, Tom Richmond, Pat King, Lucky Puhi, Stan Boteilho, Bird McIver, Ginger Towle, and Anika Glass.*

THE NIGHTINGALES

(continued from previous page)

A large caravan of volunteer trucks and trailers transported the group to Kona International Airport where they were boarded and airlifted to California. The donkeys were accompanied on the flight by Mark Meyers of the Peaceful Valley Donkey Rescue along with Dr. Brady Bergin and a stockman from Pacific Airlift. They were met by similar caravans to take them to Peaceful Valley Donkey Rescue to rest and await adoption in their new found home. The airlift reduced the existing Hawaiian herd to approximately 200, a significant reduction from the estimated 600 in the wild. (Dane 2012)

About a dozen were homed to Eagle Eye Sanctuary in Northern California. HSUS played a significant role in organizing and funding this huge undertaking. San Francisco architect, Ugo Sap, who owns Eagle Eye Sanctuary Foundation for donkeys in Northern California, generously provided substantial funding for the project, including the airlift. "I definitely wanted to save these donkeys," said Sap. "I think they are super sweet and super intelligent."

The HSUS also came through with tremendous donor funded support. Other major financial backers were Wendy P. McCaw Foundation, the Pettus Crowe Foundation, Kawaihae Harbor Gallery (customer donation jar), and Ginger Towle and the West Hawai'i Humane Society.

{ 14.14 } *Scores of gooseneck stock trailers formed a caravan delivering the California donkey shipment to Keahole International Airport.*

THE NIGHTINGALES

(continued from previous page)

{ 14.15 } *Using a hydraulic scissor lift, the operator loads a compartment of California-bound donkeys as two units stand by.*

To date, well over five hundred donkeys have been rehomed, which by far exceeded my expectations. The remainder of those treated at the clinic were to be rehomed locally. Efforts are in place to locate funding and/or land to provide a permanent local sanctuary for approximately one hundred donkeys still in the wild (see plate 13). To date, that support has yet to materialize. Until then, Boteilho will continue to trap and gather small groups and rehome them locally.

The Humane Society Wildlife Land Trust's (HSWLT) Bob Koons and Peter Bender stepped forward to assist. The trust celebrates and protects wild animals by creating permanent sanctuaries, preserving and enhancing natural habitat, and confronting cruelty. HSWLT was focused on caring for the remaining herd in Waikoloa and Waiki'i. Part of their effort involved donating and installing three domed Rainmaker Wildlife Guzzlers, which are five-hundred-gallon catchment water troughs. HSUS, on the other hand, provided funding for the flight and all supply costs for the castration clinic, including travel expenses for the team of veterinarians and technicians from Steinbeck Veterinary Clinic. The Waiki'i Ranch Homeowners Association graciously continued to accommodate the remaining donkeys.

DNA Study of the Hawaiian Donkey

The motivation for conducting DNA studies on the native donkeys was first an extension of the same research done on the Hawaiian horse. However, the driving motive for the study was a curious notion that the findings would have broader implications than that of the valley and mountain mustangs of the Island of Hawaiʻi.

This reasoning is based on early reports (late nineteenth century) of large bands of wild donkeys encircling Mauna Loa and Hualālai. Without a fence to stop migration, donkeys roamed from Kīpuka Kēkake at the top of Keauhou Ranch in the Volcano area all across Kaʻū and well into South and North Kona.

It is reasonable to surmise that the introduction in 1972 of thirty Huʻehuʻe Ranch donkeys into the plains of Waikoloa in South Kohala was, in fact, a genetic expansion of the same species from as far as 120 miles south and east. Simply put, the bands, albeit clustered in pockets surrounding the mountains, were of common genetic makeup and likely descendants of early donkey importation from 1825 forward. The DNA study of thirty-six adult donkeys, we believe, was enhanced by this commonality.

Conducted at the Texas A&M University Department of Veterinary Integrative Bioscience by Dr. Gus Cothran, the genetic analysis of this feral donkey herd is likely reflective of the entire island population. Cothran measured genetic variation of the Waikoloa subjects in comparison to other feral and domestic donkey herds in a global context. While he found that the Hawaiian donkey is closely aligned with the standard donkey, the highest genetic similarity is with the Syrian jackass, suggesting ancient relationships. Such findings made the efforts to conduct the genetic analysis of the Hawaiian donkey all the more meaningful.

Appendix B presents a complete report of the study and its results.

The Work Continues

The work to keep the pastures surrounding Waikoloa a relatively controlled environment for the donkey population requires the collective efforts of Boteilho and neighboring lessees Travis Gomes and Mark and Tony Loando and the cooperation of the WVA. Billy serves as liaison between the ranchers and the community association. All are in agreement that it will take all parties working together to keep the population at a manageable number and keep donkeys from competing for precious feed for their cattle herds.

The group first met on August 11, 2014, at the Waikoloa Clubhouse to discuss the risk of renewed overpopulation of the feral donkeys of the region. A roundtable discussion touched upon all aspects of donkey issues and the means of keeping the population under control. The present population is estimated to be less than one hundred head, located and watered at the *mauka* corner of the Boteilho/Waikoloa Village Association parcel that parallels Waikoloa Road.

Concern centers on the fact that several foals have been born due to the presence of ungelded jacks that are remnants of earlier depopulation campaigns. About half of the foals are jacks that in about a year will reach sexual maturity and begin servicing the jennies. This would accelerate herd expansion if action is not taken in the near future.

The ranchers concurred that a sanctuary should be established and came up with a three-part plan and cost estimate, as well as a projected timeline. The plan included bulldozing and building a firebreak/fence line road, restoring fence line security through repair and replacement, and establishing a working corral within the reserve to accommodate annual processing of the donkey band for culling, castration, and necessary treatment. This would eliminate the need to transport donkeys to other locations to get the job done. The estimated budget was $16,730, with the ranchers doing the physical labor and the material cost of the fencing, paneling, and bulldozing being covered by appropriate resources. As with all projects of this nature, funding is the critical element. To complicate matters, time is of the essence, as they targeted January 2015 for completion.

Cause for concern is that the present foal crop will shortly be coming of age. In addition, some of the adult jennies will already be in foal from one or two stray jacks. These jacks will be gelded and the yearlings gathered. Annual gathers are necessary as the jennies will drop new foals, about half of which are potential jacks that will reach sexual maturity.

The ultimate goal for the grazers is that within five years the band will be reduced to a permanent herd of twenty-five, made up of barren jennies and gelded jacks. Reduction will occur through periodic homing of donkeys elsewhere. Natural attrition (age, etc.) will also take its toll.

This management plan is a long-term solution to overpopulation problems of feral donkeys in the Waikoloa region. Bringing it to fruition will require the collective effort of the ranchers, stockholders, institutions, associations, and benevolent parties that wish to bring this recurrent problem under relatively permanent control in a manner that abides by humane standards and appropriate animal husbandry practices. The plan has been presented to Roger Wehrsig, general manager of WVA, for consideration and problem solving by its membership.

Support organizations were a vital component in resolving the donkey overpopulation crisis, namely Waiki'i Ranch Homeowners Association, Mālama Waikoloa Nightingales, West Hawai'i and Hawai'i Island Humane Societies, Humane Society of the United States, 'Āina Hou Animal Hospital, Veterinary Associates, Inc., Wild Life Land Trust, as well as individuals Liz Hendriks (Donkey Adoption Coordinator), photographer Mary Buckley, photographer and artist FW Hendriks, and Pacific Airlift.

Knowledgeable adopters came forth readily, including Eagle Eye Sanctuary, Hōkūkano Ranch, Chandi Hefner, Judy Hiller, Ala Lindsey, Gena Almaden, Bird

McIver, Pat King, Peaceful Valley Donkey Rescue, Mark and Cassie Richter, and 808 Equine Horse Rescue. Words are woefully inadequate to express the appreciation of the team for their combined efforts to resolve the overpopulation issues.

We continue to work closely with the Humane Society of the United States to prevent further reproduction of this feral herd and to encourage the rehoming of as many as possible. Our hope is to reduce the herd to a small, easily manageable number and work toward building a proactive alliance for a community-driven solution for consistent control and management of the feral herd, while maintaining the same united spirit that inspired individuals and organizations to come forward to resolve what appeared to be an insurmountable overpopulation issue.

CHAPTER 15

THE FUTURE OF THE HORSE IN HAWAIʻI

What the future holds for Hawaiʻi's horse community is promising on the one hand and worrisome on the other. Much of its success depends on several variables: transportation, facilities, the environment, and public awareness.

Transportation in an insular community refers to the convenience of moving horses between the islands for purposes of sale, competition, breeding, or veterinary services. Pacific Airlift primarily handles mainland transportation, but it periodically operates interisland flights from Honolulu to Maui, Kauaʻi, and Hawaiʻi Island destinations. A fee of $400 is average for a one-hour flight, counting loading and off-loading. A West Coast to Hawaiʻi flight presently costs $3,600. Both interisland and mainland services are excellent, and the comfort of the horse is more than reasonable. Air service is clearly best for the horse, but often it is beyond the pocketbook of average horse owners on both end destinations.

Young Brothers provides interisland horse transport by oceangoing barge in owner-supplied box stalls, vans, horse trailers, or modified shipping containers; the average voyage takes twenty hours. When island-to-island transport is needed, however, the round-trip doubles the cost, increases the elapsed time on board and the elapsed time of staging (delivery standby to and fro), and increases the physiological stress on the horse (and owner). The most serious factor, however, is the lack of stewardship on board, without which mishaps or more serious accidents that occur en route are left unattended until arrival at the final destination. Cost for such transport service is between $200 and $400. Despite in-stall service for watering and feeding, horses

{ 15.1 } *Dr. Billy Bergin and Tommy Goto, Parker Ranch horse foreman, receive and process a horse import via Pacific Airlift.*

arrive "shrunk" as a result of transportation stress and subsequent dehydration.

Similar problems apply to mainland-Hawaiʻi service via Matson Navigation, which charges an average fee of $800 for an eight-to-ten-day trip; the disembarking horse requires a few days rest before being used in competition.

Some transportation alternatives have surfaced: the Superferry (interisland) and FedEx (West Coast–Hawaiʻi). With the Superferry, interisland equestrian travel temporarily became convenient, inexpensive, and stress-free: the owner could drive on and drive off in a pickup truck and trailer for the three-to-six-hour sea journey, with his mount in clear view. Unfortunately, the Superferry, while a highly successful venture for local transportation needs, was shut down after a few years of existence by opposing environmentalists who cited lack of an environmental impact study.

Pacific Airlift

FedEx provides a customized, on-call, multiple venue service and a price structure very competitive with Pacific Airlift. One major advantage with the latter outfit is the high level of regulatory compliance and animal transport savvy. With

{ 15.2 } *Nine-year-old Bill Bergin holding a California-bound Thoroughbred that he accompanied on a Pacific Airlift flight with Vince Genco.*

Sheila Head's Hawaiian Transport

Ranch-raised Californian Sheila Head has been transporting horses to and from Hawaiʻi for more than twenty-five years.

Headquartered out of her Valley Ford, California, ranch, she bases her success in horse transportation to an emphasis on safety. Equally as compelling is her close attention to proper regulatory testing and paperwork, as well as certification and treatment that is accurate, legible, and timely.

About an hour's haul from the Port of Oakland, she loads at her facility into custom-built livestock containers on-ranch for the four-to-six-day voyage to Honolulu Harbor via Matson Navigation vessels. Well-qualified livestock attendants accompany the shipment, allowing for frequent care, feeding, and stall cleaning throughout the journey. While her earlier shipping containers were open-air "roll-ons," current shipments are usually in forty-foot "lift-ons" that can house up to ten adult horses. All of her shipments are destined for the Hawaiʻi State Quarantine Station in Hālawa Valley, convenient for post-import inspection and release to owners and agents. Transshipment to the neighbor islands via Young Brothers barge is usually the only alternative for those owners, an overnight trip often more arduous than the 2,400-mile trip from Oakland.

management from the early days of Bill Verdugo through the present team of Vince Genco and Andee Patterson, there have been minimal concerns or hurdles in documentation, blood testing, or animal tending and handling. Extensive communication between owners, shippers, and receivers makes the FedEx route work nearly as well as the worry-free system of Pacific Airlift. To their credit, however, Pacific Airlift has maintained its high standards and customer satisfaction rate for more than fifty years. This organization stands alone in its professional relationships with regulatory agencies of international, national, and state jurisdictions.

Perhaps the greatest dilemma and fear for the future of horse transport in Hawaiʻi is the high fuel cost. This could drive both horse and cattle transport clearly out of bounds. What then will Hawaiʻi do with seventy-five thousand weaned calves with nowhere to go in a ranching environment that over the past half century has lost not only its moisture patterns but also feedlot and slaughter facilities?

{ **15.3** } *A great-grandson of Secretariat, Salt Point came from Halfmoon Farm in Kentucky, prior to acquisition by Dr. Brady Bergin. Since his arrival in Hawai'i, he has sired many offspring destined for polo, sport horse, rodeo, and ranch circles. Secretariat, from whom he descended, was noted for his exceptional speed, outdistancing all previous winning mounts with an average speed of 37.5 mph when he won the Belmont Stakes in 1972. By comparison, Man o' War ran an average speed of 36.38 mph in the Lawrence Realization Stakes in 1920.*

Breeding Facilities

Hawai'i's horse industry can react by expanding on locally bred and trained horses. In breeding cycles, the tropics provide longer, warmer days that encourage follicular development and ovulation in mares. Frozen and chilled semen, with its tidy containerization and regulation-free status, is only an air-hop away from any of the island's state airports. A broodmare owner has a huge catalog of potential sires in all major breeds to choose from. Veterinary expertise in insemination exists in the major horse communities of the state (see plates 14–16).

Training Venues

Trainers and training facilities are treated separately. Hawai'i has reason to be proud of the many Island-born trainers in all classes of usage, many of whom have succeeded in mainland venues. Hawai'i has also attracted mainland trainers, who usually open their services at an existing facility under the auspices of an established institution. Like locally developed trainers, these horsemen often seek independent facilities as their clientele develops. As with any other profession, some choose to "come and go," while others step into the void to fill it. Hawai'i is not without well-qualified trainers, even though some discriminating owners are more comfortable flying their mounts to the mainland or flying in their retained expert for training purposes at considerable personal cost. Both systems exist to some degree.

Training facilities are a more complex matter, as location, size, availability, and cost are huge considerations in an island community, but these venues do exist.

Future rural development of Hawaiʻi's pristine landscape does not necessarily lend itself to accommodating long-range horse-oriented facilities, despite aggressive advertising to the contrary. As an example, Waikoloa Stables, the noted Big Island equine facility built in 1974, has been dormant in recent years, and the Waikoloa Village Association owners have terminated a lease to make way for a shopping center. The association, however, is currently entertaining a proposal to restore the renovated stables as an operational entity. Given the shortage of equine facilities on the Big Island, the horse community is hopeful that the latter idea comes to fruition.

The Reinsman

When the Franciscan missionaries forged north into Alta California, they developed personnel with skills in roping, riding, and training. Their finely trained horses worked the vast herds of cattle that had scattered across the coast and desert plains, high mountain meadows, and dry arroyo canyons.

The California vaquero, among the finest horsemen of all time, had developed equipment, riding styles, and training techniques that produced some of the best stock horses ever known.

Midway through the 1800s, gold was struck in California about the same time that the vast rancheros of Mexican/Spanish nobility were fractured by mandate. By the turn of the century, mechanical means seemed to have spelled the doom of the exquisite California reined horse and his skilled master.

Midway through the 1900s, however, a small group of dedicated horsemen and horsewomen gathered to virtually turn the tide in favor of the reined horse's legacy by forming the National Reined Cow Horse Association (NRCHA).

The NRCHA succeeded beyond the horizon in preserving the tradition of the Spanish vaquero by establishing a traditional training program that includes several phases. Spanning several years of training, a horse may be considered "finished" when capable of performing the standard maneuvers required on roundups and drives under bonafide cattle-ranch conditions.

The NRCHA, organized in 1949, is a performance-oriented national association with a yearly general membership meeting at the Annual Celebration of Champions in San Angelo, Texas. An annual NRCHA Colt Raffle is a highlight event that is based on the premise that a futurity competition is the premium showcase event for budding champion horses.

Philosophically, what is looked for in such a competition is a horse with innate cow savvy and quick response to the rider's commands. The ideal horse is not just a cutting horse or reining horse; it should be able to successfully execute a complex dry work pattern (maneuvers without livestock), work cattle out of a herd, and "handle cattle down the fence" (turn back at top speed and agility) in an arena.

Awarded annually during the last performance of the NRCHA Futurity is a colt donated by the Ward Ranch, the traditional epicenter of America's reining horse world. Hawai'i is fortunate to have been the beneficiary of the Ward Ranch's efforts, especially in the generosity and support of Greg Ward himself. An NRCHA Hall of Famer, he established the Ward Ranch in 1972 with the ranch-bred mare Fillinic, one of the industry's leading producers of champions. Fillinic was the mother of Sugarnic (1972 Futurity Champion) and grandmother of the 1981 champion, Sugar Remedy.

Hawai'i is also gifted with a native son, Alex Penovaroff, whose performance on a national level is remarkable, with consistent winnings both in competition as well as breeding of futurity prospects.

Alex Penovaroff, Premier Reinsman

Over the years, Hawai'i has produced some outstanding horsemen, but one accomplished individual stands out for his excellence in style and performance for more than five decades of competition. Alex Penovaroff is the epitome of the ideal cowboy in appearance, finesse, and competitive spirit, and any book about Hawaiian horses is incomplete without including his story.

Possessing an extraordinary knowledge of horse lineage in Hawai'i and on the mainland, Alex has dedicated his life to the breeding, care, and training of excellent horses and in mentoring young people today who share the same passion and love that he does for the noble steed. A thorough biography of him is included in the second volume of *Loyal to the Land: The Senior Stewards, 1950–1970* (Bergin 2006).

Alex returned home to Waimea in 1974 and developed a twenty-acre horse farm in Lālāmilo, where he stood both Thoroughbred and Quarter Horse sires.

Tellin Tales was an American Quarter Horse Association grandson of Three Bars: he stood sixteen hands and weighed in at 1,300 pounds. Alex purchased the stud from Parker Ranch as a retired sire for $1,500 and readily turned him into a talented cutting horse. He was bred to Noons Crist fresh off California Thoroughbred tracks, producing a son, Hele Kanaka Hele, a name that translates from Hawaiian into English as "Go Man Go." Hele was shipped to California, where Alex successfully competed on him in snaffle bit and cutting horse shows.

Standing a direct gray son of Ribot of distinguished Thoroughbred lineage put Alex's breeding operation at the forefront of polo circles in the Hawaiian Islands. Being a polo player himself gave Alex ample opportunity to show the stud

{15.4} *Alex Penovaroff at cutting competition.*

in competition. Amazingly, the little gray stud showed more than ample grit in the cutting and reining arena.

A college classmate and lifelong friend of Alex is Greg Ward of Ward River Ranch of California. Ward played a major role in converting Alex from a ranch/race horseman to a cutting and reining enthusiast. To his credit, Alex took the ball and ran with it, becoming the most successful and celebrated reinsman in Hawaiʻi's history. Watching Alex's fluid performance on horseback is sheer poetry in motion. He demonstrated his snaffle bit prowess at Reno's Snaffle Bit Futurities in 1994, 1995, 1997, and 1999, taking his horse into the finals in all but one instance.

Unfortunately, 1999 was a fateful year, when a filly he was training lost her footing on a sliding stop and went over backward onto Alex and shattered his pelvis, an accident that Billy witnessed. Never one to miss local (pidgin) humor, Alex was stretched out on his hospital bed when he was visited by a community character intent on cheering him up. The friend was confined to a wheelchair, so Alex queried him about what had happened. He explained that he had a bad fall from a running horse and he broke his "spatula." There was little doubt that he had indeed cheered Alex up, although he was too sore to laugh at the fellow's reference to a fracture of his scapula.

Turning to cutting was a fortuitous move. The first filly to show as a cutter was AP Aloha Friday. She made the finals as a three-, four-, and five-year-old. Friday further distinguished herself by being the only finalist to be born and trained at Alex's Lālāmilo facility before export to the mainland.

Equally proud of a pair of broodmares, JB Punxcatawny Phily and Intensive Lil Pep, both of which entered the ranks of show winnings in both snaffle bit and cutting competition on the mainland, Alex's recent program calls for their breeding and foaling at the Ward River Ranch. Shipped home as weanlings, these offspring leave for California as Alex-trained three-year-olds ready for cutting competition in California and Texas futurities.

Most recently (2011), Alex won the Amateur Class in the Pacific Coast Cutting Association, showing his gelding, I Ain't No Bum Check, a horse that was purchased by Tommy Manion shortly thereafter. Alex went on to show I'm Counting Checks at the National Cutting Horse Association's World Show in Fort Worth, Texas. In the same venue he showed Lil Miss Mauna Kea, tying for fourth place in the Amateur Division but winning the Senior Division on her. A minor setback, hopefully temporary, was the 2012 bilateral hip surgery repairing long-standing pelvic damage, a chronic sequel to his upending the filly in that sliding-stop accident a decade earlier.

Over the last twenty years, however, Alex's prowess with performance horses has been matched with unbridled passion for mentoring Hawai'i's youthful cutting enthusiasts, and through this avenue his legacy will live on for generations to come.

Equestrian Centers

Hawai'i is fortunate to have a number of equestrian centers and rodeo arenas available for use by local residents and visitors alike. Counting a couple of riding stables that are attached to hotel properties on the island of Lāna'i, the state of Hawai'i boasts more than forty equestrian centers. O'ahu leads with fifteen, followed by Maui with a dozen, Hawai'i Island with six, and Kaua'i with five.

O'ahu's larger number reflects both civilian and military populations. Waimānalo alone accommodates six equestrian facilities; New Town and Country Stables, with more than fifty years in the business, is the longest standing and the most prestigious. Bud and Katy Gibson clearly provide the most professional institution, offering a broad range of services in Western and English riding, boarding, therapeutic services, equine hydrotherapy, and horse transport on island, interisland, to the U.S. mainland, and to international destinations. Scattered throughout the island are horse centers in Hale'iwa, Hau'ula, Honolulu, Kailua, Mā'ili, Waialua, and Wai'anae.

The island of Hawai'i has been blessed with a county administration spanning more than sixty years that has supported horse activities via three facilities: Hilo's Pana'ewa Equestrian Center, the Rose Andrade Correia Rodeo Stadium in Honoka'a, and the Hōnaunau Rodeo Arena, all of which are multipurpose facilities. Except for the twenty-four-horse stall barn at Panaʻewa, all facilities are rent free. Privately owned but publically used facilities include the Parker Ranch Equestrian Center, the Anderson and Hale Kea Arenas in Waimea, and the Naʻalehu Arena in Kaʻū. North Kona boasts two private arenas available to the public—the Double D Equine Center in Kalaoa and the Puʻuanahulu Community Arena in that village community. Many horse enthusiasts throughout the island have their own arena or, at a minimum, a round pen and adjacent barn. Many of these facilities have been start-up venues for budding or established horse trainers.

Despite the downturn in the economy of 2010 and 2011, horse activities, while not thriving, have maintained a presence on the Big Island.

Riding stables on the island of Hawaiʻi are located within a fifteen-mile radius of Waimea. Dahana Ranch, owned by veteran horseman Harry Nakoa, is the oldest facility, offering rides throughout his Āhualoa ranch. Naʻalapa Stables has two venues: one at Kahuā Ranch in North Kohala that offers a ranching exposure, while its Waipiʻo Valley outfit offers rides through the verdant valley alongside two other operators, Waipiʻo Ridge Stables and Waipiʻo on Horseback. Recent closure of Cowboys of Hawaiʻi, owned by Maui horseman Alan Mendes, which offered the only horseback tours in the immediate Kamuela area, has left this historic cowtown and headquarters of legendary Parker Ranch without any commercial riding venue.

The island of Maui boasts twelve horseback-riding opportunities, with five operating in the community of Makawao and one each in Hāna, Kīhei, Kula, Kahului, Lahaina, and Nāpili. Piʻiholo Ranch offers far and away the premiere horseback-riding adventures on Maui, over wide-open ranges with panoramic views. It is owned and operated by Peter Baldwin and his family, which spans a seven-generation legacy of Hawaiʻi ranching heritage. Piʻiholo, like other ranching operations, has diversified, with activities such as zip lines.

The island of Kauaʻi is home to five horseback-riding facilities—two apiece in Hanalei and Kīlauea and one in Kōloa. The Kōloa outfit, CJM Stables, is owned and operated by Jimmy and Joyce Miranda. Beyond riding facilities, they own the island's most popular rodeo arena, complete with bucking chutes.

Highlighting Kauaʻi's equestrian facilities is Princeville Ranch Adventures, a Carswell family operation since 1978. In addition to their working cattle ranch operation, like Piʻiholo, the Princeville operation includes a variety of offerings for young and old under the leadership of David Carswell and his staff.

The Environment

Riding trails, one would think, should be discussed under horse facilities. This is not so. Horse trails require expansive tracts of land to satisfy reasonable distances that support a minimum of thirty-minute jaunts, which would provide an aerobic walking exercise of about a mile under a casual human regime.

For a horse's well-being, mildly irregular terrain in a rural setting with a four-mile round-trip conducted twice a week is an ideal exercise. Yet not many communities throughout the Aloha State boast of such a setting in a convenient, safe, and easily accessible format.

Only a few years ago, the town of Kamuela was commonly graced with horse traffic and hitching posts. Today, it would be poor judgment to ride through town from Church Row to Waimea Park. However, a rider with a Parker Ranch Arena destination could choose a route through the Ala 'Ōhiā connector road, which is an ideal bridle pathway. Horsemen and women in Honoka'a and Kailua on the Big Island face similar reservations about riding through town in these communities that historically were known as cowtowns. The same reluctance is experienced by horse folks in Makawao, Maui, Kane'ohe, O'ahu, and Kōloa, Kaua'i. Persistent riders take the risk of riding among traffic or of being charged with trespass.

The entire state of Hawai'i has limited venues for trail riding, but not because interested and responsible parties have failed to try. In some cases, real estate developers and landowners have included proposals seeking to achieve favorable Land Use Commission, Department of Land and Natural Resources, and County Planning permitting. The Parker Ranch 20/20 Plan is one such development: it carefully outlined an equestrian trail that would begin on Kawaihae Road, skirt the town safely via the Ala 'Ōhi'a connector road, and cross Māmalahoa Highway at the Church Row. From this park, one could continue on an old government road starting behind 'Imiola Church, rising through some verdant meadows and foothills, and ending at the Department of Hawaiian Home Lands (DHHL) Kūhiō Hale roadside location adjacent to Mānā Road. Mānā Road is a uniquely handled "Old Government Road" that meanders for thirty sometimes rugged miles along the northern and eastern slopes of Mauna Kea at about 4,500 feet elevation, ending at the Humu'ula Sheep Station on Saddle Road. This ride requires overnight camping at two or three intervals.

Waimea Trails and Greenways, in its early efforts, included the Parker Ranch equestrian trail as part of its pathway from Kawaihae Road to Church Row. However, Parker Ranch trustees later summarily rescinded the portion of this trail through ranch property, and Waimea Trails and Greenways discontinued the horse pathway in its entirety shortly thereafter.

Judy Ellis, a horse-trail enthusiast in the community, has kept open the segment from Church Row at 'Imiola Church along the Old Government Road along the Waimea foothills, terminating at the DHHL Kūhiō Hale location. This one-hour trail ride offers one of the most panoramic vistas of the village of Kamuela, the plains of Waimea from Hanaipoe to Waiki'i, and the western slopes of Mauna Kea, Mauna Loa, and Hualālai.

Saddle House

Formerly a line cabin of W. H. Shipman Ltd.'s Puʻu ʻŌʻō Ranch, the Saddle House, located at the twenty-two-mile marker below Humuʻula junction, is an ideal equestrian camping venue.

The DLNR originally pledged that the Saddle House facility, including a cabin and pasturage, would become an equestrian campground administered by a like-minded nonprofit corporation that would manage the public rental of the facility. Sadly, DLNR withdrew the oversight of the Saddle House facility from the Paniolo Preservation Society (PPS) in 2005 for the purpose of renovation and refencing before calling for a request for requests for proposals. Aside from installing a compost toilet and roadside fencing, no progress has been made toward public usage programs, and there is little optimism that it will happen under present economic times and political landscapes.

In years past, PPS submitted draft proposals for the conversion of the Saddle House Complex for an equestrian camping experience for up to a dozen participants over two-to-three-day excursions. Numerous archaeological features that are clear vestiges of Hawaiʻi's ranching heritage can be seen on round-trip horseback journeys of approximately two to three hours. Highlights are crossing over trails that, in part, once moved hundreds of cattle from north Hawaiʻi to Kahuku in the South Point region of the Big Island.

Since its inception in 1998, the Paniolo Preservation Society has maintained its mission to recreate Hawaiʻi's government lands for equestrian camping and daytime trail riding. As the Saddle House complex remains a top priority in dealing with the Department of Land and Natural Resources, the Department of Hawaiian Home Lands has granted PPS a limited right of entry permit for the preservation of the Humuʻula Sheep Station complex, which is a major component of DHHL's ʻĀina Mauna Legacy Program.

ʻĀina Mauna Legacy Program

Paniolo Preservation Society has the necessary expertise, personnel, and resources to assist the Department of Hawaiian Home Lands in its ʻĀina Mauna Legacy Program mission to protect approximately 56,000 acres of native Hawaiian forest toward ecological, cultural, and self-sustaining initiatives of the trust and its beneficiary community. Specifically, the society is prepared to assist with implementation of the Humuʻula Sheep Station Adaptive Reuse Plan by undertaking extensive research of the Kalaieha area and attendant buildings that supported sheep, cattle, and horse ranching over the past two centuries. Specific areas of consultative and physical support include the design and reconstruction of a historic community center, as well as ecotourism modeling and execution.

Puʻu ʻŌʻō Ranch House Restoration

The Paniolo Preservation Society received another opportunity to be involved in the reclamation of historic but worn-down ranching facilities in 2014. The Pu'u 'Ō'ō Ranch House, a nine-hundred-square-foot koa cabin built in the early 1900s by the W. H. Shipman family, was recognized by a well-established helicopter touring outfit as an ideal target site for ranch-oriented tour groups, a significant component of the ag-ecotourism movement in Hawai'i.

Though sitting on Department of Hawaiian Home Lands just seven miles north of the Humu'ula Sheep Station, the Pu'u 'Ō'ō Ranch headquarters *paniolo* heritage is enhanced by the presence of adjacent buildings such as the cobblestone stables, high-walled round pen, and spacious horse corral. Tucked away in a nearby stand of pine trees lie three cowboy bunkhouses, one of which was occupied by Billy in his youth during the summer months of 1952–1956.

PPS was asked to be the heritage resource component for the project in restoring the cabin to a workable unit for visitors arriving by helicopter to enjoy an informative presentation and tour of the historic facilities. Patience and perseverance are the vital postures needed to see this project to fruition. It will contribute significantly to the legacy of the *paniolo* and Hawai'i's rich ranching heritage.

The island of Maui, with its vast Haleakalā Crater, falls within the National Park Service, as does Hawai'i Volcanoes National Park (HVNP), which brings on some restrictions. The Maui venue is far more user-friendly for horse-trail enthusiasts, while the HVNP view of such activity is prohibitive. Unfortunately, the Big Island venues have taken away former ranch lands and cabins that offer spectacular views and experiences. These include parts of former ranch lands such as 'Āina Hou, Keauhou, Kapāpala, and Kahuku, all with established but now fallowed horse trails, some of which include cabins.

Maui's Haleakalā trails access both Kapalaoa and Palikū cabins, which readily sleep a dozen and include limited bathing facilities. From a historic ranching posture, cattle were trailed from Haleakalā and 'Ulupalakua Ranches to Wai'ōpai and Kaupō Ranch lands. Maui *paniolo* pride remains alive and well in honor of their forebears that rode these lands behind herds of beef cattle on weeklong trailing over cinder, lava, and verdant fields. The same emotion prevails on the Big Island, where teenaged great-great-grandchildren long to visit the trails and camps of their *kūpuna*.

While horse-oriented tourists ride the beaches of Mexico and South America, an experience highly advertised by the visitor industry, this privilege is beyond reach for visitors and locals alike for all of Hawai'i's shorelines. In earlier days, noted Hawaiian horse trainers such as Ben Pahinui, Naluahine Kaopua, Keli'i Kanakaole, George Napoleon, and William Paul Mahinauli Akau used the soft, wet sandy beaches to break green *hapalaka* (half-broken) colts. The soggy terrain provided excellent substance for building strength and endurance in the horse as well as a softer landing for the bucked-off cowboy. For the broncky colt, however, the deep, soft sand neutralizes the ability to buck, bolt, or misbehave to any extent without readily tiring.

The Hawaiʻi Horse Council

A genuine attempt was made in 2010 to unify Hawaiʻi's horse community into a collective voice for the equine species with a proposal to establish a Hawaiʻi Horse Council (HHC). Its purpose would be threefold: First, to serve as a voice for Hawaiʻi's equestrian community through education, communication, and representation; second, to assist in the welfare of the horse; and third, to promote access to trails and public riding venues. The Hawaiʻi Horse Council also proposed minimum horse-care guidelines.

Organizers were Ms. Bird McIver of CB Horse Rescue and Sarah Blanchard, founder of the *Mālama Lio* publication. Legitimately arguing that Hawaiʻi was the only state in the Union that lacked a formal body, a horse council, the appeal seemed to fall on apathetic ears among the island horse community, likely because it lacked a cause célèbre. Using the *Mālama Lio* periodical for genuine outreach to support founding such a body and calling for minimal membership dues of $25, the women took their appeal directly to feed and tack shops, farriers, veterinarians and their clinics and hospitals, youth rodeo associations, boarding and training stables, rescue organizations, and a litany of Hawaiʻi Horse Expo attendees over several years. Bringing these forces together proved difficult and likely needed a perceived threat to the horse via natural disaster; shipping strikes; catastrophic disease or drought; adverse federal, state, or county legislation; or statewide economic downturn.

Their aggressive campaign yielded little more than complacency, as none of these potential threats were of immediate concern or on the minds of the horse owner. Yet, hopes for public riding trails and community horse traffic is fading with every passing year, as more development and growth takes place in rural communities. Until horse owners unite in expressing their concerns for lack of vital and healthful recreational opportunities, equestrian activities will be limited to the confines of arenas, paddocks, and risky roadsides. An organization such as the Hawaiʻi Horse Council would be a legitimate and appropriate voice to further this cause.

In the spring 2012 issue of *Mālama Lio,* Bird McIver bemoaned the total lack of response to the HHC appeal, resulting in the rescinding of state legislation, the bank account, and state charter and the resignation of the founding board of directors. Until collective efforts materialize with firm commitment to a sound and safe future for the horse, Hawaiʻi will continue to struggle to live up to its early and well-deserved reputation as a haven for horsemanship.

{ 15.5 } *In establishing the Hawai'i Horse Expo in 2008, Nancy Jones effectively exposed the Islands' equine enthusiasts to the world's top authorities on all aspects of horse care, training, and breeding.*

Public Awareness

Public awareness of Hawai'i's horse interest has been genuinely enhanced by two horsewomen: Sarah Blanchard and Nancy Jones.

A resident of Hilo for several decades, Blanchard recognized the need for a regular periodical to be the collective voice of the statewide horse industry. She combined newsworthy reporting with informative articles written by local and mainland experts. Academically inclined, she published works from sound sources and reliable opinions, even those that may have conflicted with her own views. The *Mālama Lio* grew to become Hawai'i's foremost equine periodical. Adding classified advertisement was a boon to circulation. Her effort in publishing the *Mālama Lio* was seminal in terms of supporting the Hawaiian horse industry.

Upon moving to the mainland, Blanchard sold the *Mālama Lio* publication to new owners who have continued to publish the circular, availing it throughout the state electronically online as well as in feed stores, veterinary hospitals, and Western apparel outlets.

Nancy Jones arrived in the Islands, bringing a long history as a leading advocate for humane care of the equine species. Settling in Waimea on the Big Island in 2008, she quickly addressed the serious paucity of reliable and periodic seminars on horse issues. With the Hawai'i Island Humane Society (HIHS) as beneficiary, she established an annual conference on the horse, the Hawai'i Horse Expo.

Given Jones' passion for humane care of animals, the Hawai'i Island Humane Society was a logical institution with which to align. The society is contracted by the County of Hawai'i to aid in enforcing animal-related laws, while providing twenty-four-hour service for animal emergencies, conducting humane education classes, sponsoring low-cost spay/neuter programs, and providing microchipping and lost-and-found assistance services. All three Hawai'i Island Humane Society centers are equipped to provide trailer service, pen and stall space, and emergency care facilities to accommodate horse needs. The HIHS Horse Rescue Fund is the designated beneficiary of net proceeds of the annual Horse Expo event, which marked its eighth anniversary in 2015.

When it first began, Kahilu Theatre, with its splendid indoor facilities, housed informational educational presentations, while adjacent former Parker Ranch show pens provided the venue for outdoor presentations. Over the next several years, Anna Ranch, given its historic aura and beautiful setting, was host venue for the

Expo. In 2012, HIHS partnered with the Paniolo Preservation Society in hosting the event at the Paniolo Heritage Center at Pukalani Stables on Parker Ranch. This spacious facility allowed three clinics to occur simultaneously. The Hawai'i Horse Expo gained a well-deserved reputation for bringing in nationally and internationally renowned experts to the event. These experts offered their knowledge and skills in a variety of horse-related disciplines, giving clinics and demonstrations that always include opportunity for participant interaction. Among the list of national presenters were Dr. R. M. Miller, Rick Lamb (RFD-TV), Kurt Pate, and Jack Brainard. Local presenters included Brady, Lester Buckley, and Dr. Lisa Wood.

The success of the 2012 Expo led to a firm commitment from Nancy Jones and company to again partner with the Paniolo Preservation Society for the annual Expo the next year. The success of the 2013 Hawai'i Horse Expo was a resounding reaffirmation of the commitment of Nancy Jones' mission.

Jones reported, with pride, the progress made in support of horse care in the 2012 Hawai'i Horse Expo Conference program publication:

> 2012 marks the fifth anniversary of HAWAII HORSE EXPO. Through your support we have raised enough money to establish a first-class equine holding facility at the Hawaii Island Humane Society Waimea Shelter. We have developed a well-devised protocol for equine evaluation and post-rescue care. We have reason to be proud of this because we are one island in a small State with only sixteen thousand horses, and yet we have one of the best equine rescue programs in the

Lester Buckley

{ 15.6 } *Consummate horseman extraordinaire Lester Buckley has devoted his entire lifetime to working with one of the world's best-loved animals, the noble horse.*

One of the more frequent presenters at the Hawai'i Horse Expo is Lester Buckley, whose early career dealt with the Parker Ranch horse program. From an even broader platform, he expanded his horsemanship skills to international forums, especially in Germany. Considered the "Vatican of Dressage," Buckley chose this venue to hone his already expansive knowledge of fine horsemanship. From the outset, as a humble but earnest student of the highly disciplined Prussian technique, Buckley rose to become a master in German horse circles. Hawai'i, his home, has been the grateful beneficiary of his experiences, ranging from training a Hawaiian cow horse to bringing out the best of a dressage mount in an elite forum. Lester and his wife, Mary, moved to Kentucky in 2015, expanding their operation to a greater venue.

> nation. This past year twenty four horses and one donkey passed through the gates of HIHS. Six of these horses were redeemed by owners. (They had gotten out and were found wandering.) Six had to be euthanized. Three are in foster care. The remaining horses were adopted. Out of those adopted, one died and one had a baby.
>
> More good news, Hawaii's Animal Protection Laws have been changed. Horses now fall under the "pet" category, receiving the same protection as dogs, cats, domesticated rabbits, and guinea pigs. And for the first time, Hawaii has added felony penalties for cases involving extreme animal cruelty or torture. Even though Hawaii still falls in the bottom tier of States for Animal Protection Laws we are making progress!
>
> Education promotes responsible animal ownership. Most people try to do the best they know how. No one intentionally does the wrong thing. Our goal is to educate and to inspire horse owners to always do the right thing. We may not be able to change the world, but together, through our example, we can make it a better place for horses. Thank you for supporting HAWAII HORSE EXPO. (Jones 2012)

Partnerships between like-minded community organizations and foundations such as these go a long way toward building community awareness of the challenges and public service provided by the horse community in the state of Hawaiʻi.

The future of equestrian activities in Hawaiʻi rests in the hands of horse lovers who can mount a powerful collective campaign to reverse highly restrictive state and federal postures that disallow trail riding. Without a change toward more user-friendly guidelines, the vast panoramas from sea to the mountains will forever be lost to mounted residents and visitors alike who enjoy nature and exploring wide-open spaces. Highly successful ecotourism ventures such as the trail rides provided by the exclusive, internationally acclaimed groups Cabalgatas and Rancheros Vistadores could become regular features that would definitely add to dwindling tourism coffers. Moreover, present and future generations of *paniolo* could once again freely ride the countryside so beloved by their multigenerational families, thus returning pride and honor to them. Equally important is preservation of the rapidly disappearing *paniolo* heritage venues such as corrals, camps, and stables threatened by urban growth and progress.

It is time for the horse community to mobilize to protect this lifestyle for generations to come to know, appreciate, and enjoy.

Appendix A:
GENETIC ANALYSIS OF THE HAWAIIAN HORSE

In July 2010, Dr. Gus Cothran of Texas A&M released his findings in a report of the genetic analysis of the Hawaiian feral horse population based on seventy-five samples provided by the Bergin team. Excerpts of his report are provided below.

His results indicated that "no variants were observed in this population, which have not been seen in horse breeds, although there was one variant that is extremely rare in other horses."

He also found that "genetic variation in the Hawaiian horse population is quite high, both compared to feral horse populations and to domestic breeds. This indicates a population in genetic equilibrium. The high diversity is indicative of a population that originated from a diverse ancestry, possibly different breeds or even mixed ancestry populations. Thus the variability measures suggest this population has mixed origins, has not experienced a long period of small population size, and has been genetically stable for several generations."

His report further notes that the "Hawaiian horses pair with the Knapstrupper within the cluster of horses with a strong Thoroughbred influence. It is unlikely that there is any actual relationship to the Knapsrtupper which is a Danish breed known for its spotted coat. Many European breeds have been crossed to English Thoroughbreds. Here the Hawaiian horse joins just outside the Thoroughbred cluster." What the analysis indicates to Cothran is that "the origins of the horse likely include a strong component of genetics that originated from the Thoroughbred (which could come from a wide number of breeds including the American Quarter Horse), but likely has other types of horses in its background as well."

Dr. Cothran's complete report follows.

Analysis of Genetic Diversity in the Hawaiian Island Feral Horses

E. Gus Cothran
Department of Veterinary Integrative Biosciences
College of Veterinary Medicine and Biomedical Science
Texas A&M University

The purpose of this study was to analyze genetic variability in the Hawaiian Island feral horse from the Big Island in order to determine its conservation status and to understand its origins. The horses primarily derive from the Waipio Valley in Northern Hawaii.

To start out I will give a little background. First, what is genetic diversity? Genetic diversity primarily refers to variation within the genetic makeup of an individual. It also is variation in genetic makeup among individuals within a population, genetic variation among different populations of a species, and genetic differences among species. For this work I am focusing on individual and populational variation.

Why is genetic diversity important? It gives individuals flexibility to respond to different environmental conditions, it increases disease resistance, it gives populations the ability to adapt to environmental changes over time (for domestic animals this also can mean the ability to make selective improvements to a breed), and it buffers against deleterious recessive genes.

What factors act to change genetic diversity? The number one factor is population size, the smaller the size the lower the diversity. Also, inbreeding reduces individual variation. Out-crossing increases diversity when different groups are crossed. Selection, which will usually decrease variation, is another factor as is mutation which increases variation but is unimportant over short time scales.

How do we measure diversity? Individual diversity is measured as Heterozygosity (Observed *Ho*) which is the proportion of the genome that varies within an individual.

The Inbreeding coefficient also is a measure of basically the same thing but on a theoretical level. Both these measures are independent of sample size. For estimating genetic diversity of a whole population or breed we again use Heterozygosity but it is Expected Heterozygosity (*He*) which is the average proportion of the genome that varies based upon population genetic theory. Another important measure is simply the number of variants observed in the population. These measures are correlated with sample size. We determine these different measures by typing of genetic markers. A gene marker is a variable spot in the genome that we can test. The different forms the marker can take are called alleles. Each marker can have two possible alleles in an individual but many across the population. For an individual, if the alleles are

Table A1.

Genetic variability estimates for the Hawaiian Island horse herd and values for selected domestic breeds

	N	*Ho*	*He*	*Fis*	*Ae*	*TNV*	*MNA*	*Ra*	*%Ra*
Hawaiian Island horse	75	0.783	0.783	0.000	4.927	94	7.83	28	0.298
American saddlebred	576	0.740	0.745	0.007	4.250	102	8.50	42	0.412
Andalusian	52	0.722	0.753	0.041	4.259	79	6.58	21	0.266
Arabian	47	0.660	0.727	0.092	3.814	86	7.17	30	0.349
Exmoor pony	98	0.535	0.627	0.146	2.871	66	5.50	21	0.318
Friesian	304	0.545	0.539	-0.011	2.561	70	5.83	28	0.400
Irish draught	135	0.802	0.799	-0.003	5.194	102	8.50	28	0.275
Morgan horse	64	0.715	0.746	0.041	4.192	92	7.67	33	0.359
Suffolk punch	57	0.683	0.711	0.038	3.878	71	5.92	13	0.183
Tennessee walker	60	0.666	0.693	0.038	3.662	87	7.25	34	0.391
Thoroughbred	1,195	0.734	0.726	-0.011	3.918	69	5.75	18	0.261
Feral horse mean	126	0.716	0.710	-0.012	3.866	72.68	6.06	16.96	0.222
Standard deviation		0.056	0.059	0.071	0.657	13.02	1.09	7.98	0.088
Minimum		0.496	0.489	-0.284	2.148	37	3.08	0	0
Maximum		0.815	0.798	0.133	5.253	96	8.00	33	0.400
Domestic horse mean	80	0.710	0.720	0.012	4.012	80.88	6.74	23.79	0.283
Standard deviation		0.078	0.071	0.086	0.735	16.79	1.40	10.11	0.082
Minimum		0.347	0.394	-0.312	1.779	26	2.17	0	0
Maximum		0.822	0.799	0.211	5.298	119	9.92	55	0.462

Note: N = sample size, *MNA* = mean number of alleles per locus, *Ae* = effective number of alleles, *Ho* = observed heterozygosity, *He* = expected heterozygosity, *Fis* = estimated inbreeding based upon heterozygosity ratio, *TNV* = total number of variants, *Ra* = number of rare variants, *%Ra* = percentage of *Ra*.

the same, the marker is homozygous. If different, the marker is heterozygous. Heterozygosity is the proportion of markers out of all tested that are heterozygous. This can be calculated as the average of those actually observed as heterozygous (*Ho*) or by the predicted proportion based upon theory calculated from the frequency of each allele in the population (*He*).

The results of the diversity analysis of the breed show that genetic diversity in the Hawaiian horses is quite high. Both measures of heterozygosity and the allelic diversity measures *MNA, TNV* and *Ae* are very high, especially considering the relatively small population size. The genetic variability measures are consistent with a mixed breed origin for the horses. The very high levels of variation in conjunction with the overall small population size suggest high diversity of the types of horses that formed the population. The *Fis*

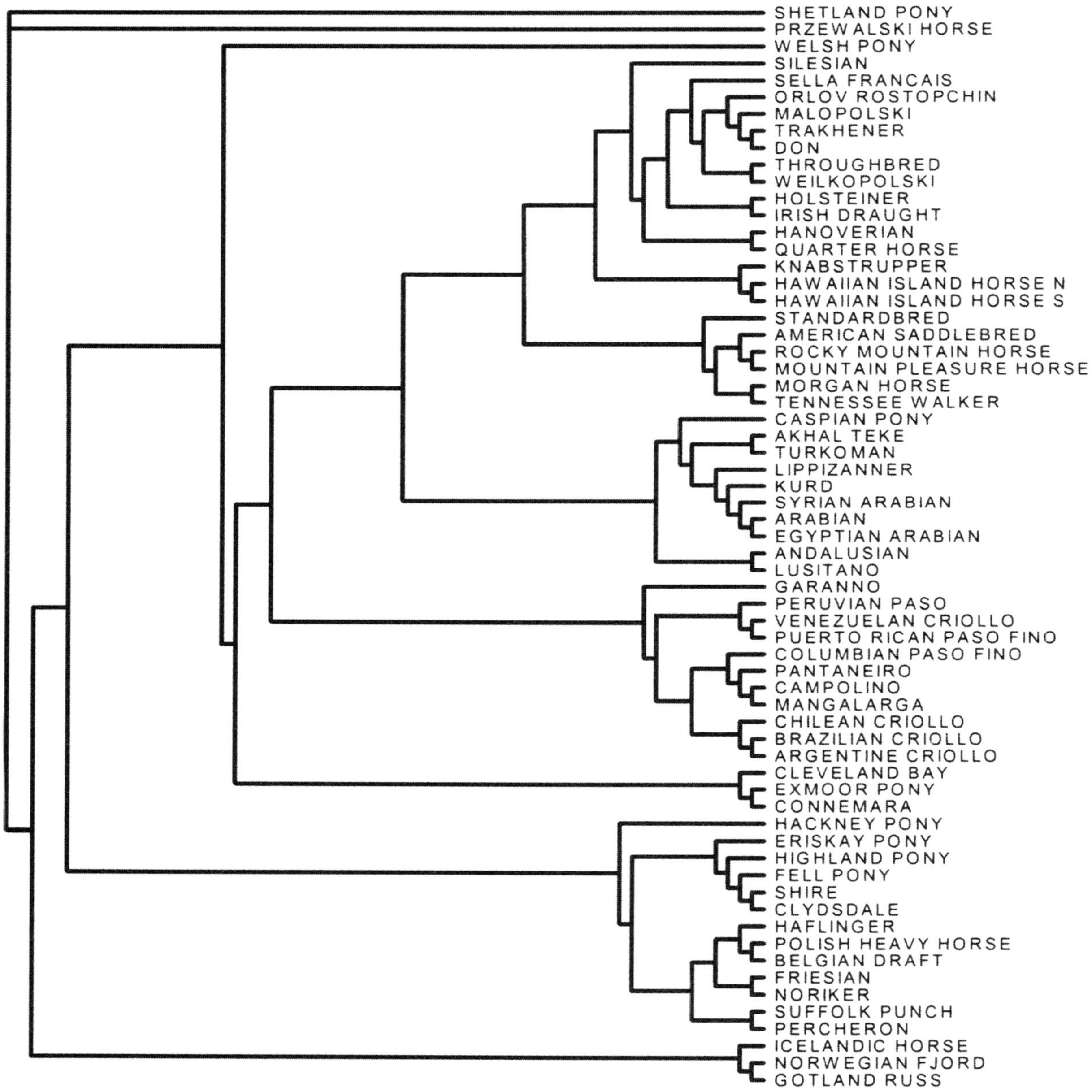

Hawaiian Island Horse N: northern (Waipi'o Valley); Hawaiian Island Horse S: southern (Mauna Kea).

Figure A. *Dendrogram of genetic similarity of the Hawaiian horses to domestic horse breeds.*

measure shows that there is not yet any indication of inbreeding or genetic variability decline in the population as a result of small population size. It will likely take several generations for a reduction in genetic diversity to become evident.

Comparison of allele frequencies can give measures of genetic resemblance and indications of ancestry. These are not true measures of ancestry but are approximations. Genetic similarity measure can be summarized by tree diagrams that give two-dimensional representations of estimated relationships. Figure A has the Hawaiian horses (divided into Northern and Southern populations) placed within the branch that is based upon the Thoroughbred. The two populations are basically identical to each other, so they will be treated as a single group in this discussion. The Hawaiian horses cluster most closely to the Knapstrupper, but this should not be taken as a close relationship, rather it shows mixed ancestry that includes Thoroughbred but it is not necessarily directly related to that breed. The Quarter Horse is another breed in this cluster. The Hawaiian horses also are very much on the outside of the Thoroughbred branch and near the branch composed of breeds developed in North America.

The overall picture of ancestry fits what was observed in the variability analysis: the Hawaiian horses appear to be of diverse ancestry. I also looked at the relationship of each individual horse of the herd in comparison to 65 domestic breeds. Just over 50% of the horses showed a breed that was largely of Thoroughbred heritage as a likely ancestor. The other influences in order of occurrence were North American, Arabian and Iberian. Many horses were clearly of mixed origins mainly in combinations of one of the four major groups above (for example Thoroughbred/North American). The general conclusion is that the Hawaiian Horse has a diverse ancestry and that much of the foundation of that ancestry comes from the Thoroughbred. (Cothran 2010)

Appendix B:

GENETIC ANALYSIS OF THE FERAL DONKEY HERDS FROM HAWAI'I

E. Gus Cothran
Department of Veterinary Integrative Bioscience
College of Veterinary Medicine and Biomedical Science
Texas A&M University

A total of 36 samples were received at Texas A&M University on September 13, 2011. Each sample was tested for variation at 12 equine microsatellite systems by use of PCR and fragment separation by an automated DNA sequencer. The systems were *AHT*4, *AHT*5, *ASB*17, *ASB*23, *HMS*2, *HMS*3, *HMS*6, *HMS*7, *HTG*6, *HTG*7, *HTG*10, and *LEX*33. A variety of genetic variability measures were calculated from the gene marker data. The measures observed were heterozygosity (*Ho*), which is the actual number of loci heterozygous per individual; expected heterozygosity (*He*), which is the predicted number of heterozygous loci based upon gene frequencies; effective number of alleles (*Ae*), which is a measure of marker system diversity; total number of variants (*TNV*); mean number of alleles per locus (*MNA*); the number of rare alleles observed which are alleles that occur with a frequency of 0.05 or less (*RA*); the percent of rare alleles (*%RA*); and estimated inbreeding level (*Fis*), which is calculated as 1-*Ho*/*He*. Data from the herd were compared to that of other feral herds and to four domestic donkey breeds. Genetic similarity of the herd to domestic breeds and other feral herds also was calculated.

Values for measures of genetic variation for the herd are shown in Table B1. Also given are data from some other feral donkey herds, domestic donkey breeds and mean values for the domestic donkey and for other feral burro populations. Genetic similarity of the Hawaiian herd to domestic breeds is shown in Figure B.

Genetic variability of the Hawaiian donkeys is relatively low compared to the domestic breeds but high compared to the feral burro mean. However, not all variability measures were higher than feral mean values, especially allelic diversity measures were fairly low for the Hawaiian animals. The Hawaiian herd had a negative *Fis,* which suggests that inbreeding is not high even though the other diversity measures suggest that inbreeding is taking place. More information is needed to interpret this result but inbreeding is likely to be taking place in these donkeys simply due to isolation. The proportion of rare variants was lower than the feral average for the Hawaiian population so that the risk of loss of alleles in the near future is moderate.

Table B1.

Genetic variability measures

HERD	N	Ho	He	Fis	Hub	Ae	TNV	MNA	RA	%RA
Feral										
Bullfrog NV	49	0.492	0.502	0.019	0.507	2.335	35	3.888	7	0.200
Blue Wing NV	28	0.252	0.268	0.058	0.273	1.487	23	2.555	6	0.260
Chemehuevi CA	52	0.353	0.426	0.171	0.430	2.111	29	3.222	6	0.206
Chocolate Mule CA	47	0.298	0.393	0.242	0.397	1.972	31	3.444	10	0.322
Clark Mtn. CA	78	0.291	0.391	0.256	0.393	1.907	36	4.000	16	0.444
East Mohave CA	30	0.416	0.508	0.179	0.516	2.475	39	4.333	13	0.333
Kingman AZ	25	0.551	0.552	0.003	0.564	2.794	37	4.111	9	0.243
Montezuma CA	25	0.111	0.095	-0.161	0.097	1.134	16	1.777	3	0.187
Picacho CA	23	0.361	0.378	0.042	0.386	1.949	30	3.333	7	0.233
Seven Tanks NV	22	0.245	0.339	0.276	0.347	1.751	24	2.666	7	0.291
Sinbad UT	30	0.466	0.430	-0.083	0.437	2.065	27	3.000	4	0.148
Twin Peaks CA	**39**	**0.487**	**0.526**	**0.074**	**0.533**	**2.484**	**31**	**3.444**	**5**	**0.161**
Yuma AZ	39	0.486	0.506	0.037	0.512	2.505	34	3.777	7	0.205
Hawaiian	**36**	**0.435**	**0.406**	**-0.007**	**0.438**	**1.902**	**26**	**2.889**	**4**	**0.154**
Domestic										
Miniature	65	0.562	0.579	0.029	0.584	3.215	48	5.333	15	0.312
Poitou	17	0.486	0.468	-0.038	0.482	2.384	30	3.333	2	0.066
Standard	63	0.503	0.588	0.144	0.593	3.300	54	6.000	20	0.370
Mammoth jack	54	0.434	0.565	0.231	0.570	3.061	51	5.666	19	0.372
Syrian	43	0.566	0.620	0.015	0.581	3.547	54	6.000	19	0.352
Venezuelan	28	0.510	0.564	0.017	0.529	3.009	39	4.333	5	0.128
Domestic mean	14	0.450	0.550	0.153	0.568	2.778	37	4.143	9	0.210
Feral mean	26	0.403	0.440	0.078	0.458	2.199	30	3.385	6	0.200

Table B2.

Genetic similarity of the Hawaiian donkey to domestic donkey breeds

BREED	SIMILARITY
Poitou donkey	.624
Mammoth jack	.665
Miniature donkey	.622
Standard donkey	.621
Syrian	.736
Venezuelan	.708

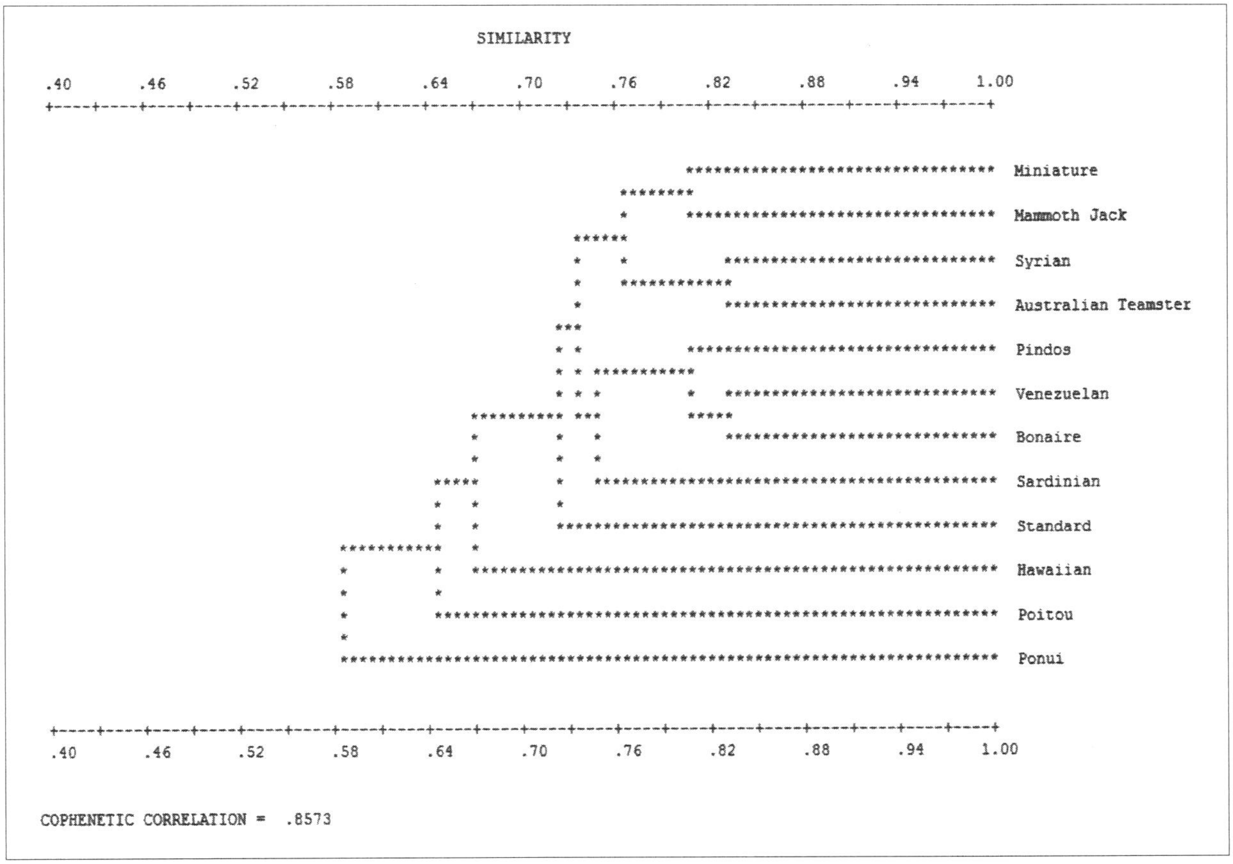

Figure B. *Dendrogram of genetic similarity among donkey populations.*

Much of the heterozygosity of microsatellite marker systems is due to a number of variants so that a loss of variants would impact heterozygosity levels.

The Hawaiian population does not cluster directly with any of the domestic breeds but appears to be closest to the Standard donkey based upon Figure B, which is not surprising as this is the most common donkey type. However, the highest genetic similarity is with the Syrian donkey, which is a type that exists near the center of donkey domestication and dispersal. This donkey breed shows highest similarity to most of the donkey populations which may represent ancient relationships. Unfortunately my reference base for donkeys does not contain many of the ancestral donkey types, so ancestral relationships cannot be clearly established at this time.

APPENDIX C:
DNA DATA FOR THE HAWAIʻI DONKEYS

Microsatellite Loci
V H A H H A H A H H H H A A L
H T H M T H M S T T M M S S E
L G T S G T S B G G S S B B X
2 4 4 7 6 5 6 2 1 7 3 2 1 2 3
ID 0 0 7 3 3

55373 HI42 ** ** DM IL II RS JK ** OO 22 QQ QR DD NN HH OO
55374 HI42 ** ** CD IJ II JS KK ** PP 22 QQ RR DD NR HH OO
55375 HI42 ** ** MM HI II RS JJ ** OP X2 QQ RR DD NN GH OO
55376 HI42 ** ** MM II II JS JK ** OP 22 QQ RR DD NN HH OO
55377 HI42 ** ** CD II II SS JK ** OP X2 PQ RR DD NN GH OO
55378 HI42 ** ** DM II II RR KK ** OP 22 OQ QQ DD NN GG OO
55379 HI42 ** ** DM II II SS JK ** MP 22 OQ RR DD NN GH OO
55380 HI42 ** ** DM II HI RS JJ ** MP X2 QQ RR DD NN GH OO
55381 HI42 ** ** CM II II RS JJ ** MO RX QQ RR DD NN GG OO
55382 HI42 ** ** MM II HI RS JJ ** OP X2 OQ RR DD NN GG OO
55383 HI42 ** ** CD IJ II RS JK ** MO 22 PQ RR DD NN HH OO
55384 HI42 ** ** MM II II SS JJ ** PP R2 QQ RR DD NR HH OO
55385 HI42 ** ** MM HI II SS KK ** OP 22 QQ RR DD NN HH OO
55386 HI42 ** ** CM IJ II SS JJ ** OP RX OQ RR DD NR GG OO
55387 HI42 ** ** DD II II RR JJ ** OP RR OQ RR DD NR GH OO
55388 HI42 ** ** DN HI II JR KK ** OP X2 OQ RR DD NR GH OO
55389 HI42 ** ** MM II II RS JK ** OP X2 OQ RR DD NN GG OO
55390 HI42 ** ** CC II II SS JK ** OP 22 OO QR DD NR GH OO
55391 HI42 ** ** DM IL II QQ KK ** PP X2 QQ QR DD RR GH OO
55392 HI42 ** ** MM II II RS JK ** PP 22 PQ RR DD NN HH OO
55393 HI42 ** ** DM II II RS JK ** OP 22 PQ RR DD NN HH OO
55394 HI42 ** ** MM IJ II RS JJ ** PP 22 QQ RR DD NN HH OO

55395 HI42 ** ** MM IJ HI SS KK ** OP XX QQ QR DD NN GG OO
55396 HI42 ** ** CM II II RS JK ** PP 22 OQ QR DD NN GH OO
55397 HI42 ** ** DM II II RS JK ** MO 22 PQ QR DD NN GH OO
55398 HI42 ** ** MM HJ IJ JO JJ ** PP RR PQ RR DD NR GH OO
55399 HI42 ** ** CM II II SS JK ** OP 22 OQ QR DD NN HH OO
55400 HI42 ** ** DM II II RS JK ** MO 22 OQ QR DD NN HH OO
55401 HI42 ** ** DM II II JJ JJ ** OP 22 OQ RR DD NN HH OO
55402 HI42 ** ** MM II HI SS KK ** PP RS QQ QR DD NR GG OO
55403 HI42 ** ** DD HI II SS KK ** OO RR QQ QR DD NR GG OO
55404 HI42 ** ** MM II II JR JJ ** MP RS QQ QR DD NR GH OO
55405 HI42 ** ** DM II II OR JJ ** OO R2 PQ RR DD NR GH OO
55406 HI42 ** ** CM IJ II RR JK ** PP XX QQ RR DD NR GH OO
55407 HI42 ** ** CM II II SS KK ** OP X2 PQ QR DD NN GH OO
55408 HI42 ** ** DM II II SS JK ** OP X2 OQ RR DD NR GH OO

GLOSSARY

aciones	stirrup leathers
aho	cord made of sennit
ahupuaʻa	designation of land extending from mountain to the ocean
alahele	pathway; trail
alakaʻi	method of leading a bull by cowboys
aliʻi	Hawaiian monarch or ruling class
ama	canoe outriggers; side bars of a saddle, also called *iama*
amala	armor, spurs, bits, hinges, tools; articles handmade by blacksmiths
ANCCE	Purebred Spanish Horse Breeders Association of Spain
Andalusian	Spanish horse from that broad geographic area
angled croup	sloping hip when viewed from the side
anquera, anquerita	leather or armor cover for a horse's rump and flanks
aparejo	pack saddle
apuapu	file
argolla	metal ring, cinch rings
armas	early chaps attached to a saddle and draped over a rider's legs
atajos	mule trains
ʻaumakua	Hawaiian guardian spirit; family or personal god
awāwa	valley
ʻaweʻawe	Hawaiian braided front saddle rigging (lit., strips, tentacles)
barb	Spanish horse likely reintroduced after Columbus' 1493 voyage
baroomby	Aboriginal word for wild
botas	jackboots
bovine	cattle
brumby	wild horse of Australia; term derived from the Gaelic term *bromaigh*
buiso	unbranded jack bull
caballero	gentleman horseman
caballo	horse
caballo *Californio*	California horse

cabeza	saddle horn
calabash	non–blood related; natural gourd or a container fashioned from wood
caprine	goat
carreta	oxcart
cat hammed	thin gluteal thigh muscle groups of livestock viewed from the rear
chaparrera	chaps
charro	exclusive form of horsemanship
cincha	cinch or girth usually made of cordage of manila, wool, or cotton
cola de pato	duckbill-shaped saddle tailpiece
corriente	a breed of cattle of feral origin
criollo	Creole
dar la vuelta	Spanish for dallying (twisting a lariat around) the saddle horn
deglutition	swallowing
DNA	Deoxyribonucleic acid test used to determine genetic match
dresser	French word meaning "to train," as in dressage
'ehu kai	sea breeze, sea spray
Equidae	family that includes horses, donkeys, and mules
Equus	horse, donkey, and mule genus
Equus asinus	donkey species
Equus asinus x *Equus*	mule species
Equus caballus	horse species
español	Spanish, Spaniard
estriba	stirrup foot piece
faldones, basto	saddle skirt
ganado	Spanish strain of cattle
garrano	type of Galician horse
glanders	highly contagious and fatal zoonotic disease transferable between animal and man caused by *Pseudomonas mallei*
gringos	white men
hacendado	owner or proprietor of a hacienda
hacienda ranchero	ranch house
hamale	hammer
hāmana	fork of the Hawaiian tree saddle
hanawai	irrigation work
haole	Hawaiian term for Caucasian or white person
haole horses	gentle horses reserved for guests
hapu	Maori extended family grouping

harriguera	rear cinch strap
hau oheohe	light, tough wood used for canoe outriggers
heiau	ancient Hawaiian temple
hiʻona	phenotype; body appearance, physical features
hippa mula	term used to urge mules forward and onward
hōau pipi	swimming cattle to longboats
hoki	Hawaiian for mule
hoʻowali	mix by hand, as with *paʻi ʻai* and water
huarache	slipper
hula	Hawaiian dance
ʻili	rawhide or leather strap
ʻili huki	rawhide or leather strap for cinching up a horse (aka *latigo*)
Īnia	pride of India tree
iukupu	Hawaiian term for lampers
jenny	female donkey; also jennet
jineta	type of combat saddle patterned after Moorish saddles
kahawai	ditches or gulches through which water flows
kaimanawa	New Zealand wild horse
kaitiaki	Maori view of the wild horse as a spiritual guardian
kalo	taro
kamaʻāina	native born (lit., land child)
kamau	card game similar to the game of trumps; also *keiki lua*
kanaka, kanaka maoli	Native Hawaiian
kanaka lio ʻāhiu	wild native Hawaiian horse
kapu	taboo
kapuahi	forge or stove
kauhale	village
kauila	*Alphitonia ponderosa;* hard wood in the buckthorn family used for spears, mallets, and tools
kaula hele	six-foot cordlike rope used to hobble stirrups together to enable a rider to stay aboard an unruly bronc
kaulaʻili	leather lariat
kaula keko	rear saddle cinch
kaula ʻōpū	cinch
kaula waha	headstall
kēkake	donkey (Hawaiian)
kiawe	mesquite; algaroba tree or wood
kīhōʻalu	Hawaiian slack key guitar style

kinohi	elegant
kīpuka	oasis within a lava bed
koa	Hawaiian acacia tree or wood
koko	genotype, blood, breed
kōkua	help or assist
konohiki	king's regional agent
koumiss	fermented mare's milk
kuahao	anvil
kualapa	ridge
kuawa	guava tree or fruit
kukui	candlenut tree, *Aleurites moluccana;* the nut produces oil used for lamp fuel and for other purposes
kūpe'e	hogtied
laina	lines, reins, or cordage
lālā	apronlike covering of the saddle from saddle horn to cantle
lampas; lampers	chronic thickening of the gum line immediately behind the superior row of incisor teeth
lariata	lariat
latigo	leather or rawhide strap for cinching; cinch strap
Latino	native or inhabitant of Latin America
lauhala	pandanus; used for weaving
lawe hānai	informal adoption in which a child is raised by other than natural parents
lina 'awe'awe	saddle ring through which *'awe'awe* is braided
Lio 'āhiu	wild horses
lio laho 'āhiu	feral stallion
lio maoli	Hawaiian feral horse
lo'i kalo	planted taro terraces
lomilomi	hand rub, massage
los caballos	the horsemen
lū'au	Hawaiian feast
luna	plantation field managers, usually astride a horse
ma'awe	rawhide strips braided to make *'awe'awe* or *kaula 'ili*
maile	fragrant vine woven into leis worn for all occasions
maize	corn
makai	direction toward the ocean
maka'āinana	commoner
makinikela	martingale, a tie-down with a breast collar

malihini	newcomer to Hawai'i
malina	Manila rope
māmane	*Sophora chrysophylla,* native leguminous tree that thrives in high altitudes of Mauna Kea and Mauna Loa; its hard wood was used for spades and sled runners
manako	mango tree or fruit
māne'ō	itch, itching
mastication	chewing
mauka	direction toward the mountain
mesteno	mustang
mestizo	bronze race; mixed ethnicity (such as Spaniard and native American Indian)
mochila	leather saddle covering, often called a mother hubbard or *lālā* in Hawaiian
montura	horse gear; *ukana lio* in Hawaiian
multiparous	litter-bearing species such as hogs
nā'ahawa	water heads
naio	false sandalwood
nā kauhale	the villages
nānā 'āina	overseeing ranch lands
neneleau	*Rhus chinensis;* Hawaiian sumac, best wood for making saddle tree parts
New Spain	Mexico and California
noho 'āmana	cross buck pack saddle
'ōhai	monkeypod tree
'ohana	family
'ōhi'a lehua	*Metrosideros macropus;* endemic Hawaiian tree that thrives in rain forests throughout the islands (*lehua* is the flower of the island of Hawai'i)
'ōkole hoki	gable-hipped
'ōkumu	saddle horn; front piece on the bow of a ship
ola mau loa	"he lives forever"; said of donkeys
'ōlelo kanaka	Hawaiian language
'one hanau	birthplace
ovine	sheep
pāhoehoe	smooth, flat lava
pa'i 'ai	cakelike consistency of pounded. undiluted taro
Pākē	Hawaiian name for Chinese

palawai	stone bruise; fetid water draining from subsolar abscesses
pāmakani	*Eupatorium glandulosum:* thick, tenacious, and leafy shrub that covers the meadows and ravines in high mountain pastures; an invasive species
paniolo	Hawaiian cowboy
Pannier packs	large basketlike side bags for packing mules
pāpale lauhala	hat woven from pandanus leaves
passage	horse gait: a slow-motion trot
pā'ū	Hawaiian horsewoman resplendent in parade dress
piaffe	horse gait: to trot in place
piha'ā	fallen logs
pini	method of leading a wild bull by "pinning" a home-raised bullock to the wild bull with a neck rope, thus encouraging the bull to follow along
pipi 'āhiu	wild cattle
piula	Hawaiian for mule; tin roofing
poe	cantle of the Hawaiian tree saddle; a semicircular splashboard at front and rear of a canoe
po'e Hawai'i	people of Hawai'i
pohā	sinkholes in lava fields; gooseberries
poi	pastelike starch from taro, a Hawaiian diet staple
pono'ī	self-owned horse
porcine	hog
po'owai'ū	tied by the horns to a stout tree
PRE	Pura Raza Española (purebred Spanish horses)
prehension	biting
prieto	Spanish breed of cattle, black in color
pūnuku	halter or noseband
Pu'u Lahohinu	Hill of the Shiny Stallion
rafter-rumped	gable-hipped; sloped hips when viewed from the rear
Real Escuela	Royal Andalusian School of Equestrian Art
retinto	Spanish strain of cattle; brown points, black body
rodeo	Mexican term meaning roundup of vast herds gathered by mounted horsemen
serape	cape, shawl
Sifrhippus sandrae	America's first horse
silladero	saddle maker
silla vaquero	Mexican cowboy saddle
skived	cut on a beveled edge

sombrero	large Mexican hat
sorraia	Portuguese horse named after the valley in Iberia
Taonga	National treasure of New Zealand
tapadero	protective foot covering the stirrup foot piece
umiʻi	tongs
ʻūpā	scissors or shears
vaquero	Mexican cowboy
vaquero *hawaiiano*	Mexican cowboys bound for the Hawaiian Islands
vog	volcanic fog or smog caused by volcanic emissions into the atmosphere
wahine holo lio	horsewoman
wailele	waterfalls
wela ka hao	"strike while the iron is hot"; originally a blacksmithing term

REFERENCES

Ahlborn, Richard E. 1980. "Horizons of the Western Saddle." In *Man Made Mobile: Early Saddles of Western North America*, Richard E. Ahlborn, ed. Smithsonian Studies in History and Technology 39. Washington, DC: Smithsonian Institution Press.

Alexander, David. 1965. *The History and Romance of the Horse: Told with Pictures.* New York: Cooper Square Publishers.

Anderson, Lieutenant Olin. 1942. "Transportation of Animals Overseas." *Army Veterinary Bulletin* 36(1): 32–37.

Ashton, Chris. 2012. "Ruddy's Polo, Rudyard Kipling and the Maltese Cat." *POLO, Players' Edition* 15(2) (October).

Barnes, Rachel, and Simon Barnes. 2011. *The Horse: A Celebration of Horses in Art.* London: Quercus.

Beckstett, Alexandra. 2012. "Behind BLM Pasture Gates." *Horse* (March).

Bennett, Deb. 2014. "The World's Most Important Horse Breed." *Equus Magazine* 446 (November).

Beresford, Lord Patrick. 2013. "Lord Patrick Beresford: An Expert Insight into the Growth of Argentina's Polo Industry." *Hurlingham Magazine* (February).

Bergin, Brady, DVM. 2009. "Not All 'Equine Dentists' Are Created Equal." *Mālama Lio Magazine* (January).

———. 2009. "Preventing Choke." *Mālama Lio Magazine* (September).

Bergin, Patricia. 1975. "Hawaiian Saddle Making." Unpublished manuscript.

Bergin, William C., DVM. 2004. *Loyal to the Land.* Vol. 1: *The Legendary Parker Ranch, 750–1950.* Honolulu: University of Hawai'i Press.

———. 2006. *Loyal to the Land.* Vol. 2: *The Senior Stewards.* Honolulu: University of Hawai'i Press.

———. 2009. *Loyal to the Land.* Vol. 3: *Agents of Change.* Honolulu: Island Heritage Publishing.

———. 2010. "Lampas, Part 1." *Mālama Lio Magazine* (April).

———. 2010. "Lampas, Part 2." *Mālama Lio Magazine* (summer).

Bird, Isabella. 1974. *Six Months in the Sandwich Islands.* 7th ed. Introduction to new edition by Terence Barrow, PhD. Tokyo: Charles E. Tuttle Company. (Originally published in London, 1890: John Murray).

Brookshier, Frank. 1945. "On the Burro Trail in Hawaii." *Paradise of the Pacific* 57(12): 17–20.

———. 1974. *The Burro.* Norman: University of Oklahoma Press.

Brown, Mark H., and W. R. Felton. 1956. *Before Barbed Wire.* L. A. Huffman, photographer. New York: Bramhall House.

Buck, Peter H. 1938. *Vikings of the Sunrise.* New York: Frederick A. Stokes Co.

Buecker, Thomas R. 1999. *Fort Robinson and the American West: 1874–1899.* Norman: University of Oklahoma Press.

———. 2004. *Fort Robinson and the American Century: 1900–1948.* Norman: University of Oklahoma Press.

Burden, F. 2012. "Practical Feeding and Condition Scoring for Donkeys and Mules." *Equine Veterinary Education, American Edition* (November).

Burris, Jon. 1977. "Airlift: Cattle Trailing in the Jet Age." *Persimmon Hill* 7(1).

Carmichael, Joe M. 1979. "Your Best Saddle is 1500 Years Old." Drawings by Paul Rossi. *Persimmon Hill* 9(3).

Cary, Pam, Christopher La Fontaine, Joyce Robins, and Angela Wyatt. 1992. *The Horse: A Complete Encyclopedia.* London: Ivy Leaf.

Chee Tsutsumi, Cheryl. 2013. "Make Polo a Part of Your Sunday, Aficionado Says." *Honolulu Star-Advertiser,* March 31.

Cima, Greg. 2012. "Vaccine Could Reduce Wild Horse Overpopulation." *Journal of the American Veterinary Medical Association* 240(8) (April 15): 921–922.

Cisco, Dan. 1999. *Hawai'i Sports, History, Facts and Statistics.* Honolulu: University of Hawai'i Press.

Clayton, Lawrence, Jim Hoy, and Jerald Underwood. 2001. *Vaqueros, Cowboys, and Buckaroos.* Texas: University of Texas Press.

Cleveland, H. W. S. 1886. *Voyages of a Merchant Navigator of the Days That Are Past.* New York: Harper. Quoted in P. Q. Tomich, *Mammals of Hawaii: A Synopsis and Notational Bibliography,* 2nd ed. Honolulu: Bishop Museum Press, 1986.

Colton, Reverend Walter. 2007. *Three Years in California* [1846–1849]. Ann Arbor: Scholarly Publishing Office, University of Michigan. (Originally published in 1850.)

Conner, Carolyn, project manager. 2013. *Introduction to Equestrian Vaulting: Selecting and Training a Vaulting Horse.* Pasadena, CA: American Vaulting Association.

Cooke, Mary. 1963. "Amy Rich Takes a Firm Stand in the Ring." *Sunday Star-Bulletin and Advertiser,* August 18.

Cooper, Jane. 1947. "Islander Profile: Amy Wight Rich." *Islander Magazine* (September).

Cothran, E. Gus. 2010. "Analysis of Genetic Diversity in the Hawaiian Island Feral Horses." Department of Veterinary Integrative Biosciences, College of Veterinary Medicine and Biomedical Science, Texas A&M University, July 29.

———. 2014. "Genetic Analysis of the Feral Donkey Herds from Hawaii." Department of Veterinary Integrative Biosciences, College of Veterinary Medicine and Biomedical Science, Texas A&M University, November 21.

Cowan-Smith, Virginia, and Bonnie Demrose Stone. 1988. *Aloha Cowboy.* Honolulu: University of Hawai'i Press.

Cummins, John A. 1913. "Around Oahu in Days of Old." *Mid-Pacific Magazine* 6(3) (September): 233–243.

Dane, Keith. 2012. "Mahalo Letter from Keith Dane, HSUS, Summarizes Everything." Malama Waikoloa Nightingales Web site (November 22). Available at http://malama-waikoloa-nightingales.blogspot.com/2012_11_22_archive.html (accessed on December 30, 2015).

Dutson, Judith. 2012. *Storey's Illustrated Guide to 96 Horse Breeds of North America*. North Adams, MA: Storey Publishing.

Edwards, Elwyn Hartley. 1995. *Wild Horses: A Spirit Unbroken*. McGregor, MN: Voyageur Press.

Elliot, J. 1905–1913. *Annual Reports of the Division of Animal Industry.* Bureau of Agriculture and Forestry, Territory of Hawaiʻi. Honolulu: Honolulu Gazette Bulletin Publishing Co.

Farren, Lee. 2005. "Cavalry Horses and the American Indian Wars." *Western Horseman* (March).

Faurie, Bernadette. *The Horse Riding and Care Handbook*. Guilford, CT: Lyons Press, 2002.

FitzGerald, J. C. 1905–1913. *Annual Reports of the Division of Animal Industry.* Bureau of Agriculture and Forestry, Territory of Hawaiʻi. Honolulu: Honolulu Gazette Bulletin Publishing Co.

Fleming, Duane, DVM, 2004. "Role of Veterinarians in Equine Welfare Cases." *Equine Medical Review* 14(3) (October).

Fletcher, Sydney E. 1951. *The Cowboy and His Horse.* New York: Grosset & Dunlap.

Flores, Dan. 2008. "Bringing Home All the Pretty Horses: The Horse Trade and the Early American West, 1775–1825." *Montana: The Magazine of Western History* (summer).

Forester, Frank. 1857. *The Horse of America.* Vol. 1. New York: Stringer and Townsend.

Frantz, Joe B., and Julian E. Choate Jr. 1955. *The American Cowboy: The Myth and the Reality.* Norman: University of Oklahoma Press.

Fry, Kathie, ed. 2015. "The History of Horse Racing in Hawaii." Hawaii for Visitors Web site, http://www.hawaiiforvisitors.com/activities/horse-racing-history.htm (accessed on November 15, 2015).

Fujimori, Leila. 2010. "Donkey Problems Increasing." *Star-Advertiser,* September 12.

Fulford, Jennifer. 2012. "Hamley & Co.: Saddlemaking Is Central to Hamley & Co., a Western Store Outpost." *Shop Talk!* (November).

Gianoli, Luigi. 1969. *Horses and Horsemanship through the Ages.* Translated by Iris Brooks. New York: Crown Publishers.

Grosenbaugh, D. A., C. R. Reinmeyer, and M. D. Figueiredo. 2011. "Pharmacology and Therapeutics in Donkeys." *Equine Veterinary Education, American Edition* 23(10) (October).

Harden, M. J. 1999. *Voices of Wisdom: Hawaiian Elders Speak.* Kula, HI: Aka Press. Excerpts in the *Waimea Gazette,* September.

Harlocker, Nancy. 1970. "A Barn Party for Amy: Nancy Harlocker's Datebook." *Honolulu Advertiser,* March 23.

Hassrick, Peter H. 1973. *Frederic Remington.* Foreword by Ruth Carter Johnson. New York: Harry N. Abrams.

Hauserman, Julie. 2011. "Hawaii Donkeys off to US Mainland in Massive Airlift." *Horsetalk* (September).

Hedemann, Ed. 2001. *Training Horses and Stories of Long Ago in Hawaii.* Published by the author.

Henke, L. A. 1929. *A Survey of Livestock in Hawaii.* University of Hawai'i Research Publication No. 5. Honolulu: University of Hawai'i.

Hockensmith, John S. 2009. *Spanish Mustangs in the Great American West: Return of the Horse.* Georgetown, KY: Fine Arts Editions Gallery & Press.

Hopkins, C. G. 1854. *Report of the Committee on Horses.* Honolulu: Royal Hawaiian Agricultural Society.

Hurlingham Polo Magazine. 2013. "Empire Games." Spring: 29.

I'i, John Papa. 1959. *Fragments of Hawaiian History.* Translated by Mary Kawena Pukui. Honolulu: Bishop Museum Press.

Jackson, Jack. 1986. *Los Mestenos: Spanish Ranching in Texas 1721–1821.* College Station: Texas A&M University Press.

JAVMA. 2014. "*JAVMA* News." *Journal of the American Veterinary Medical Association* 244(6): 628.

Jones, Nancy. 2012. Hawaii Horse Expo Conference flyer. (August).

Jordan, Terry G. 1993. *North American Cattle-Ranching Frontiers: Origin, Diffusion and Differentiation.* Albuquerque: University of New Mexico Press.

Judd, C. S. 1936. "Hawaii's Forests Winning Their Battle with Wild Animals." *Honolulu Star-Bulletin,* March 21.

Kamakau, Samuel M. 1992. *Ruling Chiefs of Hawaii.* Revised ed. Honolulu: Kamehameha Schools Press.

Kanahele, George S. 1999. *Emma: Hawai'i's Remarkable Queen.* Honolulu: University of Hawai'i Press.

Kemple, Joe. 2012. "Horse Racing in Hawaii—Why Not? The Argument for Bringing the Sport of Kings Back to the Islands." *Mālama Lio Magazine* (spring).

Kennedy, Malcolm J. 1992. *Hauling the Loads: A History of Australia's Working Horses and Bullocks.* Melbourne: Melbourne University Press.

Kidwell, Deb.,2014. "Real American Patriots." *Western Mule Magazine* 21(7) (July).

Kirkpatrick, Jay F. 2008. "The Wild Horse Dilemma." *Horse* (October).

Krauss, Bob. 2005. "15 Days of Fun with the Queen." *Honolulu Advertiser,* July 3.

Krook, L., R. H. Wasserman, J. N. Shively, A. H. Tashjian Jr., T. D. Brokken, and J. F. Morton. 1975. "Hypercalcemia and Calcinosis in Florida Horses: Implication of the Shrub, *Cestrum diurnum,* as the Causative Agent." *Cornell Vet* 65(1): 26–56.

Langrish, Bob, and Nicola Jane Swinney. 2007. *The Magnificent Horse.* Bath, UK: Parragon Publishing.

Larkin, Malinda. 2006. "Closing of U.S. Horse Slaughter Plants Still Reverberates." *Journal of the American Veterinary Medical Association* 229(4) (August 15).

Laukaitis, Algis J. 2012. "No Joey at

Nebraska's Fort Robinson, Just Thousands of War Horses." *Lincoln Journal Star,* January 29.

Layton, Elizabeth Y. 2003. *The Golden Mallet: The Story of Hawaii's Polo Great, Ronnie Tongg.* Kaua'i, Hawai'i: Grey Lady Publishing Company.

Linklater, Wayne L., Elissa Z. Cameron, Kevin J. Stafford, and Clare J. Veltman. 2000. "Social and Spatial Structure and Range Use by Kaimanawa Wild Horses (*Equus caballus:* Equidae)." *New Zealand Journal of Ecology* 24(2): 139–152.

Livingston, Phil, and Ed Roberts. 2003. *War Horse: Mounting the Cavalry with America's Finest Horses.* Houston: Bright Sky Press.

Lummis, Charles F. 1936. *The Spanish Pioneers and the California Missions.* Chicago: A. C. McClurg & Company.

Maly, Kepa, and Onaona Maly. 2005. "He Wahi Mo'olelo no Keauhou a me na Wahi Pana ma Laila: A Collection of Traditions, Historical Accounts and Kama'āina Recollections of Keauhou and Its Storied Places; with Notes from Adjoining Lands in Ka'ū and Puna, Island of Hawai'i." Report prepared for Kamehameha Schools Land Assets Division (July).

Menzies, Gavin. 2008. *1421: The Year China Discovered America.* New York: William Morrow Paperbacks.

Michener, C. B. 1907. *Diseases of the Horse.* Washington, DC: US Department of Agriculture.

Miguens, Luisa. 2008. *Passion and Glory: A Century of Argentine Polo.* Buenos Aires: Letemendia Casa Editora.

Mihlbachler, Matthew C., Florent Rivals, Nikos Solounias, and Gina M. Semprebon. 2011. "Dietary Change and Evolution of Horses in North America." *Science Magazine* (March).

Miller, Robert M., and Rick Lamb. 2005. *The Revolution of Horsemanship and What It Means to Mankind.* Guilford, CT: Lyons Press.

Monsarrat, Julian. 1918. *Annual Report of Kapapala Ranch Ltd.*

Mower, Nancy Alpert. 1972. "She Prefers a Saddle to a Rocking Chair." *Beacon Magazine* (August).

Moyer, William A. 2011. "AAEP Statement Regarding GAO Report on Horse Welfare." Available at http://www.aaep.org/info/news-room?news_id=95 (accessed on December 30, 2015).

Munro, George C. 2007. *The Story of Lana'i.* Honolulu: Native Books.

National Cattlemen's Beef Association. 2013. "Horse Harvesting and Processing Amendment." Fall 2013 Official Membership Policy Ballot.

News/Veterinary Community. 2006. "Army Veterinary Corps Celebrates 90th Anniversary." *Journal of the American Veterinary Medical Association* 229(4) (August 15).

Norgaard, Victor A., DVS. 1907–1915. *Annual Reports of the Division of Animal Industry.* Bureau of Agriculture and Forestry, Territory of Hawai'i. Honolulu: Honolulu Gazette Bulletin Publishing Co.

Phares, Crystal, and Holly Clanahan. 2014. "War Horses." *America's Horse* 16(8).

Plummer, Brad. 2013. "The West Is on the

Brink of a Wild Horse Apocalypse." *Washington Post,* September 26.

Poppe, Col. John. 2006. "Army Veterinary Corps Celebrates 90th Anniversary." JAVMAnews. Available online at https://www.avma.org/News/JAVMANews/Pages/060815i.aspx (accessed on November 4, 2015.)

Purdy, Stephen R., DVM. 2010. *Donkeys: Miniature, Standard, and Mammoth: A Veterinary Guide for Owners and Breeders.* North Pomfret, VT: Trafalgar Square Books.

Reed, Herbert. 2012. "1914: Ponies Deserve Credit." Adapted from 1914 article by Herbert Reed. *POLO Players' Edition* 15(11) (July).

Remington, Frederic. 1889. "Horses of the Plains," *Century* 37(3) (January).

Rizzo, Steven. 2013. "1920s: Polo Tactics." *POLO Players' Edition* 16(12) (August).

Roberts, Isaac Phillips. 1917. *The Horse.* 5th ed. New York: Macmillan Company.

Rojas, Arnold R. 1953. *California Vaquero.* Fresno, CA: Academy Library Guild.

Roosevelt, Theodore. 1902. *The Rough Riders.* New York: Charles Scribner's Sons.

Ryden, Hope. 1970. *America's Last Wild Horses.* New York: Ballantine Books.

Satter, Raphael. 2012. "Genetic Study Pins Horse Domestication to Steppes." *Associated Press,* May 7.

Schweitzer, Sophia V., and Michael S. Gomes. 2001. *Kohala ʻĀina: A History of North Kohala.* Honolulu: Mutual Publishing.

Sikes, Don G. 1978. "Aloha Rodeo." *Real West Magazine* (May): 29–30, 63.

Slatta, Richard W. 1990. *Cowboys of the Americas.* New Haven, CT: Yale University Press.

———. 2006. *Cowboy: The Illustrated History.* New York: Sterling Publishing Co.

Smith, Joan Irvine, and Jean Stern. 2001. *California: This Golden Land of Promise.* Orange, CA: Chapman University Press.

Smith, Max B. 1966. "Quarter Horses in Hawaii." *Quarter Horse Journal* 18(6) (March).

Sponenberg, D. Phillip. 1992. "The Colonial Spanish Horse in the USA: History and Current Status." *Archivos de zootecnia* 41 (extra): 335–348.

———. 2011. "North American Colonial Spanish Horse Update." Spanish Mustangs Web site, the Center for America's First Horse, http://www.centerforamericasfirsthorse.org.north-american-colonial-spanish-horse.html (accessed on November 15, 2015).

Spratling, Boyd M., DVM. 2012. "Bureau of Land Management Wild Horse and Bureau Program: Welfare on the Range." *American Association of Equine Practitioners Proceedings* 58.

Stewart, Robert Campbell. 1990. "My Boyhood in Paʻauilo, as Told to Liane Ulumealani Stewart." *Hawaiian Journal of History* 24.

Subica, Wayne A. 2008. *Historic Hoʻolulu Park—Hilo, Hawaii, 1899–1971.* Kearney, NE: Morris Publishing Co.

Todd, Laurence. 2012. "Hawaii's Horse Council." *Mālama Lio Magazine* (spring).

Tomich, P. Quentin. 1986. *Mammals of Hawaii: A Synopsis and Notational Bib-*

liography. 2nd ed. Honolulu: Bishop Museum Press.

———. 2008. *Hawaii: Perspectives on Hamakua History: Ramblings through an Ancient Land Division on Hawaii Island.* Published by the author.

Trotten, Ruth Ellen Patton. 2005. *The Button Box: A Daughter's Loving Memoir of Mrs. George S. Patton.* Edited by James Patton Trotten. Columbia: University of Missouri Press.

Turner, Regina M., VMD, and Sue M. McDonnell. 2007. "Mounting Expectations for Thoroughbred Stallions." *Journal of the American Veterinary Medical Association* 237(10).

USDA. 1938. "Stallion Enrollment as Related to the Horse Breeding Situation." Washington, DC: US Department of Agriculture.

Vaughn, Paddy. 1994. *The Last Forge in Lismore.* Dublin, Ireland: Poddle Press.

Wade, Nicholas. 2013. "DNA Buried 7,000 Centuries Is Retrieved." *New York Times,* June 26.

Ward, Faye E. 1958. *The Cowboy at Work: All about His Job and How He Does It.* Norman: University of Oklahoma Press.

Warmuth, Vera, Anders Eriksson, Mim Ann Bower, Graeme Barker, Elizabeth Barrett, Bryan Kent Hanks, Shuicheng Li, David Lomitashvili, Maria Ochir-Goryaeva, Grigory V. Sizonov, Vasiliy Soyonov, and Andrea Manica. 2012. "Reconstructing the Origin and Spread of Horse Domestication in the Eurasian Steppe." *Proceedings of the National Academy of Sciences* 109(21): 8202–8206.

Weyeneth, Robert R. 2002. *Kapi'olani Park: A History.* Illustrated by MacKinnon Simpson. Honolulu: Kapiolani Park Preservation Society.

Wittliff, Bill. 2002. *Vaquero: A Vanishing Tradition.* An Exhibit of Photographs. Commentary by Joe B. Franz (1917–1993). National Ranching Heritage Center, Lubbock, Texas, May 3, 2002–January 5, 2003.

Wood, Lisa, DVM. 2010. "Foaling Guidelines." *Mālama Lio Magazine* (March).

Woods, Thomas A., PhD. 2008. *Ha'ilono,* Kona Historical Society newsletter (fall).

Young, Peter. 2014. "Grand Tour of O'ahu." Ho'okuleana Web site, http://totakeresponsibility.blogspot.com/2014/11/grand-tour-of-oahu.html (accessed on November 15, 2015).

ILLUSTRATION SOURCES AND CREDITS

We are grateful to the many scholars, institutions, and horse enthusiasts who have made illustrations, photographs, and maps available for use in this book. In the rare instances in which we have been unable to track down the original photographer, mapmaker, or illustrator, we have included as much information about the original source as possible.

Figures

Frontis: *Mounted Vaquero,* by Patricia Wozniak.

Dedication: Photo courtesy of Morgan Brown.

1.1 Map courtesy of *True West Magazine,* created by the Mapinator, Gus Walker, and Rebecca Edwards.

1.2 Illustration by Fay E. Ward. Reprinted by permission of the University of Oklahoma Press.

1.3 Map by Deborah Reade, cartographer; courtesy of John L. Kessell.

1.4 Illustration originally appeared in the anonymous publication, *Famous Horses of America* (1884).

1.5 Photo by Jeff Hengesbaugh.

2.1 Photo by Ruth V. Sobeck, DVM.

2.2 Photo courtesy of New Mexico State University Library, Archives and Special Collections.

2.3 Photo courtesy of Paniolo Preservation Society Collection.

2.4 Illustration by Paul A. Rossi; originally appeared in *Man Made Mobile: Early Saddles of Western North America,* edited by Richard Ahlborn.

2.5 Photo by Ethan Tweedie Photography.

2.6 Photo courtesy of John Holi Maʻe Collection.

2.7 Photo by Michal McClure, Naturestruecolors.com.

2.8–2.12 Illustrations by Henry "Tippy" Ah Sam.

2.13 Illustration used with permission of the jmoratrust.com.

2.14 Photo courtesy of Miranda Family Collection.

2.15 Photo courtesy of Paniolo Preservation Society Collection.

2.16 Photo courtesy of Paniolo Preservation Society Collection.

2.17 Photo by Gene Balzer.

2.18 Illustration courtesy of Paniolo Preservation Society Collection.

2.19 Photo courtesy of Chris Kaaua.

2.20 Photo courtesy of Aletha Lindsey-Barkley.

2.21 Photo courtesy of Paniolo Preservation Society Collection.

2.22 Photo courtesy of A. W. Carter Collection.

3.1 Illustration originally appeared in *Man Made Mobile: Early Saddles of Western North America,* edited by Richard Ahlborn. Bancroft Library, University of California, Berkeley.

3.2 Illustration originally appeared in *Man Made Mobile: Early Saddles of Western North America,* edited by Richard Ahlborn. Bancroft Library, University of California, Berkeley.

3.3 Painting by Thomas Hedderington; Honolulu Museum of Art Purchase, 1943 (11988).

3.4 Photo courtesy of John Holi Ma'e Collection.

3.5 Photo courtesy of Territorial Division of Animal Industry.

3.6 Photo courtesy of Otto Ziegler Collection.

3.7 Photo courtesy of Territorial Division of Animal Industry.

3.8 Photo courtesy of Territorial Division of Animal Industry.

3.9 Photo courtesy of Paniolo Preservation Society Collection.

4.1 Illustration used with permission of jmoratrust.com.

4.2–4.7 Photos courtesy of Martha Bergin Collection.

4.8 Photo courtesy of Sherm Warner.

5.1 Photo courtesy of North Hawai'i Education and Research Center, Kimura Collection.

5.2 Photo courtesy of Patricia Greenwell Collection.

5.3 Photo courtesy of North Hawai'i Education and Research Center, Kimura Collection.

5.4 Photo by W. W. Williams, 1920.

5.5 Photo courtesy of North Hawai'i Education and Research Center, Kimura Collection.

5.6 Photo courtesy of Paniolo Preservation Society Collection.

5.7 Photo courtesy of T. David Woo Family.

5.8 Image by Dr. Billy Bergin.

5.9 Photo by Gene Balzer.

5.10 Photo courtesy of North Hawai'i Education and Research Center, Kealoha Collection.

5.11 Photo courtesy of John Holi Ma'e Collection.

5.12 Photo courtesy of North Hawai'i Education and Research Center, Kealoha Collection.

5.13 Photo courtesy of William Andrade Collection.

5.14 Photo courtesy of John Holi Ma'e Collection.

5.15 Photo courtesy of North Hawai'i Education and Research Center, Kealoha Collection.

5.16 Photo courtesy of Dr. Billy Bergin Collection.

5.17 Photo by Anna Pacheco.

6.1 Photo courtesy of Bishop Museum, CP 110, 161.

6.2 Photo by Howard Pierce, July 1960.

6.3 Photo courtesy of John Holi Ma'e Collection.

6.4 Photo courtesy Bishop Museum, BM CP 73308.

6.5 Photo by Howard Pierce. July 1960.

6.6 Photo courtesy of Lyman House Museum, Howard Pierce Collection.

6.7 Photo courtesy of North Hawai'i Education and Research Center, Kimura Collection.

6.8 Photo cover *Waimea Gazette,* September, 1999, courtesy of the Sproat family.

6.9 Photo by Gene Balzer.

7.1–7.3 Photos courtesy of Dr. Billy Bergin Collection.

7.4 Photo by Gene Balzer.

8.1 Photo courtesy of Edmund C. Olson Trust No. 2 photographic archives in Papaikou.

8.2 Photo courtesy of Edmund C. Olson Trust No. 2 photographic archives in Papaikou.

8.3–8.5 Photos courtesy of Otto Ziegler Collection.

8.6 Photo courtesy of John Holi Ma'e Collection.

12.16 Photo courtesy of Waikoloa Village Association and Waikoloa Rope-a-thon Sponsors.
12.17 Photo courtesy of Bergin Collection.
12.18 Photo courtesy of Bergin Collection.
12.19 Photo © James Fain.
12.20 Photo © James Fain.
13.1 Photo by R. J. Baker, courtesy of Bishop Museum SP 31476.
13.2 Photo courtesy of Paniolo Preservation Society Collection.
13.3 Photo courtesy of Paniolo Preservation Society Collection.
13.4 Photo courtesy of Haku Baldwin Center.
13.5 Photo courtesy of Haku Baldwin Center.
13.6 Photo by Sally Rice.
13.7 Photo courtesy of the Hedemann Family.
13.8 Photo by Michal McClure, Naturestruecolors.com.
13.9 Photo courtesy of Lester Maruoka.
13.10 Image courtesy of Lester Maruoka.
13.11 Photo courtesy of Lester Maruoka.
13.12 Photo courtesy of Lester Maruoka.
13.13 Photo courtesy of Lori and Bill Bergin.
14.1 *The Irish Horse Newspaper,* June 16, 2012.
14.2 Photo by Dr. Brady J. Bergin.
14.3 Photo courtesy of Dr. Brady J. Bergin.
14.4 Photo by Mary Buckley.
14.5 Drawing courtesy of Walter Slater.
14.6 Photo by Dr. Brady J. Bergin.
14.7 Photo by Elysse Butler Mallams.
14.8 Image by F. W Hendriks.
14.9 Photo by Dr. Brady J. Bergin.
14.10 Photo by Dr. Brady J. Bergin.
14.11 Photo by Michael F. O'Brien.
14.12 Photo by Dr. Brady J. Bergin.
14.13 Photo by F. W. Hendriks.
14.14 Photo by F. W. Hendriks.
14.15 Photo by Mary Buckley.
15.1 Photo courtesy of Parker Ranch Collection.
15.2 Photo courtesy of Paniolo Preservation Society Collection.
15.3 Photo by Tiffany Bergin.
15.4 Photo courtesy of Alex Penovaroff Collection.
15.5 Image courtesy of Nancy Jones.
15.6 Photo by Mary Buckley.

Plates

Plate 1 Photo courtesy of Martha Bergin Collection.
Plate 2 Photo courtesy of Bergin Collection.
Plate 3 Photo courtesy of Paniolo Preservation Society Collection.
Plate 4 Photo courtesy of Patrick Ching.
Plate 5 Image courtesy of Waikoloa Village Association and Waikoloa Rope-a-thon Sponsors.
Plate 6 Image courtesy of Hawai'i High School Rodeo Association.
Plate 7 Photo courtesy of Morag Rice Miranda.
Plate 8 Photo by Dr. Brady J. Bergin.
Plate 9 Photo by F. W. Hendriks.
Plate 10 Photo by F. W. Hendriks.
Plate 11 Photo by F. W. Hendriks.
Plate 12 Photo by Mary Buckley.
Plate 13 Photo by Dr. Brady J. Bergin.
Plate 14 Photo by Jock Goodman.
Plate 15 Photo by Gene Balzer.
Plate 16 Photo by Gene Balzer.

INDEX

Note: Page numbers for illustrations are in **bold** type; **Pl.** denotes plate; t denotes table

ABOUT THE AUTHORS

Drs. Billy and Brady Bergin, a father and son team of veterinarians, have specialized in horse care in the Hawaiian Islands for nearly a half century, combining their professional and writing skills to produce a scholarly text on the history of the equine species in a Polynesian setting.

The senior Bergin (Billy) has authored more than a dozen scientific articles on reproduction in horses. In recent years, he authored three books on the history of the Parker Ranch and is currently working on the fourth and final volume on this subject, all entitled *Loyal to the Land,* with appropriate subtitles. He has also coauthored a comprehensive biography of Parker Ranch owner Richard Smart, and another book celebrating the Hawaiian cowboy.

Dr. Brady Bergin has distinguished himself as senior author of international import in a published study entitled "Oral Hyaluronan Gel Reduces Post Operative Tarsocrural Effusion in the Yearling Thoroughbred" (*Equine Veterinary Journal,* July 2006 38(4): 375–378). For this work, he received the 2006 Literary Award at the International Equine Congress in Birmingham, England. As owner of ʻĀina Hou Animal Hospital in Kamuela, Hawaiʻi, he has led humanitarian campaigns in support of the equine species and authored publications on equine health. Currently on an interim hiatus, he is an associate professor at the University of Minnesota, where he serves as a clinical administrator at West Metro Equine Clinic in Minneapolis. He has headed the Minnesota Equine Expo and continues to lecture and publish professional articles on the equine.